JEWS IN AMERICA TODAY

Lenni Brenner

Lyle Stuart Inc.   Secaucus, New Jersey

Library of Congress Cataloging-in-Publication Data

Brenner, Lenni, 1937-
  Jews in America today.

  Includes index.
  1. Jews—United States—Politics and government.
2. Jews—United States—Attitudes toward Israel.
3. Holocaust, Jewish (1939-1945)—Causes. 4. Afro-
Americans—Relations with Jews. 5. United States—
Ethnic relations. I. Title.
E184.J5B73 1986 973'.04924 86-23028
ISBN 0-8184-0379-9

Published by Lyle Stuart Inc.
120 Enterprise Ave., Secaucus, N.J. 07094
In Canada; Musson Book Company
A division of General Publishing Co. Limited.
Don Mills, Ontario

Queries regarding rights and permission should be
addressed to: Lyle Stuart, 120 Enterprise Avenue,
Secaucus, N.J. 07094

Manufactured in the United States of America

CONTENTS

Introduction

There are several important reasons why a discussion of the status of modern American Jewry is in order. Obviously, everyone knows that the U.S., the world's mightest military force, is intimately allied to Israel, and that these financial and military links are steadily increasing. However, while Middle Eastern considerations are certainly at the core of that alliance, no election would be thought complete without the domestic politicians, down to the ranks of mayors and city council members, rushing to appear before Jewish organizations to reaffirm their fealty to "the only democracy in the Middle East." Few can have any illusions: What they are actually doing is seeking the votes and campaign contributions of a grouping now richer—on average, of course—than the Episcopalians, the classic WASPs.

However, if the military aspect of America's involvement with Israel is acknowledged, the immense socio-economic developments that have transformed Jewry since the end of World War II have not yet received proper attention from either the Jewish or the broader American reading public, although several scholarly articles and books have already been written on facets of the subject.

Authors writing on this last theme frequently begin with an apology for daring to do so. Gerald Krefetz in his *Jews and*

Money: The Myths and the Reality, and Richard Zweigenhaft and
G. William Domhoff in their *Jews in the Protestant Establish-*
ment, remark that such books automatically trigger fears that they
will be misused by anti-Semites. However, it will be noted that
their concerns did not stop any of them from publishing their
very important contributions. Here, there will be no such preliminary apologia, for none is needed. To the contrary, one of the
central assertions of this book is that anti-Semitism is a weak and
dying factor in American life, and any such hesitancy grossly
underestimates the people of this country. In fact, intermarriage is
sharply on the rise, and all signs clearly foretell further Jewish
biological and cultural assimilation into the larger community.

Since consciousness usually lags behind realities, it is hardly
surprising that there are those who squint through ideological
spectacles, and who persist in seeing both the Jews and the American people through 1920-1920 eyes. But there are others whose
material interests do not permit them to draw the full implications
arising from the actual status of today's Jews. The right-wing of
the Jewish Establishment, that is to say the bulk of the leaders of
what is referred to as "the organized Jewish community," have
committed themselves to a course of consciously linking the fate
of American Jewry to the fortunes of later-day capitalism. Worse,
they have constructed themselves an ideological Maginot Line,
from which they fire off the heavy guns in the furious war against
affirmative action. Naturally enough, these worthies are not eager
to have it widely known that a recent survey of about half of the
members of the boards of the American Jewish Committee, the
American Jewish Congress, the United Jewish Appeal, and Anti-
Defamation League, and its parent B'nai B'rith, revealed a
median annual income of $135,000. Instead, they claim that they
are merely defending the merit system against "racism in
reverse," Israel against "terrorism," and the good old 'free
world" against the Soviets, all of which they roll together into
"the new anti-Semitism."

To hear them tell it, they are not protecting capitalism, and
their positions and investments. Gracious no. They are simply
reaffirming "the Jewish heritage." But, as is always the case in
these matters, the rich and their intellectual servitors can never
uphold the best in their people's patrimony. They invariably
betray it, because those noble traditions conflict with their ambitions. In the immediate situation, the Old Testament contains

innumerable injunctions along the lines of the proverb: "The rich man is wise in his own conceit; but the poor that hath understanding searcheth him out." And the Talmud further enjoins all Jews, everywhere and for all time to come, to "always be with the persecuted, never with the persecutors."

The Establishment styles itself Jewish "survivalist." However clocks still only run in one direction, and absolutely nothing they may say or do will preserve a corporate Jewry, especially one linked to the powers-that-be in the U.S. A progressive future for American Jewry and its progeny can only be one thoroughly grounded in the experiences of the last two centuries of political and social revolution, and the lessons acquired in these battles are the communal property of all of humanity. All efforts to find the key to the Jewish future in the progressive aspects of the Jewish past alone, are doomed to come to reactionary conclusions. However, as this is a book about Jews, and these two ancient maxims are in full concordance with the conceptions which have motivated the best political minds since the age of enlightenment, this book is written in their spirit, and must be seen as standing or falling to the degree with which it carries out their mandate.

Any scholarly discussion of American Jewry must encounter another, unique difficulty, for it is immediately necessary to provide a working answer to the classic question: Who is a Jew? Thus the Orthodox Jewish religion defines a Jew as anyone born of a Jewish mother, or a convert. The largest Jewish religious sect, the Conservatives, work under similar rules. However, the Orthodox do not accept conversions done by Conservative rabbis. Reform Jews, also a larger grouping than the Orthodox, declare anyone born of a Jewish mother or father to be a Jew. Again, the Orthodox do not accept Reform conversions, and for them patrilineal descent is the ultimate in heresy.

If these differing definitions were not enough, the reality is that the majority of American Jews are not religiously affiliated. Most of these see themselves as ethnic Jews. Most would therefore consider the child of a Jewish father to be a Jew, certainly if the child called himself or herself a Jew. But, no longer religious themselves, many of these ethnics now have difficulty perceiving Sammy Davis, Jr., or Elizabeth Taylor as "real" Jews, and they categorically reject members of "Ethiopian Hebrew" cults as fellow Jews.

There are also problems going the other way. For the Orthodox, a Jew who converts to another religion remains a Jew, even
if he were to become the Pope. But Israel was once confronted
with a man who had indeed become a Catholic monk, but who
still sought automatic citizenship as a Jew. The courts ruled that
public opinion decides who is a Jew, and since the vast majority
of Jews, in Israel or elsewhere, see conversion, and particularly
conversion to Christianity, as a fundamental break with Jewry, the
high court rejected the application, quite regardless of the
Talmud's niceties. There can be little doubt that most American
Jews, religious or otherwise, share the court's view of converts to
Christianity, which they see as forever discredited by centuries of
anti-Semitism.

Here, in America, the government has traditionally seen the
Jews as a religious community. But the Census Bureau discontin-
ued religious surveys in 1957, and it does not list Jewish as a
category in its surveys of ethnicity, nor will it even accept such as
a self-definition. Insofar as the broad American public concerns
itself with such recondite matters, it sees everything with scales as
a fish. Beyond doubt, the fact that Hitler defined the Jews ethnically has helped shaped the public perception of the Jews. And
certainly the Zionists' proclamation that the Jews of the world are
a nationality has served to reinforce this. But, on the other hand,
Americans are quite used to religious conversion, and if Elizabeth
Taylor wishes to define herself as a Jew, that is acceptable to the
American people.

Generally speaking, the work at hand will follow this public
usage: everything coming into the net will be counted as a fish. In
practice, most of these marginal categories—converts, half-Jews,
cultists, etc.—are statistically inconsequential, and not to treat
them as such would lead us into absurdities. Thus Maine has a
senator, Bill Cohen, whose father was Jewish but whose mother
was Protestant. He had always assumed that he was a Jew until
the rabbis discovered that his mother wasn't a Jew. Therefore they
insisted that he would have to convert, something which he would
not do. Later he became a Unitarian. For us to go with the rabbis,
or even with Cohen's present religious orientation, would put us
in the ludicrous situation of having to insist that although the Senate has a member named Cohen, he is not a Jew. Certainly the
voters in Maine think of anyone named Cohen as some kind of
Jew, and it is crucially important to know that they do not care.

Because of the absence of official government surveys, it is frequently necessary for us to rely on private polls. Many of these, in all good faith, frequently undercount non-religious Jews, that is to say both the ethnic Jews and the completely deracinated element, particularly among the intellectuals, who no longer identify in any way with their roots. Some pollsters realize this, and alert us to the problem, but many don't, and occasionally it shall be necessary to dispute the findings of a poll, without, in any way, challenging the integrity of the scholars involved.

1

The Golden Door to the Golden Land

When Americans think of their country, they usually mean the continental 48 states, but America's Jewish history begins in the West Indies. Since Columbus thought he would be sailing to Asia, Luis de Torres, a *Converso,* baptized just before the expedition's departure, was taken on as the interpreter. Puerto Rico was discovered in 1493 and settled in 1508, and such *Cristianos nuevos* were among the colonizers.

In 1391 fanatical mobs massacred approximately 50,000 Jews in the Christian Spanish states. At least 100,000 others saved themselves at the baptismal font. As Catholics, they rose rapidly within the society, including the clergy's ranks. But their success brought a new danger. The Old Christian elite saw them as insidious competitors.

Many Conversos had indeed become extremely Catholic, but forced conversions meant crypto-Jews, and soon the Conversos were known as *Marranos*—swine—because all were reputed to avoid pork. Old Christian rivals brought the wrath of the Inquisition onto them as Judaizing heretics. If heresy was to be extir-

15

pated, unconverted Jews, providing moral examples and often material support to potential heretics, would have to be expelled, as the Inquisitors had no jurisdiction over Jews and Muslims.

The newly united Spanish Kingdom's solution was the edict of March 31, 1492, expelling all those who would not accept Christianity, thereby generating the Sephardic diaspora, *Sepharad* being medieval Hebrew for Spain. Approximately 250,000 Jews went into exile, to Portugal, North Africa, Italy and the Turkish empire. Some 50,000 remained and were converted, adding to the Converso community and particularly its clandestine Jewish element.

Many New Christians, which meant many more or less observant Jews, took part in the subsequent colonization of the new world. A Marrano, Luis de Cervaja y de la Cueva, explored New Mexico in the 16th century. Bernardo Lopez de Mendizabel, the governor of New Mexico, was arrested in 1661 as a Judaizer and died in prison, only to be posthumously exonerated.

More New Christians drifted into Texas in the 17th and 18th centuries, often to get away from the Inquisition in Mexico. Eventually these early Marrano settlers lost their Jewish consciousness, but there are a handful of descendants of 19th century immigrants from Mexico in the southwest who still retain an awareness of their Jewish background, while remaining socially part of the Chicano population.[1]

The present-day American Jewish community has its origins in New Amsterdam. Scholars differ on details, but the first Jews in the Dutch colony were Jacob Bar Simon (or Bar Simson), possibly from Germany or even Poland, and Solomon Pietersen, who, judging by his name, was also of *Ashkenazi* or Germanic background. Bar Simon most probably arrived in July, or possibly August, 1654, and Pietersen most probably came in that same period. But organized Jewish life actually had its origins in the arrival of 23 Sephardic Jews in the first week of September of that year.

For some decades the Dutch and the Portuguese had fought for control of Brazil, with the Dutch seizing Recife and holding it until 1654. A group of Marranos took advantage of the presence of Protestant masters to declare themselves Jews, and they were soon joined by traders who came out from the Netherlands.

With the Portuguese reconquest of Brazil, the entire Jewish

population had to leave. Sixteen boats set out for the Netherlands, but one was captured by pirates. These, in turn, were overtaken by a French vessel going to New Amsterdam and the Jews were rescued.

New difficulties now faced them. Governor Peter Stuyvesant hated Jews, "with their customary usury and deceitful trading with the Christians," and he did everything he could to deny them the right to stay in the colony. However, the Directors of the West Indies Company reminded him of

> the considerable losses sustained by this nation, with others, in the taking of Brazil . . . [and] . . . of the large amount of capital which they still have invested in the shares of this company. Therefore . . . we have finally decided . . . that these people may live and remain there.[2]

Stuyvesant fought a rearguard campaign against the refugees, but pressure from the Amsterdam Sephardim prevailed and the Directors usually overruled him. However, the lure of the lucrative West Indies virtually disintegrated the community by the time the British took the colony in 1664.

More Jews came out to the colonies, and while the British denied non-Christians the right to hold office, after 1700 New York's Jews could trade and pray openly. Soon there were synagogues in Newport, Philadelphia, Richmond, Charleston and Savannah, with Charleston the largest settlement. By 1720, Sephardim were no longer the majority, and few came after 1760.[3] However the Spanish and Portuguese continued to dominate the community, which numbered between 1,000 and 2,500 out of two and a half million at the time of the revolution.[4] A rare few were planters, some were farmers. Many were artisans, candlemakers, distillers, tailors; more commonly they were shopkeepers, sellers of dry goods, hardware and liquor. The most successful became "merchant shippers" in the international trade, which frequently meant West Indian rum and sometimes slaves. None were indentured servants. While some were loyalists, most were Whigs and fought in the revolution as soldiers and officers.

Post-revolutionary compromises compelled the vanguard of the founding fathers to accept a federal system, and some of the states continued to deny office to Jews, but the new government's feelings were genuinely expressed by Washington in 1789:

It is now no more that toleration is spoken of as if it were by the indulgence of one class of people that another enjoyed the exercise of their inherent natural right, for, happily, the government of the United States, which gives to bigotry no sanction, to persecution no assistance, requires only that they who live under its protection shall demean themselves as good citizens . . . May the children of the stock of Abraham who dwell in this land continue to merit and enjoy the good will of the other inhabitants, while everyone shall sit in safety under his own vine and fig tree, and there shall be none to make him afraid.[5]

Given minuscule numbers, Sephardic intermarriages with both Ashkenazim and gentiles became increasingly common, with conversions and marriages to Christians rising to 30 percent even in colonial times.[6] Harmon Hendricks, the developer of the first copper rolling mill in the 1840s, was the only Sephardic representative in the front ranks of capital, but the haughty and stagnant community continued prosperous in the century after independence. The then weakly developed intellectual professions were never their field, and even now they do not score as high on IQ tests as the Ashkenazi, who outrank all ethnic and religious groupings.[7]

In the last decade of the 19th century a new Sephardic immigration did indeed come through the golden door, this time from the Levant. Its constituents were not primarily of Grandee background, but rather descendants of those unconverted Jews who had left Spain in 1492. Between 1890 and 1907, 2,738 Sephardim arrived, with a total of 25,591 entering the country between 1899 and 1925. Most of these were from Turkey, Greece and the Balkans, and still spoke Ladino, the Spanish of 1492, with time's inevitable corruptions, admixed with the languages of their countries of historic refuge. The Marrano synagogues tried to relate to the newcomers, but they had become largely Ashkenazi in membership and even the old stock Sephardi scarcely remembered the ancestral tongue, and they could do little for the new immigrants. These, divided by the customs of their countries of origin, were not really one community. With the closing down of the weekly newspaper *La America,* in 1948, Ladino virtually disappeared.

It is estimated that there are 100,000 Sephardim in the country today. However, the number is almost meaningless as it includes people of mixed Sephardic-Ashkenazi background, as well as

Arabic speakers from Egypt and Syria, who are not really of Spanish background, but who are lumped in with the Sephardim by both Ashkenazim and Sephardim, who see any Jew who is not an Ashkenazi as a Sephardi.

Religions are perhaps humanity's most tenacious ideological productions; therefore a Sephardic detritus, a disintegrating fragment of history, will be with us for yet a while, sans future. But even most other Jews have never met an American Sephardi (over half of Israel is "oriental"). Few are aware of the subtle distinctions that divide the Orthodox. Orthoprax (correctness of practice) would be a better name for traditional Judaism, which is ritually committed to 613 laws, further Talmudized to sectarian niceties.[8] Yet not all in this obsessive world can get under one yarmulke. Sephardic rabbis allow rice on Passover, and even go so far as to permit eggs found whole inside a chicken to be eaten with milk. To Ashkenazi Talmudists such indulgence would be unthinkable. Blessings are said differently, and cantors are immediately distinguished by their use of different names for the notes of the liturgical cantillations.

In Sephardic synagogues the scroll of the law is hoisted before the service rather than following, and prayers are always said at the reading desk, whereas the Ashkenazi recite certain blessings at the side of the ark. The oldest congregation, New York's Sheareth Israel, going back to 1706, has melded these communal distinctions with vestments patterned after the Christian clergy's. The *Encyclopedia Judaica's* frank comment on the Sephardi religious establishment tells us why they lost the majority of their youth:

> Sephardim tend to be very insistent on preserving these slight distinctions, probably because they are conscious of their minority status with the Jewish community, and tend to develop the same rigorous adherence to custom vis-à-vis the Ashkenazi community as the Orthodox Jewish community as a whole does to the outside world. It is not uncommon at the present time (1972) for a deep or even fanatical attachment to Sephardi tradition to be coupled with laxity in observance of Jewish law.[9]

The German Jews

The Jewish population in the United States increased to approximately 4,000 by 1820, to 15,000 by 1840 and 150,000 by the

Civil War. There were 280,000 Jews in the country by 1880. Most were part of the second great German emigration, which began in 1828, and which was to see five million Germans come across. Others were from Prussian Poland or were highly Germanized Jews from Bohemia and Hungary.

A very few arrived wealthy, as with August Belmont—French for Schoenberg—the Rothschild representative, but thousands were from small Bavarian towns. Most gave up crafts for peddling, walking rural roads carrying a backpack full of household notions, which could be quite lucrative when country stores were a rarity. They walked six days, returning to town to pray and to stock up. The successful soon used wagons and eventually set up stores.

They arrived during a propitious economic era, when the country's population was exploding and the frontiers were being settled. Retail trade did not then require the capital that production demanded, yet could generate wealth. Soon some entered industry, as with Levi Strauss, one of San Francisco's 10,000 gold rush Jews, who invented the copper-riveted denims that became an integral part of western life. Some ventured further afield, as with Meyer Guggenheim, a peddler turned lace manufacturer, who apparently bought a debtor's flooded copper mine and promptly turned into the world's Copper King. Some went into the then unregulated banking world and their houses became some of the biggest on Wall Street.

To be sure, not all did as well as their most successful, but a survey of 10,000 Jews who arrived here after the defeat of the 1848 liberal revolution in Germany showed 1,000 having at least three servants by 1880. Another 2,000 had two servants and 4,000 made do with one. About half were in business, five per cent were professionals, one fifth were accountants and other white collar employees, an eighth were in skilled occupations, mainly tailors or cigar makers. Less than two per cent were still peddlers or in unskilled trades.[10]

They inhabited three worlds. There were never German-Jewish neighborhoods, but in midwest cities like Cincinnati they usually lived in the local Germantown. Many were active in the enclosed world of German immigrant-aid and gymnastic and musical societies. Thousands had fought in German-language units in the Union Army. It is therefore not surprising that many took no interest in narrowly Jewish affairs.

Even the rich who remained Jewishly identified sent their sons to German universities. America was their home, but America also meant "Turkey in the Straw." Germany was *Kultur,* and besides, many of the bankers here became intimately involved with Germany's banking and court circles.

Belmont was the first to intermarry, to Commodore Perry's daughter, in a High Episcopalian ceremony at Grace Church in New York. For decades the sons and daughters of the other rich married each other, but eventually increasing numbers of Guggenheims, Meyers and Speyers converted or intermarried. However, most retained a Jewish identity, brought into harmony with the liberal America they encountered.

In the early decades of the century, Germany's enlightened Jews frequently followed Heine in seeing conversion as their "passport into civilization," but as the community modernized, its youth insisted on religious freedom. But there was one charge hurled at Judaism which they thought valid. It was an *imperium in imperio,* a portable fatherland. Now, however, Germany was to be their only fatherland, and German their religious language in modernized services, usually to musical accompaniment. *Wissenschaft des Judentums,* the scientific study of Judaism, won the day against Talmudism.

Young immigrant rabbis found similar currents had evolved amongst the native synagogues, and the new immigrants made Reform the dominant element within American Jewry. In 1885 the movement drew up the Pittsburgh Platform, the Reform credo until 1937. It announced that

> the Bible reflected the primitive ideas of its own age . . . at times clothing its conceptions of Divine Providence and Justice, dealing with man in miraculous narratives . . . Today we accept as binding only the moral laws, and . . . reject all such as are not adapted to the views and habits of modern civilization . . . laws as regulate diet, priestly purity, and dress, originated in ages . . . foreign to our present mental and spiritual state . . .

They were now living in the land of the free and home of the brave. No longer were the Jews wandering in exile:

> We consider ourselves no longer a nation, but a religious community, and therefore expect neither a return to Palestine, nor a sacrificial worship under the sons of Aaron . . . We reject as ideas

not rooted in Judaism the beliefs both in bodily resurrection and in Gehenna and Eden (Hell and Paradise) as abodes of everlasting punishment or reward.

Why then should the Jews continue a separate corporate existence? They saw Christianity and Islam as "daughter religions," and Jews "appreciate their providential mission to aid in the spreading of monotheistic and moral truth," but the Jewish people still had "its mission as priest of the one God." Judaism "presents the highest conception of the God idea."

German reform had already rejected the notion that the destruction of the second temple had been a punishment for the Jews' sins. Instead it was part of a divine plan to disperse the priestly people so that they could truly be a light unto the nations. Now they were going to remake the world:

> In full accordance with the spirit of Mosaic legislation, which strives to regulate the relation between rich and poor, we deem it our duty to participate in the great task of modern times, to solve . . . the problems presented by the contrasts and evils of the present organization of society.[11]

In the real world, Reform was nothing more than the German-Jewish capitalist class at prayer, no better than their time and place. They had fought on both sides during the Civil War and rabbi Isaac Wise, who chaired the Pittsburgh conference, had maintained a discreet silence on the conflict, in keeping with the divided loyalties of his Cincinnati congregation.[12]

America was the country of religious freedom, but being Jewish parvenues had its *problematik* in a land that had known bondage and Know-Nothingism. This had been curiously sneak previewed for the Jews in Grant's Order No. 11, of December 17, 1862. The famous drinker barred all Jews from parts of three southern states, an order immediately revoked by Lincoln. However, the exclusion of banker Joseph Seligman from the Grand Union Hotel in the Catskills in the summer of 1877 converted the Gilded Age into the gilded cage as businesses, clubs, private schools and resorts followed the example. Hostility to the "hooked-nosed tribe of Shylocks and Fagins" became a factor in the nativism and populism that emerged in the next decades.

The last people these Jewish Teutons wanted to identify with were the *Ostjuden,* the Orthodox *Yidden* of the Russian empire, whose sudden migration started in 1882. Their appearance, many wearing earlocks and outlandish garb, created anti-Semitism. But it was German Jews, not gentiles, who put "kike" and "sheeny" into English.

Class antagonism added to their hostility. Some of them had started as second-hand clothes dealers, and as tailors had established themselves turning out Civil War uniforms. The mechanical cutting knife of the 1870s completed the shift to the modern world of ready-to-wear clothes. Approximately half of the new arrivals had garment trades experience in the *alte heim,* and the first of these were put to work in the "uptowners" shops. Conflict increased as the capitalists encountered graduates of Russian revolutionary movements agitating their labor force.

The Great Yiddish Migration

There were no Jews under the Tsars until the late 18th century. In 1471, two Jewish traders in the retinue of a noble of Kiev "corrupted to Judaism" two prominent Russian Orthodox clergy of Novgorod, and a Judaizing heresy spread among the monks, using Old Testament prophetic denunciations of wealth and power to critique their own establishment. The sect disappeared, but thenceforward the Holy Synod barred the "Russian earth" to Jewish merchants. It was the 18th century conquest of territory from Poland and Turkey that confronted St Petersburg with an internal "Jewish problem."

Tsarism had its liberal interlude under Alexander II, the emancipator of the serfs. While most Jews were still confined to the Pale of Settlement, the 15 westernmost provinces extending from the Baltic to the Black Sea, a few rich were permitted to live in other regions, and even allowed to enter universities. Alexander's assassination by the *Narodnaya Volya,* the People's Will revolutionaries, on March 1, 1881, was paid for by, *inter alia,* three years of pogroms in the Ukraine. The Russian *pogromit* (to devastate) tells us that the anti-Semites incited the rabble, claiming the Jews murdered the little father of all the Russias, and that the regime allowed attacks on them. The Romanoffs, later-day Byzantines, were soon devising new laws to impose upon the race of deicides.

Perhaps 7,500 of the empire's Jews had migrated to the *Goldene Medina,* the Golden Land, between 1820 and 1870, and an estimated 40,000 plus ventured to America in the 1870's but the idea of emigrating there had not really entered into the consciousness of the notoriously medieval-minded Jewish masses of Eastern Europe.[13] It was the 1881-84 pogroms, followed by additional anti-Semitic ukases—30,000 out of 35,000 Jews, three percent of Moscow's population, were expelled in 1891—which made the industrial revolution's two-week expedition across Europe by the cheapest coach, and then steerage to New York, a part of the potential life program of this most wretched of chosen peoples.[14]

In 1880 the world Jewish population was over 7½ million, with nearly 5 million in Russia.[15] Approximately 2,800,000, one-third of the Jews in Eastern Europe, immigrated into their new promised land between 1881 and 1925, when the U.S. imposed nationally restrictive quotas on immigration. The high point was 1904-08, when, following a wave of pogroms, 642,000 poured into the country, with 153,748 coming in 1905. Figures for the pre-WWI period show Russia as the place of previous residence for 71.7 percent, Austria-Hungary 16.2 percent, Rumania 4.2 percent, Germany 0.7 percent.[16] A majority of America's Jews were foreign-born until the early 1940s, and 80 percent were then of Eastern European background. In 1877 only 0.52 percent of the people, by 1927 the Jews had grown to be 3.58 percent.[17] Two hundred and eighty thousand had become 4,250,000 in 1927, out of a world Jewish population of 15,467,000.[18]

Eighty-six percent of the immigrants settled in the northeastern states, with approximately 70 percent in New York. Manhattan's lower east side became the world's largest Jewish community.

In 1900 the area had an average population density of 700 per acre, worse than Bombay's slums.[19] Five years later, some blocks held between 1,000 and 1,700 Jews, easily making them the most congested area in the world.[20] By 1915 there were 350,000 Jews living on less than two square miles.[21] At one point, one-sixth of the city's inhabitants resided on 1/32 of its land.[22] Since only so many people could be packed into even the world's champion tenements, huge Jewish neighborhoods sprang up in other boroughs, and by 1927 the 1,765,000 Jews were 29.56 percent of the city's dwellers.[23] Chicago followed with 300,000, Philadelphia with 247,000, and nationally, Jews were 11.11 percent of communities of over 100,000.

Yiddish was the glue of the immigration. The few educated Jews of Eastern Europe had dismissed the language as a stunted "jargon," preferring German or Hebrew or Russian. But only one-third of the women could read in any language, and that meant that Yiddish was the tongue spoken "on the Jewish street."

The Jews poured into the cities of the Pale in the last decades of the 19th century and a vernacular press of immense vitality suddenly emerged. Similarly, in America, a socialist daily, the *Forverts* became the dominant paper. It infuriated purists, who condemned it for anglicizing the language, but it was consciously acting as an assimilatory bridge for the masses. What is significant is not so much what it was doing as that its corruption, as it were, of "classic" Yiddish could be an important part of the critique of the paper by more radical elements.

Eastern European Jewry had been essentially a caste, with its niches in the society, but the urban population began to see themselves as a Yiddish nation. Committed linguistic nationalists became an important element in the immigration and they began to behave as if Yiddish could have a long-term future in the U.S. Logically, any reasonable person knew that Yiddish would ultimately give way to English, but for many, Yiddish had become the identifying mark of the Jews, and they could never really free themselves of their illusions. Many years later, Isaac Bashevis Singer, the venerated master of contemporary Yiddish literature, explained why they had to fail:

> Jews who speak Yiddish in the United States . . . are generally an uprooted group. Their language had become impoverished rather than enriched. They have abandoned, whether willingly or not, too many of the customs and traditions that lend a group its own special color. The Yiddish-speaking writer is in fact living in the past, both in his language and his themes.[24]

The children of the immigrants learned Yiddish at home, but their schools were in English and that became their language. The Yiddish press declined from about 5-600,000 daily during World War I, to today's three weeklies which share a circulation of 121,908, mostly elderly readers.

Today, Yiddish is a street language only in Williamsburg and a few other Orthodox neighborhoods in Brooklyn, where about 60,000 members of Chassidic or pious sects retain, in many cases, the dress and customs of their Eastern European *shtetl* or small town. Even with these, English is near universal; certainly it is with their bi-lingual children. There are a few dozen Yiddish words in contemporary English, many of them insults, but, given the extraordinary percentage of Jews in today's literary life, it is remarkable how few Yiddishisms are in our language.

Although the bulk of the immigrants were Orthodox, their rabbis rarely crossed the Atlantic, for they had heard that America was a place where Jews broke the sabbath and dietary laws. And they were right. The majority of the immigrants eventually abandoned everything—earlocks, yarmulkes, Saturday as the day of rest, the kosher laws—that made them different from the general public.

Even most of those who still considered themselves Orthodox abandoned beards and earlocks. However, neither Reform nor the halfway house known as Conservativism were ever popular with the immigrant generation. People of different class and culture are rarely religiously intimate, and the German Jews did not share their folkways. It was their native-born children who later found Reform and Conservativism in the suburbs and, if they bothered at all with Judaism, joined these Temples and Community Centers of the one Ping-Pong God.

Poverty led to many of the classic slum problems. The Jewish "white slave traffic" became of mass proportions in an age when millions of male migrants tried to establish themselves in new countries. The Orthodox religion is extremely male chauvinistic—women are considered unclean for seven days after their period and no sex is allowed, they are segregated in the synagogues—and frequently such cultures produce a stratum of women who unconsciously see sex as evil. With the bleak prospect of sweatshop labor in front of them, such women easily fell prey to pimps. John Reed, Mike Gold and other writers described streets of east side whorehouses. However, Jews traditionally had been in the liquor trade in their homelands and had come to identify drunkenness with peasant louts, therefore alcoholism never was widespread. But Jews were a considerable proportion of addicts, particularly until 1914, at which time opiates were made illegal.

Jewish violence had been very rare in Europe, but here youthful defense against neighboring anti-Semitic gangs, and the spillover from pimping, soon produced a substantial underworld, which took root in the garment industry where they were employed as strike-breakers, and then brought into several unions by bureaucrats to cow the ranks. The most notorious, "Lepke" Buchalter and "Gurrah" Shapiro, who ran a gang of over 200, were finally electrocuted in 1944. "Murder Incorporated," the prime enforcers for the Mafia, were actually Jewish, from the Brownsville section of Brooklyn. Their merger with the Mafia was, in its way, another aspect of the inexorable Jewish assimilation into the surrounding society.

The Jews had been invited into the backward Polish Kingdom in the middle ages to provide the country with merchants and artisans. In the 19th century, better medicine and sanitation produced a Jewish population explosion, which combined with anti-Semitism and competition from mass-produced factory goods to make the position of the rural Jewish lower middle class and craftsmen untenable.

Many migrated into the nearest city, where they sought work in garment and other factories, usually small, owned by Jews. Their new existance made the more thinking see three ways out of their conditions, and they brought these psychologies over with them. Some thought they could scrimp enough to set up a small shop, thus restoring their previous class status, some of the younger thought of educating themselves, and others became revolutionaries.

Adult Jews arriving between 1899 and 1910 were two-thirds skilled, a higher percentage than other immigrating nationalities. Many were tailors and seamstresses, but Jews led in 26 of 47 trades listed by the Immigration Commission. The word sweatshop means exploitation, and certainly their denizens were overworked, but they averaged $12.91 per week in 1908, while typical foreign-born workers received $11.92. Males earned $13.28 and the most skilled were paid $14.90.

A sweatshop could be started with $50 for foot-powered sewing machines. New York had more than 16,000 such contractors in 1913.[25] Typically, the contractor would receive $225 for 300 coats, turned out in a 72-hour week. After deducting minimal rent and paying his workers, he would pay himself a skilled wage and then take an additional profit of $38.10, twice the wage of a skilled worker. Up to one-third failed in a year and submerged back into the working class, but by 1914 the Eastern Europeans were employing more workers than the German Jews.[26]

Innumerable others established themselves in other fields, particularly in retail trades, which required little cash outlay. The candy stores, groceries, clothing stores, silent movie nickelodeons, dance halls, poolrooms and other stores, primarily for the poor, provided a base for the next stage, the advancement of their children.

Seventy-four percent of the Jewish immigrants could read, compared to 64 percent for Poles and 46 percent southern Italians. The Jews learned English faster than all others except Scandinavians. However, it was the sons and daughters of the emerging petty capitalists who became the first generation of scholars. While the proportion of youths who went to high school was greater than most other groups, for many years most working class Jewish teenagers did not go on to high school.[27]

Scholars debate why the Jews came to surpass all other American groupings in their pursuit of learning. Some credit the Talmudic tradition. The ordinary Jewish male was supposed to know his religion. In the theory, Talmudic *pilpul* (hairsplitting) imperceptibly passed over into a passion for secular learning. Doubtless the examples of fathers reading was a crucial factor in their children's attitude; however, secular education was a profound repudiation of the tradition, with its utter reliance upon authority. Much more important were the entrepreneurial reality and the awareness that other Jews, their equals, were rising and going to school. Additionally, the Yiddish press, particularly the *Forverts,* saw itself as an educational force, and ran vast amounts of literary works and scientific articles. Additionally, the German Jews had decided that their cousins needed "less Polish and more polish," and set up settlement houses and educational alliances.

The socialist parties also stressed theory. Many workers and shopkeepers and their student youth learned Marxist economics. Daniel De Leon, a former professor and a socialist leader of the day, actually gave lectures, "Two Pages from Roman History," which were masterful accounts of the class struggles in ancient society. People felt ennobled by such talks; they felt they understood the workings of history, that revelations were given unto them. Books became their solace in their poverty, the escape route for their children. All of these factors fueled the drive toward education, and it would be arbitrary to isolate any of these elements in the complex equation.

For several decades, the emerging capitalist and white collar stratums were a minority within the Jewish population, but by the early 1930's manual workers were only approximately 1/3 of the work force. They were still approximately 30 percent in New York as late as the early 1960s. Most blue collar workers never rose out of their class.[28] However, they wanted their children to "make something of themselves" and these soon poured into the civil service. Eventually they became a majority of New York's elementary and high school teachers.

Revolution became the major cause within the immigrant world. Since the 1880s, persecution and poverty had compelled Jewish revolutionaries to join the non-political immigrants in the U.S., but the initial groups were quite isolated. Mostly of the *intelligentsia,* they spoke Russian amongst themselves and saw themselves as exiles rather than immigrants. It wasn't until after the second wave of pogroms began, in 1903, that Yiddish-speaking radicals began to be a significant force.

In 1897 a new organization, the *Bund,* the General Jewish Workers Union, had been organized in the empire to propagandize in Yiddish, and it soon became one of the prominent groupings within the broad Marxist stream. The newly arrived Bundists were mostly workers, and as Yiddishists to the nth power, they threw themselves into the life of the community. Their fellows in the massive new immigrant wave were also sympathetic to their message, as many had factory experience in Europe, and some began to develop politically.

Domestic radicalism was now also much more conducive to the growth of a mass movement. In the 1890s, the dominant left group was the Socialist Labor Party, mostly Germans, with a few Scandinavians thrown in, and only about 10 percent Americans. Its leader, Daniel De Leon, frequently said to be of West Indian Sephardi origins (though he never declared himself such), was a profound writer at his best, but organizationally dictatorial and sectarian. His character suited the Germans, who looked down on American workers as yokels, and made no real effort to recruit them.

In 1901 a breakaway faction merged with the followers of Eugene Victor Debs to set up the Socialist Party, with the goal of escaping isolation. It was overwhelmingly native-born and it started growing in many directions. When the new Bundist arrivals joined it, the results were explosive for America's Bombay.

In the 1890s the SLP was already receiving about 10 percent of the lower east side vote, and by 1912 the SP's congressional candidate, Meyer London, took 31 percent of the vote. In 1914 he was elected with 47 percent in a three-way race. London wasn't the first socialist to go to Congress. In 1910, Victor Berger, also a Jew, had been elected in Milwaukee, but by German voters. It was that era—London was reelected in 1916, defeated in 1918 and elected again in 1920—that established the image of the Jew as leftist in the American mind. To be sure, they had their opponents, among the Orthodox and the Zionists and the new capitalists, and many inhabitants couldn't vote as they weren't yet citizens, and many others didn't vote out of indifference. Nor did the left win in any other Jewish neighborhood, anywhere in the country. However, the image was valid then, for the left controlled the predominantly Jewish garment unions, the hub of working class life.

What prevented continued left electoral progress was a split in the Socialist Party in the wake of the Bolshevik revolution, and the establishment of a rival Communist Party. The Socialist Party stagnated during the 1920s and finally lost what was left of its mass base to the New Deal. The garment unions also went over to Roosevelt. The Communist Party likewise stagnated in the 1920s, and likewise adapted to Roosevelt, in the late 30s. But unlike the SP, it remained a force in the unions, growing until it had 100,000 members at the time of the 1939 Stalin-Hitler pact, with Jews being the largest ethnic component until that point, when it lost thousands of Jewish members. It was able to recoup these losses after the Nazi invasion of the Soviet Union, and Jews again became the mainstay of party life.[29]

Prior to WWI, Zionism was little more than an offstage noise. The Orthodox saw it as a heresy: God had exiled the Jews for their sins; only the Messiah could restore Israel, and to hasten the coming was yet another sin. Most of Reform, and most of the capitalists, opposed it because it raised questions as to their loyal Americanism. The left was bitterly opposed. Zionism was—and to a considerable extent still is—a charity movement. Workers saw its fundraisers getting donations from their bosses, and felt that money that by rights should have gone to them was going to build a national museum in Palestine. Most Yiddishists loathed

Zionism, with its depreciation of their language as an "exile" tongue.

Later, having no answers to the Hitler menace, the Zionists limped through the Holocaust, only coming to dominate organized Jewish life in the late 1940s with the creation of the Israeli state.

It was the Johnson Act of 1924 which brought an end to the great migration from Eastern Europe. It limited total immigration to 154,000 per year, and within that it set quotas, two percent of a nationality living in the U.S. in 1890, before the bulk of Eastern Europeans and Mediterraneans had arrived. Starting in 1925, Poland was allowed 5,982 immigrants, Russia 2,148 and Rumania only 749. Naturally not all of these would be Jews. Between 1925 and 1932 only approximately 78,000 Jews entered the country, roughly four percent of the total immigrants.

The Emigrés from Nazi Germany

Nazism propelled German Jews into exile, but the new Democratic Administration did nothing to repeal the Johnson Act, and no more than 33,000 were admitted between 1933-37. In all, 63,000 were finally admitted. The number of Jewish immigrants, from all countries, only rose to 43,450 in 1939, with only 174,678 Jews being admitted between 1933 and 1945. In only two of those years, 1939-40, did Jews constitute a majority of immigrants.

The German Jewish exiles were not the kind of people who normally migrate. Nearly one-fifth were professionals and 41.9 percent were businessmen who, even with Nazi exit taxes, brought out $650,000,000. Naturally this then-huge sum was unevenly distributed, with early emigrés taking out sizable proportions of their wealth, fortunes in some cases, while others brought modest sums and the last fleeing virtually penniless.[30] They were history's most educated emigrés and by forcing the departure of Einstein and other scientists, Hitler unwittingly had handed technological supremacy to the U.S.

Most relocated in the "Fourth Reich," Washington Heights in upper Manhattan, but eventually they dispersed. Many were indifferent to Judaism. Even today the oldest retain an interest in things German, but because of the Nazis' bestiality, they naturally see themselves as Jews rather than as Germans. As with the previous groupings, they are Americanized and intermarry with native Jews and, increasingly, with gentiles. Henry Kissinger, who came here at age 14, is one of these last.

The Post-War Refugees

In the 15 years 1944-59, 191,693 immigrants arrived, over 63,000 of them coming in above the quota system, under the Displaced Persons Act of 1949. Most of these were Eastern Europeans and several thousands were Chassids, who significantly increased their communities in Brooklyn, particularly the Satmir sect, the most intransigent anti-Zionist wing of Orthodoxy. Between 1960-68 roughly 73,000 more Jews arrived. Some were businessmen from Cuba, others remnants of "Sephardic" communities in the Arab world that had become untenable after the creation of the Zionist state.

The Israelis Among Us

After the Holocaust, a considerable number of Eastern European Jews migrated to Israel, not out of ideological considerations but because it was open to them. Eventually many of them began to drift to the U.S. where they had relatives, and where there were better opportunities. That alone would have been an embarrassment to Zionism, but they were soon followed out by "sabras," native born Israelis.

No one is certain how many *yordim* ("those who go down") have come to the U.S., and for many years interested parties, both Zionists—who saw them as a "problem" to be dealt with—and anti-Zionists, tended to exaggerate their numbers, but recently some realistic studies have been made available.

Between 1950-79, 96,504 Israeli citizens received legal immigrant status here.[31] An additional 23,000 are estimated to be illegals.[32] Native-born Israelis have been the majority since 1966, and about 75 percent since 1978. The emigré stream increases by about 10 percent each year. A little fewer than one out of 50 Jews in America are now ex-Israelis.

Three-quarters live in New York, New Jersey, Illinois or California, with most living in areas with high concentrations of Jews. More than 70 percent are professionals and white collar employees, but about 5 percent are in services, notably as taxi drivers, and sometimes owners of fleets.

The high visibility of these has given the public the illusion that the bulk of the migrants are lower class. There is one element, however, that has deeply prejudiced many Jews against them. The April 29,1984, *Jerusalem Post* reported that a U.S. Senate Judiciary Committee study estimates that "approximately 1,000 individuals" are involved "in a myriad of organized criminal activities." Their activities are growing in New York, California and elsewhere, and include

> insurance frauds, fictitious billing, bankruptcy fraud, extortion, narcotics deals, illegal immigration and homicide . . . these Israelis are heavily involved in the importation and distribution of narcotics, especially cocaine and heroin.[33]

The yordim trouble American Jews, particularly those with Zionist sympathies, in many other ways. Israel is a settlers' laager, and can survive only if the wagons circle together to face the Indians. Committed Israeli Zionists see the yordim as, at best, a problem, and many think of them as little more than traitors. Many American Zionists see them in the same way, but have ambiguous feelings because they themselves have no intention of moving to Israel. Some Jewish organizations will not hire them, both out of loyalty to Zionism and because of their own guilt feelings. Additionally, the violence of Israeli society, generated by militarism, and slum conditions (which produce the criminal element), has developed an extremely aggressive national character.

At the other end of the social spectrum, Israel produces the world's highest percentage of university graduates, but competition for jobs there is severe, and an extremely arrogant know-it-all is frequently the end product. American Jews, primarily of humble Yiddish stock, and sharing this country's own democratic traditions, tend to be put off by many of these "ugly Israelis," whom they see as brash at best and often untrustworthy hustlers. It is ironic, but that was how the classic anti-Semites described Jews. Today such behavior is looked down on as un-Jewish.[34]

The Russians

A simultaneous source of intense agitation and humiliation for the Zionist-oriented organized Jewish community has been the Soviet Jewish immigration. Soviet Jewry's conditions have varied widely in different periods. In Lenin's time there were Jewish autonomous regions, complete with courts and schools in Yiddish. However, by Stalin's last paranoid months, he imprisoned his doctors as Zionists plotting to poison him. At present, the number of Jews in the Supreme Soviet, the parliament, has risen from six of 1,550, in 1979, to eight now, with two born Jews, declaring themselves to be of Russian nationality, sitting with them (Jews are 0.67 percent of the population).[35] Jews are over-represented in the Communist Party and their number in top committees is rising.[36] A higher proportion of Jews are party members than any other nationality.

Now primarily an intellectual elite group, Soviet Jewry's income is higher than that of Russians'. But the Bolshevik revolution degenerated into a stultifying bureaucracy, incapable of maintaining the loyalty of much of its bureaucratic and intellectual cadre. No longer inspired by the equalitarianism of classic Leninism, many Jewish dissidents have no interest in revolutionizing their society, and instead compare their status to their Western equivalents. Ultimately, economics, not discrimination, must be seen as the motive for migration to the U.S.

Stalin maintained the classic Leninist position that Zionism was reactionary until 1947, when he decided that the then-Arab regimes were hopelessly tied to Britain, and that expelling the British from the region would only begin with a Zionist victory in Palestine. Until then, the Kremlin's position was that its Jews had no homeland other than the Soviet Union. With recognition came a complete ideological change. Israel became the official Jewish homeland.

With Israeli success in the 1967 war, Zionist enthusiasm was rekindled among many Jews in the Baltic republics, Moldavia and other regions where Zionist movements had flourished in the pre-war period, before they were annexed to the Soviet Union during WWII, and in Georgia and Central Asia, where the local communities were deeply Orthodox. As a gesture towards western opinion, the regime decided to allow emigration to Israel "for family reunifications."

All observers agree that the flow of migrants from the late 1960s until 1984, when it virtually stopped, was determined by relations between the USSR and the U.S., rather than by Moscow's attitude towards Israeli policies. Obtaining advanced technology is a top Soviet priority, and if the American politicians wanted such emigration in exchange, the Soviets were willing to pay that price.

All the emigrés applied to go to Israel, and the vast majority went there until 1974, when 19 percent of those arriving at Vienna, the central transit point, decided to go to America. The percentage of *noshrim* (Hebrew for those who fall away) steadily increased to 81 percent in 1981.[37] Naturally the Soviets were aware of these statistics, but emigrés still had to declare Israel as their destination, as the right to such emigration is normally open only to nationalities with homelands outside the USSR. The U.S. didn't mind—getting Jews out of the Soviet Union was popular here—and the presence of tens of thousands of people who had chosen the "Free World" was wonderful propaganda.

It was the Israeli government which tried to stop the new emigration. Israel has always opposed Jews fighting for their rights in the Soviet Union, or joining the all-Soviet struggle for democracy. It sees the Soviets as a major factor in Middle Eastern affairs, and is afraid Moscow would take it out on them if Zionists involved themselves in the opposition.[38] Nor was Jerusalem in favor of the general right to emigrate, and it did everything it could to stop the Hebrew Immigrant Aid Society from helping those who chose America, on the grounds that their going there would provide an excuse for the Soviets to cut off all emigration, thus jeopardizing the immigration into Israel.[39]

Between 1971 and 1980, 79,806 Soviet Jews entered the U.S. Most were from the Russian and Ukrainian republics and, unlike the border region emigrés, few had any contact with Zionism prior to their signing to go to Israel, as the movement had been crushed within the inter-war Soviet borders in the 1920s. Everyone informally refers to them as "the Russians," as few know any Yiddish, which their parents abandoned after their migration from the former Pale into the major Soviet cities in the 1920s and 30s. About half are non-religious with the other half calling themselves traditional, meaning they follow some rituals or observe some holidays. Just over 40 percent attend synagogues only on a few high holidays, with only 15 percent attending more regularly and only 8 percent identifying themselves as strongly religious. The most pious are largely elderly and uneducated. Approximately one-eighth are married to non-Jews.

They have ambivalent feelings towards America. As most of them are professionals, they have a higher income than the typical American, but many feel that professional requirements here frequently compel them to work below their Soviet status.[40] They like the greater freedom, but they are quite cultured and many see

American tastes as vulgar. When urban crime touches them they are stunned: "Here, the children punch the teacher. In Russia, you hit the teacher . . . the police take you to jail."[41]

A survey showed that while most of them thought American Jews were interesting or at least acceptable, few have American friends, Jewish or otherwise, and 40 percent found American Jews politically naive, with 28.2 percent seeing them as utter bores.[42] Although a substantial minority send their children to Jewish day schools, the prime reason is not religion but simply that they have contempt for the public schools. Although they are voracious readers in comparison to Americans, the poll showed that 43.1 percent hadn't read even one book about the U.S. since their arrival, and only 31.5 percent had read anything about Judaism. Essentially, they are isolated in their narrow community, and most definitely want their children to learn Russian.[43]

Writing in the Ashes of History

Such is, in brief outline, the history of the several immigrations that produced today's approximately 5,377,000 American Jews, 2.54 percent of the country's population, and 43.9 percent of the world's Jews.[44] The past is the prologue to the present, and therefore the future, but what is its real relevance for today's Jews and today's America? The languages they brought over are dead or dying or, with Hebrew and Russian, certain to fade away. The religion? By the early 1970s only 30.6 percent of all heads of households under the age of 30 were synagogue members, and the percentage is certainly less today.[45]

Some Jews, and not only Zionists, have substituted ethnicity for religious identity, but in the same 1970s survey 62.3 percent of all adults were listed as not at all active in any Jewish organization, and 23.2 percent as slightly or doubtfully so.[46] Of all Jews who married in the last ten years, 40 percent took non-Jewish spouses, and intermarriage constantly rises.[47] The past is dead; it cannot hold the Jews together.

Are there lessons to be learned from the past? Indeed it has been said that if we don't learn from the mistakes of the past we are doomed to repeat them. True enough, except that a wag has added that the only lesson to be learned from the past is that people don't learn from it.

Scholars study the past and some, but only some, genuinely profit from their efforts. Broad masses rarely devote themselves

The Golden Door

37

to history, still less learn from it, and even fewer apply those lessons to our present situation. That does not mean that traditions have no impact on popular thinking. On the contrary, every educated person is a philosopher of a sort, and characteristically intellectuals think they know more about history than they actually do. You can do anything with the past except live in it. Whatever people may think they are doing, they operate on the basis of their contemporary status, not that of their grandparents. If their familial baggage includes an ideology, they reinterpret it to suit themselves.

In the wake of the 1984 election, when the Jews were the only white ethnics to deny the majority of their votes to Ronald Reagan, articles poured forth hailing or bemoaning the "fact" that they had stayed loyal to "their liberal tradition." The grandparents of many of the Jews who voted for Walter Mondale had supported Eugene Debs. These Mondale backers may have thought they were carrying through the progressive Jewish tradition. Were they?

One thing is certain: Debs never would have voted for an unabashed enthusiast for capitalism. At best, the Mondale vote was a final distortion of the immigrant left tradition; at worst, it was yet another sign of modern Jewry's deep assimilation into the melting pot of mainstream American capitalist politics.

The Jews came here to get away from the Inquisition, from pogroms, from Hitler, from poverty and from militarism. We will see that most of them have risen, some to the heights of their society. But while they were rising, the nation in fact was declining. A country once known for its majestic natural beauty is now notorious for its leaking toxic waste dumps. Spiritually, it is no better. Once we had a president, Thomas Jefferson, who toasted the world revolution. Today America is the world's leading counter-revolutionary force. The Jews came to what was once called the land of the free, home of the brave. We now know it as "the land of the freak, home of the knave."

Notes

1. David Nidel, "Modern Descendants of Conversos in New Mexico," *Western States Jewish History,* April 1984, p. 256.
2. Stephen Birmingham, *The Grandees,* pp. 49, 53.
3. Marshall Sklare, *American Jews,* p. 6; and Chaim Waxman, *America's Jews in Transition,* p. 6.
4. Chaim Waxman, *America's Jews in Transition,* p. 81.

5.   Birmingham, pp. 152–53.
6.   Max Dimont, *The Jews in America*, p. 58.
7.   Thomas Sowell, *Ethnic America*, pp. 76, 89.
8.   Waxman, p. 51.
9.   "Sephardim," *Encyclopedia Judaica*, vol. 14, columns 1170-1; and Marc Angel, "The Sephardim of the United States: An Exploratory Study," *American Jewish Year Book 1973*, p. 100.
10.   Dimont, p. 129; and Sowell, p. 78.
11.   "Pittsburgh Platform," *EJ*, vol. 13, col. 571.
12.   "United States of America," *EJ*, vol. 15, col. 1602.
13.   Irving Howe, *World of Our Fathers*, p. 6.
14.   "USA," *EJ*, vol. 15, col. 1608.
15.   *AJYB 1936*, p. 558.
16.   "Migrations," *EJ*, vol. 16, col. 1519-20.
17.   Waxman, p. 30.
18.   *AJYB 1936*, p. 558.
19.   Sowell, p. 83.
20.   Arthur Liebman, *Jews and the Left*, p. 139.
21.   "USA," *EJ*, vol. 15, col. 1615.
22.   Sowell, p. 83.
23.   *AJYB 1936*, p. 555.
24.   Isaac Bashevis Singer, "Jewish Peoples, Arts of," *Encyclopedia Britannica*, vol. 10, p. 199.
25.   Stephen Steinberg, *The Ethnic Myth*, pp. 97–100.
26.   Howe, pp. 158-9.
27.   Steinberg, pp. 227-8.
28.   Liebman, pp. 360-2.
29.   Ibid., pp. 57–60.
30.   "Refugees," *EJ*, vol. 14, col. 29.
31.   Aharon Fein, "The Rate of Emigration from Israel," *Forum on the Jewish People, Zionism and Israel*, Fall 1984, p. 58.
32.   Pini Herman, "The Myth of the Israeli Expatriate," *Moment*, Sept. 1983, pp. 62-3.
33.   Wolf Blitzer, "Israeli, Soviet Jewish Immigrants Involved in U.S. Organized Crime," *Jerusalem Post*, April 29, 1984, p. 9.
34.   Herman, p. 63.
35.   "USSR," *Jewish Currents*, May 1984, p. 47.
36.   W.D. Rubinstein, *The Left, the Right and the Jews*, pp. 188-9.
37.   William Blair, "HIAS Quits Israeli Plan for Settling Soviet Jews," *NY Times*, May 7, 1982.
38.   Anatole Shub, "From Russia with Chutzpah," *Harpers*, May 1972.
39.   Bernard Gwertzman, "U.S. and Israel Disagree on Giving Soviet Jews Choice Where to Settle," *NY Times*, pp. 1, 8.
40.   Ilya Levkov, "Adaptation and Acculturation of Soviet Jews in the United States: A Preliminary Analysis," *Soviet Jewry in the Decisive Decade*, 1971-80, pp. 109–43 passim.
41.   James Brooke, "Slayings Anger Russian Community," *NY Times*, Oct. 15, 1984, p. B3.
42.   Levkov, pp. 141-2.
43.   Zvi Gitelman, "Soviet-Jewish Immigrants to the United States: Profile, Problems, Prospects," *Soviet Jewry in the Decisive Decade*, pp. 96-7.
44.   Alvin Chenkin, "Jewish Population in the United States, 1983," p. 162; and U.O. Schmelz and Sergio DellaPergola, "World Jewish Population, 1982," *AJYB 1984*, p. 258.

45. Fred Massarik and Alvin Chenkin, "United States National Jewish Population Study: A first Report," *AJYB 1973,* p. 282.

46. Ibid., p.301

47. Glenn Collins, "A New Look at Intermarriage in the U.S.," *NY Times,* Feb. 11, 1985, p.16.

2

The Jews and the Left

Several questions are raised by the attraction revolution once held for many Jews, and the subsequent Jewish alienation from the left. Did Judaism predispose Jews towards socialism? When did Jewish involvement with the left become significant? What is the historic relationship between Marxism and anti-Semitism? Was Marx an anti-Semite? Is the modern left anti-Semitic? Or is the present-day estrangement primarily due to the objectively divergent evolution of the Jews and the left? Did the Jews gain or lose by moving away from the left? What was the typical evolution of those radicals who moved to the right? What will be the future relationship between the Jews and the left?

1. Did Judaism predispose Jews toward socialism?

Though the vast majority of Jewish revolutionaries were atheists, many people believe Jewish radicalism was rooted in the Bible they rejected. It is held that the left had merely secularized the prophets' cry against injustice. These people see what they want to see.

40

The Old Testament is a collection of ancient documents and legends redacted by centuries of scribes utilizing the communal theology of Israel and Judah to describe the evolution of the world around them. Far from explaining society, the Bible was itself a reflection of society and can only be explained by the evolution it attempted to interpret.

By modern standards Judaism is jarring in its ethnic and religious chauvinism, and extreme and contradictory in its social ethics, real and ideal. Contained within Moses' wilderness strictures are ample injunctions for justice or exploitation, as you will. Thus the bedouin lawgiver proclaims the jubilee, i.e, frees slaves the ex-slaves could not then have had:

> If . . . a Hebrew . . . serve thee six years . . . in the seventh year thou shalt let him go free . . . thou shalt remember that thou wast a bondman in the land of Egypt . . . if he say unto thee, I will not go away from thee, because he loveth thee . . . thou shalt take an awl, and thrust it through his ear unto the door, and he shall be thy servant for ever. (Deut. 15: 12-17)

However, the same servant of the one God instructs the chosen people that:

> Every creditor that lendeth aught unto his neighbor shall release it . . . of a foreigner thou mayest exact it again: but that which is thine with thy brother thine hand shall release; Save when there shall be no poor among you . . . Only if thou carefully hearken unto the voice of the Lord . . . thy God blesseth thee . . . and thou shalt lend unto many nations, but thou shalt not borrow, and thou shalt reign over many nations, but they shall not reign over thee. (Deut. 15:2-6)

Orthodox Judaism is notorious for its obsessive-compulsive ritualism, but Isaiah's deity demands to know:

> To what purpose is the multitude of your sacrifices unto me? . . . bring no more vain oblations . . . your hands are full of blood . . . Learn to do well; seek judgement, relieve the oppressed, judge the fatherless, plead for the widow. (Isaiah 1: 11-17)

Ancient Jewry was sharply divided by class and sect. On the mass level religion indeed was a psychological opiate, Marx's "heart of the heartless world," a world which debated the beginning and end of things, and justice in between, but had not yet invented the stirrup. A profound longing for justice developed, for all its natural and social limitations and concomitant fanatic expressions. However, neither justice nor grounded realism were genuinely attainable in an epoch of sybaritic luxury amidst primeval ignorance.

Zeal for justice sometimes took national form against foreign oppression, but just as often the mighty amongst the Hebrews were excoriated. Nationalist fervor was extinguished in the blood and fire of the revolts against Rome in 66-70 A.D. and 132-35 A.D. Popular hatred of the Temple priests and the rich became the basis of Christianity, and the New Testament must be seen as the last major production of the Jewish religious genre. It too contains the same incongruities; denunciations of the rich and powerful stand side by side with bleating homilies admonishing slaves to obey their masters.

The New Testament does not explain the evolution of Christianity. The church's transition from a heretical plebeian Jewish sect into a pillar of the emerging feudal order explains the many contradictions of its holy book. But modern Judaism is not the heir of either of these urges. It is the direct descendant of the school of Yabneh, set up by Johanan ben Zakkai, a Pharisee opposed to the first revolt, whose disciples carried him out of besieged Jerusalem in a coffin, bringing him to the Roman general Vespasian, who allowed him to set up his quietist academy.

After the destruction of the Temple in 70 A.D., the rabbis, who now dominated the surviving communities in Palestine and elsewhere, saw the defeat as God's judgment upon the Jews, who he exiled for their sins. The Talmud commanded them never to try to retake their land or rush the coming of the Messiah who, alone, would restore them. Nor could they add to their sins by rebelling against the gentiles in whose midst they found themselves.

Although there are some dignified social statements within the Talmud, as with the insistence that Jews should always stand with the oppressed, in fact Orthodoxy was in principle for accommodation with the powers that be. Jewish liberalism, and then radicalism, are modern phenomena, brought about by the bourgeois enlightment in Europe, and the subsequent decline of Orthodoxy. Individual Jews may have been inspired by selected Biblical passages, exactly as Christian liberals were influenced by New Testament rhetoric, but the modern concern for social justice goes side by side with repudiation of religion. Immigrant leftists mocked the synagogues, organized Yom Kippur balls and ate pork before the scandalized eyes of believers. Contrariwise, the religious, be they Orthodox, Conservative or Reform, never were in the front ranks of social protest throughout the entirety of the American Jewish working-class era.

2. When did Jewish involvement with the left become significant? What is the historic relationship between Marxism and anti-Semitism? Was Marx an anti-Semite?

The internalized ghetto of medieval Jewry began to collapse with the rabbis' impotent excommunication of Baruch Spinoza (1632-77), the lens-grinder pantheist of baroque Amsterdam. However, the Jewish role in the classic age of bourgeois revolutions, in Holland, America or France, was not significant. It was only in the lifetime of Heinrich Heine, with his poetic passport of conversion, that Jews began to be significant on the left.

Several Jews, loosely defined, played a crucial role in the emerging 19th-century working-class movement, and one of these, Karl Marx, certainly is the central figure of socialist intellectual history. Marx's father had converted so as to have a career with the Prussian civil service, and Karl was baptized a Lutheran at six.

In recent years the Zionist right has taken to writing much about "the anti-Semitism of the left," and have proclaimed Marx as its father. They point to a very few lines in his enormous writings, mainly in his letters, and a scattering of remarks on Jews and Judaism in his published works, to prove their case. Among other things, in his letters to Engels he referred to Ferdinand Lasalle, a rival socialist, as a "Jewish Nigger," meaning he was stubborn and stupid, and in an exposé of a Tsarist agent he ridiculed a hostile editor, Moses Levy, whom "Mother Nature in extravagantly Gothic writing had inscribed his family tree in the middle of his face."

Though such evidence is real, the charge is false. Marx was developing a materialist historical methodology, but by no means did he or his collaborator Fredrich Engels completely emancipate themselves from their epoch and its prejudices. To us they are upper-class Victorians, albeit with revolutionary politics. By our standards they are both male chauvinists, but so was virtually every male of their time. Again, by our lights, they were racists, but so was Lincoln. By modern criteria, Marx's slurs are anti-Semitic, but this likewise has little meaning.

From the start Marx's practical politics were progressive on the Jewish question. In his early 1840s essay "On the Jewish Question," Marx portrayed Judaism as completely capitalistic, nevertheless the piece is a polemic in favor of granting full rights to the Jews. The Zionists do not tell us that Theodor Herzl, the founder of the World Zionist Organization, attended a synagogue in Paris in 1894, and told of his disgust at his fellow Jews and their "bold, misshapened noses, furtive and cunning eyes." He denounced one of the Rothschilds as "Mauschel"—kike in English. Today no enlightened gentile would use the kind of language the Jewish founders of Marxism and Zionism used in their time, but we live in the post-Holocaust epoch, they did not.

Marx and Engels's bilious utterances, re Blacks, Jews, Russians, and others, have long been found in their collected letters and writings, and their later-day followers disassociated themselves from their slurs, while developing their dialectical historical analysis. The need for scientific precision on ethnicity only became apparent to revolutionaries in the late 19th and early 20th century, when they had to compete directly with nationalists for the allegiance of the masses.

The fight against anti-Semitism and all other forms of chauvinism became central to Communism. Lenin became positively prudish on the matter, opposing even the most harmless ethnic and dialect humor. Certainly Marx would never have been accepted into the Bolshevik Party with his crude remarks, any more than he would be admitted into any modern Marxist group with his sexism. However, looking for the roots of Stalinist anti-Semitism in Marx is simply peeping down the wrong end of the historical telescope.

Stalin's later-day paranoia was not in any direct line from Marx's offhand remarks. Lenin's writings on nationality, not Marx's statements, became the touchstones of Communism on the Jewish question. Stalin's anti-Semitism is to be seen as another aspect of his repudiation of Leninism, not as an extention of Marx's philosophy.

3. Is the modern left anti-Semitic? Or is the present-day estrangement primarily due to the objectively divergent evolution of the Jews and the left?

If "who is a Jew?" arouses debate, "who is a leftist?" equals it
for argument. The left is a very broad church, with most of the
congregations in conflict with each other. Neil Kinnock's British
Labor Party, Mikhail Gorbachev's politburo and Ernest Mandel's
Trotskyist 4th International differ on Jewish matters, but none
now command a growing mass following among Jews. The BLP
is in the same reformist Socialist International as Shimon Peres's
ruling Israeli Labor Party, and Kinnock and the reigning bureaucrats are pro-Israel, yet increasing numbers of Jews cross over to
the formerly anti-Semitic Tories.

In America, Michael Harrington's Democratic Socialists of
America are likewise strongly pro-Israel and share the Jewish
majority's Democratic Party politics. Although Jews are a substantial minority, at least, of its ranks, Harrington would concede
the DSA is nit-sized in terms of influence among the broad Jewish public. DSA's inability to establish a mass Jewish base is
explainable in terms of the sociology of Jewry, rather than by
DSA's ideology. Absent anti-Semitism, not even pale pink social
democratic reformists will find a strong perch among upward-
moving Jewish intellectuals. It is that mobility which is the sociological motive force behind the alienation of the left and post-
Holocaust diaspora. The only country with a blue collar Jewish
proletariat is Israel, and even there unskilled labor is "Arab
work."

The international capitalist conglomerates welcome Jews at all
levels except in matters involving Arabs. Anti-Semitism and
poverty pushed much of Jewry to the left; neither now goad
western Jews. Hatred of Jews is a factor of varying importance in
the Soviet and Islamic worlds, but even there intellectualization is
extinguishing the Jewish manual trades. The drift from the left is
true of the entire diaspora except Argentina, with its intense Yid-
dishism and domestic populist passions. "The people of the book"
have become central to modern economic and intellectual life.
America's wealth meant the upward turn developed more
vigorously than elsewhere, and the weight of its 5.5 million Jews
has given the organized community disproportionate clout in a
country overwhelmingly inhabited by apathetic political naifs, but
the same result appears everywhere Jews are free of extreme
and/or government-sanctioned anti-Semitism: acceptance and ultimate assimilation into the mandarin stratum and business elite.

All left currents were a minority within the Jewish milieu after the post WWI split in the Socialist party, but it was Stalinism that was, by far, the most influential left tendency from 1927 until after the 1956 Khrushchev revelations. There is no exact figure, but certainly the Jewish proportion of the Communist Party of U.S.A. exceeded that of any other ethnic community. An educated estimate would be that between 40 and 50 percent of the party was Jewish between the late 1930 and mid-1940s.[1] Subsequent to the Kremlin's acknowledgment of Stalin's crimes, particularly against Jews, the last substantial numerical linkage between the left and the immigrant generations was severed.

The CPUSA had already declined from about 100,000 in 1944 to 20,000 in 1956, due to public exposure, McCarthyite intimidation, and a self-purge which expelled all but a hard core. The party shrank to under 10,000 after the revelations, and many of the remaining Jews left it. A rump Jewish party apparatus remained intact, with the *Freiheit* continuing on as a Yiddish daily and *Jewish Currents* as a monthly English-language journal. But these now catered to what amounted to a hermetically sealed, increasingly elderly, Yiddishist working-class Communist subculture.

Unable to withstand the justifiable contempt of Jewish opinion in the post-revelations period, the ethnic hacks around the two publications eased out of the party in 1970, although neither they nor the party thought to inform the public of the fact until the party finally broke the silence in 1977.

Jewish Currents now completely identifies with the Democratic Party, and while it is critical of right-wing elements within Zionism, its special venom is reserved for those on the left who oppose Zionism in principle.

Today's CP is virtually unrepresented among Jewish youth. It now has another magazine, *Jewish Affairs,* but its intellectual quality is poor, and the publication has few readers outside the ever-aging Party. That a party which defended anti-Semitic murders is now the only major left tendency with a journal devoted to Jewish matters is ironic, but even with that, such a grouping can never attract Jews again, on a mass basis, no matter how sincerely it attempts to apologize for or atone for its crimes.

While many Zionists claim that Trotskyist anti-Zionism equals anti-Semitism, few Jews believe the fable. Given the fact that their families emigrated from what is now the Soviet Union, it is scarcely surprising that a minority of Jewish youth have an

interest in Russian history. But as is typical of descendants of
immigrants, generations removed from "the old country," almost
invariably their actual knowledge is minimal, disjointed and
stereotyped. However, if they know anything, they know Trotsky
as the organizer of the Red Army, which ultimately routed the
pogromists.

While today's Trotskyists clearly support the Palestinians, they
have Israeli and American Jewish members. Their literature
rarely even discusses American Jewry except occasionally in the
context of dealing with Zionism, and not even their Zionist
opponents accuse them of making the slightest attack on the
equality of Jews with other Americans.

It is not their pro-Palestinian stance or their attitude toward
America's Jews that is the basis of Trotskyist isolation from the
modern Jewish intelligentsia. As we shall see, Jewish academics
are by and large not interested in either the rump American Jewish community or Zionism. The Socialist Workers Party came to
play a pivotal role in the organizing of Vietnam anti-war demonstrations, and many Jews worked with them, utterly indifferent to
their middle-eastern politics.

Two factors are involved, beyond the sociological evolution of
Jewry. It has been 69 years since the Bolshevik revolution, 46
years since Trotsky's assassination, and 12 years since the final
fall of Saigon. For today's youth, Trotskyism is History, without
visible impact on the present. Even more important is the fact that
the Trotskyists, along with almost all other left currents, abandoned the universities, where young Jews congregate, to march
off to the factories, looking for a working-class base. Ultimately
we see here again that it is sociology, not ideology, that puts most
Jews and the revolution on different paths.

4.   Did the Jews gain or lose by moving away from the left?

It was the Democratic Party, "the immigrant's party," that
gained from the rightward drift. "Poor people have poor ways,"
and the naive poor were grateful to the New Deal with its unemployment compensation and work projects. But, of course, the
Democrats were only giving them crumbs from their table. The
party remained what it always was, an instrument of the capitalist
class, and as such, it never had the interests of the Jewish masses
in mind. The Democrats made not the slightest effort in the 1930s
to open the gates to German Jewish refugees, and during the

ensuing war, the party's role was disgraceful. Jimmy Carter was only conceding what the scholars had already exposed when, decades later, he said that "We," *i.e.,* Roosevelt and his party, "turned our backs on the Jews."

The Democrats subsequent post-war importation of Nazi scientists and the utilization of war criminals such as Klaus Barbie was motivated by anti-Communism rather than anti-Semitism. Nevertheless, it was criminal, and demonstrated the impotence of Jewry vis-à-vis the party, despite its overwhelming support for Roosevelt and Truman. The latter was willing to allow a substantial post-war Jewish refugees influx, but Congress was dominated by Republicans and Dixiecrat racists and the 63,000 Jewish Displaced Persons eventually admitted scarcely qualifies as a Jewish victory.

The Democratic Party's patronage of Israel since 1948 is the beginning of the modern American Jewish political era, and will be dealt with in detail in a subsequent chapter, but it is sufficient to emphasize here that the immense change in the relationship between the Jews and the larger American society in the subsequent years could never begin to compensate for the Democratic Party's share of culpability in the Jewish catastrophe during the age of the dictators.

For the apolitical masses, the turn toward the Democrats did not alter their relationship to reality. For the most part, they had only a tangential connection to the left, voting for an occasional candidate, paying their dues to a left-led union or a socialist-run insurance co-op, and they were to be equally passive in their new relationship to the Democratic Party.

But what of the reformist socialist and Stalinist and Trotskyist party leaders, union presidents, and intellectuals who abandoned their opposition to capitalism to enter the Democratic Party? To be sure, some few arrived politically, in the most cynical, most American sense. And, eventually, the Jews' status in the society did rise, but these changes are to be seen throughout the west in the post-Holocaust, cold-war world and cannot be credited to the activities of any Jewish ex-radicals. If the majority of Jews here prospered, those who embraced the enemies of their youth disgraced themselves. For the umpteenth time the Old Testament proverb proved true: "The prosperity of fools shall destroy them."

The garment union leaders led the retreat to the Democrats, splitting from the Socialist Party in 1933. In 1936, David Dubinsky, head of the International Ladies Garment Workers Union, and Sidney Hillman of the Amalgamated Clothing Workers, joined Alex Rose, a long-time Zionist and leader of the Millinery Workers Union, to set up New York's American Labor Party.

Many Jewish workers still thought themselves socialists but wanted to vote for Roosevelt. However, they could not get themselves to vote the Democratic ticket, as they identified the local party with the notorious corruption of Tammany Hall. The ALP provided Roosevelt with a "clean" ballot position. Later the CP captured the ALP and the union tops broke off to set up the Liberal Party in 1944.

While the Liberals play the field in local politics, endorsing Democrats and occasionally Republicans running as such, and sometimes backing maverick Democrats and Republicans running on the Liberal line against their own party machines, nationally they are committed to the Democrats. Dwindling for decades, isolated from the masses, the Liberals ended up a patronage machine, pieced off by the major parties in return for providing the extra ballot position for deserving Democrats and Republicans.

Behind the scenes, the realities were sinister, with the garment bureaucrats being among the first into the cold-war trenches. In 1944, Jay Lovestone, an ex-Communist Party leader, who later made his peace with Dubinsky, was put in charge of their front, the American Federation of Labor's Free Trade Union Committee.

The *Encyclopedia Judaica* article on Lovestone tells the tale of the degeneration of the Jewish labor movement:

He constructed a world-wide intelligence network which, throughout the Cold War era, worked closely with the CIA. When the AFL and CIO merged, Lovestone continued his anti-Communist activities within the merged labor movement's Department of International Affairs. During the 1960s he vigorously supported American military intervention in Cuba, the Dominican Republic, and Vietnam, and opposed the concepts and practitioners of neutralism and revolutionary nationalism.[2]

Readers who have seen the movie *Reds* will recall the Socialist Party's leaders calling the cops against John Reed and the pro-

Bolshevik majority at the SP's 1919 convention. But no amount of police protection could hide the party's sharp decline in the ensuing 1920s. Norman Thomas received more than 900,000 votes in the 1932 Depression election, but the vote declined to 187,342 votes in 1936 and 99,557 votes in 1940.

The SP survived the 1933 withdrawal of the bureaucrats. Its ranks witnessed the shameful defeat of their co-thinkers of the reformist German Social Democratic Party that same year (the giant SDP did not fire a shot in defense when Hitler suppressed it), and the now much smaller party lurched to the left. The militants opened the party to the Trotskyists, and the suddenly charged-up SP entered into a phase of intense activity. However, the forces around Thomas were still muddled reformers, bent out of shape by the German events, and they could never co-exist in one party with the gifted intellectuals drawn to Trotskyism in the 1930s. (Hal Draper, Sidney Hook, Irving Howe, Irving Kristol, Seymour Martin Lipset, George Novack, to name only Jews among them, each with his present politics, are still in the front ranks of America's older political intellectuals.)

The SP split again in 1938, with the Trotskyists forming the more active Socialist Workers Party.

Thomas scandalized Jews in 1941, when he shared America First platforms with Charles Lindbergh, an open anti-Semite. But he was merely a naive semi-pacifist semi-radical in so doing. He continued on as the party's perennial presidential candidate, with fringe celebrity name recognition, but the reality of the SP was perfectly summed up in a James Thurber cartoon in *The New Yorker,* where someone asked: "What ever happened to the Socialist Party?" It wasn't until the mid-1950s, when it united with a rightward moving current around Max Shachtman, one of the founders of the Trotskyist movement, that the party revived, in time to play an important role in the organizational engine rooms of the civil rights movement.

Again the behind-the-scenes story was sordid. On February 22, 1967, *The New York Times* reported that Thomas's Institute for International Labor Research had received $1,048,940 between 1961 and 1963 from a CIA conduit. Thomas was 82 in 1967, and the impression he tried to give in the *Times* interview was that he was just a foolish old dupe rather than an active hustler after CIA bucks, but he had personally solicited "the company" in the mid-1950s for the American Committee for Cultural Freedom.

The ACCF had become a catch-basin for failed leftists turned anti-Communist, with Thomas and Sidney Hook among its most prominent members. Hook, who abandoned Trotskyism in the early 1930s, is today the chairman of Social Democrats USA, a successor organization to the SP. In the July 1982 *Commentary* he revealed what he knew, then, of Thomas's connection to the CIA:

> When it was unable to pay its rent . . . Thomas . . . telephoned Allen Dulles of the CIA and requested a contribution . . . he said that he and Dulles had been friends and classmates at Princeton . . . and that he had solicited the contribution purely on the basis of his personal friendship.[3]

The CIA's policy was to support any group that might draw people away from the left, and that meant that they frequently subsidized reformist socialists, here and abroad. The CIA understood that for one of their fronts to attract would-be leftists it would have to occasionally struggle against the system, hence it was unconcerned about the SP's involvement in the civil rights movement. But the Vietnam war destroyed the SP.

It had a curious line: America shouldn't have gone into South Vietnam but—alas—Ho Chi Minh was invading the country. Therefore, the anti-war movement had to oppose "both Washington and Moscow," otherwise the American people would think we were a bunch of reds. There were stormy meetings and everywhere the activists told these "State Department socialists" the same thing: "Go to hell. Ho is Vietnamese, he has a right to fight a regime created by French imperialism and then subsidized by the U.S. Washington invaded Vietnam, not Moscow." Despite the yelping from Thomas & Co., hundreds of thousands poured into the anti-war movement, and it was the SP that became utterly isolated, splitting once again, and finally vanishing into history.

The faction fights in and around the SP in the 1950s and 1960s generated many of the left currents in the civil rights and anti-war movements. In 1953 Bogdan Denitch and Michael Harrington led a split from the party's Young People's Socialist League, joining Max Shachtman's Independent Socialist League, a heterodox Trotskyist grouping, calling itself "third camp," i.e., opposed to capitalism and communism, unlike the SP, which was clearly tilted toward capitalism, as were its sister parties in Europe. In 1956, in the wake of the Khrushchev revelations, Shachtman concluded there was a possibility of recruiting some of the newly disillusioned ex-Stalinists, but to the SP, which they had heard of, not his obscure grouping, and in 1958 he dissolved his ISL into the all but publically non-existant SP.

The inevitable split developed in the ISL's Socialist Youth League over the entry into the reformist mausoleum. A minority joined the Socialist Workers Party, then less than 400 strong, and built the Young Socialist Alliance, which eventually turned the SWP into the organizational motor force behind the largest Vietnam-era demonstrations. However, the bulk of Shachtman and Harrington supporters, including this writer, followed them into the SP. All of the Shachtmanite youth were well intended, if reformist, and played a crucial role in the offices of the NAACP, CORE and, later, as assistants to the then pacifist Bayard Rustin, central to Martin Luther King's organizational entourage. The activists rejuvenated the Student League for Industrial Democracy, but by the early 1960s it slipped out of the control of Thomas and Shachtman and Harrington. Castro's triumph, the mass Black struggle and Malcolm X propelled the organization leftward, and it broke off to become Students for a Democratic Society.

The again-isolated SP degenerated into an employment agency, providing functionaries for ossified noble causes. The AFL-CIA, as its detractors called it, was opposed to political philosophizing, which it identified with its internal radical opponents, but its leaders had to keep up appearances and, on ceremonial occasions, look like they could think. Ghosts were in demand and even the most boring union puff sheet must have an editor. Tom Kahn became George Meany's assistant, and has stayed on as Lane Kirkland's Edgar Bergen.

Rustin finally settled down as the reactionary and isolated director of the A. Philip Randolph Institute, cozily ensconced in Albert Shanker's United Federation of Teachers headquarters. Shachtman became Shanker's adviser. Irwin Suell, once the SP's secretary, became the information director—head spy—for the B'nai Brith Anti-Defamation League. These forces became the organizational drive behind the Coalition for a Democratic Majority, down-with-the-ship Vietnam hawks and electoral "Jew wooers," identified with Scoop Jackson, Washington's "Senator from Boeing."

Much of the minuscule party wouldn't follow the hawks. Harrington and his friends could see which way the war was going, and their ties were with William Winpisinger of the Machinists and other union pie cards, whose ranks were anti-war. They finally fell out over George McGovern. Harrington backed him for the U.S. Presidency but the hardcore labor imperialists couldn't, as Meany was still pro-war and the Israeli ambassador, Yitzhak Rabin, toured the synagogues hustling votes for Nixon. Their Labor Zionists friends heard one of the century's champ demagogues denouncing Nixon as not pro-Israel enough. But they looked at his supporters, who were for peace everywhere else, and realized they could never rely on a McGovern Administration, dependent on such a clientele, to rush arms aid to them in a crunch.

A large party can combine hostile factions held together by the hope of power, but an isolated sect is in deep trouble if there is no practical unity. The party collapsed and the hawks went on to become the Social Democrats USA, kenneled down in the ultimate CIA safe house, ILGWU headquarters, while Harrington and Irving Howe's clique eventually recycled as DSA.

The decades-long ideological drift of these quondam radicals has not received the scholarly analysis it richly deserves. Certainly the evolution of their attitude toward Zionism is distinctive. Characteristically, Thomas has never been clear on Zionism, but he was critical of it in the 1930s. Shachtman once loathed Zionism. On February 20, 1939, he had led a huge demonstration protesting a Nazi rally at Madison Square Garden, and the SWP had tried to involve some self-styled left Zionist youth in the fight. They refused, saying, "Sorry we can't join you, our Zionist policy is to take no part in politics outside Palestine." Shachtman wrote a furious editorial about this, "An End to Zionist Illusions!"[4]

Later, in 1948, during the first Arab-Israeli war, his group took the position that Zionism was reactionary but that the Jews in Palestine had no choice but to critically support the creation of the Israeli state, given the racist character of the then-Arab resistance to Zionism. Nevertheless, in the ensuing years the Independent Socialist League frequently exposed Zionist racism, even if they were not clear as to the resolution of the question. Adaption to organized Zionism on the part of Shachtman and Harrington began only after their merger with the SP, and particularly after they entered into the Democratic Party. They were intensely active people, and once committed to a party that never stops demagogically howling for the Jewish vote, they learned to scream as shrilly as the best of them.

The SP had jumped into Democratic politics with both feet flying. All their initial chatter about converting the liberals to socialism soon ceased. Instead, the differing Democratic cliques, devoted to fundraising demagoguery re the Middle East, ended up recruiting from the SP. Suell's tie to the ADL would also seem to have been crucial. The ADL considers most anti-Zionists to be anti-Semites, therefore it routinely spies on left organizations. The morbid mentality of both the SDUSA and DSA wings of social democracy was perfectly summed up in Irving Howe's racist remark that he has "lived long enough to recognize a portion of truth in the sour apothegm: *In the warmest of hearts there's a cold spot for the Jews.*"[5]

SDUSA cannot in any way still be thought of as left or even liberal. Articles by Carl Gershman in Norman Podhoretz's *Commentary,* the organ of the wealthy American Jewish Committee, landed him the post of assistant to Jeane Kirkpatrick at the UN, and Bayard Rustin testified as a character witness for Ariel Sharon in his libel suit against *Time* magazine. But DSA's leaders have also fanatically committed themselves to Zionism.

DSA supported Ronald Reagan's arming of Israel up to the day Lebanon was invaded. Even then, Harrington has said they still had the "feeling that a case should be made for the initial action," but the invasion proved unpopular even among many of Israel's most devoted liberal apologists, and they had to call for a temporary U.S. embargo on arms to the region.[6] The Beirut massacre compelled Irving Howe to shamefacedly confess that "American Jews opposed to Begin-Sharon have hesitated and waffled before going public."[7]

Once attention shifted to other parts of the world, DSA retreated from its embargo position, instead calling for a "mutual, balanced reduction of arms sales by the superpowers in the region."[8] The phrase is borrowed from the freeze movement. It is, of course, a trick. They know that the U.S. is not interested in any such agreement with the Soviets. In practice a formula for a hypothetical arms freeze in the sweet by and by permits them to freely operate in the Democratic Party in the here and now, despite the party's dead-end support for Israeli militarism.

In 1984, a referendum measure, Proposition E, appeared on the ballot in Berkeley, California, calling on the U.S. to reduce aid to

Israel in proportion to the amount of money Israel spends on settlements on the West Bank. The local congressman is Ron Dellums, a member of DSA. When he was questioned about his
stand, he replied that his

> gut reaction is that the problems of the Middle East are so com-
> plex that it is of questionable value to approach solutions in such a
> piecemeal fashion. Such efforts seem better calculated to cause
> anguish and divisiveness than to move us to a realistic position of
> solving these problems. On a personal level I resent being pushed
> into kneejerk positions on ballot initiatives that are irrelevant to
> any political solution to the problem; when I think of it in that
> vein, a neutral position makes perfectly good sense.[9]

"Jewishness" is a central factor in the private ideologies of
DSA's leading figures. Thus Jack Newfield of the *Village Voice,*
one of DSA's journalistic stars, has confessed that:

> I share . . . an identification with the tribal suffering. I don't
> know why, but if I read of Russian Jews waiting outside a visa
> office, if I read that a synagogue is blown up in Brussels, or I read
> Timerman's book, it affects me more on a certain level than when
> I read about a massacre in El Salvador or if I read about some
> atrocity in South Africa. There is a sense that those are my broth-
> ers and sisters.[10]

Howe fears that "the extreme alternative always beckoning in
America—the alternative of assimilation—is morally and cultur-
ally sterile."[11] Even Harrington has chimed in on this bizarre
theme. According to David Twersky, who interviewed him for
Jewish Frontier, a Labor Zionist monthly:

> Harrington is married to a Jew and claims one of his two sons has
> "a Jewish identity," He . . . lured me into a conversation on inter-
> marriage, a subject on which he is more conservative than I! He
> signed one of his books, "the first autobiography of a Jew from
> Irish grandparents."[12]

Such statements are, of course, incompatable with modern
liberalism and Marxism. Neither have favorite races or nationalities whose sufferings are more important than that of others, nor
do either see any tragedy in the voluntary assimilation of ethnic
groups, and certainly neither have the slightest hesitations about

intermarriage. These racist opinions have nothing to do with the real world, still less with the needs or interests of America's Jews, who will continue to assimilate and intermarry without so much as a by your leave to the leaders of DSA. Instead, they clearly reflect their authors' total abandonment of their past radicalism.

These are intellectuals. When such people retreat from the left, they rarely completely abandon politics. Instead they have a strong tendency to revert to the ideology of their youth, which they touch up to make it do service in defending their present politics. Once, in their youth, the Jews were victims. Therefore, in their minds, in supporting the Democratic Party, which arms Israel to the teeth, they are, in their fantasies, only coming to the aid of the oppressed. It is to be understood that they are not trying to trick anyone. This is simply self-deception, the tragic final stage of their decades of political decomposition.

5.   What of the future relationship between the left and the Jews?

A portion of the intelligentsia always comes over to the revolution, as they understand that the status quo is an obstacle to progress. As we shall see, young Jews are the most intellectualized stratum in our society. Therefore, individual Jews, including individuals of mixed descent, will always play a role in the socialist struggle. However, these individuals will not amount to a majority of Jews. We have no reason to be surprised at this because the Jews are now, on average, the richest ethnic group in the country. Class illusions and interests usually immunize upper- and middle-class youth against the revolutionary message. And while the Zionist movement is everywhere a minority of Jewish students, this increasingly fanaticized element is unlikely to produce more than a few individual converts to the left. The same must be said of those still bound to the Orthodox synagogues. Worse yet, many more Jews are part of the narcissistic walking wounded of their American generation.

Some of the future Jewish revolutionaries will be "red diaper babies," but this is an ever-shrinking pool of recruits. In fact, as we have seen in the cases of *Jewish Currents* and the social democrats, the organizational remnants of the mass Jewish left are now virulent opponents of the present-day anti-Zionist left, and, again, few youth from their milieu will come over to the revolution.

Naturally the percentage of Jews in the coming American revolution is a variable. The larger left organizations are returning to the campuses now that the schools are erupting with anti-apartheid demonstrations, nevertheless it will take time before they reestablish themselves. When they do, they will find that they will have a head-on collision with Zionism, which is one of the best-organized anti-revolutionary movements on those campuses.

Moreover, the Israel-Palestine issue is the one topic that most sharply differentiates the left from the professorial liberals, with their dead-end lesser-of-two-evils support for the Democratic Party, the demagogic patrons and defenders of Zionism. The task of building support for a democratic secular Palestine, an Arab-Jewish Palestine, will be seen for what it is: an integral component of the struggle for a democratic secular world.

Notes

1.   Arthur Liebman, *Jews and the Left,* p. 59.
2.   Kenneth Waltzer, "Lovestone, Jay," *Encyclopedia Judaica,* vol. 11, col. 531.
3.   Sidney Hook, "My Running Debate with Einstein," *Commentary,* July 1982, p. 47.
4.   "An End to Zionist Illusions!," *Socialist Appeal,* March 7, 1939, p. 4.
5.   Irving Howe, "Thinking the Unthinkable About Israel: A Personal Statement," *New York Magazine,* December 24, 1973.
6.   David Twersky, "Michael Harrington: A Vision Writ Large," *Jewish Frontier,* August 1983, p. 14.
7.   Howe, "Warm Friends of Israel, Open Critics of Begin-Sharon," *NY Times,* September 23, 1982, p. 27.
8.   "Resolution on the Middle East," (DSA).
9.   Jock Taft, "Sifting the Berkeley Left," *Merip Reports,* January 1985, p. 27.
10.   Martha Ackelsberg, "Pride, Prejudice, and Politics: Jewish Jews on the American Left," *Response,* Autumn 1982, p. 19.
11.   Howe, "The problem of Jewish Self-Definition," *Reconstructionist,* October 1983, p. 6.
12.   Twersky, p. 13.

3

"A Minnow Can Swallow a Whale"

Although the wealth of the German-Jewish bankers began to attract comment in the 1850s, Simon Baruch, the former Quartermaster-General of the Confederate Army, and father of Bernard Baruch, was a post-Civil War member of the KKK. Anti-Semitism did not become an ideological plank for any mass movement until the second, 1915 KKK, which added anti-Catholicism and anti-Semitism to the traditional white supremacy.

The Russian revolution triggered a nation-wide fear of "international Jewish banker-bolsheviks," and by the mid 1920s the klans had four million members. Soon, however, scandals wracked the KKK. From 1920 until 1927, Henry Ford's *Dearborn Independent* waged a campaign against the Jews. Lawsuits, by Bernard Baruch, among others, forced Ford to apologize for his libels. Although anti-Semitism was still quite strong, for a brief interval its momentum slowed. Suddenly, in 1933, the Jews were confronted with the triumph of their greatest enemy, and Hitler's German success raised renewed questions among wide circles here, as to the extent of Jewish influence in the country's economic life.

It was in response to this heightened interest that the editors of *Fortune* ran a long essay on the Jewish economic role in their February 1936 issue. "Non-Jews," they maintained, tended to complain of the Jews' "aggressiveness, sharp business practices, clannishness and lack of sensitivity to the feelings of Gentile groups." But they insisted that

> there is no basis whatever for the suggestion that Jews monopolize US business and industry . . . the great mass of . . . Jews . . . is made up of workers . . . Jews *seem* to play a disproportionate part for two reasons: the Jews . . . are the most urban . . . of all peoples, and the favored occupations of Jews . . . are those . . . which bring them into most direct contact with the great consuming public . . . if appearances are disregarded . . . the general impression of Jewish . . . power disappears.

Sixteen per cent of the members of the New York Stock Exchange were Jews, but the carefully researched article minimized Jewish influence on Wall Street, insisting that "very definitely, they do not run banking." They played "little or no part in the great commercial houses." It was in investment banking that the Jews were important, with Kuhn, Loeb & Co., Speyer & Co., J. & W. Seligman, Lehman Bros., and Dillon, Read & Co., among the most influential houses. But of these only Kuhn, Loeb and Dillon, Read were really important. And even then the editors commented on the fact that several of these houses had ceased to be exclusively Jewish.

Jews were underrepresented in heavy industry. Only the Blochs were important in steel, controlling Inland Steel, the number seven company. There were very few Jews in autos, almost no Jews in coal, rubber, chemicals, shipping, transportation, light and power, telephones, engineering or lumber. To be sure, there were a few important individuals here and there in those industries, as with Sam Zemurrey of United Fruit, with its huge shipping holdings, but it was in light industry that the most important concentrations of Jewish wealth were found.

Jewish-owned firms produced 29 percent of the country's shoes, half its hard liquor, and they *were* the clothing industry. Again and again the same story was repeated. They were "most frequently to be found in those reaches of industry where manufacturer and merchant meet." However, even in the department store field, Jews were by no means as important nationally as they so obviously were in New York. Woolworth, Kress, Marshall Field, to name some of the country's most prominent retail outlets, were not Jewish, nor were most drugstore chains.

The article didn't say so, but it was clear that the Jewish proportion of the rich was already higher than the Jewish percentage of the population. However, their importance was exaggerated. Only in the media were they really significant. But aside from *The New York Times* and *Washington Post* (whose owner had converted to Christianity), very few papers were Jewish. While book publishers such as Simon and Schuster, Knopf and Random House were Jewish, Macmillan, Scribners, Doubleday were not. It was in radio that Jews were dominant. CBS was Jewish, NBC was headed by David Sarnoff. Half of New York's theatrical producers were Jews, and of course

> they do . . . exert pretty complete control over the production of movies. . . . At the very most half the opinion-making and taste influencing paraphernalia in America is in Jewish hands.

Nevertheless, the magazine concluded, quite correctly, that

> Jews do not dominate the American scene. . . . what is remarkable . . . is not their industrial power but their curious industrial distribution, their tendency to crowd together in particular squares of the checkerboard.[1]

Many of the leading companies of the day discriminated against Jews in employment, and even the richest Jews were usually excluded from the social life of the WASP establishment. Some rich Jews, as with Bernard Baruch, had Roosevelt's ear, but exceptions aside, the Jewish rich were then a sort of pariah elite. As a group they were not even junior partners within American capitalism.

"It's Hard to Believe That Jews Are Discriminated Against If You Have These Myths"

Even decades later, long after Hitler's defeat, the Jewish Establishment still feared that discussion of the wealth of the richest Jews would lead to anti-Semitism. Max Geltman, a reactionary identified with the *National Review*, revealed, in his book, *The Confrontation*, that:

> It's by now an open secret that in 1957 the American Jewish Com-
> mittee interceded with the Bureau of the Census in Washington
> and besought it not to ask questions about income related to
> national groupings in the 1960 census, for fear that the compara-
> tively high income levels of the Jewish minority would lead to
> anti-Semitic outrages. The Bureau complied.[2]

In his *Course of Modern Jewish History,* Howard Sachar wrote
of the Jewish rich of 1957 that "some 20 percent of
America's . . . millionaires were Jews." but he immediately
depreciated these statistics by adding that "These latter were
rarely multimillionaires, however, for they were little involved in
the key capital industries . . . that produced America's staggering
fortunes."[3]

Given that the myth of the "all-powerful Jew" is identified with
Nazi propaganda, it should not surprise us that there are still
many people who are squeamish about bringing attention to the
sociological changes that have converted a community once
unique in America for its mass radicalism into a pillar of capitalism. However, there are others who have less legitimate reasons
for evading a discussion of Jewish wealth. Thus Jack Newfield,
long associate with the reform wing of New York's Democrats:

> There is a kind of devil theory, that the Jews control the media, or
> that Jews control the Democratic Party through money, which I
> think is inflated. And therefore it's hard to believe that Jews are
> discriminated against if you have these myths.[4]

The Poor, You Shall Not Always Have With You

Those who do not want to confront the reality of the wealth of the
richest portion of modern Jewry tend to overemphasize the
poverty of the poorest section. Thus, in 1983, we were told by
the Jewish Telegraphic Agency that "An estimated 13-15 percent
of the total Jewish population is economically disadvantaged and
vulnerable.[5] This would seem to be comparable to the 15 percent
of the American population with incomes below the official
poverty line. Except that the Jewish statistic is from an American

Jewish Committee study which defined "poverty among Jews at 150 percent of the Federally defined poverty level."[6]

Two-thirds of the Jewish poor are elderly. A large proportion of these are widows. Most of the other Jewish poor are also women, many of these divorcees with dependent children.[7] But even here the percentage is less than the national average.[8] The unemployment level in 1984 was below that for whites, because few Jews hold the blue-collar production jobs most severely hit during the last recession. However, it must be assumed that Jewish poverty, as defined by the AJC study, will increase in the next period, given that the average Jew is older than the average American and, of course, medical expenses are rising.

Not more than 10 percent of adult American Jews are in unions, compared to approximately 18 percent for the nation as a whole. Very few are in blue-collar trades, with Brooklyn's Jewish plumbers the major exception. Jews are distinctly under-represented in the "physical" civil service—police, fire fighters, postal clerks or soldiers. Most Jewish unionists are social workers or other governmental desk bureaucrats or teachers. Twenty per cent of all Jews are in teaching, at all levels.[9]

In 1969, 18 percent of Jewish women trained as elementary school teachers, with another 12 percent planning high school careers. In our new feminist world, only 6 percent expected to be elementary teachers in 1980 and only 1 percent high school instructors. Jewish women are now pouring into law with a spill-over into academia. Now 10 percent of all U.S. professors are Jews, and the number is increasing. Even more decisive for the self-image of the young Jew, increasingly it is not enough to be an ordinary professor of origami. For the more ambitious, nothing less than the chair in late medieval origami, at Columbia or Harvard, will do. At least 20 percent of the faculty at America's leading universities are Jews, with over 25 percent in the prestige medical schools, 38 percent for similar law schools, rising even higher at Harvard, where half the law faculty is Jewish.[10]

Today Jews are 20 percent of the nation's doctors and lawyers.[11] They have long been drawn to accounting, and barriers against Jews in engineering are a thing of the past. Computer pro-gramming is a new field, with few reactionary traditions, hence Jews are increasingly important within the profession.

It was the fallout from the civil rights revolution that finally opened up the entirety of American business to Jews as employees. While many, if not most, Jews in the corporation bureaucracies are accountants, lawyers, programmers or scientific workers, they are increasingly found in direct managerial positions with non-Jewish firms.

In a 1984 work for the American Jewish Committee, *Who Gets to the Top?*, Richard Zweigenhaft declared that:

> Jews make up between 5 percent and 7 percent of the corporate directors on *Fortune* magazine's annual list of the largest corporations. These figures, slightly higher than the frequency of Jews in the population at large, but slightly lower than their percentage in the college-educated population, indicate neither Jewish control of the economy, nor gross discrimination against Jews.[12]

More important, two-thirds of the directorships held by Jewish trustees of charitable foundations were with corporations neither founded by nor presently controlled by Jews.[13] The reality of Jewish acceptance within the broad business world was best expressed by Zweigenhaft's Jewish women informants. They were absolutely "unanimous in their conviction that being a woman was more likely to impede their careers than being Jewish."[14]

The shift into the mainstream of corporate life will mean a decline in the present Jewish middle class. In his 1982 book, *Jews and Money*, Gerald Krefetz informed us that three-fourths of the retail stores in New York were Jewish-owned.[15] At first, his figure seems somewhat excessive, until we remember that there may not be a single Fifth Avenue store, from 59th Street to Greenwich Village, or a single 34th Street store, or a single Fulton Street store in downtown Brooklyn, that is owned by either a Black or a Puerto Rican, and the number of such shops owned by either Irish or Italians on any of those streets is very small. If we eliminate Chinese restaurants, Hispanic bodegas and the like, retail trade in the city is indisputably Jewish, in a manner unheard of since pre-Holocaust Eastern Europe. Nevertheless, most children of these petty (and sometimes not so petty) merchants will not replace their fathers. At present at least 15 percent of all business school graduates are Jewish youth, and with the exception of a few yuppie entrepreneurs, these will blend into the cocaine world of the large corporations.[16]

"So? Is it good for the Jews?" It certainly would seem so. If they are 2.54 percent of the population, they take in approximately 5 percent of the national income.[17] Jews are almost 7 percent of the country's middle and upper classes, taken together.[18] In 1972, almost 900,000 Jewish families out of two million were middle and upper class, while only 13.5 million out of 53 million American families were so classified.[19] According to Krefetz, 43 percent of all Jews earned $16,000 plus, in contrast to only 25.5 percent of all Americans.[20] And while only a little under 5 percent of the Jewish population is in millionaire families, Jews constituted a fluctuating 23-26 percent of the 400 richest Americans between 1982 and 1985, and perhaps more of the taxpaying millionaire population, which was estimated at 574,342 in 1980.[21]

There is no doubt that, on average, American Jewry is the richest ethnic or religious grouping in the country. According to the June 1984 *American Demographics,* the average annual Jewish household income is $23,300, compared to $21,700 for Episcopalians. Presbyterians received $20,500, religiously unaffiliated took in $17,600, Catholics made $17,400, Methodists $17,000, Lutherans averaged $16,300. White Fundamentalists and southern Baptists earned a piddling $14,000 plus.[22] Statistics show that Jews have been earning more than Episcopalians and Presbyterians, the archetypical WASPS, since the late 1960s.[23]

Whales—and an Occasional Shark

How many of the country's richest people are Jews? The play on words will be forgiven, but we are fortunate today in having that perfect "capitalist tool," *Forbes* magazine, and its annual four hundred edition for 1985 to tell us who the richest Americans are. I've modified that list only to include some of its "near misses," members of the common herd, who came in with under $150 million. As with the 1985 issue, I've retained the "drop outs" from 1984, because many are certain to return. The only exception is for death, because inheritance taxes and many heirs disintegrate a fortune. Additionally, there were a very few names dropped from 1984 without explanation, which I saw no reason to omit.

The special issue's staff are justifiably proud of their year-long effort and have willingly discussed their immense project. Again the American Jewish Committee asked that they not focus on the ethnicity or religion of their subjects. *Forbes* decided that such forebearance is prudent, not so much, the staff insisted, out of special concern for the AJC's fears, but because of the endless problems such discussions would create on classificatory grounds. Who is a Jew would then be joined by who is a Catholic and who is an Irishman? However, many Jews are immediately identifiable by their first and/or last names, characteristic of their Jewish generation. And since the Jewish percentage is of such magnitude that even these self-described capitalist tools had to take note of it, they have satisfied themselves with a sort of in-group code for Jews. Thus we are frequently told of a mogul's "Latvian" familial origins, or that the family arrived here in the late 1930s as fugitives from Hitlerism, or as a DP, or that dad or a grandfather was a garment worker.

Verifying *Forbes* with other sources, we get the following list. Errors are inevitable, given that many of the very rich are extremely private people who shun publicity, fearing everything from anti-Semitism to revolution and kidnappers. However, I will be forgiven if some gentile is inadvertently included, as it certainly is no shame to be thought of as a Jew in today's America. Nor will the omission of some assimilated Jew alter the statistical reality in any meaningful way, nor will any such errors change the sociological implications of these statistics: No longer a pariah elite, the modern American Jewish rich are the full partners of their Christian equivalents.

1. Leonard Abramson, 53. U.S. Health Care Systems Inc. Estimated wealth $140 million plus.
2. Charles, Herbert and Herbert Anthony Allen. Charles was "raised in a Manhattan cold-water flat." Stock market and real estate. Together worth $549 million.
3. Walter Annenberg, $850 million.
4. Enid Annenberg Haupt, $180 million.
5. Esther Annenberg Simon, $180 million.
6. Jeanette Annenberg Hooker, $180 million.
7. Lita Annenberg Hazen, $180 million.
8. Evelyn Annenberg Hall, $180 million.

The Annenbergs' Triangle Publications is worth approximately $1.6 billion, with Walter holding 35 percent of the shares and voting his sisters' 9 percent each, worth $180 million. Heirs of two deceased sisters own another 18 percent. Triangle's *TV Guide* is the most profitable magazine in the U.S. They also put out *Seventeen* and the *Daily Racing Form*. Walter has other widely scattered stock, real estate, and huge art holdings.

While capitalism has its devotees, there are few who would give the entire class all A's on its report card. A convention has arisen, on the left and right, of dividing the class into two broad camps. Thus, in journalism, there is the "responsible bourgeois press," as with the *Washington Post,* which allows its reporters to pretty much say what they want, without editorial censorship. Then there is the yellow press. When Annenberg sold the *Philadelphia Inquirer,* the staff cheered like slaves watching the Union Army coming through the gate. It may well have been the worst daily produced in the U.S. in the 20th century.

Annenberg's father, Moses or Moe, started as a newsboy on the streets, and fought his way up through the circulation network of the Hearst press, frequently using goons to push out distributors for rival papers. Eventually he went into publishing on his own, and set up a national bookies' racing wire service. In 1939 he and Walter were indicted for tax evasion. Moe pleaded guilty on the condition that the charges against Walter were dropped, and he went to prison as the biggest tax cheat in American history.

In recent years, Walter has tried to clean up the family name by utilizing the Moses Annenberg Foundation for colossal philanthropic donations. One of his least significant grants was a million bucks to Israel in 1967, after the six-day war. Annenberg eventually became Nixon's ambassador to Britain, and even today, when Nixon just wants to relax and be Mr. Nice Guy, he falls by Walt's Sunnylands pad in Palm Springs. Reagan always tries to make New Year's Eve at Walt's. Not for nothing is Annenberg's name among the first to come up in any educated discussion as to who has been the wickest Jew since Herod Antipas.

9.   Edmund Ansin, 50. Father Sydney became a Florida realtor in the 1940s. Then the family branched into TV. His Sunbeam TV Corp. is valued at more than $200 million.

10.   Ted Arison, 62, fourth-generation Israeli, now a U.S. citizen. Shipping, Miami real estate, gambling casinos. Worth minimum of $300 million.

11.   Robert Arnow, 62. Real estate. Shares $450 million with brother-in-law Alan Weiler and Weiler's father, Jack.

12.   Arthur Belfer, 79, "Polish-born." Peruvian oil, huge New York real estate. Big contributor to Jewish and Zionist causes. Worth $475 million plus.

13. Belz family, Memphis. Philip, 82, "from Austria." Real Estate. Family worth $250 million. Or more.

14. Charles Benenson, 73. Real estate. "Father built Bronx apartments." Worth at least $200 million.

15. Morton Blaustein, Ruth Blaustein Rosenberg, Henry Rosenberg, Jr., Louis Thalheimer. Founder of fortune, Louis Blaustein, invented precursor of metered gas pump, anti-knock gas. Eventually merged with Standard Oil of Indiana. Collectively worth an estimated $850 million. Morton is large donor to Jewish charities.

16. Paul Block, Jr., and William Block. Publishing. Joint wealth, a soft $300 million.

17. Neil Bluhm, Judd Malkin. Real estate, Chicago. Worth about $300 million each.

18. Ivan Boesky, 49. America's leading arbitrager. (An arbitrager buys stock in companies in takeover situations, gambling that he can sell his shares to the real competitors for control for more than he bought in at. To be polite about it, a parasite's parasite.) Big bucks to Jewish causes. Two million to Jewish Theological Seminary (Conservative sect) for Boesky Library. Martin Peretz, fanatic publisher of pro-Zionist *New Republic,* is big investor in Boesky's Wall Street firm. Boesky was the United Jewish Appeal New York 1985 fund drive chair, and is a leading supporter of NAT PAC, the leading Zionist election fund. Worth an estimated $150 million plus.

19. Donald Bren, 54. Real estate. Father, Milton Bren, was Hollywood producer. Worth $525 million.

20. Edgar Bronfman, 57. Worth $665 million. President of the World Jewish Congress. His Seagram Company is the world's largest distiller and marketer of spirits and wines. Bronfman tried to take over Conoco Oil in 1983, but eventually the company went to Du Pont. However Conoco shares were converted to Du Pont stock, and Bronfman ended up owning 22 percent of the giant chemical company, twice as much as the Du Pont family. An agreement was reached between the two interests, and Bronfman pledged not to try to take over the management of the firm for at least 10 years.

If there was any lingering doubt about the present status of the Jews within the higher circles of America's capitalists, Bronfman's friendly deal with the Du Ponts laid them to rest. The requirements of business compel even such giants as Du Pont to seek merger partners, and to refuse such partners because they are Jewish would be financially suicidal. Once a capitalist society rejects anti-Semitism as its official policy, the eventual assimilation of Jewish and gentile capital is inexorable. To be sure, American capitalism is still lustily vicious, as witness its foreign policy, now or under previous administrations; but, particularly with the marked decline of religiosity among the younger capitalists, anti-Semitism is on an ever-downward spiral within the dominant class.

21.   Edward and Sherman Cohen. Real estate and construction. $330 million.

22.   Seymour Cohn, and his brother Sylvan Lawrence's heirs. Real estate. $550 million.

23.   Henry and Lester Crown, 90 and 61. "Henry, son of Latvian immigrant." Lester is now the largest shareholder in General Dynamics and the two own about 23 percent of the nation's largest defense contractor. Together worth $1.1 billion. In 1974 Lester, a Chicago Democratic contributor, was named an unindicted conspirator in an attempt to bribe members of the Illinois legislature. He was granted immunity in exchange for testimony. In September 1985 the Defense Department instituted proceedings to revoke his security clearance because he concealed the Illinois scandal from them for eight years.

In 1985 American newspaper readers came to know the company well: It was to corruption what Michelangelo was to marble. The new scandals are a terrible embarrassment to Reagan. They are too huge to conceal. However, a Republican business regime is always full of fast-buck operators and, at most, the government will punish a few fall guys. But the company's name is mud to informed newspaper readers. However, there is one place in the world where they still know quality. In February 1986, Lester was named an "honorary fellow of Jerusalem" for donating an undisclosed sum for a huge cultural center. Did that government know of Lester's and General Dynamics' little legal problems? Of course. Why then did they honor him? Because that is the morality of modern Israel. They couldn't care less how he got his money, or what he did with it, as long as he gave some of it to them.

24.   Joseph Morton Davidowitz, a.k.a. Morton Davis, 57. Son of kosher food distributor, he graduated Harvard Business School with honors, went into D.H. Blair brokerage firm and ended up its owner. $200 million and rising.

25. Leonard Davis, 62, Colonial Penn Group, insurance. Has donated substantial sum to Hebrew University. $230 million is minimum estimate of wealth.

26. Marvin Davis, 61. "Father onetime boxer from Manhattan garment district, got into oil . . . after WWII." His Denver-based Davis Oil Company is second only to Standard Indiana in discovery of new gas and oil fields. Davis's net worth at any given time is difficult to estimate, given the drop in oil prices, and his recent sale of his half of 20th Century-Fox. But *Forbes* 1985 says "still a billionaire."

27. Clarence Douglas Dillon, 76. Banker. The 1983 *Forbes* had "father was son of Polish immigrant." Owns Chateau Haut-Brion vineyard, massive art collection. Worth at least $150 million.

28. Richard Dinner, brother-in-law of San Francisco real estate Swigs. Two Swigs and Dinner share $450 million.

29. Sherman Dreiseszun, Frank Morgan. Kansas City real estate and banks. Dreiseszun was sportswear manufacturer. Morgan sold surplus war goods. They opened small bank in 1964. Now they are into suburban banking and shopping malls. Extremely secretive, but traceable wealth above $300 million.

30. David, Roy and Seymour Durst. Real estate. $550 million.

31. Jane Engelhard. Father was Brazilian, but her second husband, Charles Engelhard, the "platinum king," was Jewish. Worth more than $365 million.

32. Harold Farb, 63. Houston real estate. Houston slump means that his worth is probably a bit less than $150 million.

33. Larry and Zachary Fisher. New York real estate. $600 million, or more.

34. Max Fisher, 78. Oil refiner. Worth at least $225 million. Max is a Republican, and the leading Jewish political fundraiser. Although he does not consider himself a Zionist, he funded Israel's initial petro-chemical projects, and has been president of the United Jewish Appeal, the Zionist charity. He once called Nixon "a Jewish delight" for his support for Israel.

35. Michael Fribourg, 72. "Completed move (to U.S.) after France fell in 1940." Controls 20 percent of world grain trade. At least $700 million.

36. Alfred and Monte Goldman. Father Sy invented the shopping cart. Now primarily in real estate. $400 million plus.

37. Sol Goldman, 69. Was once New York's biggest landlord,

but his holdings have since declined. He was indicted in 1985 for perjury re illegal demolition of buildings in Times Square region. Notorious as a terrible landlord. Worth $450 million minimum.

38. Catherine Graham. Her father, Eugene Meyer, converted to Christianity and she was raised a Christian. Owns *Washington Post, Newsweek*. Late husband Philip got involved with the CIA, but that ended years before it exposed Watergate. Family fortune over $350 million.

39. Pincus Green, Marc Rich, commodities traders. Started in mail room of brokerage house, went on to become traders. During hostage crisis they bought Iranian oil, beat U.S. tax man out of $48 million. Fled to Switzerland in 1983. Made a $150 million settlement in 1984 so that their company could do business here. Biggest tax fraud arrangement in American history. Deal permitted Rich to sell his half of 20th Century-Fox (to Marvin Davis, who then sold out to Rupert Murdoch). Both still face fraud, racketeering and tax evasion charges if they set foot in this country. They now hustle out of Switzerland. Wealth is about $200 million. Each.

40. Haas family. Levi Strauss heirs. World's largest apparel manufacturers. Equity valued at $775 million.

41. Armand Hammer, 88. Only one on *Forbes* list with a Moscow address (also New York and Los Angeles). "Bronx-born son of Russian immigrants . . . father active in Socialist Labor Party." Its symbol was an arm and hammer. Our Armand was a 1920 capitalist trader in Soviet furs and U.S. grain. Learned fluent Russian. Took over Occidental Petroleum in 1955 and built it into 9th largest oil company and 17th largest firm in country, selling Libyan oil. He was trained as MD and is an immense art collector. By any standards, one of the few genuinely impressive people on the 400 list. Worth more than $150 million.

42. Leon Hess. *Forbes* 1984: "Lithuanian father." Amerada Hess Oil refinery sales were $8.3 billion in 1984. Owns Jets football team, one-third of New Jersey's Monmouth racetrack. At least $360 million.

43. Horvitz family. Unaccountably completely omitted from 1985 list. But estimated $250 million was listed on 1984 list for five papers, cable service in Cleveland, Florida real estate, construction firm.

44. Peter Kalikow, 43. Real estate. Worth at least $375 million.

45. Paul Kalmanovitz, 80. Falstaff and Pabst beers, real estate. He and wife are childless and almost all of his $250 million estate will go to charity.

46. Howard Kaskel, 48. Real estate. Worth more than $250 million.

47. Ewing Marion Kauffman, 69. Started as drug salesman in 1948. Began Marion Labs 1950. Owns Kansas City Royals. Wealth about $190 million.

48. George Kozmetsky, 68. Teledyne and other investments. Wealth is more than $175 million.

49. Carl and George Landegger. "Father . . . escaped Hitler 1938." They build and run paper mills. Carl, 56, runs marathons and is serious amateur archeologist. Worth about $250 million.

50. Estée, Leonard and Ronald Lauder. Estée Lauder Inc. is the third largest cosmetics and perfume firm in the country. Ronald became Ronald's assistant defense secretary. Over $700 million.

51. Norman Lear, 64. Television. Famous for *All in the Family, Jeffersons.* Organizer of major opposition group against Moral Majority. $175 million.

52. Sam LeFrak, 67. America's largest apartment landlord, with 87,000 units. TV production: *Fame.* Broadway: *Cats.* At least $800 million.

53. Leon Levine, 49. Family Dollar stores. Worth more than $315 million.

54. Leonard Litwin, 70. Real estate. $200 million.

55. John Loeb, 82. Merged his Loeb Rhoades brokerage firm into Shearson Lehman/American Express, of which he is honorary chairman. Was on jury of ultra-right Zionist Jabotinsky Prize in 1984. Worth $150 million.

56. Robert Lurie, 56. Real estate. Owns Giants baseball team. More than $200 million.

57. Mack family. "Russian immigrant Phillip Mack began construction demolition company." Also owns Minnesota Twins baseball team. More than $250 million.

58. Jack, Joseph and Morton Mandel. Premier Industrial Corp. More than $260 million. Morton is huge contributor to Jewish causes.

59. Leonard Marx, 81. Real estate. Over $300 million.

60. Bernard Mendik, 57. Real estate. $180 million.

61. Dominique de Menil. "Daughter of Conrad Schlum-

berger . . . with husband John (son of French baron) fled Nazi occupied Paris 1941." World's largest collection of surrealist art. More than $200 million.

62.   Sy Sims (Merns), 60. Legally changed his names to Sims. Cut-rate clothing stores as well as prestigious A. Sulka & Co. At least $210 million. But he once was a radio announcer and still does all his own television spots.

63.   Paul and Seymour Millstein. Real estate. Over $375 million.

64.   Stephen Muss, 57. Real estate. At least $200 million.

65.   Donald and Samuel Newhouse. Grandfather "Russian." One of the largest media chains: *New Yorker, Vogue, Mademoiselle, House and Garden, Vanity Fair, Parade,* 28 newspapers, Random House. Worth $2.2 billion. But tax man wants $914 million in estate taxes, including $305 million in penalities for fraud.

66.   Robert Olnick, 71. Real estate. $200 million, plus.

67.   Max Palevsky, 61. Computers. Big backer of liberal causes and Democratic Party. More than $200 million.

68.   William Paley, 85. CBS. "Grandfather had thriving lumber firm in Russia." Chairman, Museum of Modern Art. At least $290 million.

69.   Jack Parker, 70. "Son of blouse manufacturer." Real estate. More than $300 million.

70.   Milton Petrie, 83. Petrie Stores, clothing stores, shopping centers. Was on jury of ultra-right Zionist Jabotinsky Prize in 1984. Worth $585 million.

71.   Victor Posner, 68. Investor. Indicted 1982 for $1.25 million in tax evasion and filing false returns. His Sharon Steel is in bad way, and he had to sell his National Can interests to save Sharon. Was worth $250 million, but given his present difficulties it is hard to say what he is worth at any given moment.

72.   Sol Price, 70. Merchandiser. At least $200 million.

73.   Abram, Jay and Robert Pritzker. Worth $1.5 billion. Hyatt Hotels, *McCall's,* Hammond Organ, Braniff Airlines, real estate, timber. Jay says he has been to Israel three times, on the way to some other place: "I've been there, but not really."[24]

74.   Pulitzer family. *St. Louis Post-Dispatch* and other papers, TV stations. The family may be bought out by A. Alfred Taubman, another multimillionaire, who is offering $500 million for Pulitzer Publishing. Listed at $475 million.

75. Resnick family, real estate and construction. Minimum $250 million.

76. Meshulam Riklis, 62. Page 65 of the May 1985 *Penthouse* was a boring display of a woman playing with her genitalia. Pages 66 and 67 are a photo of Riklis, illustrating an interview with the man *Penthouse* says is synonymous with "entrepreneurial balls." Riklis, born in Turkey in 1923 but raised in what was then Palestine, came here after WWII, and put himself through college teaching Hebrew. He is the inventor of the leveraged buy out, or conglomerating. While doing a business school term paper, he discovered that there was a whole industry whose stock was selling for less than the cash the companies had in their till:

> here was the greatest possible bonanza: that a minnow can swallow a whale. In those days you could control a company with maybe only 25 or 30 percent of the stock. . . . If I could get control of a company, liquidate it, then buy control of a larger company, I'd start the string going and at the end buy control of a very large company. . . . If you have three marbles, you can control seven marbles, and seven marbles can control 100 marbles. . . . My scheme was that if I could get American Jews to give me their money instead of turning it over to the UJA, their investment would not only work out brilliantly, but subsidiaries could be established in Israel. This is Riklis's brilliant scheme for peace in the Middle East! . . . with every company being an American subsidiary; then the United States will make sure that there is peace and tranquility. . . . I . . . was using the list of all the wealthy Minneapolis Jews who were contributing to the UJA. . . . Each one . . . comes out of his shell of mediocrity . . . each one became pillars of industry. And it happened! . . .

Riklis's corporate vehicle, Rapid-American, has had its ups and downs, thanks to his unstable personality, and *Forbes* says that by the mid-1970s he was commonly called "Meshugener Reckless of Rancid-American" (*meshugener* is Hebrew and Yiddish for crazy). As *Penthouse* delicately put it, "your press coverage at the time implies that you were screwing your brains out," and Meshugener freely agrees with that diagnosis:

> I was cracking up . . . sometimes I felt suicide might be the better solution. . . . I wouldn't let the goyim enjoy it, and by "goyim" I do not necessarily mean gentiles. What I'm talking about is that

mythical "establishment." I wasn't about to let *Forbes* or *Business Week* have the pleasure of seeing me fall.

Eventually Meshugener settled down, that is to say he met a 17-year-old actress (he was 50), and married her. But his reputation was clearly established, with *Forbes* calling him "a stunning case of the American Dream gone wrong." However, Meshugener is a fair man, he doesn't think it's "because somebody has it in for Riklis because he's Jewish. . . . It's because the establishment was against *anyone* who's an originator."[25]

Its easy to understand why Malcolm Forbes despises Riklis. Capitalism is under severe challenge, morally no less than materially. Forbes knows that if a prominent Soviet started screwing his brains out and ended up marrying anyone 33 years younger than himself he would be flung out of the Party. Forbes wants capitalism with a human face. Meshugener is just a mite too human. But then, what is $150 million for? In the end, capitalist playboys are as American as chorus girls with their panties down, and nothing Forbes can say or do will change that.

77. Rose family. Real estate. More than $250 million.

78. Rosenwald family. Still owns stock in Sears, Roebuck. William owns 90 percent of American Securities Corporation. Family has other investments, art. Famous for philanthropy, mainly towards Jews and Blacks. Family was outspokenly anti-Zionist until the 1940s. $300 million plus.

79. Jack and Lewis Rudin. Real estate. More than $700 million.

80. Arthur Sackler, 73. Identified histamine as hormone. Medical publisher. Perdue-Frederick drug company. Ad agency. Celebrated for art collections valued at half or more of $175 million fortune. These are all organized around scholarly themes; archaic jades from China, Inca and other pre-Columbian artifacts. He is now giving these collections away. A documentary about his collections revealed him as extremely insightful about art. Unknown to public, but obviously one of the country's best examples of a well-lived life of the mind.

81. Schnitzer family. Sons of junkman. Now into steel, shipping, real estate. At least $250 million.

82. Shapiro family. Started in ice cream, went into making cones, cups, disposable paper goods. At least $350 million, but shared by 70 family members.

83. Peter Sharp, 56. Real estate. $250 million plus.
84. Leonard Shoen, 69. U-Haul. $300 million.
85. Walter Shorenstein, 69. Real estate. $300 million. Was the finance chairman of the hosting committee for the Democratic convention in San Francisco.
86. Lawrence Silverstein, 55. Chairman New York Real Estate board. $180 million, plus.
87. Herbert and Melvin Simon. Shopping centers. Herb is worth about $135 million, Melvin $250 million.
88. Norton Simon, 79. Industrialist. Famous L.A. art museum. $200 million.
89. Sheldon Solow. Real estate. $250 million. Big art collection.
90. Stanley Stahl, 61. Real estate. $250 million.
91. Ray Stark, 69. Movies, investments. $150 million.
92. Saul Steinberg, 47. Financier, insurance (Reliance). Worth $400 million in 1984, but has made major purchases since. Debt load is huge, but he seems to be on the move.
93. Leonard Stern, 47. Hartz Mountain pet food company. In 1984 Hartz pleaded guilty to obstructing justice (lying under oath, destroying evidence). Company used prostitutes, got deep into bribes, violated anti-trust laws, etc. Fined $20,000 big bucks. Bought *Village Voice* in 1985 for $55 million. Worth estimated at $550 million.
94. Stone family. Stone Container Co. *Forbes* 1984 had "father left Russia about 1890." Worth $200 million. Completely omitted from 1985 list.
95. Sulzberger family. *The New York Times,* other papers, TV stations, book company, cable. More than $450 million.

Historically, the *Times* was an outspokenly reactionary paper, supporting Mussolini within months of his coming to power in 1922. Always afraid of being identified as having a "Jewish" slant, the *Times* was absolutely craven during the Hitler era, and particularly during the Holocaust, and it did nothing to mobilize public opinion to press Roosevelt to rescue Jews in Europe. It developed a later-day reputation for liberalism during the Vietnam War, when it published the purloined Pentagon papers. Now it has reverted to its old tricks. Anything connected with editing is ultra-conservative,

The same mentality that made them into do-nothings during the Holocaust made the family into anti-Zionists until the U.S.

government decided to back Israel. To say they are not pro-Zionist ideologically, even now, would be an understatement. If one of the family were to go off to live in Israel, they would call in a psychiatrist. For them, as highly class-conscious American imperialists, Israel is strictly an airstrip 2, in Orwell's sense of the term, just another piece of anti-Soviet real estate. The paper has editorialized in favor of a grand middle-eastern anti-Soviet alliance, tying together Israel and the right-wing Arab regimes, and it understands that Israeli territorial greed stands in the way of such a concord. Therefore, the paper has no hesitation in discussing Israeli crimes, including torture.

96.   Swig family. Real estate. $300 million, at least.

97.   Sydney Taper, 83. First Charter Financial Corporation, Los Angeles. $300 million.

98.   Laszlo Tauber, 70. Real estate. $250 million. Tauber is certainly atypical of the 400. Born in Hungary, he was a champion gymnast. Sent to a concentration camp in 1944, he escaped. Trained as a surgeon, he came to the U.S. after WWII under a special program, and was supposed to teach medicine in North Dakota. Instead he went to Washington, D.C. While working as a doctor, he started investing in real estate, and is now the government's largest landlord, but still runs his own hospital. "Surgery is the satisfaction of my life." Endowed Holocaust Studies center at Brandeis University. Wealth estimated at over $300 million.

99.   A. Alfred Taubman, 61. Real estate, fast food chain, Sotheby's, Michigan Panthers football team. Trying to buy Pulitzer Publishing empire. In excess of 600 million.

100.   Lawrence and Preston Tisch. Loews Corporation, 25 percent of CBS, Bulova Watches, Lorillard Tobacco, real estate, securities. Share $1.7 billion.

Larry Tisch is the ultimate old-fashioned petty Jewish capitalist, and although he has struck it rich, intellectually he is still stuck in an old country *shtetl*. Adamantly against assimilation, he opines:

I think that the tragedy of the Jews, once they get affluence, and mingle in the non-Jewish world, they think there's something socially more desirable perhaps over there. I don't think so, and it concerns me as far as the future of the Jewish community in America.

Readers will be reassured that assimilation is a "disaster":

> The joke of it is that they're still Jews no matter what they do in the non-Jewish world, even though they may not consider themselves Jews.[26]

Tisch is an "ethnic" Jew: "I'm not really involved in synagogue affairs. I'm on the board of the Jewish Theological Seminary, but I'm not a religious person as such."[27]

Why then would the Conservatives put him on the board of their rabbinical school? The synagogues of the Pale were dominated by the rich, as comically described by Mendele Mocher Sforim, Mendele the bookseller, in his 1892 story, *Unease in Jacob:*

> This is the way of Jews, the nature imbued in them from time immemorial, that whenever they see a fellow with a gold coin, let him be what he will, even a calf, a beast in human form—he becomes their God, and they bow down to him, dance and frolic before him, giving glory to his name.

Those who attempt to conserve the past usually end up preserving the vices of that past. It is with the Conservatives as it is in the old proverb: "To a dog with money, people say 'my lord dog.'"

101. Lew Wasserman, 73. MCA talent agency. $220 million.

102. Weiler family. Real estate. Three brothers share at least $450 million. Jack Weiler is a former chairman of the United Jewish Appeal. A district in Jerusalem is named after him.

103. Harry Weinberg, 78. Real estate, securities, bus companies. Richest individual in Hawaii, worth over $550 million. Most to go to charity.

104. Leslie Wexner, 49. Owns 2,500 specialty clothing stores. Part owner of Sotheby's. Donates to Jewish causes. "With immediate family, worth $1 billion."

105. Lawrence Wien, 80. Real estate. Owns big piece of Empire State Building. Worth $150 million.

106. Wirtz family, Chicago. Real estate, liquor distributorships, Chicago Black Hawks, Bulls. At least $350 million.

107. Wolfson Family, Miami. *Forbes* 1984 list set their worth at $240 million. Movie houses, TV stations and other media properties. Became unpersons in 1985.

108. William Ziff, Jr. Father was author of book, *The Rape of Palestine,* which favored a Zionist alliance with Mussolini. Co-founder Ziff-Davis Publishers. Son now liquidating many properties. Over $650 million.

109. Ezra Khedouri Zilka, 60. Father was Baghdad banker, "The Rothschild of the east." Came to U.S. in 1941 to escape war. Family lost much of its fortune in Arab world in the wake of the creation of the Israeli state, but enough was left to continue on in investment banking in U.S. Worth at least $150 million. Director New York's Metropolitan Opera. Said to be religious.

110. William Zimmerman, 66. Pic 'n' Save bargain stores. $150 million.

111. Mortimer Zuckerman, 49. Real estate, publishing. *Atlantic Monthly, U.S. News and World Report.* Owns New York Coliseum site. Paid $8.5 million for 5th Avenue penthouse triplex, highest co-op apartment price ever in Manhattan. Heavy Democratic contributor, including to Gary Hart. Increasingly becoming ultra-rightist fanatic, favored U.S. military aid to Nicaraguan contras. Worth $200 million.

The Characteristics of the Jewish Capitalists

Fortune thought it remarkable that Jews tended to congregate in certain occupations. Today's Jewish rich are much more widely dispersed, with real estate and sports being the only distinctive Jewish fields. As a group, the realtors have one notorious characteristic. In his 1974 *Jews in American Politics,* Stephen Isaacs, one of America's leading journalists, described them:

> In localities across the country, Jews like non-Jews have been known to invest in candidates in return for government contracts, favorable rezonings on potentially valuable plots of real estate. . . . Jews have tended to be active in such instances of bribery. . . . Yiddish, had a word for the bribe: *shmeer* [to grease], a word that has somewhat come into the American English idiom.[28]

In an American court of law, the defendant is supposed to be presumed innocent until proven guilty. In the real estate business, people must be presumed guilty until proven innocent, for it may safely be said that real estate and construction are the most corrupt industries in America. At every level politicians, inspectors, fire marshalls, union officials and others have their hands out for bribes. In many cities a realtor who did not pay off would be hounded out of business by these characters, and therefore many real estate and construction contracts set aside an automatic percentage for such graft. Given that Jews are so prominent in the field, it is certainly true that shmeer is universally understood, but it is false to see these Jews as more corrupt than the non-Jews in the profession. Was any politically literate American surprised when John Zacarro, husband of Geraldine Ferraro, the 1984 Democratic vice presidential candidate, and a realtor of Italian descent, pleaded guilty to financial irregularities? Of course not.

Similarly with the other instances of criminal behavior among the Jews on the 400 list. Only a purblind "tribalist" like Newfield could brazenly write that "Jews do not own any of the corporations that have become symbols of greed and misconduct."[29] Steven Cohen, one of the Jewish Establishment's best sociologists, was only being candid when he wrote, in the *American Jewish Year Book 1980,* that the

> resulting shifts in type of work (from business to professions) and sources of income (from self-employed to salaried) mean that younger Jews will less often enter the pool of potential multimillionaires, that group which has most generously supported federation [Council of Jewish Federations and Welfare Funds—LB] drives in the past. The shift in source of income also means that a smaller fraction of . . . income . . . will be of the disposable variety. One need not be overly cynical to realize that self-employed entrepreneurs have a greater ability to hide their income from the Internal Revenue Service than do most salaried professionals.[30]

Nevertheless America's distinctive corruption pre-dates the mass Jewish immigration by several decades, and its constant graft scandals clearly demonstrate that these rich Jews are not any more corrupt than their class. Cynicism and corruption pervade America. All literate Americans know that "it's not what you know but who you know," and that "America has the best Congress that money can buy." Indeed, America's intellectuals find idealism naive, at best to be tolerated in callow student activists. Worldly types are expected to be "realists," with the smarts to vote for a bone fide "lesser of two evils."

Are There Too Many Rich Jews?

The magnitude of the Jewish proportion among the wealthy automatically raises questions for modern Americans, for whom affirmative action is an immensely controversial topic: Are there too many rich Jews, and should something be done to lower their percentage? Affirmative action need not be debated here; for now it is sufficient to recognize that it can be implemented, wisely or foolishly, on a level where it raises the position of an exploited minority of the poor. However, it is philosophically impossible to fairly dish out privilege, and any such effort would end up in disastrous or ludicrous situations if applied to property ownership under capitalism.

Europe's anti-Semites harped on similar statistics, and frequently attracted middle-class followings from those who saw themselves succeeding to the Jews' positions. Such efforts to restrict the Jews economically paved the way for the Holocaust. We are well advised to draw a few lessons from that: As a rule, restrictions on ethnic or religious *minorities* must be looked upon with profound suspicion.

Capitalism as such is anti-egalitarian. Each of the 400 enjoy a pharaonic luxury that beggers the vast mass of the people, including the overwhelming majority of America's Jews. In 1984, the 400 were worth $125 billion, almost equal to the $126 billion in all savings accounts in all commercial banks in the U.S., a nation of over 238,000,000 people.[31] In 1985 their wealth went up by another 9 billion. That this elite is additionally inegalitarian ethnically and religiously should not surprise us even if it is indeed noteworthy. It demonstrates that full equality for the economically deprived minorities is impossible within the system. But this is a secondary phenomenon. It is the expropriation of the capitalist class as a whole that is the order of the day. Or else those proclaiming themselves for human freedom must cease pretending they are also for full equality. Only expropriation coupled with democratic control of management by the workers in each and every place of work can lead to the ultimate equality of all ethnic groups.

Be that as it may, the future of American Jewry is in the intellectual field, and this will be true for the children of the very richest as well. They will not, for the most part, make their careers within the companies owned or operated by their fathers, though they certainly will hold onto their stock. Even Riklis's mother "would have preferred that I be a teacher or professor."[32] He understands that a surgeon is in fact a more prestigious member of society than a brassiere manufacturer, no matter how rich. However, in the present, the bulk of America's Jews are tied to capitalism in myriad ways. Certainly Zionism, with its fatal addiction to military handouts from the Pentagon, has propelled a substantial minority into a political alliance with the most reactionary elements within American life. Orthodoxy's hatred of atheists, characteristic of all intense sectarians, has served the same purpose. But in general, their relative wealth operated to draw the bulk of middle-aged Jews into the orbit of the system's ideological values. They share the culture of the very rich, they are a massive component of the audience in the fossilized worlds of classical music and the plastic arts, so dependent on the philanthropy of the richest Jews.

In some respects, these middle-aged Jews are the most philistine stratum within the American middle and upper classes. Aside from a few landed southern families, the majority of rich Americans with full-time servants are Jews, and half of all middle-class Jews have their "shvartze," their once-a-week Black cleaning lady, in contrast to no more than five percent of the Protestant middle class.[33] This element may be more cultured than most of the American middle class; certainly on some secondary political questions, as with separation of church and state or abortion, they are far more enlightened than the general public. Nevertheless, it may be said, with scientific certainty, that in this day and age a social stratum with such a vastly disproportionate addiction for maids can never again be the cutting edge of ideological progress.

Their children are another matter, as many will evolve away from the West End Avenue culture of their parents; but the cocaine and quiche and hanging plants world of the gentrified yuppies is scarcely a serious alternative value system. Nor is academia, with its own crackpot realist propensity for lesser evilism. Only a minority of the Jewish intelligensia will be found in the trenches in the final battles against exploitation and oppression.

Notes

1. Text in *The Aliens: A History of Ethnic Minorities in America,* Leonard Dinnerstein and Frederic Jaher (editors), pp. 229–47, passim.
2. Max Geltman, *The Confrontation,* p. 112.

3. Howard Sacher, *The Course of Modern Jewish History*, p. 346.
4. Marta Ackelsberg, "Pride, Prejudice and Politics: Jewish Jews on the American Left," *Response,* Autumn 1982, p. 15.
5. Murrey Zuckoff, "Study Shows Jewish Jobless Is Growing, Despite Improved Economy," *Jewish Telegraphic Agency Daily News Bulletin,* Nov. 22, 1983.
6. Helen Ginsburg, "Holes in the Safety Net," *Jewish Currents,* November 1984, p. 16.
7. Ibid., p. 13.
8. Ibid., p. 14.
9. Gerald Krefetz, *Jews and Money,* p. 17.
10. Charles Silberman, *A Certain People, pp. 23, 99, 124.*
11. Ibid., p. 124.
12. Richard Zweigenhaft, *Who Gets to the Top?,* p. 6.
13. Ibid.
14. Ibid., p. 17.
15. Krefetz, p. 18.
16. Ibid., p. 256.
17. Ibid., p. x.
18. Ibid., p. 11.
19. Ibid.
20. Ibid., p. 10.
21. Silberman, pp. 143–4.
22. Tom Smith, "America's Religious Mosaic," *American Demographics,* June 1984, p. 20.
23. Stephen Isaacs, *Jews and American Politics,* p. 279.
24. G. William Domhoff and Richard Zweigenhaft, *Jews in the Protestant Establishment,* p. 105.
25. "Meshulam Riklis," *Penthouse,* May 1985, passim.
26. Domhoff and Zweigenhaft, "Jews in the Corporate Establishment," *NY Times,* April 24, 1983, sec. 3, p. 2.
27. *Jews in the Protestant Establishment,* p. 99.
28. Isaacs, pp. 127–8.
29. Jack Newfield, "Blacks and Jews," *Village Voice,* March 20, 1984, p. 15.
30. Steven Cohen, "Trends in Jewish Philanthropy," *American Jewish Year Book 1980,* p. 33.
31. "The 400 Richest People in America," *Forbes,* Oct. 1, 1984, p. 156.
32. *Penthouse,* p. 76.
33. Seymour Martin Lipset, "The Left, the Jews and Israel," *Encounter,* Dec. 1969, p. 33.

4

Israel, Its American Jewish Supporters, and American Politics

Although "organized Jewry" is extremely divided in its conceptions of Jewishness, the one thing that does loosely unite the vast majority of Jewish organizations is their support for Israel. Therefore, before it is possible to understand fully the modern "community," it is obligatory to analyze Zionism. What is more, Israel has become so intimately connected with official Washington that it is also necessary to understand the overarching relationship of American Zionism to the American political structure before we can fully grasp the inner dynamics of American Zionism.

The Lovers of Zion

Throughout the middle ages, a trickle of pious Jews had migrated into Palestine. None of these believers came with any political pretensions. On Passover and the Day of Atonement Jews would cry out *"leshono hobo Birusholaim"* (next year in Jerusalem), but it would be the Lord, in his own good time, who would deliver them up to their ancestral seat. On one thing the Talmudists were very clear: It was—and is—blasphemy to come up to the Holy Land in a column, to take it by force. That would be substituting human agency for God.

Modern Zionism evolved out of—and away from—that tradition only in the last decades of the 19th century, in the wake of the first Tsarist pogroms, when some thousands of *Hovevi Zion,* lovers of Zion, departed the "prisonhouse of the peoples" for the land of their fathers.

Although this proto-Zionist current clearly had its roots in religion, the newcomers were bitterly opposed by the "old *yishuv,"* the genuinely pious old settlement. The new element did not come to pray but to work, with many becoming farmers, unlike their religious adversaries, who were, for the most part, content to live on charity from overseas Jews and from a scandalous begging at the Wailing Wall. What is more, the traditionalists only used Hebrew in their prayers. For them, it was the holy tongue, never to be profaned by common discourse, for which they used Yiddish or Ladino or Arabic. The later arrivals were nationalists, and it was they who revived the long dead language. Nevertheless, they were still without political ambitions.

The World Zionist Organization

It was Theodor Herzl who put the movement onto a political footing. Although he occasionally attended the synagogue, this was only to make his new World Zionist Organization appealing to believers. Hebrew meant nothing to him, and he didn't care whether his state was to be in Palestine or Argentina or even Kenya. He would accept whatever any imperial patron would offer. Herzl understood that the Jews did not have the strength to create their own state, and it could only begin as a colony of some empire.

After setting up the WZO in 1897, he embarked on a diplomatic campaign, meeting some of the most important figures of the day. If the Turkish Sultan would give him an autonomous Palestine, he would ensure him Jewish funding for the imperial debt. He tried to gain the support of the Tsarist pogrom Minister, Vyacheslav von Plevhe, telling a revolutionary that:

I have just come from Plevhe. I have his positive, binding promise
that in 15 years, at the maximum, he will effectuate for us a charter for Palestine. But this is tied to one condition: the Jewish revolutionaries shall cease their struggle against the Russian government. If in 15 years from the time of the agreement Plevhe does
not effectuate the charter, they become free again to do what they
consider necessary.[1]

The Kaiser was assured that Jewish Marxists would be diverted
to Palestine; the Italian king promised aid in colonizing Libya, if
he would help Herzl obtain Palestine; London was told unwanted
immigrants would be diverted to a far away colonial outpost.

From Balfour to Hitler

None of Herzl's ploys were successful, but Zionism's hour struck
with WWI. The war was not going Britain's way in 1917. Revolutionary Russia looked as if it was going to pull out of the
imperial carnage. London thought Russian Jewry could use its
influence to hold the Kerensky regime in the war, and perhaps
American Jews could help bring the U.S. into the slaughter if
Palestine were dangled before them. Whitehall's hopes were fantasy, but the surviving result of its scheme was the Balfour
Declaration, establishing a Jewish national home in Palestine.

Zionism finally had its patron, but most Jews still showed no
interest in the enterprise. Naturally the Palestinian Arabs thought
their country was their national home, and they rioted against the
unwanted colonizers in 1920 and 1929. The British, knowing they
needed local catspaws to maintain the empire, planned to use the
Zionists against the natives, but even with their patronage the
Jewish population had only risen from 8 percent in 1917 to 18
percent in 1931.

Hitler's rise to power really set Zionism on the road to ultimate
control of Palestine. The Nazis were still too weak in 1933 to
murder German Jewry, and the regime had to content itself with
pushing them out of the country. Ever since Herzl, Zionism saw
the anti-Semites as potential patrons; now the WZO made a deal
with the Hitlerites.

In August 1933 the WZO and Berlin signed an agreement, the
Ha'avara, or Transfer, which was the least painful way a Jew
could get wealth out of the Third Reich. The Jew put money into
a special account in Berlin, the money was used to purchase Ger-

man export goods, which were then sold in Palestine or elsewhere in the Middle East. When the emigré arrived in Palestine he would receive repayment, from the WZO, after the wares had been sold.

The Jew still lost on the deal, but not as much as if he had tried to ship capital to any other country. The Zionists gained because approximately 60 percent of all Jewish investment in Palestine in the 1930s came through the *Ha'avara,* and the Jewish population rose to 29.9 percent in 1935.

Of course it was the Nazis who were the big gainers from the transaction. The pact punched a hole in the Jewish boycott of German goods, and the WZO did nothing to organize resistance to Hitlerism.

With the sharp rise in the Jewish population, the Palestinians saw their country slipping away and a popular revolt broke out in 1936. The British thought they could restore order by partitioning the country and creating Jewish and Arab statelets attached to the empire. They announced their plan in 1937. But suddenly they realized that once such a Jewish state was established, the Arab world would always hold them responsible for their action.

London feared that such a policy would throw the Arabs towards the Nazis in the event of another war, and they immediately abandoned the proposed dismemberment of the country. Eventually, by 1939, the British had crushed the revolt, but, that same year, they further sought to reassure the Arabs by curtailing Jewish immigration. Zionism was at an impasse.

Throughout the subsequent Holocaust, Britain kept all but a trickle of Europe's Jews from gaining refuge in Palestine. The laws of inertia apply in politics, and the WZO, which did nothing to mobilize the Jews before the killing time, remained supine and did nothing to put pressure on America or Britain to rescue the Jews in Nazi-occupied Europe. With the end of the war it became still clearer that London's abandonment of their erstwhile clients was irrevocable. For Zionism to achieve its ambitions it would have to fight both Britain and the Arabs.

The Establishment of the Israeli State

The post-war constellation of forces presented Zionism with immense opportunities. As long as the Nazis could use the WZO, they were indifferent to the Arab cause. But once the war broke out they openly identified with the Palestinian leader, the Mufti of Jerusalem, who eventually recruited Soviet and Yugoslav Muslims into the SS. Now he was a wanted war criminal and the Palestinians were totally discredited in the eyes of the world.

Britain had emerged a pyrrhic victor; it was the beginning of the end for her globe-girdling empire. Aramco had begun to exploit the Saudi oil fields in the late 1930s, and now the State Department saw itself as an active arbiter of Middle Eastern affairs, succeeding the slowly retreating British and French. Communism was dominant in Eastern Europe, the historic heartland of Ashkenazi Jewry. And much of Western opinion felt that the creation of a Jewish state would be the belated silver lining after the black cloud of horror that was the Holocaust.

It is still widely believed that this international sympathy for the Holocaust's survivors was the decisive factor in the new political equation, but this was true only in the most restricted sense. No one was thinking of a haven for survivors *per se*. With the exception of some thousands of German Jews who found temporary refuge in what had been the International Settlement in Shanghai, few of the pre-war exiles who were not already in Palestine were interested in uprooting themselves for a second time. And barely any Western European Jews thought to abandon their now liberated countries. It was Eastern Europe's "Displaced Persons" whose plight troubled the world.

About 85,000 Jews survived the war in Poland, and they had been joined by approximately 175,000 more Jews who returned from the Soviet Union in 1946. The new Communist regime had come into the country on Soviet gun carriages and had no popular base. The new government was still too weak to protect the remnant community, and right-wing fanatics murdered 351 Jews between November 1944 and October 1945. That same month, David Ben-Gurion, then Zionism's leading figure, journeyed to the American Zone in Germany, where he asked Eisenhower to admit Jews coming out of Poland into the Displaced Persons Camps. He outlined his stratagem in a November 21 memo to his headquarters:

> If we can succeed in concentrating a quarter million Jews in the American Zone, it will increase the American pressure [on Britain—LB]. Not because of the financial aspects of the problem—that does not matter to them—but because they see no future for these people outside Eretz Yisrael.[2]

On July 4, 1946, the reactionaries slaughtered 42 Jews in Kielce, and 100,000 Jews fled Poland and other eastern European countries in the wake of the pogrom. Hebrew University professor Yehuda Bauer candidly conceded that:

> The Zionist leadership feared that the masses concentrated in the displaced persons camps . . . would seek a way of reaching countries overseas rather than waiting until the gates of Palestine were opened to them. . . . It is probable that if the people had been given equal opportunities to go to Palestine or to America, 50 percent would have joined the Diaspora Jewry in America. . . . A mixture of deep shock, feelings of guilt, and perhaps even a touch or more of anti-Semitism led to the support of the U.S. Army for Jewish emigration from Eastern Europe to a country the Jews wanted to build up as their own.[3]

"I Do Not Have Hundreds of Thousands of Arabs Among My Constituents"

Large numbers of America's Jewish capitalists had opposed Zionism, fearing it would raise questions as to their loyalty to the U.S. Now, however, they had a greater concern. Samuel Halperin, a Jewish Establishment historian, described their behind-the-scenes cogitations in his *Political World of American Zionism:* The American Jewish Committee, then as now the publishers of *Commentary,* and the Joint Distribution Committee

> were much concerned with anti-Semitism and other such threats to their personal security. Admitting concentration camp survivors would perhaps mean importing more anti-Semitism. Emigration to Palestine would be better for good Jewish-Christian relations in America.[4]

Truman had once been in business with a Jew, Eddie Jacobson, and was no anti-Semite, but he knew Jew-hatred was endemic in the Dixiecrat wing of his party. He believed that patronage of Zionism in remote Palestine would be more palatable to this group than admitting Jews into the U.S. The Administration decided to publicly support the creation of a Zionist state.

Behind the scenes, Truman's own State Department opposed the venture. They needed London as a cold war ally, and their ambassadors in the Arab world warned that the U.S. would never be forgiven if it was seen to be pro-Zionist. A UN special committee called for partition, but it needed a two-thirds Assembly vote to become official policy. The diplomats decided on a little fancy footwork. Roy Henderson, Director of the Department's Office of Near Eastern and African Affairs, explained their thinking, in a October 22, 1947, memo to his superiors:

> If we carry the flag we shall inescapably be saddled with the major . . . responsibility for . . . enforcement . . . important Departments of the Government are unwilling . . . to accept the losses to the U.S. position in the Middle East which would be bound to follow an aggressive partition policy. . . . On the assumption that we are going to follow our present policy of supporting partition without waving the flag, we agree that partition will probably fail of a two-thirds vote . . . if partition fails, we do not see that the U.S. . . . would be inhibited from retreating to some compromise plan which would receive a two-thirds vote.[5]

George Butler of the Department's Policy Planning Staff explained that the U.S. delegation "took the position that this government should not use U.S. . . . influence . . . upon other countries against their will to support partition."[6]

However these intriguers had not reckoned with the Zionists, who called in their chits with their American friends. Walter White, for one, the leading personality in the National Association for the Advancement of Colored People. He later described his role in the creation of Israel:

> Haiti had announced that she would vote against partition as had . . . Liberia. I was bombarded by pro-partition organizations . . . to persuade Haiti to change her vote . . . both the wisdom and the practicability of partition were doubtful. . . . I did not like the self-segregation of Zionism. . . . But I reluctantly supported partition only because Palestine seemed the only haven . . . for nearly one million Jews. . . . I talked with representatives of Haiti, Liberia, the Philippines . . . [they] voted for partition. . . . Those three votes decided the issue.[7]

The State Department did not give up. The UN, it said, had voted for partition as the only way to obtain peace. Soon it became plain that carving up the country only guaranteed war, and the diplomats tried to get Truman to announce that the U.S. would not support partition. However, historian John Snetsinger has told us, in his *Truman, the Jewish Vote and the Creation of Israel*, that:

> Following Truman's Yom Kippur statement in 1946, the Democratic National Committee received large amounts of money from grateful Jewish contributors. . . . On September 4, 1947, Postmaster-General Robert Hannegan told the president that another statement favorable to the Jews would be of great assistance to the committee in raising needed campaign funds.[8]

Truman had everything going against him in the 1948 election campaign. The South Carolina racist Strom Thurmond had bolted the Democrats to run on the States Rights Party ticket. Henry Wallace had teamed up with the Communists to set up the Progressive Party.

The UN partition had been supported by Stalin, who had decided that the Arab princelings were too dependent on London to ever break with the empire, and he figured that only the example of the hated Zionists forcing the British out of Palestine could compel the Arab states to follow suit. Once word came from Moscow, the local Stalinists threw their all into pandering to the emotions of the Jewish masses, now purblind chauvinists in the wake of the horror visited on their kin during the Holocaust.

On February 17, 1948, a Wallaceite upset the Democrats in a special election in the 24th congressional District in the Bronx. Thomas Dewey, the Republican, saw his opportunity, and started making pro-Zionist noises. The leaders of the big city Democratic machines knew that if the rich Jews swung over to the Republicans and the masses voted for Wallace, not only would Truman lose, but their local tickets would be swamped. They screamed for Truman to support partition. The president vacillated, but in the end he stuck to the position he had taken in an October 1946 meeting with his Middle Eastern ambassadors.

William Eddy, the Minister to Saudi Arabia, later wrote of the meeting:

> Truman summed up his position with the upmost candor: "I'm sorry, gentlemen, but I have to answer to hundreds of thousands who are anxious for the success of Zionism; I do not have hundreds of thousands of Arabs among my constituents."[9]

That the UN had no more right to partition Palestine than it had to partition the U.S. is a settled point. Therefore, American support for the creation of Israel was undemocratic. But even domestically, philo-Zionism was part of an undemocratic cluster of policies vis-à-vis the Jews and their needs and interests.

The same U.S. passed the Displaced Persons Act in 1948. West Virginia Senator William Revercomb, one of the prime supporters of the bill, summed up the majority feeling in Congress when he said that "we could solve the DP problem all right if we could work out some bill that would keep out the Jews."[10]

That same legislation required that 40 percent of the DPs be from the Baltic states and/or *volkdeutsch,* and under it hundreds of war criminals found refuge here. Additionally, between 1945-55, some 800 German rocket scientists were brought here, under Project Paperclip. Among them were SS Major Werner von Braun, the developer of the V-2 and later head of the U.S. space program; Walter Schreiber, whom Washington helped to escape from the U.S. to Argentina after his role in the euthanasia gassing of mental defectives was exposed in 1952; and Arthur Rudolph, who had to give up his American citizenship in 1984 rather than face charges here that he had worked slave laborers to death in Dora-Nordhausen.

It is now admitted that Klaus Barbie was helped to escape to Argentina by his employers in military intelligence. Government rules barring admittance of war criminals were violated so frequently and by so many agencies that we must conclude that the highest levels in Washington didn't care to enforce their own regulations. And certainly both the Democrats and the Republicans later knew that every single general in the "democratic" West German army that they ultimately brought into NATO had served Hitler.

Anti-Semitism was not a motive in the patronage of these Nazis, they were just useful in the fight against Communism, and anti-Arab sentiment was not a motive in the support of Zionism. The Democratic Party, then as now, wanted Jewish money for its campaigns. It had no more real interest in creating "the only democracy in the Middle East" than it had in creating democracy in Germany.

"Out of Evil, However, Good Came"

With the U.S. and the Soviet Union on its side, the victory of Zionism in Palestine was assured. Although Jews constituted no more than one-third the population, the partition gave them over half the country. Yet this did not satisfy the Zionists.

Terror was their weapon to widen the conquest. On April 8, 1948, the right-wing Irgun and Stern Gang militias stormed the village of Dir Yassin on the outskirts of Jerusalem. Five Zionists were killed, and 254 Palestinians, half of them women and children. The rival Labor Zionist Haganah denounced their action as a monstrous atrocity, but soon merged the murderous Irgun and Sternist forces into the new Israeli army. Begin, the Irgun's commander, was not present, but defended his men in his *Revolt*. As per usual, the world, Arab, Jewish, neutral, was lying about the Irgun. But, "out of evil, however, good came."[11] Yes, indeed, much good:

> Arabs throughout the country, induced to believe wild tales of "Irgun butchery" . . . started to flee for their lives. . . . Of the about 800,000 Arabs who lived on the present territory of the state of Israel, only 165,000 are still there. The political and economic significance of this development can hardly be overestimated.[12]

Of course Begin knew the mentality of the troops that night. One of the assault's leaders, Yehuda Lapidot, wrote an account of their attack and inserted it into the movement's archives in the 1950s. The Stern Gang had "put forward a proposal to liquidate the residents of the village after the conquest." Benzion Cohen, the overall commander of the Irgun that night, wrote that:

> When it comes to prisoners, women, old people and children, there were differences of opinion, but the majority was for liquidation of all the men in the village and any other force that opposed us, whether it be old people, women or children.[13]

The Haganah was loud in denunciations of their rivals, and no one then believed the Arabs, who told of the Haganah's own crimes that year. It took until 1979 for much of their charges to be verified.

Yitzhak Rabin, now Israel's Defense Minister, had published his memoirs in Hebrew and then in English in this country. Except that, according to *The New York Times*, a panel of five cabinet ministers had censored out "a first-hand account of the expulsion of 50,000 Palestinian civilians from their homes near Tel Aviv." The translator, Peretz Kidron, gave the *Times* the unexpurgated manuscript:

We had to grapple with a troublesome problem . . . the civilian population of Lod and Ramle . . . we could not have Lod's hostile and armed populace in our rear . . . (Yigal) Allon repeated his question: "What is to be done?" B(en)-G(urion) waved his hand in a gesture which said, "Drive them out!" . . . There was no way of avoiding the use of force and warning shots in order to make the inhabitants march the 10 to 15 miles to the point where they met up with the [Jordanian] Legion . . . the Yiftach Brigade included youth-movement graduates. . . . There were some fellows who refused to take part. . . . Prolonged propaganda activities were required . . . to . . . explain why we were obliged to undertake such a harsh and cruel action.[14]

Israeli soldiers are not fools. If they were endangered there would have been no outcry. Although the Haganah's cold pogrom was less brutal than Dir Yassin, the effect was the same: land was cleared of Arabs.

The vast majority of refugees were never permitted to return and their property was turned over to Jews. The remaining natives were placed under military rule, and a racist social order was set up, which remains fundamentally intact to this day.

Every Tree Is Judged by Its Fruit

Central to Israeli racism are the Jewish National Fund and the Israeli Land Authority. The JNF, a British chartered firm, had been the pre-state Zionist land purchasing agency, and in the 1950s it was rechartered as an Israeli company. The problem that then arose was described in an internal discussion paper (CZA 36.911/90d):

In the Memorandum of Association of the existing company it is emphasized . . . that the JNF is permitted to act for the benefit of Jews only. One clause specifies that the . . . company is to purchase lands for . . . settling Jews. . . . Another . . . specifies that the company is permitted to lease its lands only to Jews. . . . Although the object of the JNF will continue to be to assist in the settlement of Jews only . . . should we allow this explicit prohibition to remain, the undesirable impression might be created of so-called racist restrictions, which are opposed by Jews throughout the world. It is therefore proposed that in the new Memorandum . . . the clause specifying the object . . . remain unchanged . . . to purchase lands for the purpose of settling Jews.

The other clauses will be modified so as to remove the prohibition against the leasing of lands or the allocation of cash advances to non-Jews. One can assume that even without these explicit prohibitions, the JNF Board of Directors will know how to administer the work . . . in accordance with the explicit object as specified in the aforementioned clause which remains unchanged.[15]

Professor Uzzi Ornan has described the relationship of the JNF to the Israel Land Authority, in a letter to *Ha aretz,* the country's leading paper:

The parliament [Knesset] also approved the agreement signed between the ILA and the JNF, according to which the lands belonging to that authority shall be administered according to the JNF's principles, which means: a Jew has a right to receive land, or an apartment on lands controlled by the Authority, but a non-Jew doesn't enjoy that right, unless the apartment or plot of land are located in a special "zone of residence" assigned to non-Jews.[16]

The ILA administers 92 percent of the land within the pre-1967 borders, and it built Jews-only towns, as with Carmiel and Upper Nazareth in Galilee, to dominate areas with Arab majorities. Arabs cannot legally own homes in these towns. However, Jews have discovered that Arabs are willing to pay extra to get the flats, and by now a substantial minority of Arabs lives in Upper Nazareth. Fear of adverse American reaction prevents the government from expelling them, but it tried to keep them out by offering to match the Arabs' key price bids if the Jewish flat dwellers would give the keys to the state.

For all the propaganda about the kibbutzim as Zionism's answer to Communism, these are racist institutions. Professor Yosef Goell has written an article for the *Jerusalem Post* discussing the exclusionary policies of the kibbutzim operated by the Mapam party, the strongest "left" Zionist grouping:

The movement's struggle for more far-reaching integration of the Arab minority into the mainstream of Israeli life has, however, stopped at the gates of its kibbutzim . . . occasional applications on the part of individual Arabs to be accepted as kibbutz members have uniformly been turned down.[17]

"Israel," that is to say Israel within its pre-1967 borders, is not South Africa. There are Arabs in the Knesset. The proper analogy is to Northern Ireland before its parliament was abolished. There are free elections, but they do not prevent massive communal discrimination. When some of the natives go too far in their resistance, the government applies an updated version of the Mandatory's Emergency Military Regulations, which in their original form had been copied, word for word, from Northern Ireland's infamous Special Powers Act: rebels are arrested without charge, and held without trial.

The occupied territories are infinitely worse. On July 19, 1977, the London *Sunday Times* issues a report, "Israel Tortures Arab Prisoners," after a five-month investigation. The authorities brazened it out and denied the charges, but as everyone knows that the *Sunday Times* is not exactly a Pennysaver, the *Jerusalem Post* came up with an unofficial cleanup that would, hopefully, satisfy Israel's cynical public. According to David Krivine:

> In order to get information from a particular recalcitrant suspect, rough treatment may be used. He may, according to my information, be pushed about, he may have his face slapped, he may be blindfolded. He may be stripped and have his manliness mocked by a girl soldier to make him feel small. He can be kept in isolation; he can be threatened with a dire fate; he can be subjected to other psychological pressures.[18]

Note well that this was in an article denying the charge that torture was "widespread and systematic." To this apologist, all that was going on was merely "routine manhandling." Certainly if any American police force tried what Krivine says was routine, the police would themselves go away to the penitentiary for many years, for violating the civil rights statutes.

Of course Krivine was deceiving himself, if not others. He claimed that all of this was unfortunately necessary to get information on terrorist plots. Except that you can push an Arab from here to Mecca, slapping him all the way, and he will tell you nothing. You must torture him, and it is hard to think Krivine didn't know it.

The sordid essay sought to play on the modern intelligentsia's characteristic cynicism. If war is hell, fighting terrorism is heck itself. And the unofficial "realistic" defense ultimately comes down to that: Aren't all Arabs unreconciled to a Jewish State? How dare they then turn around and expect equal treatment—and why should they get it? In fact however, Zionism discriminates against Jews as well.

The Messiah Just Might Come—Any Day Now

In 1953 a man named Cohen married a divorcee in a civil ceremony under a law still on the books from British Mandatory days. The marriage nearly brought down the cabinet. Our man may have been a butcher-baker-candlestick-maker, but a Cohen is a descendant of the priests of the ancient Temple of Jerusalem, and all Cohens are supposed to be on stand-by, ready to perform the ritual animal sacrifices, when the Messiah comes and restores the sacred Temple. Cohens are polluted by sexual contact with divorcees and converts, and the religious party threatened to walk out of the ruling coalition if civil marriage was not abolished. Henceforth, all marriages and divorces in Israel were to be religious. Under prevailing Orthodox law, no woman can initiate a divorce, nor testify in a divorce proceding, nor are there any women judges in such cases. Nor can a Jew substitute a Conservative or Reform divorce. Their synagogues are allowed, but their rabbis' marriages and divorces are not recognized.

Criticism of Israel focuses on racism against Arabs rather than on these discriminations against Jews. But these medievalisms actually tell us a decisive fact about Israel. For what are the mathematical odds that a Jewish state that discriminates against Jews would ever stop discriminating against Arabs? Of course there is no chance. Can a Zionist state secularize itself? Again, there is no chance.

Why so? Because there are only two kinds of Zionist parties: the religious fanatics, and those secular parties that habitually form coalitions with them. What then is to prevent liberal Zionists from forming a new party, decisively winning an election, and changing the laws? Logically, nothing. Except that Israeli liberals are no better than American liberals. In the June 28 issue of *The New York Review of Books,* Avishai Margalit, the chairman of Hebrew University's Philosophy Department, denounced Noam Chomsky because the American did not understand that, in practical terms, Zionist policies are divided between "the sane hypocrisies of the Alignment and the self-righteous brutality of the Likud." And, of course, he "would not hesitate to prefer the Alignment."[19]

In Israel's case the resident lesser evil is the Labor Party, which led the Alignment in the last election. Except that it was the same Labor Party which was in power when our friend Cohen decided to make an honest woman out of his girlfriend, and it was they who abolished civil marriage.

Modern liberals have no insight into themselves. In any society with more or less free elections, such crackpot realists delude themselves that they are true to liberal principles, when in fact they are actually voting for the enemies of such principles. It must be said with certainty that the only way Jewish women can ever get equality with Jewish men is when they unite with the Palestinian masses and replace the Zionist state with a democratic secular Palestine.

Ever since the American revolution, the doctrine of human equality has been the central axiom of progressive thought. To be sure, the Bill of Rights was the work of slaveholders. Nevertheless the first shot at Lexington was indeed "the shot heard around the world." Today we, and the Communist states as well, take the principle for granted in our domestic legal life.

Never mind, for now, that our president is a fanatic who invariably is on the side of the rich, or that Communism frequently means tyranny. In the end, these undeniable facts merely mean that history has granted the singular privilege of finally utterly destroying inequality to our undeserving generations. The point is that if Israel were America's 51st state, Washington would not send it arms, it would have to send the army, exactly as it did to our southern states in the 1950s and 1960s. And this is the utterly counter-revolutionary movement that commands the allegiance of that minority of American Jews who style themselves "the Jewish community."

How U.S. Policy Makers See the Middle East

Prior to WWI, American involvement with the Arab world was minimal, largely confined to Christian missionary and educational organizations. Later, when the Standard Oil interests moved into the Saudi oil fields in the 1930s, their potentials were not appreciated, and the region was still far from central to the oil cartel's concerns. Even in the 1940s, when the State Department had to determine policy towards the emerging Zionist state, fear of antagonizing London, rather than the Arab princelings, was the prime consideration.

Once it was decided that the Democratic Party's electoral fate was to be the crucial factor in the equation, the U.S. rushed to grant de facto recognition to the new Zionist state, and a $100 million Export-Import Bank Loan was made in 1949. But direct U.S. grants, as opposed to loans, did not pass the $1 million mark until 1952, with $86.4 million that year.

The U.S. adhered to the April 17, 1948, UN Security Council embargo on arms sales to the Palestine region, and Washington did not provide Israel with any direct military aid until the late 1950s, and it was only in 1962 that such aid exceeded the paltry sum of $1 million. Although the domestic politicians had already become virtuoso demagogues, in practice it was the State Department, not the stump orators, who determined policy toward the region.

With Dwight Eisenhower's victory in the 1952 election, Washington put considerable distance between Israel and itself. Secretary of State John Foster Dulles saw the creation of an anti-Communist wall on the Soviet border as his prime regional goal, and to achieve that he needed the participation of Turkey, Iran and Pakistan, as well as Arab Iraq, in the February 1955 Baghdad Pact. He made it clear that the U.S. was not in Israel's corner in the wake of the 1956 British-French-Israeli invasion of Egypt, when Washington joined Moscow in commanding an Israeli withdrawal from Gaza and Sinai. However, the Eisenhower Administration was not "pro-Arab." Eisenhower openly proclaimed that the U.S. had a unilateral right to intervene in the internal affairs of any Arab country it thought threatened by "Communist aggression," and he sent the marines into Lebanon in 1958.

Israel wanted U.S. support, and had no scruples about how to get it. On July 14, 1954, Israeli Intelligence firebombed the U.S. Information Center Libraries in Alexandria and Cairo. They hoped the attacks would be blamed on Egyptian nationalist elements. Then, they thought, the U.S. would lessen its pressure on Britain to withdraw from the Suez.[20] A firebomb went off accidently in the pocket of one of their agents in a public place in Cairo, and the ring was broken up by the Egyptian police.

The Israeli authorities tried to escape Washington's ire by blaming the whole affair on Pincus Lavon, the Defense Minister, who, it was alleged, had acted on his own. Today it is no longer disputed that the government was responsible for the attacks.

After Eisenhower's hostility towards Israel in the 1956 Sinai adventure, Israel persuaded the Jewish Establishment here to decisively step up its lobbying in Washington.

We may speculate as to whether a Democratic President would have been so quick to condemn the 1956 invasion, given the Democrats' dependence on Jewish fundraisers. There is no doubt that, at that time, a commitment to Israel was seen as a regional liability by virtually all the foreign policy makers.

Republicans are never as concerned about the Jewish vote as the Democrats. The Republicans have always received the support of a significant proportion of the Orthodox, who see them as opponents of liberalism and its loose morals, as well as an ever-increasing segment of the Jewish rich, who prefer the party for cut-and-dried class reasons. But as they are the party of the overwhelming majority of America's capitalists, they are not dependent on these rich Jews for campaign contributions.

The leaders of both parties see the Persian Gulf as the center of the universe. The world capitalist system is dependent on oil. In its propaganda, the U.S. never stops talking about the threat to the Middle East from "Soviet imperialism." Since the Soviets are massive exporters of gas and oil, it is difficult to believe our politicians take this line seriously. What "Soviet imperialism" really means, to them, is social revolution in the region.

It was the development of the radical nationalist orientation towards the Soviet Union, in the wake of Washington's refusal to fund the building of Egypt's Aswan High Dam, that finally moved the U.S. to make a strategic turn towards Israel. Prior to the Kennedy Administration there were no military ties, and the economic links were limited. Between 1951 and 1961, economic assistance to the Zionist state totaled only $594.5 million (excluding Export-Import Bank loans), with only $349.3 million taking the form of outright grants. The earliest military connections were largely clandestine shipments utilizing West German and Belgian covers.[21]

No open military aid was given until 1962, and even in that year only $13.2 million in military-oriented loans was given. This was followed by $13.3 in 1963, nothing the next year and only $12.9 million in 1965. However, by 1963 Kennedy was willing to sell Israel a clutch of Hawk anti-aircraft missiles, and in 1965 Johnson sold Israel its first A-4 Skyhawk fighters.

It was Israel's stunning triumph in the 1967 war that proved decisive for the American-Israeli alliance. The Johnson Administration, itself fanatically committed to a military solution in Vietnam, gave Israel the OK to start the war (the Arab states had made bellicose threats, but there is no disputing that Israel was in no military danger, or that it struck first). The war itself convinced Washington of two things. The Arab armies were worthless, certainly in any potential war involving the Soviets. And Israel would dominate the region for decades to come.

Johnson's conception of the way to get ultimate peace in the region was for Israel to hold the newly conquered territories until the Arabs came to terms, and therefore he backed Israel to the extent of selling no less than 50 F-4 fighter-bombers to Israel. This marked the only time any had been sold to a non-NATO state. The "Black September" affair in Jordan in 1970, when the U.S. and Israel saw the "Soviet client" PLO in a death struggle with King Hussein, the CIA's man in Amman, clinched the relationship, and U.S. military sales jumped from $140 million in 1968-70 to $1.2 billion in 1971-73.

Nixon not only increased the sales, but also changed their terms, and with this the present relationship can be said to have begun. With Johnson the sales had been for cash. Nixon agreed to let Israel, and only Israel, utilize a "cash flow" method to pay for the weaponry. Normal buyers under Foreign Military Sales agreements are required to set aside the full cost of all items upon first placing the order. Israel only was permitted to set aside just the yearly payment. In 1971 technical assistance was provided so that Israel could produce advanced weapons parts, and this proved to be the basis of Israel's present military exports industry.

For all of Washington's patronage of Zionism, there were still important figures within American imperialism's inner circles who refused to accept the notion that Israel was Wall Street's only reliable perch in the region. These groups preferred to rely on the reactionary regimes, notably the Saudis. In 1976, General George Brown, the head of the Joint Chiefs of Staff, insisted, in public, that, "from a purely military point of view," Israel has "just got to be considered a burden," because it was absorbing so much of America's current weapons production and, more important, he thought it would drag the U.S. into a fight with the Arabs for its special interests.[22]

The years between the 1967 and 1973 wars were the high point of the "special relationship." The 1973 war forced Washington to drastically revise its perception of the problem. Sadat had broken with the Soviets even before the war, and he saw the war as the ultimate form of political pressure to make the U.S. compel Israel to come to terms with the Arabs.

The 1977 shift of Egypt, by far the militarily most important Arab state, away from the radical nationalist states, permitted the U.S. to conclude that it could ride two horses at the same time. Previously, the conventional wisdom within ruling circles had been that the closer you got to Israel the worse off you were politically within the Arab world. The end result was that weapons and money were poured into the region to both Israel and the Arabs.

In the end, all such hopes of utilizing both Zionism and Arab reaction are utopian, as America is slowly discovering. Sadat was assassinated, to the pleasure of tens of millions of ordinary Arabs. Bashir Gemayel was likewise assassinated, certainly for his pro-Israeli stance. The ill-concealed glee in Washington when Israel destroyed the PLO's military base in Lebanon turned into utter despair when Reagan had to withdraw from Lebanon in the face of the nationalist onslaught against the Marines in Beirut. And the notion of Israel as imperialism's cop in the region became ludicrous in the wake of Israel's own forced retreat from its northern neighbor.

"War is the continuation of politics by other means." This is the central doctrine enunciated by the Prussian military theoretician Karl von Clausewitz. All modern military establishments declare themselves to be his disciples, yet few generals, and fewer politicians, really understand this simple axiom. In the end, if you have nothing to offer the masses except a bullet you cannot win, quite regardless of your military successes, because you have no solution to your political problems. Zionism can never come to terms with the Arab masses, no matter if their rulers try to come to an agreement with Israel, because of its racism towards the Arabs held in its claws. There is a broadly progressive camp within every Arab state, opposed to the regimes, and if a revolution takes place in any of these states, any enlightened government will automatically have as its foreign policy a resolute struggle against an anti-Arab racist enclave within the Arab sphere, as well as a no-compromise position on breaking the economic and military connection to the U.S.

Indeed, given that Zionism and U.S. imperialism are so hated by the Arab masses, it must be said that the only reason that both have not yet been defeated is due to the failings of the Palestinian movement, whose leaders certainly qualify as among the least competent leaders produced by any colonized nationality in the post WWII epoch.

For a Democratic Secular Palestine You Need a Democratic Secular Movement

The Palestinian movement has gone through an immense metamorphosis in the decades since the 1948 debacle. The Mufti represented the landlord class, and with the expulsion of hundreds of thousands from the area that became pre-1967 Israel, that class effectively ceased to exist. The areas that did not immediately fall into the Zionists' hands languished under the tyrannical control of the Hashemite kingdom of Jordan and the Egyptian monarchy, with the people mired in dreadful poverty, and demoralized by their terrible defeat.

Modern ideological currents began to emerge among them as they witnessed Britain and France finally being expelled from the Arab world. The Soviet Union slowly began to regain credibility with the Palestinians and the broader Arab public after it became the economic and military patron of Nasser's Egypt. A considerable intellectual stratum emerged among the refugees as their UN benefactors stressed education as the only economic hope for the younger generation.

The Arab League was eventually obliged to establish a new movement, the PLO, in May 1964, to channel the growing determination to challenge the permanency of the Zionist entity. Initially, however, the organization was little more than the catspaw of the Arab states, and, as with his masters, the PLO's leader, Ahmad Shukeiry, became a byword for irresponsible demagoguery, with his call for driving the Jews into the sea.

The crushing defeat for the blustering Arab states in 1967 was also the turning point for the PLO. Shukeiry had to step down, and was eventually replaced by Yasser Arafat, head of the Fatah guerrilla grouping. The PLO then adapted a strategic line of protracted people's war. Politically it still could go no further than its new Palestinian National Covenant, which declared that all of historic Palestine still belonged to the Palestinians, and that only those Jews "who were living permanently in Palestine before the beginning of the Zionist invasion will be considered Palestinians."[23]

It did not take very long for it to become obvious to the elements of the leadership who had to deal with the outside political world that the Covenant was an absurdity. Everyone asked them what would be the fate of the rest of the Jews, those whose families came after 1917 or 1948, the varying dates given for the start of the invasion. Eventually, the leadership came up with the far more palatable slogan of a democratic secular state. But the Covenant was never amended. Instead it was allowed to become a dead letter, rarely cited or read, except by Zionist propagandists, who delighted in utilizing it to discredit their foes.

The PLO's leaders genuinely called for a democratic secular state, but their organization remained Arab only, and never even tried to publish in Hebrew. They were not being hypocrites. The PLO constantly works with Jewish sympathizers, all over the world, and many of these have met with Arafat himself. It is safe to say that he has certainly met more Jews than the average American non-Jew ever meets. The PLO leaders' difficulties in this regard flowed from a thoroughly incorrect general political perspective which they adapted early on, and which led them to inadequate and incomplete postures on a range of strategic possibilities.

The Palestinians suffer from national oppression. Their small capitalist class, and the socially much more important intelligentsia, want to end that oppression, but they have no equivalent fundamental quarrel with the class nature of the surrounding Arab society, in which these elements among the refugees have long ago found their niches. On the contrary, they wished to utilize the surrounding countries as bases for guerrilla attacks on Israel, and for this they needed the benevolence of the regimes. Although they fully understand that they are only a branch of the Arab nation, the Fatah leaders took a position of non-intervention in the "internal affairs" of the Arab states. That is to say, for all their rhetoric about a democratic secular Palestine, they were not part of the larger struggle for a democratic secular Arab nation.

They understood that the states would never support a movement that would seek to abolish private property in a liberated Palestine, so they never talked about what their liberated Palestine would look like socially. Therefore they could never seriously become a bi-national movement of Arabs and Jews because, were they to do so, it would have been a signal to the Arab regimes that they were in fact going to create a revolutionary state. The last thing the Arab governments want to see is a democratic secular Palestine, which would inevitably inspire their own masses to seek the same for themselves.

Within what might appear to be a narrower field, military tactics, the same pattern of avoiding ideological conflicts likewise emerged. The leadership soon became aware that attacks on Israeli civilian targets were counter-productive. The Israeli masses saw the PLO as madmen who slaughtered children, and rallied behind their government.

The world left takes a principled position in support of any colonized people, regardless of the form of their resistance, be it civilized or savage. But neither their military patron, the Soviet Union, nor any other important left tendency ever encouraged such acts of terrorism. And the Western capitalist press naturally had a field day with such atrocities.

The PLO's leaders saw the popular mood of blind despair culminate, in 1981, in avowedly kamikaze attempts to cross the Israeli border using a motorized hang glider and even a weather balloon. But any attempt to educate their ranks would have required them to counterpose an alternative strategy, and this they could never do. If you impose ideological limitations on yourself so as not to offend some despots, it is impossible to develop a realistic alternative to military fanaticism and martyrdom.

In retrospect, it is clear that the tendency toward development of a genuinely progressive ideology ceased after "Black September" in 1970, when the Popular Front for the Liberation of Palestine, the PLO's left wing, skyjacked four planes to Jordan. Hussein decided that he had to crush the PFLP or lose control over the country.

The PFLP's defeat was naturally enough a defeat for the entire PLO and the entire organization became demoralized in degree in the wake of the debacle. The various PLO factions became pessimistic and began to operate on the assumption that they would be lucky if they saw a West Bank-Gaza ministate in their lifetimes. Once they began to think in terms of an Arab ministate as their practical goal, even the PLO's left factions locked into an irreversible Palestinian nationalism that belied their Marxist-Leninist pretentions.

The PLO's next defeat in Lebanon in 1982 further demoralized the moderates around Arafat. They have concluded that they have fought and lost, and now they only seek to salvage what they can. They hope that Reagan will throw them a bone to finally quiet them—a Bantustan attached to the Jordanian police state they had rejected back in their heroic days in the late 1960s.

It seems that President Reagan would like to wrap up the whole Palestinian matter by exactly such an arrangement. Except that the Israeli government sees no reason why they have to give the defeated Arafat anything. He can do them little harm now, and Hussein will never fight them again.

Arafat no longer has anything to offer the Palestinian people. However it remains to be seen if any of the rival forces within the present PLO can come up with a viable alternative strategy. If not, they too will, eventually, be superseded by younger forces.

It is to be understood that any Democratic or Republican Administration would be opposed to the Palestinians, regardless of their ideology or tactics. Both parties proclaim themselves to be for capitalism and opposed to revolution. But there can be no doubt that the profound failings of the PLO have made it infinitely easier for them to get their counter-revolutionary support for Israel accepted by the American people.

Similarly, while there is no doubt that many of Israel's Jewish supporters have grown restive as Zionism has increasingly identified itself with Reagan and Falwell here, and Botha and other reactionaries abroad, nevertheless they will not break with Jewish chauvinism unless they see a viable alternative. None of the PLO's present factions present them with that alternative.

"Israel Draws to It the Insane, the Fanatics, the Extremists"

The most important thing about American Zionism is that the least important thing about it is "Zionism." About 1,700 U.S. Jewish WWII veterans fought in the 1948 war. No more than 5 percent had been Zionists and only 370 settled, even if only temporarily.[24] Only 59,103 *olim,* no more than two-thirds of 1 percent of American Jewry, migrated to Israel between 1948 and 1976, and of these an estimated 60 percent to 80 percent returned to the U.S. as the vast majority of U.S. settlers prudently keep their U.S. passports.

There has always been a small stream of elderly foreign-born, to whom America is just another country in which they have lived, who retire to Israel, in no small measure to stretch their retirement pensions. Some 1,000 to 2,000 supporters of the *Neturei Karta,* an ultra-Orthodox sect who consider Zionism a blasphemy against Judaism, have also settled in "Palestine" or *"Eretz Yisrael,"* the land of Israel, but not *"Medinat Yisrael,"* the State of Israel, which they refuse to recognize.

The olim are far from typical of America's Jews. No more than 8.9 percent of American Jewry, at the outermost, are Orthodox, and not many more keep the dietary requirements. Yet a 1970s survey showed the migrants to be 37 percent Orthodox, 20 percent Conservative, 22 percent Reform. At least 53 percent observed some dietary laws, and no less than 75 percent fasted on Yom Kippur.[26] Only half of these emigrés had been in American Zionist organizations, and less than half of these had been activists. Formal organizational Zionism is not crucial in such emigration. A chauvinist interpretation of the religion is increasingly central.[27]

As Israel veered sharply to the right, after Begin's accession to power in 1977, the character of the U.S. emigrés also moved in that direction. Today many of the emigrés become part of the Israel ultra-right, with thousands of Americans settling on the West Bank and forming much of the cadre of the *Gush Emunim* (Bloc of the Faithful), the *Kach* (Thus!) Party of Meir Kahane, and of the even more bizarre underground religio-nationalist terror groups.

When, on April 11, 1982, a madman stormed the Dome of the Rock mosque, built on the site of the ancient Temple, but centuries after it had been destroyed, no one in Israel was surprised that the murderer was an American, Allan Goodman. According to Ehud Ben Ezer, writing in *Ha aretz,* the equivalent of the *Times,* modern "Israel draws to it the insane, the fanatics, the extremists and the violent, from all over the Jewish world, and probably mainly from the U.S.A."[28]

"I Wouldn't Be Caught Dead With Those Creeps"

If Zionism were nothing more than its most devoted practitioners, it would be nothing more than an offstage noise in American politics. But of course it is far more than the full-regalia fanatics, although it would be very difficult to give an up-to-date figure for its actual membership. Virtually all ideological groups, political or religious, lie to themselves, if to no one else, when it comes to their membership figures, and on November 7, 1974, the *Jerusalem Post* ridiculed those Zionists who had plucked a 700,000 figure straight out of thin air.[29]

Hadassah is, by far, the largest Zionist grouping in the U.S. It claims 375,000 dues payers. It has more members than the rest of the movement combined. But in many cases when a woman joins the sisterhood of a synagogue she automatically is counted as a member of its Hadassah branch. In fact it is a charity and a social club on the local level, and most members take no interest in ideological Zionism and do not vote for delegates to the World Zionist Congresses.

In recent years, a Movement to Reaffirm Conservative Zionism (MERCAZ) and an Association of Reform Zionists of America (ARZA) have similarly enrolled whole synagogues, and thus their figures, like Hadassah's, are largely meaningless. In 1977, 218,000 votes were cast for delegates to the 29th World Zionist Congress, far less than Hadassah's membership alone. Even that statistic is out of date. The WZO allows national sections to waive elections if enough of the constituent organizations can agree on a division of the delegates, and there was no election for the 1982 congress.

Hadassah is non-partisan regarding internal Israeli politics, as are ARZA and MERCAZ. There is a Labor Zionist Alliance affiliated to the Israeli Labor Party; an Americans for a Progressive Israel tied to the Mapam or United Workers Party; a Mizrachi (East) group, connected to the National Religious Party; Herut Zionists of America is the national section of Begin's party; and the Zionist Organization of America is connected with the Liberals, allied to the Israeli Herut in a close coalition called the Likud.

There are several small parties in the Israeli parliament that have followers here who work outside the framework of the American Zionist Federation. Kahane's *Kach* is actually an outgrowth of his original movement here, the Jewish Defense League, and the JDL and *Kach* only parted company organizationally in 1985. Presently, Kahane works through a new grouping, Friends of *Kach*.

The ultra-Orthodox Agudath Yisrael has been in the Israeli cabinet, but does not consider itself ideologically Zionist. However, it has several thousand followers here, and the Brooklyn synagogue of its most prominent supporter, the so-called Lubavicher rebbe, is a mandatory stop for many Israeli politicians.

Generally speaking, Israeli politicians can be said to harbor no illusions as to the AZF's real strength, aside from the efficient women of Hadassah. For audiences they go to the synagogues. If they are looking for money they go to a few hundred wealthy individuals or to the broad local Jewish community federations and/or the State of Israel Bonds Development Corporation for Israel.

American Jewry is the most educated ethnic and/or religious community in the country, if not the world, and there have always been a few first-rate scholars in and around the American Zionist movement, but these have never put their stamp on it. To the contrary: American Zionism is strictly the Philistines against the Palestinians. As we have said, Hadassah is organizationally the most efficient constituent of the AZF, but its intellectual level was best described in a report in its own *Hadassah Magazine* of its 1975 convention:

> Climaxing the opening session was the premier of the 1975–76 Israeli fashion show, featuring haute couture clothes designed and produced by students of Hadassah's Seligberg-Brandeis Comprehensive High School in Jerusalem. I. Magnin's, San Francisco's leading store of fine fashion, coordinated and staged the show with professional models and musical accompaniment. The knockout evening gown was adopted from a Yemeni (Jewish) bridal dress.[30]

In a very significant sense, Zionism has always had to preach to the converted. In America at least, it never has been able to develop a mass base independent of the synagogues. Orthodoxy is male chauvinist to the depths of its soul, and it has only been in recent years that the Reform, and later the Conservatives, began to admit women to the rabbinate. Hadassah evolved within that context as a pre-feminist women's auxiliary.

Just as the Israeli Labor Party produced a female Prime Minister, Golda Meir, while denying women the right to initiate a divorce, so the AZF produced a "chairman," Charlotte Jacobson, out of Hadassah. Today all but the most Orthodox women insist on organizational equality, but for Hadassah to dissolve itself as a separate women's group is equally out of the question. Its base is too unpolitical to merge directly into an ideological Zionist organization, and it is rich Jewish businessmen, not their wives, who will always be the dominant force in the Jewish community federations and the other Jewish charities.

In fact, the menfolk of "organized Jewry" are every bit as politically vulgar as Hadassah with its fashion shows. Nahum Goldmann, for 12 years the President of the WZO, perfectly described the official community in his 1969 *Autobiography,* and if anything has changed in the intervening years it has been for the worse:

> It reacts emotionally . . . it is more susceptible to sentiment, slogans, and passions than to ideas. Among no other Jews in the world does the public speaker, especially the demagogue, play such a role. . . . The Jews share another characteristic of the general American mentality: the excessive importance they attach to material assets, the dominance of the rich man. . . . Thus the "big giver" almost inevitably and automatically becomes a leader in Jewish life. . . . Any organization representing all of American Jewry must, by its very nature, be democratic. The handful of big givers will never assent to this. . . . The consequence . . . is the quite inadequate, not to say negligible, role the intellectual plays. . . . How often have I reproached American-Jewish intellectuals for their inadequate participation in Jewish life, only to hear the answer: I'm not a big giver; what part could I play? But the whole thing goes much further. The aloofness of tens and hundreds of thousands of intellectuals impoverishes Jewish life, makes it boring, shallow, and devoid of spiritual impetus.[31]

These pro-Zionist organizations draw their leaders and funds from the wealthiest community in the country, and Zionism is therefore one of the most powerful influences in American politics. But that same overwhelming dominance by shallow millionaires makes the movement into a sociological disaster, doomed to long-term defeat. Jewish youth are now the most intellectualized stratum in the world, and the philistine rich have become repulsive in their eyes. Manheim Shapiro, an official of the wealthy American Jewish Committee, discussed their hostility to the whole edifice of modern Jewry in a 1965 description of Harvard,

> where Jewish students form about a quarter of the student body, only about a tenth of these Jewish students join the local Hillel Foundation (of the B'nai B'rith, Sons of the Covenant). Similar patterns prevail at most other campuses. . . . The vast major-

ity . . . do not affiliate . . . and many of them say, "I wouldn't be
caught dead with those creeps." . . . Jewish membership organizations are either losing their membership, barely holding their own,
or increasing at a tiny rate. . . . They complain of what looks to
them like hypocrisy in their parents. . . . An older girl said, "They
keep telling us about Jewish ethics, but who gets the most important job in the synagogue? The man who gives the most money."
And a college student: "All my life, my parents were talking
about how everybody is equal, but they never wanted me to be
friends with anybody but Jewish kids." . . . they see the goal of
most Jewish activity as narrow and parochial.[32]

Nothing has changed in this regard in 20 years. According to a
1985 article by Don Gilbert, co-chair of the Israel Action Committee at the University of California at Berkeley, again, one of
the most prestigious schools in the world, only "approximately
150 students . . . are involved with campus Jewish activities" out
of a population of "between 5,000 and 6,000 Jewish students."[33]

The Self-Chosen Leaders of The Chosen People

American Jewry is a tiny minority of the American people, and
organized Jewry is a minority of that minority. The activists of
the Zionist movement are yet an even more infinitesimal sliver of
the Jews. In 1973 the *American Jewish Year Book* reported the
results of a National Jewish Population Study, which was the first
scientific effort to study all of American Jewry. Since then there
have been a few refinements in the statistics, but the general
trends seen then still remain true.

The study showed that 60.2 percent of all Jewish adults were
"not at all" active in any temple or synagogue, and 69.4 percent
of all household heads under the age of 30 defined themselves as
"not at all" active in any religious congregation.[34] We may legitimately assume that the figure for activity in all Jewish organizations is similarly low for young Jews. Another 22.3 percent of all
adults described themselves as only "slightly" active in any Jewish organizations, and another 1 percent were listed as "doubtful." The "quite" active were 7.9 percent and the "very" active
were 6.4 percent. Combined, they total 14.3 percent of all American Jewish adults.

According to the NJPS, 34.7 percent of all adult Jews had
never dated a non-Jew, with 28 percent saying they had only

dated non-Jews "once in a while" and 21 percent saying "sometimes."[35] It is a certainty that the percentage of Jews who never dated a non-Jew sharply declines as the older generations pass. But, while some present-day organizational activists have dated non-Jews and—rarely—intermarried (usually to a woman who then converts to Judaism), nevertheless the vast bulk of activists are the ultimate in ethno-religious fanatics. That is to say they never seriously consider 97 percent of Americans of the opposite sex as potential bed partners. The most important study of the younger activists leadership is Brandeis professor Jonathan Woocher's "The 'Civil Judaism' of Communal Leaders," in the 1981 *AJYB*. He looked at 309 middle- and upper middle-class participants in leadership development programs of the United Jewish Appeal and the community federations. According to the professor:

> 85 percent see assimilation as the greatest threat to Jewish survival. . . . Responses to other questions . . . reveal that intermarriage and the alienation of youth from Jewish life are widely regarded as among the most critical questions confronting the American Jewish community.

Again, according to Woocher,

> nearly 65 percent deny that Jewish values are basically the same as those of all religions, and more than three-quarters acknowledge a "special" Jewish responsibility to work for justice in the world. . . . Nearly 60 percent . . . view the Jewish contribution to modern civilization as greater than that of any other people . . . 70 percent . . . claim that they feel more emotion listening to "Hatikvah" (Israel's anthem) than to the "Star-Spangled Banner" . . . a majority reject the proposition that an American Jew owes his/her primary loyalty to the United States. Further, while all but a handful . . . are glad to be Americans, only 54 percent are strongly so, compared with 86 percent who strongly assert that they are glad to be Jews . . . 63 percent . . . explicitly affirm that Jews are the chosen people (and only 18 percent actually disagree).[36]

Pressures Are Indeed Mounting

As can only be expected with a movement appealing to the richest grouping in America, fund-raising is the chief strength of the

Zionist movement. Israel could never have absorbed the massive immigration of its early years without the aid of American Jewry and others in the Diaspora, who donated 28 percent of capital imports between 1950–55.

Between 1945 and 1967, American citizens, not all of them Jews, sent no less than $1.5 billion to Israel.[37] As late as 1978, donations constituted 11 percent of Israel's capital imports and almost 4 percent of its GNP.[38] In 1985, the United Jewish Appeal/Jewish Community Federations received $598 million in pledges.[39] The biggest recipient of the UJA's slice of the pie is the United Israel Appeal. Technically, the money goes to Israel's civilian budget, but it is war that brings in the real *mesuma*. Gottlieb Hammer of the UIA once put it bluntly: "When the blood flows, the money flows."[40]

The bonds are the world's second most widely held securities, only U.S. paper is more widely distributed. From 1951 through 1985, the bond organization had taken $7.2 billion, world wide.[41] Over 3,000 U.S. banks bought them. Savings banks are forbidden from investing in foreign issues, yet a number of state legislatures have specifically permitted them to buy Israel Bonds. They are a charitable investment, not a reasonable business proposition and in New York and other states, legislation was required to declare them investment grade so that financial institutes operating under the "prudent man" rule, prohibiting purchase of low interest securities, could legally buy them.

Because they pay so little, the bonds are strictly a "good will" proposition for the immense majority of the thousands of banks who hold them. They usually buy them because they are afraid local Jewish merchants will take their cash elsewhere if they don't make a nominal purchase. Unions are really the most important non-Jewish purchasers. The Teamsters, who must divert attention from their proverbial grafting, purchased $26 million at 5½ percent. U.S. bonds paid 6.9 percent at that time. Thus the bonds cost $26 million plus the $7.2 million extra they would have received on American paper over 20 years.[42] The Teamsters, who now have between $35 and $40 million invested, and are among the world's largest holders, and AFL-CIO unions, hold over $250 million.

Union bureaucrats are organized into the National Committee for Labor Israel, and Trade Union and Public Service Councils for Histadrut, the Zionist company union. Top labor bureaucrats are frequently "honored" by local Israel Bonds organizations as a way of forcing the other local bureaucrats to attend these utterly boring dinners—where they get hit up for purchases.

The prime Bonds pushers within the AFL-CIO are of course Lane Kirkland and his henchman, Tom Kahn. There is even a statue of Golda Meir in the AFL-CIO headquarters in Washington. In some places the local bureaucracy opposes the CIA contingent on other foreign policy questions, particularly regarding Central America, but virtually the entire union leadership, excepting the top Teamsters, is deeply involved in the Democratic Party, and they see many of the Zionist fundraisers as their party cronies. Until the bombing of Libya, they never differed with Kirkland and "the company" over the Middle East.

In 1984–85 the Machinists struck El-Al airlines, the Israeli carrier, and the Histadrut sent scabs to America to break the strike. This proved embarrassing to the union's president, William Winpisinger, a member of the fanatically pro-Zionist Democratic Socialists of America, who had been a featured speaker at Bond rallies during the Lebanon war. The Machinists tabled a resolution before the AFL-CIO council, calling on unions to divest their bonds unless the strike was settled. However, everyone knew this was simply a bluff. The AFL-CIO tops are too committed to the CIA to pass such a resolution, and the local leaderships are too involved with the Democratic Party for any portion of the officialdom to break with the Zionists.

Wolf Blitzer, the well-informed *Jerusalem Post* correspondent in Washington, reported that:

> According to Israeli officials and their supporters in American labor, pressures are indeed mounting to distance the United States labor movement from Israel—and these pressures are coming from the rank and file.[43]

Opposition comes from Arab workers, a powerful force to be reckoned with in the United Auto Workers in Michigan, and from various radical groups. The more militant Black workers see Israel allied to South Africa. But, for the most part, the American working class is extremely backward politically, and most workers don't even attend union meetings, much less care about what their leaders say or do about the Middle East.

The "Millionaires"

Who are the Jews who fill the coffers of the UJA? The great experts on this are the Zionists themselves, as they must know who to appeal to for the bucks. For, although the sums taken in are still enormous, things do not bode well for the future. Steven Cohen, one of the Establishment's best sociologists, pessimistically analyzed the situation for the 1980 *AJYB:*

> Jews who are generationally removed from the immigrant heritage less frequently undertake expressions of religious or ethnic attachment such as Jewish charitable giving. . . . Younger Jews . . . are entering the salaried professions rather than becoming independent entrepreneurs. The resulting shifts . . . mean that younger Jews will less often enter the pool of potential multi-millionaires, that group which has most generously supported federation drives.[44]

Differing figures are mentioned by knowing Zionists, but "the 200" is the term within the movement for the biggest donors. An Israeli Zionist writer declared that between one-third and one-half of contributions come from 0.5 percent of contributors, those who give over $25,000.[45] Charles Silberman, an American, states that 1 percent of the donors, roughly 7,000 individuals giving $10,000 and up, provide 60 percent of the take.[46] Eight percent give 77 percent.[47] The 20 percent who give $1,000 and more give 80 percent. Those giving $100 or less contribute only 5 percent of the money.[48] In 1973, Pincus Sapir, then Israel's chief fundraiser, told of the money taken in after the 1973 war:

> Most of the money comes from a relatively small number of big buyers (of bonds) and contributors . . . termed the "millionaires" since they participate in the amount of a million or more. There were several dozen of these . . . a prominent woman . . . notified me . . . of a contribution of $5 million which she increased after a few days to $7½ million. There were some whose individual contributions amounted to $5 million and many more whose individual contribution exceeded the sum of $1 million.[49]

Who doesn't give is equally significant. Hirsh Goodman, one of the *Jerusalem Post's* leading writers, spent a year in the United States and described the realities of Zionism's isolation. One of the more disturbing problems was that the liberal communities in the universities have become alienated from the official Jewish organizations, which they associate with despised wealth. The few Jewish students who will agree to head the UJA campaign on campus often do so because prior to the campaign they were shuttled off to Israel on a 10-day fact-finding mission, which included accommodation at the best hotels. . . . What return does the UJA get on its investment? One example: the total collected by the UJA at Washington University in St. Louis in 1974/75 from over 5,000 Jewish students was $600. . . . The average American Jewish family will give less than one percent of its income to Jewish causes in general, and far less than that to Israel . . . the vast majority will give absolutely nothing. . . . There is no better job for a student . . . than being a professional Zionist. Some . . . make $5,000 or more a year for 10 months of work, while other Zionist activists . . . make as much as $20 an hour working as youth movement guides.

The charity statistics reveal much about the class nature of modern Zionism, but in the end it is not class that determines whether or not a Jew gives to the UJA. The amount he or she will give, if money is given, is economically related. However, the initial decision, whether to give at all, is now increasingly related to the degree of religious identification.

In the past, a Jewish businessman would frequently come to despise the religion, but he still saw Jewishness as the center of his personality. He spoke Yiddish, if not to his children then to his own parents. He lived in a Jewish neighborhood. His business friends were usually all or overwhelmingly Jewish.

Today all the youth speak English and many were born in mixed suburbs. Given the traditional weakness of the specifically ideological Zionist organizations, only a distinct minority come to Zionism through a previous familial connection.

The synagogue is the basis of today's Zionism. If there is no religious link, there is no other communal connection that can be the modern substitute. Cohen is very clear in this regard: By 1975, when the Boston Jews were surveyed, philanthropy had become

increasingly confined to those Jews who regularly act out their Jewishness. . . . Less observant Jews (measured by ritual performance and synagogue attendance) had largely dropped out of organized Jewish life. . . . The correlation ratios . . . [do] not

bode well for the future of Jewish philanthropy. The proportion of
Jewishly involved Jews is declining, while the growing segment of
relatively assimilated Jews is giving less frequently and gen-
erously.[51]

Two things are slowly but inexorably defeating Zionism among
American Jews: Israel and the United States. Zionism is
encountering increasing opposition from students on American
campuses, where Jewish youth are found, and few are interested
in challenging that opposition. However, exposure of the oppression of the Palestinians is not what is alienating the youth, at least
not yet, because the pro-Palestinian sentiment is by no means
presently overwhelming, and because the Palestinian movement
here is extremely ideologically mediocre and has little contact
with Jewish youth. It is the fact that Israel has nothing to offer
these youth except religion, and these are the best educated, most
urbanized youths in the country; therefore, axiomatically, they
are furthest removed from religion.

In many ways, America is repulsive to any sensitive person.
Exploitation, poverty, crime, mass ignorance and many other
gross faults exist here. But all these exist in Israel as well.
America's sins do not drive a single Jew to Zionism. The key
factor is that anti-Semitism is on its last legs in America. Given
that, and their education, young Jews are the least likely stratum
to be personally demoralized by the social decadence.

Young Jews are now the most successful stratum, profession-
ally, and it would be amazing if the most successful element in
the country would be preoccupied with the doings of another
country, thousands of miles away, which speaks another
language, and prays to a god few of America's Jewish youth
believe in. The vast majority are not anti-Zionist, they are a-
Zionist. To them, Zionists are creeps rather than sinister figures,
bores rather than war criminals. Zionism directly impinges on the
lives of young Jews in Israel, but here it has no state power, it
can do nothing to harm American Jews. You do not have to fight
creeps and bores, you only have to get out of the way when you
see them coming, and that is what the youth do.

Notes

   1. Samuel Portnoy (ed.), *Vladimir Medem—The Life and Soul of a Legendary Jewish Socialist*, pp. 295–8.

2. Yehuda Bauer, "The Holocaust and the Struggle of the Yishuv as Factors in the Establishment of the State of Israel," *Holocaust and Rebirth*, p. 120.

3. Ibid.

4. Samuel Halperin, *The Political World of American Zionism*, pp. 216-7, 380.

5. *"Pentagon Papers"—1947* (American Jewish Alternatives to Zionism, publisher), p. 20.

6. *Report #30*, (AJAZ), Nov. 1947, p. 15.

7. Walter White, *A Man Called White*, pp. 352-3, 357.

8. John Snetsinger, *Truman, the Jewish Vote and the Creation of Israel*, p. 72.

9. Harry Ellis, *Challenge in the Middle East*, p. 91.

10. Charles Allen, Jr., "War Criminals as 'Quiet Neighbors,'" *Jewish Currents*, April 1985, p. 7.

11. Menachem Begin, *The Revolt*, p. 164.

12. *Who Is Menachem Begin?*, p. 14.

13. Eric Silver, *Begin*, p. 90.

14. David Shipler, "Israel Bars Rabin From Relating '48 Eviction of Arabs," *NY Times*, Oct. 23, 1979, p. 3.

15. Uri Davis and Walter Lehn, "And the Fund Still Lives," *Journal of Palestine Studies*, Summer 1978, p. 9.

16. Uzzi Ornan, "The Regime of Privileges," (Letter to the editor), *Ha aretz*, March 26, 1975.

17. *Jerusalem Post Magazine*, May 28, 1976.

18. David Krivine, "Flawed Insight on Torture," *Jerusalem Post Magazine*, Aug. 5, 1977, p. 4.

19. Avishai Margalit, "The Fateful Triangle: The US, Israel and the Palestinian by Noam Chomsky," *New York Review of Books*, June 28, 1984, p. 14.

20. Moshe Brilliant, *"Portrait of Israel,"* p. 300, *Encyclopedia Judaica Yearbook 1973*, column 180.

21. Joe Stork, "Israel as a Strategic Asset," *MERIP Reports*, May 1982, p. 4.

22. Ibid.

23. "Israel, State of (Historical Survey)," *Encyclopedia Judaica*, Vol. 9, p. 470.

24. Harold Isaacs, *American Jews in Israel*, p. 82.

25. Melvin Urofsky, (Reply to letters), *Midstream*, June 1977, p. 96.

26. Calvin Goldscheider, "American Aliya: Sociological and Demographic Perspectives," in Marshall Sklare, ed., *The Jew in American Society*, pp. 335-384.

27. Gerald Berman, "Why North Americans Migrate To Israel," *Jewish Journal of Sociology*, Dec. 1979, pp. 142-3.

28. Ehud Ben Ezer, "The Insane Immigrate—the Sane Emigrate," *Ha aretz*, April 20, 1982.

29. "Zionist Elections," *Jerusalem Post*, Nov. 7, 1974, p. 8.

30. *Hadassah Magazine*, Oct. 1975.

31. Nahum Goldmann, *The Autobiography of Nahum Goldmann*, pp. 195-8.

32. Manheim Shapiro, "Jewish Youth and Their Parents," *Pioneer Woman*, Jan. 1965.

33. Don Gilbert, "De-Activism on Campus," *Ha'Etgar*, Winter, 1984-85, p. 10.

34. Fred Massarik and Alvin Chenkin, "United States National Jewish

Population Study: A First Report," *American Jewish Year Book 1973*, pp. 282, 301.

35.   Ibid., p. 302.

36.   Jonathan Woocher, "The 'Civil Judaism' of Communal Leaders," *AJYB 1981*, pp. 157–61.

37.   Joe Stork, "Israel as a Strategic Asset," *MERIP Reports*, May 1982, p. 4.

38.   Haim Ben-Shahar, *Israel and the Diaspora: A New Strategy*, p. 9.

39.   Interview with Ronnie Horn, Public Relations Department, UJA, Sept. 20, 1985.

40.   Lawrence Mosher, *Zionist Role in the US Raises New Concern*, p. 2.

41.   "Israel Bonds Aims to Raise $1 Million in N. California," *Northern California Jewish Bulletin*, Sept. 6, 1975, p. 2.

42.   Norman Dacey, "For Owners of Israel Bonds . . . Danger Ahead!," *American Jewish Alternatives to Zionism Report*, #29, July 1977, p. 62.

43.   Wolf Blitzer, "Love of Labor: Israel's Constant Friend," *Hadassah Magazine*, Feb. 1983.

44.   Steven Cohen, "Trends in Jewish Philanthropy," *AJYB 1980*, pp. 32–3.

45.   Israel Alman, "U.S. Jewry's Financial Set-up: A Centralized Philanthropy," *Al Hamishmar*, Nov. 24, 1977.

46.   Charles Silberman, *A Certain People*, p. 194.

47.   *Ha aretz*, Jan. 26, 1975.

48.   Alman.

49.   Pincus Sapir, "Paying for the war," *Israel Industry and Commerce and Export News*, Dec. 1973.

50.   Hirsh Goodman, "Wasted Dollars," *Jerusalem Post Magazine*, Oct. 1, 1976, pp. 7–8.

51.   Cohen, p. 43.

5

The Chosen People Choose the Politicians

Inasmuch as the Jews are only 2.54 percent of the population, it would seem that the Jewish vote should be of no interest to anyone except possibly a few sociologists. Everybody knows better. Jews are the most urbanized people in the country and they form a far more substantial minority in the crucial metropolitan areas. They are 19 percent of both Manhattan and Brooklyn, and the 1,133,100 Jews in New York City are 16 percent of the total population.

It will be immediately understood that their political weight is even greater if one realizes that Jews are 31 percent of all white, non-Hispanics in the city.[1] There are an additional 537,600 Jews in suburban Westchester, Nassau and suffolk, 15 percent of the population, with the Jewish percentage for Nassau being 23 percent, the highest for any county in the nation.

Jews are 10.6 percent of New York State's population. They are 5.9 percent of New Jersey with 100,000 in Bergen County

119

and another 95,000 in Essex county. Jews are 4.8 percent of the District of Columbia. They are 4.7 percent of Florida, with 225,000 in Miami alone. They are 4.6 percent of Maryland with 100,000 in Montgomery and Prince Georges Counties and 92,000 in Baltimore, 4.3 percent of Massachusetts with 170,000 Jews in Boston. They may be only 3.2 percent of Californians, but there are 500,870 Jews in the Los Angeles area and 75,000 Jews are roughly 10 percent of San Francisco. There are 295,000 Jews in metropolitan Philadelphia and 253,000 in greater Chicago.[2]

As the Jews are the most educated stratum of the electorate, they vote in greater proportions than any other ethnic or religious grouping. Ninety-two percent of all Jews vote in national elections compared to only 54 percent for the people as a whole. Jews may only be 10.6 percent of New York State, but they are between 16 percent and 20 percent of the voters. More important, they were 30 percent of the voters in the April 1984 New York State Democratic primary, when they made up an estimated 41 percent of Mondale's vote.[3] They are customarily nearly 50 percent of the Democratic primary voters in mayoral contests.

Jews are also disproportionately represented among political activists. Although they were only 2 percent of the delegates at the 1984 Republican convention, Jews made up 9 percent of the Democratic confab.[4] America's Jews are only 2.54 percent of the people but there were eight Jews—four Democrats and four Republicans—in a Senate of 100 in 1985. Contrary to what might be expected, none were from New York State. There were 30 Representatives, 24 Democrats and 6 Republicans, out of 435 seats, roughly 7 percent of the House.[5]

The strategic location of the country's Jewish population and the high degree of organizational activism do not exhaust the Jewish role in the political system. Huey Long's quip, about Louisiana's legislature, has stayed in the language as a national proverb, one that every intelligent American knows—and knows is true: "America has the best Congress that money can buy." Therefore, the Jews being the richest grouping in the country, it is only to be expected that, as Will Maslow, general counsel of the American Jewish Congress, has written:

> The percentage of Jews . . . who involve themselves in party affairs as policy-makers and fund-raisers, is probably higher than that of any other racial, religious or ethnic group. The result is that Jews play a role in the political life of the country whose

significance far transcends their proportion of the total population.[6]

"As a Dog Returneth to His Vomit, So a Fool Returneth to His Folly"

A whole literary genre has developed, debating whether there is an incongruity between the Jews' domestic liberalism and their pro-Zionism, given Israel's unconcealed connections with right-wing militarism in America and the world. The discussion frequently takes the form of questioning whether the Jews will continue to soldier on as the mainstay of Democratic Party liberalism. However, for the most part, this literature is deformed by an inadequate interpretation of American politics, and illusions about the Democratic Party and liberalism. This inexorably leads to a sterile description of the Jewish relationship to the larger political scene. Therefore, if the present critique is to bear better fruit, it is obligatory to accurately portray—without mincing words, without evasions, without hypocrisy—the wretched thing called the American "two-party system."

Political parties, even the Nazis, proclaim themselves to be idealists. Nevertheless, such groups almost invariably end up committing enormities that far exceed the crimes of all the common criminals in their country's prisons, and this is absolutely true for America. With the Republicans, things are cut and dried. For them it isn't enough to like capitalism or even to love it fondly. You must marry it, and preferably in an eternal Catholic marriage. And they never stop talking about that great capitalist—and great American—in the sky, their intimate friend God. In practice they are not quite so angelic—they gave us Nixon—and now they have further blessed us with his pal Reagan, with his own double talk about "constructive engagement" with Pretoria and the vast distinctions between capitalist gorilla dictatorships and totalitarian communism. Given the GOP's sentiments, it should surprise no one that 90 percent of Wall Street's stockbrokers backed Nixon in 1972, or that these sterling patriots once again are equally rapturous about Ronnie.

With the Democrats, things are different. From 1933 through the 1984 election they strenuously projected themselves as the party of the common man. Nevertheless they are a pro-capitalist party. Domestically the two parties' differences boil down to this:

The Republicans give nothing to the poor, and now they are trying to take away what little they have. The Democrats are more
suave. They use the velvet glove and the mailed fist. They know
the middle ages are over. If you squeeze the poor too hard they
will go over to the left.

In foreign affairs the differences are less distinct. It was Kennedy who invaded Cuba—and then sought to have the Mafia
assassinate Castro. It was the Democratic Party that invaded the
Dominican Republic. The party's leaders were fully responsible
for the murder of 55,000 Americans in Vietnam, to say nothing
of one million Indochinese. Even McGovern, the self-styled anti-
war candidate, voted for the war budgets, so he couldn't be
accused of being unpatriotic.

Carter supported Lieutenant Calley, the My Lai mass murderer, and later brought the Shah here with full knowledge that he
had run a torture regime. Mondale not only backed the Vietnam
War, and the Shah, he shouted for arms to Begin even after Sabra
and Shatilla, and supported sending the Marines to Beirut. He
backed the Grenada invasion. In 1984 he declared he would not
"pull the plug" and withdraw all U.S. troops from Honduras. He
favored placing American missiles in Europe.

Who is a liberal? Someone who opposed Johnson and Hum-
phrey and Carter and Mondale and their murders in Vietnam—
and voted for them, felon after felon. The September 12, 1984,
Times presents Mondale deciding to move right during his campaign in vain hope of picking up conservative votes. And why
not? Woolsellers know woolbuyers. Mondale knew liberals. He
could have had horns on his head and danced them down to hell
as long as he stayed one step behind and to the left of Reagan.

As the present discussion is of liberal Jews, here is Victor
Nevasky, editor of *The Nation*, endorsing Mondale:

> Mondale enthusiasts should remember that the present political
> direction was prefigured by the sharp turn toward cold-war-
> making and social retrenchment taken by the Carter-Mondale
> Administration midway in its term . . . though his criticism of
> Reagan's failure to negotiate on arms . . . was a welcome quarter-
> turn. . . . But a ringing Reagan triumph would surely make
> matters worse. . . . For that reason and because of Mondale's
> more enlightened domestic policies, we urge *Nation* readers . . . to
> vote against Reaganism.[7]

Nevasky's logic—if it is logic—is the best liberalism comes up with. Alas, the liberal pundit rues, Mondale in his prime has killed many innocents, yet he is not without his virtues. For he was and is for saving the redwoods, every blessed one. Voting "against Reaganism" was mandatory, if not heroic. Except that there was no life-saving "against Reaganism" lever in American poll booths. You had to pull down the "for Mondaleism" handle.

The liberals are played out cynics. They knew their tiger too well to be "enthusiasts." Besides enthusiasm, for any cause, does not appeal to these licensed realists. They know we are damn lucky to have honest-to-goodness lesser evils to play the golem against the Reaganism they dread but lack the grim-visaged resolve to bring to earth.

Today the demoralized Democratic leaders are openly discussing abandoning their populist mask in an effort to out-Reagan Reagan. Many commentators question whether such a spavined party can continue on. Perhaps such talk is premature, but certainly the liberals will never leave it as long as it staggers on. Reformers, ideologically brain-dead, they could never create a viable new party. Reagan's 1984 triumph was an American tragedy but the Democrats' rout was low farce. History can now pass final judgement on liberalism. As the discussion is of Jews, an Old Testament proverb—26:11—is appropriate. Truly, the far-seeing prophet had them fully in mind when he set quill to scroll, for indeed "As a dog returneth to his vomit, so a fool returneth to his folly."

What Great Event Happened in 1776?

According to rabbi Arthur Hertzberg, former President of the American Jewish Congress, only "perhaps 10 percent" of the Jewish vote "is really determined by the issue of Israel—but that is the maximum."[8] However, a 1983 American Jewish poll showed 20 percent of America's Jews have written at least one letter to an elected official on Israel's behalf. Since then polls show a considerable minority of Jews here support Israel's rightist hardliners. Certainly such fanatics take seriously the Middle East stands of candidates. On September 22–3, 1982, days after the Beirut massacre, Gallup compared 258 Jews with a cross-section of the broader public:

Compared with a year ago, would you say you are more sympathetic or less sympathetic to the Israeli position?

	National Sample	American Jews
More	24%	33%
Less	51%	36%
Same	10%	28%

Israel cannot be held responsible for the massacre . . .

National Sample	American Jews
8%	28%

Israel must bear partial responsibility . . .

National Sample	American Jews
49%	54%

Israel is very much responsible . . .

National Sample	American Jews
32%	11%

Do you think anti-Semitism in the U.S. is likely to increase because of recent developments in the Mideast?

	National Sample	American Jews
Yes	51%	77%

Do you think U.S. aid to Israel should be suspended or reduced in order to force a pullout of Israel forces from Lebanon?

	National Sample	American Jews
. . . suspended	50%	18%
. . . not be suspended	38%	75%

Which of these proposals for the West Bank would you prefer to see implemented

	National Sample	American Jews
Israeli sovereignty with military and civil control by Israel	9%	19%

Military control by Israel but civil control by the Palestinians	12%	39%
Jordanian sovereignty and . . . a demilitarized zone	31%	16%
An independent Palestinian state	23%	7%

The pollsters asked the Jews what they thought is "the most appropriate role for American Jews":

Take an active role in trying to affect Israel's policies	36%
Support Israel's government regardless of the Israeli government's actions	24%
Try to remain neutral	30%[9]

The poll permits us to put Jewish opinion re Israel in an American perspective, but only if we take it *cum grano salis*. Its weakness re Jews is that a telephone sample would undercount younger liberals. Call the Ginzberg residence and you get Grandpa, not the dope smoker with the unlisted phone. Nor are all the rightwingers poll-wise organized Zionists. Like most folks, most Jews are hot air politically.

Does anyone believe most of those who thought they should influence Israel communicated their feelings to that government? Note also that 77 percent thought anti-Semitism would rise, yet it continued to diminish as a real factor. In fact, many of Zionism's adherents are so fixed in their illusions that not even a visit to their holy land can cure them. According to a Zionist scholar,

16 percent report a sabbath ban on the use of the main roads by private cars and 18 percent claim that terrorists kill at least one citizen each day . . . 46 percent of the visitors overestimate the number of terrorist-caused casualties.[10]

It is fortunate that, as the proverb has it, "God looks out for fools, drunkards and Americans." In the days of mass illiteracy, few educated people could have naive democratic illusions. However, pollsters still find tens of millions of Americans to be factual ignoramuses. Gallup reports 20 percent are functional illiterates and another 50 percent just get by.[11] In 1975, 30 percent didn't know what great event happened in 1776.[12] In 1981, the *Washington Post*/ABC poll asked "which country, the United States or the Soviet Union, was a member of NATO?" only 47 percent gave the right answer.[13] In 1983 a *Times*/CBS poll found only 25 percent knew Reagan supported the government in El Salvador, only 13 percent knew he favored the Contras in Nicaragua, and only 8 percent knew both at the same time.[14]

In 1984, after the mining of Nicaraguan harbors had been discussed for days on TV, "only 19 percent . . . could answer that the U.S. supported the opponents of the Nicaraguan government."[15] In 1986 only 38 percent could identify Reagan's side.[16] Polls show great misapprehensions re the Middle East. A 1985 *Times* poll showed the public thought the Camp David negotiations of 1978 was "the most successful foreign policy venture of recent years."[17]

Almost all Americans still support the capitalist system and they see the outside world through ideologically naive eyes, even if after Vietnam they no longer will ever again uncritically accept direct U.S. military intervention abroad. Therefore, they think Camp David was a step towards peace, not even beginning to ask why tens of millions of modern Arabs, ordinary people like themselves, not fanatics, thought Sadat was a traitor and were jubilant when he was assassinated.

Many of the thinking portion of the population were repelled by Israel's crimes in Lebanon in 1982, but their disgust could not take a political form. The pro-Palestinian movement was too weak to reach them, and the liberals who normally articulate the anti-war sentiments of the public, however hesitantly they may do this, are locked into a dead-end pro-Israel position. Reagan's subsequent debacle in Lebanon reconfirmed the public's opposition to military adventurism, but the liberals could not utilize the fiasco against him because they could not even begin to critically analyze Reagan's Middle Eastern politics without exposing their own criminal collusion with the Zionists.

Only a few sectors of the American electorate are movers on the Middle East. The committed Zionists are the most important element. The "AFL-CIA" leaders and Jerry Falwell of the Moral Majority are strongly for Israel but their followers don't concern themselves about the region to any serious degree. Arab-Americans are demographically insignificant everywhere except in Detroit, and they are divided, with many of Lebanese descent supporting the Phalangists. The oil companies are naturally unsympathetic to Zionism, which complicates their relations with the Saudis and other reactionary Arab regimes. But they are scarcely friends of the Palestinian revolution.

There is an ever-growing minority of Blacks who sympathize with the Palestinians as a colonized people, and who see the Jewish Establishment as their own enemies because of its opposition to affirmative action. But popular Black intervention in politics beyond the electoral sphere declined after the civil rights movement. Jesse Jackson's campaign showed that the masses were willing to move if someone provided leadership. But Jackson has no clear American perspective, nor do any of the more militant Black Democrats. They ended up supporting Mondale in 1984 regardless of their profound differences with him on the Middle East and Grenada.

It was left to Louis Farrakhan to articulate the mass hostility to Israel over its alliance with Pretoria, but of course his program is a utopian amalgam of theology and a quite American shopkeeper mentality. Black militancy is certain to grow on the apartheid question, and in the end that struggle will have explosive ramifications here, but for the present, community action is still only developing.

The left is small and divided and doesn't put much energy into the Palestine question, especially as there is presently no significant motion in Palestine by the Palestinians. Therefore, while the Jewish Establishment is locked in battle with the Black militants, and is beginning to lose the fight on the campus, nevertheless it can still afford to put its main effort into influencing the politicians, and in this it is still immensely successful.

"If the Messiah Comes, on That Very Day We'll Consider Our Options"

The *Times*/CBS poll reported that the Jews voted 66 percent–32 percent for Mondale, the *Washington Post*/ABC poll had it 70 percent–30 percent. Mondale and Hart made demagogic statements in New York that they would move the U.S. embassy from Tel Aviv to Jerusalem, but no one believed they would do it if elected and the Establishment rushed into print to disassociate itself from the witless proposal.

Hyman Bookbinder of the AJCommittee declared from the *Times's* Op-ed page that "It gives the impression that these two candidates are pandering to the state's Jewish voters."[18] Most Jews voted for Carter or Anderson in 1980 and would have voted "against Reagan" again under any circumstances, but in fact Reagan's vote declined, from 39 percent. Observers are unanimous in crediting his intimacy with Falwell and the campaign to "Christianize America" for the drop, rather than attributing it to Mondale's demagoguery on the embassy non-issue.

Traditional Christian anti-Semitism has so discredited Christianity among Jews that the vast majority are now instinctively hostile to any political current that bases its opinions about Jews on the New Testament, regardless of whether or not it is "pro" Jewish. But the leaders of the AJCommittee and the Anti-Defamation League take a cynical line toward the Moral Majority.

William Rubenstein, a right-wing pro-Zionist sociologist, has reported that " a very well-placed source" told him that "75 percent" of "the leaders of America's Zionist organizations . . . supported Reagan over Carter."[19] They know the Democratic tops are for Israel, but they don't have any confidence in the party ranks, which are generally opposed to U.S. military intervention abroad. What would happen, in the event of another Yom Kippur War, if Israel needed emergency military equipment? Would the ranks let their leaders send it? So the right-wing of the Jewish Establishment has thrown in with the likes of Falwell, who is for total military support for Israel because be believes the "ingathering" of the Jews in the Holy Land is the essential precondition for both their conversion and the return of Jesus.

Nathan Perlmutter, National Director of the ADL, and his wife Ruth Ann know this world. Truth to tell, it is divided between idiots and useful idiots, and in their book, *The Real Anti-Semitism in America,* they had no doubt about either Falwell's utter stupidity or his utility:

> It is neither our intention to be flippant nor disrespectful when we say, when the day comes, we'll see. . . . No matter. . . . Falwell's friendship for Israel is rooted in the New Testament, we've an open mind. If the Messiah comes, on that very day we'll consider our options. Meanwhile, let's praise the Lord and pass the ammunition.[20]

"The Only Group So Identified by a Majority of Respondents"

But how liberal are the Jews? In fact, Jewish voters were sharply divided by age, education, religion and lifestyle. An analysis of seven of the more plebeian Jewish state assembly districts in the outer boroughs of New York City showed that while Carter had taken them by 17,826 votes, Mondale lost one of them and won the others by only 8,122 votes. Reagan gained almost 2,000 votes in the Chassidic section of Borough Park in Brooklyn, winning by two to one.[21]

Mondale's increased Jewish strength in New York largely came from Manhattan's Jews, yuppies and "limousine liberals," professionals and businessmen who ignored the urgings of Irving Kristol and the neo-conservatives around *Commentary,* which had tried to convince them that Jews had to pander to the Christian neanderthals on church-state issues to keep their support for ever-increasing arms and money to Israel.

In 1984, sociologist Steven Cohen conducted his annual National Survey of American Jews for the AJCommittee. His 959 respondents were 7 percent Orthodox, 32 percent Conservative, 23 percent Reform, 2 percent Reconstructionist. However, the 1973 National Jewish Population Study had already listed 69.4 percent of household heads under 30 as having "No membership" in any congregation and 53.1 percent of all household heads as non-members.[22] We may reasonably assume most of these remained unaffiliated, while many of the older, more religious, generation has died off.

While all observers agree that the intermarriage rate is no less than 40 percent, by comparison 56 percent of Cohen's Jews said their three closest friends are Jews and 22 percent said two were. Cohen's Jews are clearly more representative of the insular older generations and the rump "organized" community than the broad Jewish population, and the poll therefore is tilted to the right. Indeed Cohen himself concludes that those with the most Jewish friends tend towards conservative stands. However, he also found a conservative stratum with no Jews in their social circle. He did not further describe these, but it is reasonable to believe they are businessmen and professionals of German heritage.

In 1981 Cohen's poll listed 2 percent as "radical or socialist," 32 percent liberal, 49 percent middle-of-the-road, 16 percent conservative and 1 percent "very conservative." In 1984, they were 1 percent socialist, 35 percent liberal, 38 percent middle-of-the-road, 24 percent conservative, and 1 percent very conservative. In 1984, Cohen's Jews were 57 percent registered Democrats, 31 percent independents and 12 percent Republicans. Their opinions revealed that their liberalism was both selective and relative:

	Agree	Disagree
Persecution has made Jews sensitive to minority groups needs	80%	11%
Affirmative action	70%	20%
Job Quotas for minorities	22%	64%
Support goals of welfare programs	75%	17%
Welfare programs have hurt recipients	64%	23%
Should be reduced because of fraud and waste	43%	45%
Death penalty	68%	20%
Permit to buy gun	90%	7%
Pro-homosexual rights	87%	9%
Troubled by homosexual rise	49%	43%
Government aid for abortions	81%	13%
Adultery is wrong	73%	16%
Tax credits for private schools	29%	63%
Religion's decline has hurt morals	44%	42%
Silent meditation in schools	21%	70%
Build more nuclear power plants	31%	48%
More plants to lessen dependence on Arab oil	38%	42%
Be more forceful with USSR	29%	55%
Reagan accurate on "evil empire"	50%	35%
Reagan showed poor judgement	66%	27%
Use of military if USSR invades Western Europe	56%	19%
If Arabs cut off oil to U.S.	38%	37%
Maintain strong military to back Israel	61%	24%
Cut military spending	59%	27%
Nuclear freeze	84%	10%[23]

Clearly even these Jews are far more liberal than any other white ethnic group, but the conservative element, which is far larger than the 25 percent who call themselves that, is visibly rising within the more traditional Jewish grouping. If anyone could be expected to support total church-state separation it is Jews. Therefore, it is startling to see 29 percent of Cohen's sample favoring tax credits for private schools, which is just a hustle to get the state to indirectly foot the bill for religious schools. And the 44 percent who think morals decline along with religion are certainly naive. Do they mean that their pot-smoking children are less moral than they are? Or do they mean that today's Americans, who overwhelmingly accept intermarriage with Jews, are less moral than their bigoted predecessors? They are perhaps at their most rightwing in their belief in capital punishment. Israel has few redeeming features but one of them is that it has only executed one person, Adolf Eichmann. Does anyone doubt that it would be a dramatic step to the right for Israel to start executing terrorists, let alone wife murderers, as the majority of American Jews seem to favor?

American Jewry has one of the weakest militaristic traditions in America. Many Jewish immigrants came here to get away from conscription. Hatred of Tsarism, and then a growing socialist movement, made the Yiddish community a stronghold of anti-war sentiment during WWI. While Jews certainly favored the war against Hitler, the army was not popular with them, as barracks life meant a too-close contact with the then still quite strong anti-Semitism.

The Korean War came as the next generation was fully intellectualizing itself and a military career was too plebeian for them. Certainly the majority of Jews, including Cohen's largely ideologically backward elements, opposed the Vietnam War before the majority of their compatriots. Yet now, even after Vietnam, a majority of these traditionalists show they have not developed any ability to generalize about the American political system from what most of them thought was a criminal war, and are in favor of a strong military.

A number of factors have contributed to the development of their relative later-day militarism. Most Jews disapproved of the Vietnam War but only a minority had demonstrated against it. Moreover, most who did were liberals and, as liberalism is notoriously superficial, they promptly abandoned the anti-war movement after that immediate war.

While most Jews, as educated people, are among those who know which side Reagan favors in Central America, far fewer Jews have demonstrated on that issue than did on Vietnam. As they have completed their total transition into the intelligentsia, a considerable vulgar embourgeoisification has set in, and it is unrealistic to expect them to be more anti-war than others in their economic status, simply on the basis of any vestigial traditions.

Anti-war sentiment is increasing among students in the wake of
the ever-widening anti-apartheid movement, which has exposed
Reagan and his "constructive engagement" hustle, but how many
of the older generations will revert to a more critical stance is
problematic. Cohen also asked what groups—Blacks, Big Business, Fundamentalists, etc.—were anti-Semitic, and 17 percent
said most Blacks were anti-Jewish and another 37 percent said
many were. Cohen pointed out that Blacks were "the only group
so identified by a majority of respondents."[24]

In his *Breaking Ranks,* Norman Podhoretz, the editor of *Commentary,* had figured out that it was easier to swing Jews to the
right by focusing on Israeli security rather than on domestic
American questions. [25] Cohen asked several questions to try to
test the hypothesis. Certainly the 38 percent who favor using the
U.S. military if the Arabs cut off oil to the U.S. are so motivated.
(It must be remembered that an oil embargo would be completely
legal). Nor can there be any other explanation for the difference
between the two percentages on the questions re nuclear plants.

Cohen found that the more religious opened "a gap of about 10
points" between them and the more secularized when he
rephrased the question.[26] When he asked if the U.S. should cut
military spending, about three-fifths said yes, and when he asked
if the U. S. should retain a strong military to be a reliable sup-
plier of Israel, about three-fifths replied yes. Cohen concludes
that about 28 percent are "pure" doves who don't want a strong
military and do want cuts, while 27 percent are hawks. Roughly
40 percent fall in between, wanting a strong military but favoring
cuts.

The two questions regarding nuclear plants should warn us
about the value of such polls. The queries are really identical yet
received conflicting answers from 6 percent of respondents
because they are in no way active on the issue and therefore can
hold contradictory opinions on the subject. Similarly with the
explicitly military questions. Such polls would have more value if
they asked how many people "put their money where their mouth
is," if they asked how many demonstrated for any cause, wrote a
letter to their senator or gave money to a political party.

Cohen remarks that readers with differing orientations can
"draw comfort" from his findings. Conservatives should be
pleased with the majority views on capital punishment and a
strong defense, and the substantial minorities with rightwing posi-

tions on other issues. But he thinks liberals will take comfort in
that the majority are still generally liberal on most issues. In fact,
even if the broader Jewish population is yet more liberal than his
sample, as is hypothesized herein, Cohen is still profoundly in
error. For whatever the percentage of Jewish liberals, those who
are actively so on any issue are a minority. And these "liberals"
duly voted for Mondale who, even the Jewish Establishment con-
cedes, played the irresponsible demagogue towards Jews. (What
conceivable comfort can any humanist take in self-proclaimed
liberals voting in someone to the right of Reagan on the Middle
East?)

"Legalized Political Prostitutes"

The so-called "Jewish lobby" has a domestic agenda. All but the
Orthodox are against government aid to church schools, and most
of the Jewish Establishment is against affirmative racial quotas.
However, Israel, not domestic questions, hold them together.

America's rulers only give aid to forward their imperial
designs, hence Israel is sold as the only militarily meaningful
anti-Soviet bastion in the Middle East. Nevertheless, the Arab
reactionaries have a case—they have the oil—so the lobby also
sells itself as a domestic prop for the warmongers. In 1965 the
ADL gave an award to Lyndon Johnson, and Israeli politicians
tried to get American Jews to mute their opposition to the Vietnam War, claiming Washington might cut off aid if they persisted.
Eventually, in 1970, rabbi Arthur Lelyveld, President of the
AJCongress, publically complained:

> Does Israel have the right to ask us to be silent on Vietnam
> because it thinks that in its relationship to the current government
> of the U.S. it would be tactically helpful for us to do so?[27]

In 1972, Golda Meir quite correctly decided that Israel is best
served by a criminal in the White House, and her ambassador,
Yitzhak Rabin, openly campaigned for Nixon. Israel, he said,
"must see to it that we express gratitude to those who have done
something for Israel and not just spoken on behalf of Israel."[28]
The Democrats complained about Rabin's intervention, but not
too loudly, as they feared losing Jewish votes if they criticized
Israel.

After Watergate Israel realized such endorsements could only hurt Zionism. American Jews could not be told who to vote for. But Israel did not abandon intervention in our affairs. On November 24, 1974, the government's *Jerusalem Post* reprinted a Joseph Alsop article:

> It is an obvious fact that the Jewish-Americans are this country's single most successful racial group. It is equally obvious that their political influence, more particularly in the Democratic Party, is at least proportional to this group's well-deserved success. Everyone knows these things, even if there is a convention that one must not say them. . . . The Israelis have a way of answering the laments of the U.S. military about their hard-pressed defense budget by the somewhat arrogant promise: "Don't worry about the Congress. We'll take care of the Congress." But the Israeli promise has always been kept! . . . If it had not been for Israeli and Jewish-American pressures, that national defense . . . would have been cut to ribbons by the new anti-defense posture of American liberal-intellectuals. . . . The Israeli Ambassador, able Simcha Dinitz, is now the strongest and most effective lobbyist on Capitol Hill for a serious American national defense.

Israel lobbies Congress, particularly its Jews, for State Department policies in its interest. For some years Congress, under Greek-American pressure, embargoed arms to Turkey. Like Israel, Turkey had driven many thousands of refugees from northern Cyprus. A Turkish retreat would inspire Palestinians, therefore Israel lobbied on Istanbul's behalf. As South Africa's ally, Israel lobbied Congress to allow CIA intervention in Angola, and on behalf of aid to its own client state, Zaire.

However, while its lobbying power on its own behalf is legendary, it has little ability to get its way on these other issues, even with the Jewish Congressional contingent. They know Greek constituents would be furious if they appeared pro-Turkish. Besides, most Jews in Congress are liberals who rationalize support for Israel's hardline policies as "politics." They think they must do this to get Jewish votes and funds so as to play the liberal on other questions.

The lobby understands realities. Although the Jewish Establishment is now overwhelmingly right-wing Republican, since they understand every victory of the left inspires the Palestinians, they know their unpolitical supporters will never draw the full implica-

tions of Zionist politics. Ordinary Jews neither know nor care to
know about Cyprus. They aren't going to punish politicians who
vote against Israel's wishes there. The lobby knows most Jews are
dovehawks. They want the U.S. to defend Israel but are not generally warlike, and don't want the CIA in Angola or New Jersey.
The lobby is content to back any in Congress, of either party,
who will keep giving more and better boomsticks to the Israelis
than to the Arabs, and they do this the good ol' A-murican way:
legal bribes, campaign contributions and huge speakers' honorariums.

The voting strength of the Jews in New York City, particularly
in Brooklyn—the Belfast of American Jewry—as well as in Los
Angeles and elsewhere, must not be minimized, given the
demagogic nature of our politics. Nevertheless, money is the real
basis of Zionism's strength. In the wake of the Watergate
reforms, the December 4, 1974, *Jerusalem Post* reported Yitzhak
Rabin, then Prime Minister, as warning that

> it did no good to exaggerate the political power of American
> Jewry . . . Israelis had still not realized the effect of the new U.S.
> laws on political financing upon Jewish political influence there.[30]

That same month, Leonard Fein, now editor of the liberal
Zionist *Moment,* wrote that he

> had not seen any study which tries to trace the importance of cam-
> paign spending reform proposals to Jewish political power, but
> inherent in such proposals may be consequences a hundred times
> more significant than any of the more immediately obvious cir-
> cumstances of the Jews.[31]

Congress had enacted federal financing of presidential elections, but rich individuals are still the official fund-raisers for both
major parties, and still massive contributors. G. William
Domhoff's 1972 classic *Fat Cats and Democrats* described a reality that has not essentially changed:

> The gentile financial community is almost exclusively Republi-
> can . . . it is the Jewish financiers who by default provide the
> Democrats with their handful of essential money raisers among the
> super-wealthy of Wall Street. . . . We found no big Democratic
> donors among the leading partners of the largest gentile firms. . . .

> Jewish investment bankers combined with other Jews around the
> country . . . to provide the financial leadership of the Democratic
> Party in every major non-Southern city except Boston. . . . Esti-
> mates from informants supposedly knowledgeable about the party
> range from a low of forty percent to a high of sixty-five percent
> for the total Jewish contribution to non-Southern Democratic can-
> didates. . . . The most prominent fund-raisers in many large
> Northern cities are Jewish.[32]

There are no "official" statistics as to how many rich Jews are
Republican contributors. A significant proportion of the German-
Jewish rich have always been Republicans. Most of the Eastern
European rich grew up in the Democratic Party when it was seen
as the immigrants' champion, but many have drifted to the
Republicans, particularly since Golda encouraged a Nixon vote.

A reasonable estimate would be that about half of the Jewish
millionaires are now Republican. However, as the immense
majority of Christian rich are Republican, the party is in no way
dependent on rich Jews, although it would not be pleased if too
many Jewish contributors went Democrat over some Israeli issue.

The GOP draws up its Mid-East strategy on the basis of what it
thinks is best for American capital, sometimes leaning more
towards Israel as their regional bouncer, sometimes necessarily
accommodating their feeble Arab reactionary clients, who are
subject to mass pressure on the Palestine question.

The Democrats get their funds from some very heterogeneous
groupings. Domhoff calculated that:

> Labor unions provide as much as twenty to twenty-five percent of
> the war chest in some states, racketeers and gangsters—some of
> whom are amazingly intimate with respectable Democratic
> fundraisers—provide ten to fifteen percent in certain metropolitan
> areas (and perhaps more in Chicago and Nevada), and little people
> from the middle class pick up about fifteen percent of the tab.[33]

In his 1974 *Jews and American Politics,* the *Washington Post's*
Stephen Isaacs explained that many such crooks were Jews:

> On the level of local politics, the *quid pro quo* is likely to be more
> tangible than on the national scale. . . . Jews like non-Jews have
> been known to invest in candidates in return for government con-
> tracts, favorable rezonings on potentially valuable plots of real
> estate. For two reasons, Jews have tended to be active in such

instances of bribery. One has been that their types of livelihoods—real estate, for instance—have been like those of the Mafia, entrepreneurial and speculative. Mere mention of such activity tends to throw "establishment" Jewish agencies into a tizzy. . . . But . . . America has had such "achieving" Jews as . . . Meyer Lansky, "Bugsy" Siegal, Mickey Cohen. . . . The second is that bribery has been an essential part of Jewish history . . . Yiddish had a word for the bribe: *shmeer* (grease) . . . that has somewhat come into American English idiom.[34]

The shmeer artists are an outcroping of the notorious "shtetl mentality" of the Pale. The shtetl or small-town merchants could get nothing done in that anti-Semitic environment without bribing the authorities, and they developed a hypercynical and provincial narrowness. But for there to be a bribe giver there had to be a bribe taker. When the Eastern Europeans arrived here they found a country as corrupt as the one they had left.

The Swedish sociologist Gunnar Myrdal, a deep student of America, eloquently described

the country that leads the whole western world in violence, crime, and corruption in high places. Fragmentation and passivity on economic and political issues among the lower strata of the American nation are part of a much larger problem: the relatively low degree of institutional and psychological integration of its people. Associated with this is the high degree of American tolerance of corruption.[35]

The union bureaucrats almost all come from Democratic families, and usually start out believing the claptrap about the Democrats as the party of the common man. But eventually they settle into another set of American values: "politics" as wheeling and dealing rather than the expression of principles, which they identify with the left and unpopularity. They have to justify themselves to their members, and one way is by bankrolling the Democrats their members support in return for reforms, or at least the feeling that the Democrats are less likely to take back reforms already achieved. However, their positions as bureaucrats depend on apathy in the ranks, and this weakens them vis-à-vis the party. They have difficulty getting their members to go along with subsidizing primary candidates and therefore they are never party kingmakers. They need allies with money to back the

national candidates they want. The crooks are parish pump orien-
tated; many Jewish realtors don't give a damn about Israel. That
leaves those rich party Jews who are pro-Zionist as the only
significant capitalist stratum who are interested in national politics
and do not have an *a priori* hostility towards labor.

It is difficult to keep up with the constantly changing laws and
court decisions regulating national elections. Besides, many are
obviously designed and written so the wealthy can beat them.
Thus an individual is only supposed to be able to give up to
$5,000 to a Political Action Committee in any year, and only
$20,000 to a party. But so can the wife and so can all the tod-
dlers. After all, is nothing sacred? Brave men died at Valley
Forge so that kids could give $20,000 per year to the party of
Daddy's choice—and don't you forget that! Then there are what
are jokingly called independent campaign expenditures. A mil-
lionaire can spend all the money in the world on an election as
long as his activities are not directly coordinated by a candidate's
campaign committee. So, inasmuch as our politicians are to graft
what Paganini was to the violin, we must look through the
cobweb of laws to the realities.

Zionists funnel cash to the politicians through both PACs and
individual contributions. They dread attention, therefore 54 PACs,
most with anonymous names like San Franciscans for Good
Government, Arizona Politically Interested Citizens or the Joint
Action Committee for Political Affairs, divided the task of allo-
cating funds to various candidates in elections all over the country
in the 1980s.

The public is not aware of the con, but it is easily traced in
the Federal Election Commission's records. Rolled together, the
pro-Israel PACs gave out $1,873,623 in the 1982 election
period, more than the Realtors PAC—$1,536,573; United Auto
Workers Volunteer PAC—$1,422,731; American Medical PAC—
$1,348,985; Auto and Truck Dealers PAC—$1,035,276.[36]

The Zionists have learned who it is important to shmeer. By
August 1984 these PACs collected $4.25 million. They handed
out at least $851,873 to sitting senators who were not even up for
re-election. At least $576,000 went to incumbent members of the
Senate Foreign Relations Committee.[37] More than $2 million
went to 223 candidates, with the largest amount going to Paul
Simon who successfully opposed incumbent Charles Percy of Illinois, the committee chair who frequently criticized Israel. Other

funds went to members of the military and appropriation committees.

There were 158 Democratic and 65 Republican recipients. About 20 times as much went to incumbents as to challengers, but some PACs gave out cash to rival candidates and in a few cases four and even five candidates for the same seat were given money by a single PAC.[38]

In 1974, Congress enacted legislation for federal financing of Presidential elections. To be eligible, a primary candidate must raise $5,000 in donations of $250 or less in 20 states. This sounds good, but realities are far different, as shown in the December 18, 1983, *Times*. It talked about a $1,000-a-plate dinner in Manhattan for one of the would-be candidates of the party of the common man. The chairman of Mondale's state fund-raising effort was Robert Rubin, a partner at Goldmann, Sachs brokerage house. Vice-chair was Roger Altman of Lehman Brothers Kuhn Loeb investment bankers. One of the co-chairs of the dinner was Arthur Krim, chairman of Orion Pictures, whose largest shareholder is Warburg Pincus Capital. There was nothing subtle in Mondale's fund-raising. According to Altman:

> Mondale appeals very broadly in New York . . . because he has supported issues that are important here, domestic issues, urban policy and foreign policy issues, like Israel.[39]

The story is the same in Los Angeles, the other major Democratic fund-raising center. According to the July 16,1984, *New York Times*, the chair of the Democrats' convention planning committee, Mrs. Rosalind Wyman, is "married to a lawyer who became one of California's most influential Democratic fundraisers . . . especially . . . among Jewish Democrats in West Los Angeles. The couple, ardent Zionists, raised money for and fought hard for American support of Israel."[40]

According to the July 16, 1985, *New York Times*, "Nathan Landow, a wealthy Maryland real estate developer . . . was the single largest raiser of funds for Mr. Mondale's campaign."[41] The biggest of those "independent" campaign spenders was a Californian, Michael Goland, who spent nothing less than $419,573 on advertising against Percy—in Illinois![42]

As is said, there is more than one way to skin a cat—or bribe an American congressman. Common Cause has revealed that the

United Jewish Appeal put up more money in speaking honorariums to U.S. Senators in 1983 than any other organization in the country. Senator Christopher Dodd of Connecticut, the most popular speaker on the kosher chicken banquet circuit, is—beyond doubt—the greater orator since Demosthenes. Why else would the UJA, a charity no less, give him $32,000? And why else would other Jewish groups give him another $14,000?[43]

John Oakes, former senior editor of *The New York Times*, a journal not exactly given to wild statements, once said all there is to be said about both America's system of campaign contributions and speakers' honorariums, in a 1984 Op-ed:

> The PAC handouts on a newly gigantic scale are only the most spectacular form of legalized bribery of members of Congress. The "honorarium," which should be called the "dishonorarium," is another. . . . The power of money threatens increasingly to turn members of Congress into legalized political prostitutes.[44]

"A Wave of Revulsion"

Historically Jews were frequently victimized by demagogues, today they are courted for their money. However, foreign readers would be wrong to conclude that all the Zionists have to do is just walk right into an ol' Democrat's office and buy him. No. First they must make an appointment. Indeed for many years there were prominent Democrats who opposed Zionism because it complicated relations with the Saudis and other Arab despots. But today the only serious Democratic opposition comes from an occasional Congressman of Arab descent who is elected out in the boondocks, and from some—but only some—of the Black Congressional caucus. The party's dominant elements are Zionism's dead-end partisans. An article from the July 21, 1982, *New York Times*, six weeks into Begin's invasion of Lebanon, tells the story. To put it into context, it must be recalled that by then tens of thousands of Israelis had already demonstrated against the war:

> Both critics and long-time supporters of Israel talk freely of "a wave of revulsion" caused by pictures of civilian casualties in Lebanon and a shift in the almost automatic support Israel has enjoyed in Congress. . . . Some members . . . say the mood . . . is already sufficient for a sizable group to endorse a cutoff in ship-

ments of cluster bombs. . . . "It's the kind of thing that could
carry," said . . . Dodd. . . . "That would satisfy those who are
critical of Israel without significantly altering our basic relationship." . . . Dodd . . . contend(s) that the current displeasure with
Israel amounts more to "rhetorical criticism" than any substantive
shift of support. . . . Ambassador Arens said many of Israel's
traditional supporters remained unshaken by recent events, citing
conversations with . . . Kennedy . . . Hart . . . Metzenbaum . . .
and . . . Levin. . . . But few of them have spoken out on Israel's
behalf.[45]

A few plain truths are in order here. As the Jewish scriptures
would put it, the Democratic Party goes toward murder "as
sparks to heaven fly." These hacks oppose the PLO for only two
reasons: The Palestinians are the oppressed and they are conscious imperialists; the PLO terrorizes Jews and Jews are their
moneybags.

If the PLO were to bomb Vietnam, the liberals would vote for
them, as they did for Johnson. And the truth about the Jewish
liberals is that they would also vote for Arafat if he bombed
Hanoi, providing he ran on the Democratic ticket. The politest
thing that can be said about American liberalism, Jewish or otherwise, is that it is twisted like a pretzel.

Myrdal was correct: apathy and toleration of evils is characteristic of America, and this is particularly so of its intellectuals,
of whom not a few are Jews. Exceptions aside, professors always
lag behind students in terms of activism. Cynicism is never out
of fashion in literary circles. However, Myrdal's formulation was
incomplete. Only a minority of the educated are for corruption
just so they can get their snout into the trough. And of course
there is always the minority of muddle-headed specialists who can
never understand politics.

What ties most intellectuals to the corrupters is their unshak-
able addiction to the unprincipled doctrine of lesser evilism. This
leads many, if not most of them, to thralldom to the Democratic
Party. Whatever their public rhetoric, *minus malum* is the closet
ideology of the liberals, Jew or gentile, and this can be easily
verified by anyone who takes them aside and asks hard questions.

Unfortunately Myrdal's and Oakes's denunciations of American
politics are completely true and cannot be conjured away. They
command resolute action or, to be precise, revolution. For to irrevocably end the power of money over politics in the richest coun-

try in the world is to make a revolution, or that word has no meaning.

It was Karl Marx, naturally enough the great expert on such things, who once explained that only a portion of the intelligentsia will ever go over to the revolution. The rest of the learned are the hustlers, the a-politicals and, as in the case of the modern young educated Orthodox, all those who are psychologically unable to emancipate themselves from the fossilized cultural values of their families.

As a social stratum, modern American Jewry's progressive political role is played out. Henceforth only a minority, greater or lesser, will involve itself in the struggle for social and political change. In any advanced society, intellectuals will necessarily play a central part in any such process, and, given their weight within the intelligentsia, Jews, as individuals, will be prominent in any forthcoming left upsurge. But, barring a universal catastrophe analogous to the 1929 Depression, it is virtually impossible to foresee a majority of Jews, the richest grouping in the richest country in the world, coming over in a body to the fundamental opponents of the system, quite regardless of any ethical or political heritage they may still retain. And this would be so even if Israel did not exist.

As for that majority of the most educated ethnic group in the country, we can only go with the poet who once said that some things would be tragedies, if they weren't so hilarious. For it is not exactly a state secret that many Jews think Jews are smarter than other people. Yet they have ended up, for all their *Yiddisher kops,* as the playthings of demagogues and the financial prop of a party which their old high school history books had already told them was as crooked as a dog's hind leg.

Notes

1. Paul Ritterband and Steven Cohen, "The Social Characteristics of the New York Area Jewish Community, 1981," *AJYB 1984,* pp. 128–9.

2. Alvin Chenkin, "Jewish Population in the United States, 1982," *AJYB 1983,* pp. 130, 133–8.

3. Cheryl Rubenberg, "The Conduct of U.S. Foreign Policy in the Middle East in the 1983–84 Presidential Election Season," *American-Arab Affairs,* Summer 1984, p. 33.

4. "Delegates and Ordinary Partisans: Differences and Similarities," *NY Times,* Aug. 24, 1984, p. 10.

5. "Around the World," *Jewish Currents,* Jan. 1985, p. 45.

6. Will Maslow, *The Structure and Functioning of the American Jewish Community,* p. 39.

7. "Now, We Begin," *Nation,* Nov. 3, 1984, p. 435.

8. Arthur Hertzberg, "Jewish Voters' Interests," *NY Times,* Sept. 16, 1980.

9. *"Newsweek* Poll: Israel Loses Ground," *Newsweek,* Oct. 4, 1982, p. 23.

10. Albert Goldberg, "Visions of Zion: The Visitor and North American Aliyah," *Forum on the Jewish People, Zionism and Israel,* Fall 1984, p. 48.

11. George Gallup, Jr., "Commentary on the State of Religion in the United States Today," *Gallup Report,* March 1984, p. 2.

12. *San Francisco Chronicle,* D2, 17.

13. *Herald Tribune,* Oct. 22, 1981, p. 1.

14. Adam Clymer, "Poll Finds Americans Don't Know US Positions on Central America," *NY Times,* July 1, 1983, pp. 1–2.

15. *NY Times,* April 29, 1984.

16. David Shipler, "Public is Confused on Contra Aid Issue, Poll Indicates," *NY Times,* April 15, 1986, p. 4.

17. Adam Clymer, "Camp David at Top in U.S. Policy Poll," *NY Times,* April 1, 1984, p. 4.

18. Hyman Bookbinder, "The Wrong Appeal to Jewish Voters," *NY Times,* March 30, 1984.

19. William Rubinstein, *The Left, the Right and the Jews,* p. 175.

20. Nathan and Ruth Ann Perlmutter, *The Real Anti-Semites in America,* p. 172.

21. Wayne Barrett, "Sonic Boom Over City Hall," *Village Voice,* Nov. 20, 1984, p. 5.

22. Fred Massarik and Alvin Chenkin, "United States National Jewish Population Study: A First Report," *AJYB 1973,* p. 282.

23. Steven Cohen, "What We Think," *Moment,* Jan. 1985, pp. 34–42.

24. Ibid., p. 40.

25. Norman Podhoretz, *Breaking Ranks,* p. 334.

26. Cohen, p. 40.

27. Gerald Strober, *American Jews: Community in Crisis,* p. 26.

28. Isaacs, p. 192.

29. Joseph Alsop, "The General and the Ambassador," *Jerusalem Post,* Nov. 24, 1974, p. 8.

30. "PM: Trim our sails for next seven years," Ibid., Dec. 4, 1974, p. 2.

31. Leonard Fein, *Analysis,* Dec. 1, 1974.

32. G. William Domhoff, *Fat Cats and Democrats,* pp. 46, 58, 62-63.

33. Ibid., pp. 13–4.

34. Isaacs, pp. 127–8.

35. Gunnar Myrdal, "The Case Against Romantic Ethnicity," *Center Magazine,* July 1974, p. 27.

36. Rubenberg, p. 40.

37. "Study Finds Pro-Israeli PAC's Active in '84 Races," *NY Times,* Aug. 16, 1984, B10.

38. "Pro-Israel PACs Hand Out Over $2 Million," *ADC Times,* Dec. 1984, p. 4.

39. Bernard Weinraub, "Mondale Is Ahead in Campaign Funds," *NY Times,* Dec. 18, 1983, p. 24

40. "A 'Born Democrat' Makes the Plans," *NY Times,* July 16, 1984.

41. "A Democratic Selection," *NY Times,* July 16, 1985, p. 11.

42. "Conservatives Took '84 Lead in Independent Political Aid," *NY Times,* Sept. 9, 1985, p. 13.

43.   Rubenberg, p. 41.

44.   John Oakes, "The PAC-Man's Game: Eating Legislators," *NY Times,* Sept. 6, 1984, p. 23.

45.   Hedrick Smith, "In Congress, the Invasion Has Erased Israel's Almost Automatic Support," *NY Times,* July 21, 1982, p. 8.

6

Six Million
Skeletons in the
Closet

As long as the public only remembered what Hitler did *to* the
Jews, many people hesitated to denounce Israel's actions vis-à-vis
the Palestinians. But once they started asking what Zionism and
the Establishment did *for* the Jews, they were both in deep trouble. And indeed the world is beginning to discuss their real part
in the Holocaust horror, still more so abroad than here, but
increasingly in the U.S. as well. Facts are stubborn things, and
any political grouping that denies the undeniable or justifies the
unjustifiable is a candidate for ultimate oblivion. Truth to tell,
they have six million Jewish skeletons in their closet, skeletons
that are now beginning to bang—and bang loudly—on the door.

Pro-Russian Communists admit Stalin's crimes; Catholics and
many Protestants will confess that their denominations were anti-
Semitic; Democrats don't defend segregation or the Vietnam war.
But most pro-Zionists simply cannot cope with the shocking truth

145

about their movement's role during the Hitler era. They have convinced themselves that they are Jewish history on the hoof. If you attack them you are attacking the Jews, and it does not matter if you are a Jew or even a Zionist.

Perfidy

There has been sporadic controversy over the wartime role of the Jewish Establishment and the World Zionist Organization ever since the Holocaust. In 1961 Ben Hecht, one of the most famous writers of his day (he was co-author of the celebrated stage play and movie *Front Page*), published *Perfidy*, describing the collaboration of Rezso Kastner, a Hungarian Labor Zionist, with Adolf Eichmann in 1944-5.

During the war, Hecht had become a partisan of the Irgun, an ultra-rightist terror group in Palestine, then organizationally separate and opposed to the WZO's own Haganah. When the public became aware of the full extent of the Holocaust, in 1942, Hecht and his Irgun friends here became intensely active trying to get the U.S. to set up a rescue commission, and for their pains they had been relentlessly sabotaged by their mainstream Zionist foes. *Perfidy* was Hecht's revenge.

In 1953, Kastner was an Israeli public official, when an obscure pamphleteer accused him of collaboration in the deportation of 450,000 Jews. The government brought the elderly accuser into court as a libeler. However, the case exploded in the face of the Israeli Labor Party when the trial judge declared that the charges had indeed been true.

The Attorney General appealed, but in the interim Kastner was assassinated. After his death, the Supreme Court ruled 3-2 that Kastner had not been guilty of most of the accusations, but voted 5-0 that he had perjured himself in providing a post-war alibi for a Nazi war criminal. The Israeli public was still deeply divided, on party lines, over Kastner's dealings with the exterminator. Hecht's book, which was based on the lower-court trial transcript and the Supreme Court's appellate statements, provoked similar discussion here.

The essential facts of the case were never in dispute. Kastner, the head of the WZO's rescue committee in Budapest, knew that Eichmann planned to ship Hungarian Jewry to Auschwitz, and he did not warn the Jews in return for a special exemption for a trainload of Jews whom he could pick for escape to Switzerland. In his argument before the Supreme Court, the Attorney General had insisted that:

> You are allowed—in fact it is your duty—to risk losing the many in order to save the few. . . . It has always been our Zionist tradition to select the few out of many in arranging the immigration to Palestine. Are we therefore to be called traitors? . . . There was no room for any resistance . . . if all the Jews of Hungary are to be sent to their death he is entitled to organize a rescue train for 600 people.[1] [In fact there were ultimately approximately 1,684 Jews on the train—LB]

The Supreme Court majority's most forceful argument was put forth by Judge Shlomo Chesin:

> The question is not whether a man is allowed to kill many in order to save a few, or vice-versa. The question is altogether in another sphere and should be defined as follows: a man is aware that a whole community is awaiting its doom. He is allowed to make efforts to save a few, although part of his efforts involve concealment of truth from the many; or should he disclose the truth to many though it is his best opinion that this way everybody will perish. I think the answer is clear. What good will the blood of the few bring if everyone is to perish?[2]

Hecht insisted that the pre-war Zionist leadership, Chaim Weizmann and the Labor Zionists led by David Ben-Gurion, had been

> stirred by the Jewish dream of a New Zion, which somehow did not include the Jews of reality. . . . He offered the world a picture of a Zionism toiling to turn Palestine into a Tiffany's window for glittering Jews, and not another ghetto for pushcart vendors and lowly tallith-wearers.[3]

Hecht was correct. Never having been interested in recruiting the Jewish masses before the Holocaust, in their souls the Zionist leaders were not suddenly loyal to them in their hour of peril. Throughout the Holocaust, they thought primarily about their hopes for a post-war state. It was only after the Holocaust, when they needed cannon fodder to obtain their ambitions, that they encouraged mass immigration.

Perfidy is not without weaknesses. Hecht was a dead-end polemicist, forever glorifying Menachem Begin and his Irgun in the 1944-48 revolt against Britain. At times he became simply absurd, as when he proclaimed that "a handful of Irgun and Lehi fighters won its [Israel's] independence from Britain."[4] Nevertheless, all intelligent readers recognized that, though he was wildly opinionated on intra-Zionist matters, Hecht was scrupulous in citing the testimony at the "Kastner" trial, as it came to be known.

Not so the defenders of the then mainstream of Zionism. Shlomo Katz poured out his bile in a scurrilous diatribe called "Ben Hecht's *KAMPF*," in *Midstream:* "It is an evil book, in every sense of the word. It is a McCarthyite book . . . the question of motivation arises." And he answers his own question, suggesting a "possible motivation: Profit . . . a book smearing Israel and Jews is almost certain to sell."[5]

The American section of the Executive of the WZO snarled that "he is engaged in political pamphleteering. . . . It is the hatred of the self-exiled. . . . The method used by Hecht would not put to shame the most notorious falsifiers of history, past or present."[6]

In fact, Elie Wiesel, scarcely an anti-Zionist, or an Irgunist, wrote in 1959 that Hecht had written the book and then hesitated for years to publish it because he feared it would discredit Israel in the eyes of the world.[7]

He was right. Kastner condemned himself, repeatedly, in his testimony. But so did Zionism's Attorney General and the majority of its Supreme Court. No one has the right to turn himself into a dog for the sake of a bone, and no judge, not in this world or the next, has the right to sanction the betrayal of hundreds of thousands of innocents, sent to their deaths with the connivance of such a creature.

Eichmann in Jerusalem

Paradoxically, the next challenge to Zionism's Holocaust bona fides came precisely as it seemed to have become truly the avenger of the martyrs, with the *Mossad's* (the secret police) capture of Adolf Eichmann. Hannah Arendt covered Eichmann's trial for the *New Yorker* and converted her articles into a book, *Eichmann in Jerusalem.* One phrase from it is justly famous, "the banality of evil," for certainly Eichmann was history's ultimate clerk. He had accidently become the SS Security Service's specialist on Zionism in the pre-war period, when Nazi policy was to encourage Jewish emigration to Palestine, and he would have been happy to do that forever. But he who told the court that "officialese is my only language" killed Jews with just as much happiness when the order came down.[8] Arendt was no lawyer, but a graduate of Mittel Europa's genius factories feels called upon to fault everything, and she quibbled with the terminology of the indictment, the prosecutor's argument's, the court's opinions and procedures, and those of the later appellate court as well; but, in the end, her caveats and cavils amounted to nothing and she ultimately upheld the court's jurisdiction and, of course, its verdict.

Her carping could be cosmic—and ludicrous—as when she treated readers to a digression wherein she discussed a post-war declaration by the *Evangelische Kirche in Deutschland*. These good folk had proclaimed "before the God of Mercy we share in the guilt for the outrage committed against the Jews." Arendt gave their paper an F: "If the churches shared in the guilt for an outrage pure and simple, as they themselves attest, then the matter must still be considered to fall within the purview of the God of *Justice.*"[9]

Why then did the Zionists savagely attack her book? The answer is that she had been a Zionist functionary in the 1930s and was familiar with the movement's trade links with the Hitlerites in that period. She therefore was concerned with the one facet of the Holocaust which the prosecutor did not want to go near: Zionist collaboration with the Nazis. In her treatment of Eichmann's career in the 1930s, she quoted a Zionist functionary's remark that in that period the Nazis "thought it proper to adopt a pro-Zionist attitude." She added that it was during these first stages that:

> Eichmann learned his lessons about Jews. . . . During its first few years, Hitler's rise to power appeared to the Zionists chiefly as "the decisive defeat of assimilationism." Hence, the Zionists could, for a time, at least, engage in a certain amount of non-criminal cooperation with the Nazi authorities; the Zionists too believed that "dissimilation," combined with the emigration to Palestine of Jewish youngsters and, they hoped, Jewish capitalists, could be a "mutually fair solution." . . . There existed in those first years a mutually highly satisfactory agreement between the

Nazi authorities and the Jewish Agency for Palestine—a *Ha'avara* or Transfer Agreement, which provided that an emigrant to Palestine could transfer his money there in German goods and exchange them for pounds upon arrival. . . . The result was that in the thirties, when American Jewry took great pains to organize a boycott of German merchandise, Palestine, of all places, was swamped with all kinds of goods "made in Germany." . . . He [Eichmann] remembered a visit he had received in Berlin from a Palestinian functionary . . . because this visit ended with a formal invitation to Palestine. . . . Eichmann, together with a journalist from his office, a certain Herbert Hagen, had just enough time to climb Mount Carmel in Haifa before the British authorities deported both of them to Egypt.[10]

The first into the lists against her was Jacob Robinson, with his *And the Crooked Shall Be Made Straight.* He had been an aide to Chief Prosecutor Jackson at Nuremburg, as well as Israeli Attorney General Gideon Hausner's assistant at Jerusalem, and he subjected her to a microscopic critique which, beyond dispute, created an all-time unbreakable world record for pedantry. He corrected her spelling: "Belzec (not 'Belzèk,' as she has it on pp. 96, 265)"; she had said that the inhabitants of the Lodz ghetto called their Jewish Council Elder 'Chaim I,' he set the record straight: "but it is not true, as Miss Arendt writes, that he was called 'Chaim I,' as if the head of a dynasty. According to Emmanuel Ringelblum he was nicknamed 'King Chaim.'"[11] He was at his maddest in a footnote running almost four pages in which he carefully demolished her passing references to Hungarian history in her introduction to her chapter on Eichmann's activities there. He, not Arendt, took us on a guided tour of Magyar history, all the way back to 1155 A.D.[12]

Robinson naturally had his excuse for the *Ha'avara* pact: "It also led to the grants of permits allowing some 50,000 Jews to emigrate and settle in Palestine at a time when each certificate or visa meant rescue for a person or a family."[13] More will be said about such "rescue." For now it is sufficient to say that his answer simply begs the question. It is the same argument given by Judge Chesin in defense of Kastner: Collaboration with Nazism was justified if a few were saved, Devil take the hindmost. And sure enough Robinson even talked of the "relative success" of Kastner's Rescue Committee, and claimed that 35,000 Jews had been saved by the committee.[14] Some of these were part of the deal Eichmann struck to ensure Kastner's cooperation in the deportation of the other Jews, and some were rescued by neutrals, who began to take initiatives to save Jews in the last months of the war, and who can scarcely be said to have moved because of Kastner.

Justice in Jerusalem

Next to attack Arendt was Attorney General Gideon Hausner, whose *Justice in Jerusalem* was published in the U.S. in 1966. He disposed of her with a deft hand:

> Hannah Arendt's *Eichmann in Jerusalem* has been refuted by many reviewers, most recently in a comprehensive point-by-point rebuttal in Dr. Jacob Robinson's *And the Crooked Shall Be Made Straight.*[15]

Only the oldest generations among the Israeli population still recalled anything about the *Ha'avara* pact, as Eichmann sat in his Jerusalem courtroom, but there had been other aspects of alleged Zionist collaboration with him that most definitely were of interest to some of the survivors. Hausner wrote of how he had long discussions, before the trial, with Zivia Lubetkin Zuckerman and Yitzhak Zuckerman, two leaders of the Warsaw ghetto rising.

> "What will you say about the Jewish Councils?" Yitzhak asked me. . . . He still remembered the bitter internal strife. "This is going to be the trial of the murderer, not of his victims," I replied. "But you will not be able to avoid the issue," Zivia said. . . . "No," I replied, "and what we shall bring forth will be the whole truth."[16]

It should be obvious from his statement that Hausner never intended to deal with Jewish collaboration, and he did not, certainly not in any depth, either at the trial or in his book. He did not dare to do so because one of the central concerns of his Labor Zionists was that what they had planned as a show trial would not explode in their faces. They knew exactly what Eichmann would say if he were to be asked about Kastner.

In 1955-57, the Nazi, hiding in Buenos Aires, met a Dutch Nazi journalist, Willem Sassen. Their interviews ran to 67 tapes, 659 pages in Sassen's transcription, which was corrected by Eichmann. The transcript was introduced into the trial as evidence. After Eichmann's capture, Sassen sold some of the tapes to *Life* magazine, which ran excerpts in its November 28 and December 5, 1960, issues. Eichmann discussed Kastner in the *Life* tapes, which Hausner knew were genuine.

> This Dr. Kastner was a young man about my age, an ice-cold lawyer and a fanatical Zionist. He agreed to help keep the Jews from resisting deportation—and even keep order in the collection camps—if I would close my eyes and let a few hundred or a few thousand young Jews emigrate illegally to Palestine. It was a good bargain. For keeping order in the camps, the price of 15,000 or 20,000 Jews—in the end there may have been more—was not too high for me. . . . I believe that Kastner would have sacrificed a thousand or a hundred thousand of his blood to achieve his political goal. He was not interested in old Jews or those who had become assimilated into Hungarian society. But he was incredibly persistent in trying to save biologically valuable Jewish blood— that is, human material that was capable of reproduction and hard work. "You can have the others," he would say, "but let me have this group here." And because Kastner rendered us a great service by helping keep the deportation camps peaceful, I would let his groups escape. After all, I was not concerned with small groups of a thousand or so Jews.[17]

We must presume the judges also knew of the *Life* articles, and much other material from the Sassen papers that was discussed before them, but, from the beginning, the court insisted it was not a commission of inquiry, which can investigate a broad area and command that evidence be brought before it.

The Israeli secret police had kidnapped Eichmann in violation of Argentine and international law. Israel did not exist when Eichmann committed his crimes, and they did not occur in Israel. Eichmann's sole legal defense rested in these niceties. The court was determined that he not be able to shake world respect for the proceedings, and therefore they were very concerned that, now that they had him before them, he was given due process of the law.

A court, the judges announced, is a passive instrument. It is up to the adversaries before them to present any evidence that would vindicate their side. If Hausner would not bring up the Kastner affair, no one would, and he deliberately excluded the matter from the trial, and then justified his decision (and the decision of his government) in his book:

> There were many others, however, who had never acquiesced in the Supreme Court's considered verdict exonerating Kastner and continued to condemn the leaders of martyred Hungarian Jewry. I knew they were fairly active in an attempt to use our trial as a platform for reopening the whole issue. I had appealed to everyone to abstain from internal reckonings, since this was the trial of the exterminator and not of his victims. The issue was so heavily laden with emotions, however, that I could not be sure. . . .
>
> I told him [assistant Gabi Bach] that we would not call any witness who might use the platform for a pro-Kastner or anti-Kastner demonstration. Two witnesses were disqualified by this criterion. One came to me saying that he would now show the whole world that Kastner was one of the greatest Jews who ever lived; it was for that purpose, he said, that he had come from Europe to testify. . . . Although we might have otherwise called this man as a witness to supplement some aspects of the Budapest story, I refused to have him testify. . . . Another witness . . . was given up for the opposite reason. We knew that the man would not be able to overcome a vitriolic hostility towards some members of the Jewish Council, particularly Kastner. . . . Bach . . . managed to steer clear of highly explosive possibilities.[18]

Hausner would not pursue the Kastner angle even when Eichmann brought it up on cross-examination. He had mentioned the fact that he sometimes had to lie to everyone, including his superiors:

> "Yes, that is so with one reservation. The Jews did not always accept what I said. Toward them, I should rather say, toward one of them, I had to be more outspoken." Eichmann was obviously trying to drag Kastner into the circle of "the initiated."[19]

Hausner confessed that the question of whether the WZO did enough "will continue to plague our national conscience," but he carefully listed all the reasons he thought might explain why the Zionists did not make the struggle against Hitler their prime focus in the pre-war period:

> The Zionists themselves suffered from internal strife; politically they were mainly engaged in a conflict with Great Britain over the carrying out of the Palestine Mandate; emotionally and physically

they were involved in the huge enterprise of building the Jewish-State-in-the-making. And all this was in addition to their active engagement in the day-to-day activities in their own communities. Busy with these responsibilities, the Jews did not perceive in time from where the immediate danger to their survival was to emerge.[20]

In other words, the Zionist leaders were too busy being Zionists to concern themselves with Hitler. In the end, isn't that just putting a little minus where Hecht had put a big minus? He had said that they had been fanatics constructing a Jewish Utopia, and that is, in short, exactly what Hausner finally mumbled.

Of course Arendt replied to Robinson and her other detractors, but she had written a book about Eichmann, not Zionism, and he had attacked her on so many points that the questions of Zionism's role in the pre-war period and Kastner's Holocaust role were lost amid his mad footnotes. Arendt was amazed that people took him to be an authority, and that even her friends began to doubt her. She defended herself and in fact did reestablish her credibility. Robinson sank back into oblivion, while she ended up a cult figure to much of the American intelligentsia, who think that *Kaffee mit Sahne* tastes better than coffee with cream The controversy over Zionism's role died away, or so it seemed.

Who Shall Live and Who Shall Die

These first post-war controversies had been battles between those who either had been directly struck by the Holocaust as victims/survivors, or were veterans of the different Zionist movements of that epoch. Eventually, a new interlocutor · emerged. Professor emeritus Marie Syrkin of Brandeis, herself a veteran labor Zionist leader, discussed this in a 1982 article in *Midstream:*

> Since the sixties, young students with memories of civil rights protests have often asked me pointedly why American Jews were so craven: Why did we not rage in the streets when the *St. Louis* with its freight of 1,000 men, women, and children moved along our shores in 1939. . . . Why did we not leap into the Atlantic to free the passengers? Why did we not stage sit-ins in the halls of Congress. . . . This failure appears base and inexplicable to a generation conditioned to direction action.[21]

Perfidy had only devoted five pages to Hecht's own efforts to get the U.S. government to rescue Jews. The first effort focusing primarily on American Jewry's reaction to the Holocaust was *Who Shall Live and Who Shall Die,* a documentary movie by Larry Jarvik, who started working on it at the age of 20, while a student at Berkeley in 1977. The movie was an instant success, playing at the prestigious Carnegie Hall Cinema in New York in 1982 and then on PBS-TV in 1983, each time gathering respectful and deeply troubled reviews from *The New York Times,* and furious denunciations from the Jewish Establishment and its intellectual hangers-on.

Times critic Vincent Canby described "the still angry Peter Bergson of the Emergency Committee to Save the Jewish People of Europe" as being

> especially harsh on American Jewish leaders who dragged their feet because, he charges, they were afraid that too much publicity on behalf of the victims would prompt a backlash of anti-Semitic feeling against American Jews.[22]

Frightened out of their wits by domestic anti-Semitism, the Establishment either did nothing, as with the then-assimilationist American Jewish Committee, or tried to get Britain to admit refugees into Palestine, as with the American Jewish Congress. Bergson and Hecht and their friends understood that the public wanted to rescue Jews. It was not interested in a fight with Britain, in the middle of the war, over Palestine. They simply proposed a rescue committee (the Emergency Committee to Save the Jewish People of Europe), leaving the question of Zionism until later.

Fanatic factionalists who were bitterly opposed to the Emergency Committee because of the Irgun's terrorist history, the mainstream Zionists actively fought them. Jarvik showed a May 19, 1944, State Department memo, obtained decades later under the Freedom of Information Act, describing how rabbi Stephen Wise of the American Jewish Congress had gone to a government official and told him that "he regarded Bergson as equally great an enemy of the Jews as Hitler, for the reason that his activities could only lead to increased anti-Semitism." The same memo reported that Nahum Goldmann "could not see why this government did not either deport Bergson or draft him."[23]

Syrkin, a leading propagandist for the mainline American Zionists during the Hitler epoch, clearly has learned nothing in the ensuing decades, as she demonstrated in her *Midstream* piece, wherein she denounced Jarvik's movie, the Bergsonites, and her own later-day students, who had obviously faulted her for her role during the horror:

Who Shall Live and Who Shall Die peddles a simple thesis: only the Irgun group tried to save Jews. . . . Why were Bergson and company not welcomed with the enthusiasm their zeal merited? Because they jeopardized the cause they sought to serve through a penchant for publicity and provocative gestures. Those who cite the civil disobedience of the sixties as a feasible tactic draw no meaningful parallel. . . . Civil disobedience and disruptive protest are only tolerated when they enjoy wide public support, as in the case of the Blacks.[24]

Veterans of the civil rights movement will no doubt be surprised to know how much support they "enjoyed." In fact anti-Semitism here was never, at any time, even remotely as strong as the mass hatred of Blacks, even after their victory in the 1960s. Further, anti-Semitism declined as a result of the revelations of Hitler's atrocities, as witness the support Christians gave Hecht and Co. in their efforts to rescue Jews.

Lucy Davidowicz also denounced Jarvik, in the most vitriolic terms, in *Commentary:*

There is no one at all in the film who speaks . . . about the work of the American Jewish organizations during the war. Failing that, there is no one even to read the heartrending letters that Rabbi Stephen Wise . . . wrote to Roosevelt . . . nothing of the masses of information about the fate of the European Jews with which Jewish organizations deluged America's newspapers. . . . Anti-Semitism did not intimidate the Jewish organizations . . . they did speak out . . . it is Jarvik and his companions on the left who have turned the Holocaust into a stick with which to beat the Jewish community for its "sin" of supporting Israel. . . . The Holocaust's bitter history is now being transformed into a vehicle of anti-Semitism. . . . The anti-Semites of the Left blame it on the Jews.[25]

Indeed. Here is part of a "heartrending" letter from Wise to Roosevelt, dated December 2, 1942, describing the rabbi's "deluging" of the media with the atrocity:

> I have had cables and underground advices for some months, tel-
> ling of these things. I succeeded, together with the heads of other
> Jewish organizations, in keeping them out of the press.[26]

The stark reality, discussed by many scholars since, was that
Wise suppressed a report from the World Jewish Congress's agent
in Switzerland that the Nazis had embarked on a systematic gassing campaign. He did it for 88 days, at the request of the State
Department, and he got other bureaucrats to go along with him.

In 1983 Alex Cockburn asked Jarvik why today's Establishment was so hypersensitive to any candid examination of their
WWII predecessors' failings. Jarvik explained that

> They feel the Holocaust is a useful thing to browbeat the Gentiles
> with: that as an organizational technique it's helpful to say, Look
> at what the Christians did to us. . . . If one admits that there is
> some Jewish responsibility for what happened . . . then one
> changes the rules of the game. . . . What they have tried to do is
> to say that in questions of Israel and the relation between Israel
> and other countries, Israel and the United States, "this is a Jewish
> issue." And they say it's a Jewish issue because of the Holocaust,
> and because the Goyim can't be trusted, because they are all anti-
> Semites.[26]

American Jewry During the Holocaust

The story of the American Jewish Commission on the Holocaust
would make a droll play: Jack Eisner, a Warsaw ghetto fighter,
came to the land of opportunity, and made his fortune. He
decided to spend some of it trying to find out what American
Jewry did to get him and Europe's Jews out of Hitler's claws, and
he got a Professor, Seymour Finger, to help him.

Finger was no Holocaust scholar, but he was the head of the
Institute for Mediterranean Affairs, whose director was Sam Mer-
lin, who had been one of Bergson's and Hecht's lieutenants in the
Emergency Committee. Finger had also been an Assistant
Ambassador to the UN for Johnson and Nixon during the Viet-
nam War. Finger's boss then, Ambassador Arthur Goldberg, had
gone on to even greater glories, and later become President of the
American Jewish Committee. So, in September 1981, Finger put

together Eisner's bucks, Goldberg, who lent his name to the Commission as its Chairman, and Merlin, who signed on to do the basic research.

In addition to Goldberg and former Senators Jacob Javits and Abraham Ribicoff, who represented American Jewry in all its political glory, the Commission included Morris Abram, a former President of the American Jewish Committee (and later a Reagan hack on the Civil Rights Commission); rabbi Arthur Hertzberg, Vice-President of the World Jewish Congress; Charlotte Jacobson of the Jewish National Fund; Frieda Lewis, President of Hadassah, Jack Spitzer, Honorary President of B'nai B'rith; rabbi Marc Tannenbaum of the American Jewish Committee; rabbi Morris Sherer, President of the ultra-Orthodox Agudath Israel; Milton Himmelfarb, and Martin Peretz, owner and editor of *The New Republic*.

All went well until June 1982, when the full Commission discussed an edited version of Merlin's report. Frankly, it is difficult to understand how Finger could have thought that today's hacks would ever certify their predecessors to be fools and knaves. At any rate, according to a series by Yaakov Rodan for the right-wing *Jewish Press*, it was Martin Peretz who led the pack against Merlin's report, " and after the meeting he had sharper words for those associated with the commission."[27] Goldberg and Finger agreed to further revise the offending paper.

Eisner was not about to pay for a whitewash and he stopped funding the group; it went out of business in August 1982. Eventually, in January 1983, *The New York Times* broke the story, on page one, and Goldberg had to insist that it wasn't the Jewish Establishment's censorship that killed the Commission, but rather Eisner's tardiness in coming up with the money. Whereupon Muhammed Medhi, a gifted free-lance Palestinian publicist, announced that he was willing to put up the bucks. He was bluffing, but Goldberg had to say that, rather than accept filthy Palestinian lucre, he, Goldberg, would front the money. The age of miracles is not over, and the Commission arose from the dead, in February 1983.

American Jewry During The Holocaust, released in March 1984, was the result. But the Establishment honchos were still not about to sign anything criticizing their groups, and the independent figures on the panel were unwilling to sanction the paper, given that the Commission hadn't dared to hold even one public hearing. The final work had to be designated "A Report by the Research Director, his staff and independent research scholars."

To say that it is mediocre would be an understatement. A professor might, charitably, give an undergraduate a B on it, at best. Balfour Brickner, a Reform rabbi and liberal Zionist, one of the independents on the Commission, appeared on a TV talk show with Finger, after its release, and bluntly told him that "there's nothing new in it." Morris Sherer had Finger add a statement by him as an appendix, in which he explained that the final product had two contradictory goals: to be candid about "the guilt of the American Jewish leaders," and, at the same time, to be "graciously protective" of those same leaders.[28]

Finger and Goldberg were primarily concerned to limit the political damage. They knew they could hardly get away with saying "the operation was a success; the patient died," and said just enough in the way of criticism so that they could point to something when the inevitable word "whitewash" would be thrown at them. But they said nothing that hadn't been said before, many times, and better and in far more detail. Each major organization gets a dollop of blame, but Sherer was correct: Nixon's henchman, Finger, always came up with excuses in the good old days, and he wasn't going to stop now.

The American Jewish Committee instantly strikes Holocaust scholars of all persuasions as the most arrogantly upper class and cowardly of the Holocaust Jewish groupings. With their former president as the chair of the Commission, it would have been too clearly a cover-up if Finger hadn't gone along with the consensus. Besides, the AJC doesn't really care what people with incomes of under a million think; they don't pay the rent. So we were told that, in the 1930s "the upper class leaders of the Committee . . . responded to each new Nazi outrage by practicing their traditional style of discreet 'backstairs' diplomacy. . . . With each worsening event, the Committee reacted by contacting yet another [American] official."[29] Finger is quick to divert the reader's indignation away from the AJC to the politicians: "That their efforts made little impact may, in fact, be an indictment of that government's attitude rather than of the Committee's aims."[30]

As Johnson's and Nixon's accomplice during the Vietnam War, Finger is not enamoured of demonstrations, and therefore he had no explanation as to why the AJC opposed the anti-Nazi boycott and demonstrations against the new and still-weak Berlin regime.

But Samuel Untermeyer, a spokesman for the boycott, did explain the AJC's stance, in 1933. Boycott, he said,

> conjures up to them images of force and illegality, such as have on occasions in the past characterized struggles between labor unions and their employers. As these timid souls are capitalists and employers, the word and all that it implies is hateful to their ears.[31]

During the Holocaust proper, the Joint Distribution Committee, one of the organizations that eventually merged to form the present-day United Jewish Appeal, was "dominated by the wealthy philanthropists who also composed the leadership of the Committee" and it "scrupulously observ[ed] all government regulations, despite the consequences for the Jews of Europe."[32]

These rules forbade sending money into enemy occupied territory. Not breaking the regulations meant not providing the wherewithal for bribes to German officials or the cash nexus that would have induced the resistance movements to make Jewish rescue a priority. But Finger again leaps in to say that the JDC's field reps often ignored their home office's commandments, as if these individual actions could, somehow, compensate for the JDC's cowardly policy. Similarly, he tells us that the B'nai B'rith (then also non-Zionist) went along with the AJC's futile policies, and then says, "Yet, it could point to a number of accomplishments, however small these might appear against the enormity of the loss . . . they reflected concern and effort."[33]

Rabbi Wise has been repeatedly denounced for his 88-day silence about the gassing program. Here is Finger's description of Wise:

> An uncertain Wise accepted what he privately termed "the great responsibility," lest he lose the WJC's only sympathetic audience in State and contact with Riegner [the WJC rep in Switzerland]. The tormented WJC president . . . shared this and related information at meetings with Jewish organization leaders."[34]

Of course Finger (and Goldberg) knew that, far from "sharing" this information, Wise was swearing these others to similar silence. Tucked away, on the 23rd page of the 8th Appendix, by another scholar, is the incriminating statement from Wise's letter to Roosevelt: "I have had cables and underground advices for months, telling of these things. I succeeded, together with the heads of other Jewish organizations in keeping them out of the press."

It is interesting to compare Finger's sympathetic picture of Wise with the comments of Saul Friedman, the independent scholar who, unlike Finger, quoted the damning letter, and Walter Laqueur, who has also written on the Holocaust:

> Wise agreed to stifle the information until State obtained confirmation from the Vatican. "In ancient times," Walter Laqueur has commented, "kings and rulers used to consult the Delphic Oracle, with similar results." . . . Meanwhile, five to ten thousand Jews, victims of what Laqueur terms the ineptitude and naivete of Jewish leaders, were being evacuated daily from the Warsaw Ghetto to Treblinka.[35]

What about Merlin and Bergson and Hecht and their efforts? To discuss how Wise and Co. sabotaged their work would be to set the cat among the pigeons, and Finger deftly evaded his responsibility:

> The Emergency Committee . . . posed a special problem for the Commission. This group does not belong within the terms of reference of the Commission, which deals with the leadership of the *American* Jewish organizations. The Bergsonites were outsiders, all of them Palestinians. . . . On the other hand . . . their activities cannot be ignored. . . . The Commission decided *not* to undertake a special study . . . of the "Bergson Group" . . . but instead to reproduce documents or excerpts from official Government agencies [and] evaluations of works by historians who cannot be suspected of having a particular bias for or against this group.[36]

Of course Hecht was American, and many of the leaders of the mainline Zionists, such as Nahum Goldmann, were foreigners. And one document Finger did not dare reproduce was the State Department memo wherein Goldmann was cited as asking for Bergson's deportation.

Paradoxically, the zeal shown by the Irgunists during their rescue campaign stemmed precisely from the terrorist element of their Zionism which Wise despised. They had abandoned the notion that either London or Washington would give Palestine to the Zionists for good behavior. They understood that they would have to rip it out of the hands of Britain. This same independent spirit allowed them to understand that the only way Washington was ever going to set up a rescue agency was if they mobilized public opinion to compel Roosevelt to do it.

The bankruptcy of mainline American Zionism in the crisis related to the original sin of its ideology. As the State Department memo demonstrates, they were extremely fearful of domestic anti-Semitism. To be sure, American anti-Semitism greatly increased in the wake of Hitler's 1933 triumph, and was still significant in 1944. But they had never fought American anti-Semitism. On February 20, 1939, the German-American Bund— the Nazis—rallied in New York's Madison Square Garden, and the Zionists had opposed Jews demonstrating against them. Thousands of people, most of them Jews, did in fact slug it out with the Nazis and the cops, and the fascists had to call off other planned rallies in other cities as a result. Further, there is not the slightest evidence that the Emergency Committee's drive in any way stimulated anti-Semitism. Hitler's murderous efforts were discrediting the domestic anti-Semites, and a mass mobilization of the Jews and their allies, from 1942 on, could have easily dealt with the domestic problem as well.

The failure to resist domestic anti-Semitism highlights Zionism's congenital indifference to the real needs of Diaspora Jewry. The mainstream Zionists could never have mobilized American Jewry for rescue because Zionism had to have the patronage of western capitalist governments for its Palestinian ambitions. It was always impossible to simultaneously lobby Washington for Zionism's position in Palestine vis-à-vis the British and Arabs, and rally Jews against America's racist immigration laws.

In the ultimate crunch, during the Holocaust, the mainstream Zionists could not press for governmental support of a post-war Zionist state, and embarrass that same government with a demand for a wartime rescue operation. The Democratic Party was fighting only to preserve American investments and markets abroad from challenge by the Axis, and the Roosevelt Administration had no interest in humanitarian distractions like rescuing Jews.

In his foreword to the Finger folly, Goldberg declared that the aim of the Commission "was not to make moral judgments but rather to enable later generations to learn from this experience whatever might help prevent a similar tragedy from ever again befalling the Jews or any other people."[37] A miserable thing, without morals or judgments, the report has sunk without a trace.

What was most disgraceful about the sordid Commission was that these hacks were unwilling to admit the full guilt of their predecessors even though Nahum Goldmann, one of the most culpable of the wartime leaders, wrote, repeatedly, in his *Autobiography* and other places, about their—and his—shame. Indeed, so that later generations may learn, we shall counter the hypocrisies of Finger and Goldberg with Goldmann's candid confession, from a Paris platform, in 1964, as reported in the *Jerusalem Post:*

> "They are moral bankrupts," declares Dr. Goldmann, "and I have no qualms in saying 'they,' for this 'they' includes myself." He goes on to indict, first and foremost, the American Jews who 30 years ago (1933-34–LB) refused to campaign against the Nazis for fear of "spoiling relations between the United States and Germany." . . .
>
> Dr. Goldmann remembers, aloud, how at the height of the calamity he and the late Dr. S. Wise received from the Jewish Resistance Movement in Poland a telegram exhorting "twelve top American Jews to go and sit day and night on the steps outside the White House until the Allies are moved to bomb Auschwitz and Treblinka."
>
> Instead, the Jewish leaders made discreet, if pressing representations to Roosevelt and Churchill, who had other things to do than to knock out the gas-chambers. . . . Dr. Goldmann does not dwell, though, on the responsibility of other people. He insists that the Jews must, if only to find their future bearings, make a spiritual self-reckoning, a *heshbon ha nefesh.*[38]

The Transfer Agreement

Edwin Black, author of *The Transfer Agreement,* is the son of Holocaust survivors. His father was a pre-war member of the Betar Zionist-Revisionist youth movement in Poland, when Menachem Begin was its Warsaw leader, and Black is himself a perfervid member of the American branch of Herut, the modern-day party of Begin and Yitzhak Shamir. Nevertheless, his book has created immense problems for American Zionism, and Zionist critics have either been extremely wary of the book or intensely hostile.

When he first heard of the *Ha'avara* pact with the archenemy of his people, it was a nightmare: "The possibility of a Zionist-

Nazi arrangement for the sake of Israel was inconceivable."[39]
Even after he collected his wits, and decided to write about it, he
understood that he was walking straight into a political minefield:

> My greatest worry is that the revelations of the book might be
> used by enemies of the Jewish people. For those who seek to
> besmirch the Zionist movement as racist and Nazi-like, this agree-
> ment might seem to be perfect ammunition.[40]

His Zionist critics share his anxiety. Arnost Lustig, writing in
The Jewish Monthly, the organ of the B'nai B'rith, said that
"sometimes he gets into dangerous, carefree formulations that the
critics will return to him like a boomerang."[41]

Henry Feingold declared, in the *Congress Monthly,* that

> both Nazis and Zionists had something in common. Neither
> believed that Jewish life in the Diaspora was desirable. They were
> both dissimiliationists. It was that shared belief which made the
> Transfer Agreement possible. . . . For a propagandist who seeks to
> strike at the very core of Jewish sensibility, awareness of the
> Transfer Agreement is like a dream come true.[42]

One can imagine Black's dismay when he read of Muslim minister Louis Farrakhan's June 1984 speech, in the wake of Jesse
Jackson's "Hymietown" remarks:

> I'm not anti-Jew. I am pro-truth, but in this serious hour, the truth
> must be told. . . . The Zionists believed that they should get a
> homeland for the Jews and maintain that homeland, but they
> wanted to fulfill the vision without fulfilling the preconditions. So
> Zionists made a deal with Adolf Hitler. These are the same people
> that condemn me for saying Hitler was a great man, but a wicked
> man. . . . So for me to say that Hitler was great, I've made no
> mistake at all. He was great, but wickedly great, and the Zionists
> made a deal with Adolf Hitler according to a book called *The
> Transfer Agreement* by Edwin Black, one of their own kind. . . .
> This transfer agreement let 60,000 German Jews into Palestine
> and $100 million of their money into Palestine, where they began
> to take the land away from the Palestine people and little by little
> they gained strength and power and with the backing of the
> nations, they claimed that land to be theirs and they called it
> Israel. I say to the Jewish people and to the Government of the
> United States: the present state called Israel is an outlaw act. . . .

Now that nation called Israel never has had any peace . . . and she will never have any peace, because there can be no peace structured on injustice, thievery, lying and deceit and using the name of God to shield your gutter religion under His Holy name. . . . It is the black people in America that is the chosen people of Almighty God.[43]

Black, his Zionist critics, and Farrakhan are all correct, on one level or another. It is instinctual for us to suspect any group of the oppressed who try to make a deal with their oppressor. Nevertheless, Black tried to vindicate the *Ha'avara*. To be sure, he was well aware of what they did:

It was one thing for the Zionists to subvert the anti-Nazi boycott. . . . But soon Zionist leaders understood that the success of the future Jewish Palestinian economy would be inextricably bound up with the survival of the Nazi economy. . . . If the Hitler economy fell, both sides would be ruined.[44]

However, he is so fanatically committed to today's Israel that he is psychologically driven to deceive himself with a totally false after-the-fact explanation for the traitorous pact:

As many Jews as possible had to be brought over from Germany as fast as possible—not to save their culture, not to save their wealth, but to save their lives [p. 374]. . . . The only way to continue the transfer and rescue was to bring over large groups of so-called capitalist emigrants [p. 376].[45]

In a subsequent article in the May 1984 B'nai B'rith magazine *Jewish Monthly,* Black tried his own rescue operation—on the Transfer. Everyone knows that modern liberation movements are not supposed to be concerned only with saving capitalists, so he rushed to tell us that the wealth of these German Jews "opened the gates to hundreds of thousands of working class Polish and Eastern European immigrants."[46]

Black hired 50 people to help him research the period. He is completely familiar with the standard Holocaust literature. Yet he knowingly omitted anything from other scholars which would contradict his rescue fable. In 1983 this writer discovered that Black was working on his book, and inasmuch as my own *Zionism in the Age of the Dictators* was about to be published, I contacted his editor, Ned Chase, who was good enough to put me in contact with Black. He presented me with his rescue theory. I asked if he was familiar with Abraham Margaliot's article, "The Problems of the Rescue of Germany Jewry During the Years 1933-1939: The Reasons for the Delay in Their Emigration from the Third Reich," found in *Rescue Attempts During the Holocaust,* a tome issued by the Yad Vashem Institute, Israel's Holocaust study center. Of course he had read it, but our youthful author was quick to tell me that he was "the person who knows more about the transfer than any person alive," and that Margaliot—like every other scholar who differed with him—was wrong in his treatment of 1930s Zionism. Margaliot is mentioned in Black's Acknowledgements, but the article is nowhere cited in the incredible 38 pages of notes. Readers will understand why when they read Margaliot's description of a speech by Chaim Weizmann, in 1935, while the *Ha'avara* was in full swing:

> He declared that the Zionist movement would have to choose between the immediate rescue of Jews and the establishment of a national project which would ensure lasting redemption for the Jewish people. Under the circumstances, the movement, according to Weizmann, must choose the latter course.[47]

Margaliot directly quoted Labor Zionist leader Berl Katznelson's 1933 statement that "we know that we are not able to transfer all of German Jewry and will have to choose on the basis of the cruel criterion of Zionism."[48] Margaliot went further, telling us that two-thirds of those German Jews who applied to the WZO for immigration certificates in 1933-35 were rejected.[49] They were either not Zionists, or, if Zionists, were too old (usually meaning over 35), or didn't speak Hebrew. Or their profession wasn't in demand in the utopia in the desert, or they weren't rich. To put this in context, it must be appreciated that no less than 6,307 Zionist cadre were brought into Palestine in those years from Britain, Turkey, South Africa and the western hemisphere.

Rescue was never the WZO's priority, and Black knew it. Again, any Holocaust scholar reads the *Yad Vashem Studies* series. He knew of Yoav Gelber's article in volume XII. The noted Israeli savant had quoted a speech by Ben-Gurion, on December 7, 1938, uttered in the wake of the dreadful *kristallnacht* pogrom.

Immediately following Crystal Night in Germany, the British, hoping to ease the pressure for them to admit more immigrants into Palestine, had offered to take in thousands of children directly into Britain. Said the future first prime minister of Israel:

> If I knew that it would be possible to save all the children in Germany by bringing them over to England, and only half of them by transporting them to Eretz Yisrael, then I would opt for the second alternative. For we must weigh not only the life of these children, but also the history of the People of Israel.[50]

The curse of our century has been state building. There have been any number of ideologues prepared to justify anything and everything if it led, or might have led, to the creation of their particular Holy Land. However, serious scholars cling to a conception—normative history—in dealing with the past. We do not debate settled points, one of which being that Hitler was evil, another being that collaboration with him was, in every case, likewise evil, or stupid, or both. Anyone—a Jew no less— defending such collaboration, and by Jews, must be summarily dismissed with contempt, and this is particularly so when it is falsely claimed that such traffic was motivated by humanitarian considerations of rescue.

Black's Zionist reviewers have almost all been hostile to him, but not one criticized him for his bogus rescue tale. What they disliked was that he was so blunt in putting down the fact that the WZO did not fight Hitler, but rather accommodated him. They know where this kind of thinking can lead. Ben Halpern attacked him in *Moment,* normally a liberal Zionist publication: Archival searches, he said,

> should be used to help us understand why policies were adapted, not to judge those who adopt them . . . before undertaking to judge, one should surely seek to empathize. . . . Labor Zionists and Revisionists . . . agreed that anti-Semitism is a structural feature of the Jewish problem, not to be remedied by palliative action . . . both were prepared to fight or to deal with enemies of the Jews, basing their decisions on their assessment of national interest rather than on emotions alone. . . . Socialist Zionists . . . placed the building of the Homeland and the resettlement of Jews above the emotionally fulfilling impulse to fight the new Haman at every turn.

So they got what they wanted from Hitler, millions of dollars in German Jewish wealth, which proved crucial in providing the economic base for the eventual creation of the Zionist state. Of course, Hitler got what he wanted: the WZO broke the Jewish boycott of Germany, and did nothing to mobilize world Jewry against the new Haman. Six million died and all that, but not to worry:

> Israel's existence is the rainbow that marks the Jewish vow to history that we shall not give Hitler posthumous victories[51]

Arnost Lustig wrote perhaps the blandest review, for *The Jewish Monthly,* in a piece accompanying an article by Black:

> Nothing has divided the Jewish public more than the Transfer Agreement. . . . The author also concludes that in 1933 the agreement was necessary for the future establishment of the Jewish state. This is impossible to prove or disprove. . . . Sometimes he gets into dangerous, carefree formulations that the critics will return to him like a boomerang. . . . But in the end, everyone who reads Edwin Black's book will be wiser. It is a book written from a desire for a clear conscience.[52]

A.J. Sherman, who reviewed the book for *The New York Times,* was out of sorts with Black for asking, rhetorically,

> whether the Jewish architects of the agreement were men of madness or of genius. They were of course neither . . . they left to others the self-indulgence of ringing denunciations and posturings for the press, delivered in the comfort of first-class Swiss hotels or the heady atmosphere of a crowded Madison Square Garden.[53]

Having told us that "The Transfer Agreement is like a dream come true" for anti-Zionist propagandists, Henry Feingold went on, in his *Congress Monthly* piece:

> Those anxious to participate in what has become a veritable popular sport, accusing the Jewish leadership of betrayal during the Holocaust, will find Zionism an easy target. But this particular facet of the emerging indictment goes beyond reading betrayal back into Jewish history. It plays into the hands of those who seek to destroy the state of Israel. . . . That is why such demagogues as Lyndon LaRouche and Louis Farrakhan have both found it so useful to cite his book.[54]

In many ways, Richard Levy's critique in *Commentary* was the most reactionary:

> The Zionists' motives . . . were clear and cold-blooded. Recognizing the peril of the Jews trapped in Germany, they worked to build a Jewish state in Palestine. . . . In doing so they rejected . . . a broadly-based rescue mission; they short-circuited attempts to relocate Jews to countries other than Palestine; they often spoke of the "rescue of assets" rather than of people. . . . This was a rational analysis, whatever one thinks of its ethical dimension . . . the historian's job is to explore and explain, not to sneer. . . . To the historical record Black has added conspiracy-mongering, innuendo, and sensationalism, but nothing new, and much that is both factually wrong and morally shabby.[55]

We got two for the price of one with Jack Riemer's double review of Finger's report and Black's book, for *Judaica:*

> These are two disturbing books that I think we could have lived well without. They both expose old sores—it seems to me for no good purpose. . . . Both are unfair in that they judge historical events with 20-20 hindsight. . . . At a time when we hear enough at the United Nations from Arab and Soviet spokesmen about how the Jews were partners with the Nazis or about how the Israelis are the new Nazis we don't need to have a book like this that rakes up old wounds and creates new tensions, especially not in this tone.[56]

Lastly, we have Eric Breindel, who took on Black in Martin Peretz's *New Republic:*

> Black draws absurd and insidious conclusions: his thesis is that Zionists leaders revived and stabilized Adolf Hitler's ostensibly faltering regime. Moreover, The Transfer Agreement has been put to unsavory political uses, thanks in no small measure to this thesis . . . Farrakhan invoked Mr. Black. . . . By negotiating the transfer, the Zionist leadership deliberately (consciously may be a better word) undermined the boycott *not* because these Jewish leaders wanted to help Hitler, but rather because they and others judged the notion that a boycott might topple the Nazis sheer fantasy. . . . As for the book's admirers, Louis Farrakhan is by no means alone; he is joined by Lyndon LaRouche . . . among others. . . . Black cannot evade responsibility for the uses to which his book is now being put by simply asserting, in his text, that suggestions of Zionist complicity in the Holocaust are "absurd."[57]

Such are the thoughts on the Zionist-Nazi trade pact of intellectuals representative of the differing sectors of today's Jewish
Establishment. We will again contrast them to Goldmann, who
was the WZO's representative during that period at the League of
Nations' headquarters in Switzerland:

> "I was never so ashamed in my life," Dr. Goldmann recalls, "as
> when I had to admit to Benes how passive the Western Jewish elite
> were. This was the day after promulgation of the Nuremberg laws.
> Benes, who was not yet President of Czechoslovakia, called me to
> his hotel in Geneva. He shouted: 'Don't you Jews see that this is
> not only the end of German Jewry, but a threat to all of you and
> to all humanity? You Jews are powerful in finance, in the press, in
> other walks of life. Why don't you act? Why don't you summon a
> world conference?' I had to explain to him that it would do more
> harm than good to call such a conference since the most influential
> Jews would stay away, causing a fiasco."[58]

Zionism in the Age of the Dictators

In 1979, the present writer sent out the standard chapter and outline for a book on Zionist-Nazi collaboration to 10 American
publishing houses. All sent back the standard rejection slip:
"Thank you for considering our house, but the book is not suit-
able for our list." I then met a leading agent, told him of the proposed book, and he sent the material to five more houses. Agents
are a real part of the literary world, and they get more or less
honest critiques with rejections. There were two basic replies:
Brenner is too scholarly, he's not popular enough; or Brenner is
too popular, he's not scholarly. As none suggested the obvious,
that we discuss such stylistic questions, I understood these were
polite brushoffs. No one was going to let an unknown, who had
only written a handful of unremembered articles for journals they
had never heard of, write a book that was certain to engender
hatred towards any house foolhardy enough to publish it.

In 1980 two books on Zionism, one pro, one con, both published by the same British firm, came into my hands. Although
Croom Helm Ltd. is one of Britain's most prestigious scholarly
houses, I had never heard of them until then. But no longer
expecting to find an American publisher, I sent them my material,
and *Zionism in the Age of the Dictators* was the result. Later,
Lawrence Hill & Co. signed on as American co-publisher, and
the book was released in the U.S. and Britain in 1983.

The only advance publicity the book received was in three of Alex Cockburn's columns in the *Village Voice* between 1981 and 1983. Given my experience with the 15 American publishers, I presumed it would get few reviews outside the specialized journals. I was wrong. It was reviewed by some of America's and the world's most important journals. As a result it will always be a razor at Zionism's jugular. A description of how the Zionists have responded to the book will, it is hoped, further illuminate both the role of the Zionist movement and the American Jewish Establishment during the Holocaust, and the difficulties their present-day epigones have defending them.

Commentary

Attacks were not long in coming. Lucy Dawidowicz took it on in the course of her omnibus defense of the Holocaust Jewish Establishment in the June 1983 *Commentary:*

> The Left . . . bays loudly against the "Jewish establishment." . . . It appropriates the cruel and ill-founded charges . . . which . . . Arendt . . . leveled . . . and applies them to the Jewish leadership. . . . In a retrospective alliance with the Irgun . . . Brenner echoes the Soviet-Arab line about "Zionist collusion with the Fascists and the Nazis." . . . Brenner . . . says of them [Bergson and Merlin] . . . that they "did more than all other Zionists to help the Jews."[59]

My reply appeared in the September issue:

> I praised *and severely criticized* Bergson and . . . cited Merlin as among those Zionist-Revisionists who "admired" Mussolini. . . . I criticized the Stalinists, I condemn the Mufti. . . . Her charge is vintage red-baiting, nothing more.

I challenged her to debate the issues at her school, Yeshiva. Her reply, I thought, was quite witty:

> Lenni Brenner denies that he echoes the Soviet-Arab line. . . . Maybe it's the other way around, and the Soviets echo *his* line. Just lately . . . *Izvestia,* not customarily well-disposed to Trotskyites, gave Mr. Brenner's book a rave review.[60]

Since reviews are to a writer what heroin is to a junkie, I wrote her, asking in what issue I might find the offending piece. Turns out she had never read it (Reaganites do not trouble to read communications from the evil empire). She had read a brief mention of the review in London's *Jewish Chronicle*.

I turned to the Soviet's TASS news agency for help, and discovered that the reviewer, Vladimir Kikilo, was one of their American correspondents. His piece, "Zionist Collaborationists: A Journalist unmasks dirty deal with Nazi chiefs," had appeared in the July 5 issue. I sent it to Dawidowicz, remarking that I saw nothing improper about it. He had said, among other things, that "during the world war, Brenner points out, Zionism showed its real meaning: for the sake of its ambitions, it sacrificed the blood of millions of Jews."

Kikilo had taken the book very seriously and had written an additional six-page essay on the book, which TASS distributed to libraries throughout the Soviet Union. Having had the offending *Izvestia* review translated, I wrote Dawidowicz that:

> I am reinforced in my belief that you . . . took refuge in a stale red-baiting. All I know is that when I went to the Yad Vashem, and met with Yoav Gelber on the day that Shamir had been nominated to be the Prime Minister [of Israel], he told me that the scholars there were in utter consternation at the thought of Israel having a Prime Minister who wanted to go to war on Hitler's side. Tell me: do you think he was also echoing the Soviet and Arab line?[61]

It need not be said that she never accepted my challenge to debate the issues before her students.

Choice

In July 1983, *Choice,* the publication of the American Library Association, ran an unsigned attack: "The proverbial kernel of truth is here, but historical context and objectivity are not . . . most sources are quoted out of context, others are unreliable."[62] Librarians are a major market for scholarly books, therefore in a pound, shilling and pence world reviews in such magazines are more important to authors than the vast majority of reviews, and again I replied.

Choice's policy was to send such authors' letters to their reviewers, who could rebut if they wished, but if so their names must be signed. Sure enough, the reviewer did not dare to up periscope, and the magazine ran my protest in their April 1984 number:

What possible "context" can possibly erase the treason of today's Israeli Prime Minister, Yitzhak Shamir, whose "Stern Gang," in 1940 and again in 1941, sought to go to war on Adolf Hitler's side?[63]

Britain

Their debacle in the U.S. did not prevent the Zionists from trying to utilize the offending review in Britain, where no one knew of the scandal. The situation there had gone from bad to worse for the local Zionists. I had lectured there in October-January 1983-84, and they did everything they could think of to stop the truth from getting out. The *Jewish Chronicle* libeled me in their November 18 issue, falsely writing that:

> Brenner's latest thesis as impeccably reported by none other than the *News Line,* Workers' Revolutionary Party journal, is how Jews control the American political process . . . as in "Hispanics and blacks give votes, Jews give money."[64]

There is nothing like the threat of being hauled into court to make honest folk out of Zionists, and the paper had to run a letter from me and a retraction from their scribbler:

> Brenner's accusation is technically correct insofar as the quote about Jews controlling the political process in the United States was a distillation which I made for space reasons. . . . He said: "Truman was told by his advisers that he had to have the Jewish vote and campaign contributions from rich Jews. I stress rich Jews, of course."[65]

Everywhere I toured, Zionists tried to ban me from the universities. Off campus, some of them tried to use strongarm tactics, which, fortunately, backfired on them, as reported by the December 12, 1983, *Guardian:*

> Police are investigating an attack by right-wing Zionists on the American author Lenni Brenner at Lambeth Town Hall last week. Mr. Brenner is . . . promoting his book which shows how the Stern Gang (former member Israeli premier Shamir) offered to fight for the Nazis in 1940. Two people, including the elderly chairman of the meeting, were hospitalized and Mr. Brenner was bruised on his arm and leg when a small group started throwing punches. They were thought to be members of British Herut . . .

in London, at least, known for their rough tactics. Their escape—
and the registration numbers of their cars—were noted by John
Fraser, the local MP who happened to be in the town hall.[66]

As if things weren't bad enough, Britain's Zionists woke up on
February 11, 1984, to find that their nemesis, Edward Mortimer,
editorialist for the London *Times,* had favorably reviewed the
book. If you are a Zionist it is hard to get down your morning tea
if you must read that "Mr. Brenner is able to cite numerous
cases where Zionists collaborated with anti-Semitic regimes,
including Hitler's."[67]

The Jerusalem Post

The difficulties Zionism has with the book are clearly shown in
another review, which came out only six days later, in the
Jerusalem Post. The reviewer, Louis Rapoport, an American, a
former leftist, had once been an editor of the San Francisco
Express-Times, which had devoted the front page of its first issue,
in January 1968, to a laudatory article on—guess who? Right.
Me. Now—finally!—Louis had come to his senses, and was able
to see me for—let's face it—the despicable rogue that I always
was. However, although he solemnly declared the book to be
"leftist babble," he had to denounce "the so-called historians who
defend the Zionist and Jewish leadership" against "very real
charges that will continue to haunt until they are dealt with
honestly."[68]

It is my policy to reply to hostile critics, and I sent a response
to the *Jerusalem Post.* As every author knows, there are two
kinds of journals: responsible publications and rags. Responsible
periodicals print replies from anyone they criticize, with the
reviewer then having the last word. Rags attack people and do not
let them respond. The *Jerusalem Post* is a rag. It is easy to see
why they did not run my letter, which said, in part:

> Rapoport is not above some mathematical sleight-of-hand in his
> effort to portray me as some kind of fanatic: "it seems odd that
> Trotsky and his movement have more entries in a book 'about'
> Zionism than does Ben-Gurion." In fact, Trotsky is indexed four
> times (and quoted only once), while Ben-Gurion is listed seven
> times (and quoted 4 times). It's that trick "and his movement" that
> gives "Trotsky and his movement" more entries than Ben-Gurion

alone. Trotsky, Trotskyists, the Socialist Workers Party, the *Militant, Socialist Appeal,* and the one other named Trotskyist, get a total of 13 entries, while *Davar* has three, the Haganah four, the HaPoel one, Hechalutz five, the Histadrut four, the Israeli Labour Party one, *Jewish Frontier* three, the *Labor Zionist Newsletter* two, the Po'ale Zion 24, and 17 named Labourites received 40 index entries, in addition to Ben-Gurion's seven. That's 94 for Ben-Gurion *and his Labour Zionists.*[69]

The Village Voice

It was not long before a chance to hit back at Rapoport availed itself. Rapoport and Sol Stern, another renegade leftist, who had once been an editor of *Ramparts,* published an article on Yitzhak Shamir in the July 3, 1984, *Village Voice,* and I commented on it in a letter.

David Schneiderman, the editor of the paper, had been quite unhappy when Alex Cockburn had used material from the book in his columns. Later, after Cockburn's 1984 suspension from the paper, Schneiderman gave orders that neither I nor the book were to be mentioned again, and no letters from me were to be printed. I'm a prolific letters-to-the-editor writer, used to seeing them run in major publications, and at first I couldn't understand why I was having no luck with the *Voice*. But once I learned of Schneiderman's *diktat*, I wrote letters under an assumed name.

Edwin Krales is an anti-Zionist Jew, who joined me in co-authoring a pamphlet, *Problems of the Palestinian Revolution,* as well as a previous letter to the paper. Given that fact, and the topic, Zionist-Nazi collaboration, the Letters editor, Ron Plotkin, knew that I was the one challenging the two apologists for Shamir, but having more integrity than Schneiderman, he ran the letter in the July 24 issue:

> They concede that the Stern Gang tried to ally itself with Hitler, but insist "contact with the Germans was never made . . . and the plan was abandoned." They then cite, without demurral, Shamir's claim that he opposed the scheme, and only joined after it was dropped. . . . [in fact] . . . a Sternist agent, Naphtali Lubenczik, met with Otto von Hentig . . . in Beirut in January 1941. . . . If Hitler would let them train the Jews he had penned up in the ghettos, they would go to war against Britain and establish "the historic Jewish state on a national and totalitarian basis." Gerold Frank's *The Deed* tells of Shamir recruiting for Stern . . . in

August or September 1940. And Shamir was a leading Stern Gang member in December 1941 when, according to the *Encyclopedia Judaica,* Nathan Yalin-Mor was arrested trying to reach the Nazis again.

The two replied:

Lubentchik was arrested after he met one German official; Yalin-Mor was arrested in Syria before meeting anyone. Several Lehi veterans told us that Shamir held back for six months before joining Stern, and Gerold Frank gives no sources.[70]

Readers will have noticed that in the original lie "contact with the Germans was never made," while in the second lie the Stern Gang agent "met one German." The world is often unkind. Just because you meet one, just one, Nazi you are called a traitor. Now in fact he had met two, von Hentig and Alfred Roser, but even one is more than none, which is what they had originally pretended.

Gerold Frank was a reporter who covered the trial of two Stern Gang youths who assassinated Lord Moyne, the British High Commissioner for the Middle East, in 1944. It is universally agreed that Yitzhak Yizernitsky, known from then on by his underground name, Shamir, organized the slaying. He is a major personage in the book, and Frank, a pro-Zionist, whose book is quite sympathetic to the two youths, at least on the human level, definitely gives his source for Shamir's recruiting speech.

The Stern Gang evolved out of a split in the Irgun. Two factions were led by David Raziel and Avraham Stern, each claiming the command of the movement. The political mentor of the Irgun was Vladimir Jabotinsky, then in New York. In August 1940 he declared for Raziel as commander, and called upon Stern to step down, but Stern refused. Suddenly, on August 3, Jabotinsky died. Frank relates that

the movement all but disintegrated. In September Stern walked out and set up his own group . . . Eliahu [Bet Zouri—LB] and David Danon . . . were summoned to a remote schoolhouse . . . they were to be addressed by a representative of each faction . . . the entire group of fifty were ordered to proceed . . . to another classroom. Here a short, square-shouldered, square-faced, muscular man awaited them. Itzhak Yizernitsky . . . spoke tersely, summing up the reasons behind Stern's decision to walk out. . . . "Men!"

His deep voice rumbled. "If you want to smell fire and powder, come with us!" [pp. 91–3] . . . David, for his part, could not forget Yizernitsky's "fire and powder" remark in the days immediately following the Raziel-Stern split. [p. 139][71]

Bet Zouri, one of the assassins, was hanged for the killing. The source of the incident re Yizernitsky-Shamir is obviously David Danon. It was a minor episode in the book, and it only takes on significance now because of Shamir's later importance. When Frank wrote this, in 1963, Shamir was an operative of the Israeli secret police, and there was no reason for Frank to make up the incident, which had occurred 23 years before.

Yediot Ahranot, an Israeli daily, interviewed Shamir on his accession to the Prime Ministership in 1983, and he gave them his version of his relationship to the collaboration attempts. The London *Times* ran the story:

"There was a plan to turn to Italy for help and to make contact with Germany on the assumption that these could bring about a massive Jewish immigration (to Palestine). I opposed this," he told the Tel aviv newspaper *Yediot Ahranot,* "but I did join Lehi after the idea of contacts with the Axis countries was dropped."[72]

Even if we were to believe him, he convicts himself of joining a pack of traitors, with knowledge that they were such. But of course he was lying. He was with them from the beginning, before they sent Lubenczik. Frank had no reason to make up his account; Shamir had the best reason in the world to make up his tale.

The world is still naive. It isn't ready for an Israeli Prime Minister who would admit to wanting to ally himself with Hitler. He must at least go through the motions of denying the truth. Rapoport and Stern are converts to Zionism. They have broken with their past. For them to admit that the leader of their new found Holy Land was a Jewish Nazi was impossible. So they made up their two little *maiselas,* their little fairy tales, "contact with the Germans was never made " and "Gerold Frank gives no sources."

"Extremists of Right and Left Meeting"

Some Zionist scholars invented an ingenious formula for disposing of my claims. In November 1984, an article appeared in the

National Student, the organ of Britain's National Union of Students. It seemed the Union of Jewish Students were "stepping up their fight against racism" in the wake of my tour: "Brenner, like extreme right-wing writer David Irving . . . rewrite[s] the history of the Hitler era, denying or playing down Nazi atrocities."[73] Protests came into the paper from students who had heard me, and the paper ran a rebuttal from me:

> That the Nazis murdered six million of my fellow Jews is a certain fact, and readers of my book . . . may see . . . there is not one word in it that even remotely challenges that truth.[74]

Matthew Kalman, former head of UJS, and Neil Cohen tried the same argument in an attack in the June 17-18, 1985, issues of the *Jerusalem Post:*

> as you move towards the outer edges of the political spectrum it becomes a circle, with the extremists of right and left meeting . . . the Holocaust . . . stood as the major link. . . . Arguments have been employed . . . delegitimizing Jewish suffering under the Nazis and proving that the Jews blackmailed the Europeans into giving them . . . Israel by playing on their guilty conscience for a mass murder . . . for which the Nazis were not responsible. . . . Ideologues have begun to argue that it was actually the Zionists, as much as the Nazis, who were responsible for the Holocaust. . . . The anti-Zionist left has built a monolithic and documented case for Zionist collaboration with the Nazis. The original material for this slander originated in the Soviet Union, and its two chief promoters—Tony Greenstein in Britain and Lenni Brenner in the U.S.—are both Jewish Trotskyists.[75]

Again I replied, for the record, fully realizing that if the paper would not print my rebuttal to Rapoport's review, it would not run my latest letter:

> This is monkeychatter: The neo-Nazis deny the Holocaust happened. Not one word in my books casts doubt . . . that six million Jews were murdered. Of course the Nazis were responsible for their deaths, and nowhere do I imply the Zionists were responsible "as much as the Nazis" for the Holocaust. It eludes me how the Soviets rate credit for originating the "material for this slander" . . . the Revisionists . . . proclaimed the World Zionist Organization to be traitors for their *Ha'avara* . . . the WZO's

leaders thought Stern—and Shamir—wanted to collaborate . . . the Revisionists . . . insisted that Kastner was a traitor. . . . Let's go further . . . Louis Rapoport denounced "the so-called historians who defend the Zionist and Jewish leadership" against "very real charges" . . . and Cohen and Kalman concede that my book "has not been seriously rebutted by Jewish historians."[76]

As we have seen, Martin Peretz led the fight against Sam Merlin's initial report for the Holocaust Commission, and he opened *The New Republic* to Eric Breindel's attack against Black. That "review" turned into a diatribe against me:

A word should be said about the larger context in which *The Transfer Agreement* is best considered. . . . Moving from the truth that anti-Semitism was a principle impetus to Zionism, some (the Soviets have figured prominently among them) have tried to show that an early common interest, Jewish departure from Europe, led to genuine collaboration. *Zionism in the Age of the Dictators* . . . a recent example of the left-wing effort to defame the Jewish national movement, and *The Iron Wall,* a new study of Revisionist Zionism by the same author, seek to document the purported collaboration. Brenner's work has been applauded, and made available by the Institute for Historical Review, a pseudo-scientific flat-earth society which endeavors to prove that the Holocaust was a hoax.

Brenner and others like him seek to have it every which way. The mainstream Zionists collaborated with Hitler by undermining the boycott—unlike Jabotinsky. But Jabotinsky and his Revisionists followers were the *real* collaborators, because, it is alleged, they admired the fascists (not at all true . . . Jabotinsky himself was a classic 19th-century liberal), and early on sought Mussolini's support. . . . A favorite new case . . . is the 1941 attempt by members of the Stern group . . . to make contact with the Germans in order to propose a deal: the mass shipment by the Nazis of European Jews to Palestine in return for Sternist aid in ridding Palestine of the British. This hopeless, desperate effort speaks for itself: it was born of sheer despair and carried out by one lone disciple of the hunted Stern before the Holocaust was underway. The purpose of the mission: to rescue the doomed.

In view of what actually happened, is not absolutely every attempt to save European Jews, however misguided, at least understandable?[77]

Naturally, I responded to the attack in *The New Republic,* but it did not print my rebuttal. I then wrote directly to Breindel:

You know the established custom in scholarly debate: authors attacked in reviews get the right of reply, with the reviewer getting the last word. . . . You well know why there can be *NO EXCEPTIONS* to this rule: . . . 100,000 potential readers are now prejudiced against my books, as they do not know that I responded to the review, or what I wrote in my defense. And they do not know any of this because *The New Republic* does not want them to know this. Your duty in this matter is crystal clear: you are to demand that the magazine run my response, with whatever rejoinder you wish! . . . Do I have to tell you that the vast majority of writers will, automatically, come to my side on this question, regardless of their opinions on Zionism or its role during the Holocaust . . . the *NR*'s reputation will be severely damaged. It is for you to determine if you wish to go down with Peretz's ship.[78]

Not having seen anything on the book by the Institute, I wrote them for such a statement. I received a letter from Tom Marcellus of the IHR. They had "promoted" the book on two occasions. They sent me a booklist:

397. ZIONISM IN THE AGE OF THE DICTATORS: A REAPPRAISAL by Lenni Brenner. An astounding, bombshell exposé of the *active collaboration between Nazis and Zionists,* by a courageous anti-Zionist Jew who spent years piecing together the story. Details the close links between the "Revisionist Zionism" movement (to which both the young Menachem Begin and Yitzhak Shamir belonged) and the Jewish Question experts of the Nazi Party. Brenner's charge, overwhelming documented: that Zionism and its leaders from the beginning were prepared to go to any lengths to achieve their goal of a state in Palestine—lengths that included fostering and exploiting anti-Semitism in Europe, and proposing an alliance with Germany at the zenith of that nation's power. This book has certain surviving WWII-era Zionists quaking in their boots—including the present Prime Minister of Israel![79]

The letter went on:

We also promoted it in an *IHR Newsletter* of a couple of years ago, but the remaining copies of that issue and the records concerning it were all lost in an arson that completely destroyed our business address and inventory on 4 July last.[80]

I replied as follows:

The depravity of the Institute is clearly expressed in a box, "The Holocaust," in the same booklist: "A catch-all term to identify the alleged extermination of European Jewry which insists on the following presumptions: (1) The Nazis executed a deliberate plan to destroy (not resettle) European Jewry, (2) Six million or more Jews perished as a result, and (3) A majority of these were killed by poison gas (Zyklon B) in gas chambers designed for the purpose of taking human life en masse. This is the "orthodox" or Establishment view. A subscriber to this view could be called an EXTERMINATIONIST: whereas one who endeavors to show that one or more of the above presumptions is not factual is a REVISIONIST."

All of the above is bullshit. I share not one iota of your mad ideology. I am your implacable opponent. I do not believe you have any right to exist . . . and I support any and all attempts, by any and all, Zionist or anti-Zionist, to bust up your institute and your meetings.[81]

I sent copies to Breindel and *The New Republic,* but of course I had no illusions that the *NR* would now see its way to running my response to Breindel's review. However, no matter how much they might have hated Black, he is a Zionist-Revisionist, and they are in the Israeli government; therefore, the magazine ran his rejoinder to Breindel:

Breindel links me with the anti-Zionist efforts of Arab propagandists, Soviet anti-Semites, and the anti-Zionist work of Lenni Brenner. This is so far from the truth, it is laughable. Indeed, Jewish leaders have felt that my book provided the precise document-by-document rebuttal to Brenner's distortions, and encouraged the distribution of my book overseas. . . . As for misuse by the likes of Lyndon LaRouche and Louis Farrakhan . . . I am unable to stop any of them if they want to distort my book. . . . The fact is that nearly all published anti-Zionist material is based upon the research from Holocaust and Zionist sources.[82]

I sent the *NR* a response to Black, but knowing that they would not run it, I also sent it to him via his publisher, with a challenge:

If you . . . believe that my books . . . are in need of refutation, the best way to try to do that is in debate. . . . My associates . . . in Chicago are willing to meet with you . . . to arrange such an event.[83]

By now it should come as no surpise that he did not accept my

offer. However, I had told Breindel and Peretz that I was determined to expose them, and did so, thanks to Alex Cockburn,
who, on June 29, 1985, gave the story to the *Nation*'s readers:

> Some journals automatically allow those who have been subjected
> to criticism to respond. . . . Others routinely refuse to run
> replies. . . . Among the worst . . . is *The New Republic*. . . . Eric
> Breindel attacked Lenni Brenner's books . . . for accusing . . .
> Shamir's Stern Gang of seeking to ally itself with Hitler in 1940-
> 41. All they really did, Breindel maintained, was "propose . . . the
> mass shipment . . . [of] . . . Jews to Palestine in return for Sternist
> aid in ridding Palestine of the British. . . . The purpose [was] . . .
> to rescue the doomed."
>   In the letter Brenner sent *The New Republic,* he directly quoted
> the Sternists' incriminating proposal, which stated that "common
> interests" could exist between the "new order in Europe in confor-
> mity with the German concept" and the establishment of the "his-
> toric Jewish state on a national and totalitarian basis." The Ster-
> nists' National Military Organization . . . "offers to actively take
> part in the war on Germany's side" . . .
>   Breindel had also suggested . . . that the Institute for Historical
> Review . . . likes Brenner's work, thus insinuating that Brenner
> and the Institute are in sympathy. . . . Brenner, a self-described
> hard-core Trotskyist . . . has encouraged people to bust up meet-
> ings of the institute.[84]

When you are dead you are dead and, but for our Savior, most
corpses have agreed to abide by that prudent axiom. But not so
Breindel. A letter from him appeared in the August 31, 1985,
Nation. "Cockburn," he wrote, sneeringly,

> chides *The New Republic* and me for denying Lenni Brenner the
> right to reply. . . . Brenner receives only passing mention in my
> rather long review. His letter . . . to me took the imperative form,
> as in: "You are to demand that the magazine run my
> response." . . . Brenner further issued to me what I can only take
> as a threat, warning: "It is for you to determine if you wish to go
> down with [Martin] Peretz's ship." . . .
>   I wrote nothing of Brenner that can be construed as either abuse
> or distortion. I called his work "part of the left-wing effort to
> defame the Jewish national movement." I would think from having
> read his books, and from Cockburn's comment that Brenner is a
> self-described "hard-core Trotskyist," that Brenner would regard
> defaming Zionism (i.e. the Jewish national movement) as a noble

endeavor. . . . I made no "suggestion" or "insinuation"—just a simple statement of fact: "Brenner's work has been applauded and made available by the Institute for Historical Review." . . . My point was not that Brenner and the I.H.R. are in sympathy. Rather that the various contributors to the "debate" over an essentially fabricated issue—Nazi-Zionist collaboration—while coming from disparate points on the political spectrum, as do Edwin Black, Louis Farrakhan, Lenni Brenner and Lyndon La Rouche . . . find each other useful. . . .

If it is indeed the case . . . that Brenner "has encouraged people to bust up meetings of the institute," this affords an edifying perspective on someone seeking to cause a great ruckus over his right to be heard. Still, Brenner's unfriendly attitude towards the I.H.R. is unlikely to diminish the positive view these Neo-Nazis take of his work.[85]

As the letter was in response to an article by Cockburn, he, not I, had the right to reply. Anyone reading the letters columns of, first, the *Village Voice,* and then the *Nation,* will see that more hostile letters came in on his work than on any other writer for either publication. Such epistles almost invariably turn into disasters for their hapless perpetrators, and such was the case with Breindel. Cockburn replied:

Breindel's letter reminds me of the old proverb, "The wise man sits on the hole in his carpet." At the center of the row . . . is the alliance . . . Shamir proposed in late 1940. . . . Breindel doesn't deal with this because, like most American Zionists, he seems incapable of acknowledging that Israel has as its Foreign Minister someone who was once eager to collaborate with the Nazis. . . . So, squatting on the great hole in his carpet, Breindel quibbles over whether he was reviewing Brenner or only attacking him and says he isn't sure whether *The New Republic* routinely refuses to run replies from its victims. I am. Although Martin Peretz once claimed that it is "axiomatic" that the right of reply is given . . . the assertion, like almost everything Peretz writes, is false. . . . Chomsky's replies . . . are routinely, indeed almost axiomatically, suppressed . . .

Breindel is fond of saying that the Institute . . . applauds and disseminates Brenner's work, though he denies that he is thus trying to saddle Brenner with the institute's views. But of course that is what Breindel has been trying to do, as anyone looking at his remarks in *The New Republic* . . . will instantly perceive. The Institute lists Brenner's book as it does books by such diverse people as A.J.P. Taylor, former Israeli Prime Minister Moshe Sharett and *New Republic* contributors Ronald Radosh and Allen Weinstein. Breindel used the same type of attack on Edwin Black, linking him to Louis Farrakhan and Lyndon LaRouche. This has about as much relation to reality as if I were to link John Z. DeLorean, Jimi Hendrix and a victim of Agent Orange because they all have had unfortunate encounters with toxic substances.[86]

Alex Cockburn is a hard act to follow, but a few words must be said regarding one of Breindel's points. It is in order to dismiss the Institute's praise of the book by saying it is no more important than the fact that roaches like gourmet cooking, but the reader is entitled to know why these wackoes liked *Zionism in the Age of the Dictators*. Essentially, their line is to minimize the Holocaust. "Aw right, so Hitler didn't exactly like the Jews, and he rounded them up, as enemies, and some of them died of disease. An' besides, what about Roosevelt rounding up all the Japanese on the West Coast? An' look at Stalin's Katyn massacre, and Churchill's dreadful bombing of Dresden, or the A-bombing of Hiroshima and Nagasaki. Well now, whaddaya know? Here the Yids have been yellin' all these years about Hitler, an' their own leaders were fascists jus' like him. It sure 'nuf is a wicked world, damn it if ain't everybody got skeletons in their closet. Why go on pickin' on po' ol' Adolf?" Given this mad psychology, their catalogue is full of books on Allied crimes, no less crimes for being emphasized by such as these.

"Seemed Determined Not to Dwell on Criticism of Mr. Reagan"

Most people do not focus on contemporary politics, still less on history, but 1985 was remarkable in how the Holocaust impinged on the public consciousness, even if fleetingly. For it was both the year of Bitburg and the exhumation of Josef Mengele. Each revealed the hypocrisy of the American Jewish Establishment.

That Bitburg proved Reagan an idiot was universally agreed. Ordinary Americans had to wonder at a political pro who first refused to make a ritual visit to a concentration camp, but insisted on going on with a wreath-laying at a cemetary holding SS graves. But for typical Americans that war was over a long time ago, and they were not going to complain if the Jews didn't. Even for most Jews, the Holocaust is a dead issue, as it were. Midge Decter was right when she wrote, in *Commentary*, after Bitburg, that "the word 'Holocaust,' even for Jews, induces by now a mostly dead sensation."[87]

Not so for the Jewish Establishment. What Jarvik said of them is absolutely true. It's their *shtick*, their bit, their act. For them it's a growth industry, with Holocaust commemorations, monuments, scholarly institutes, museums. They are on a President's Commission on the Holocaust, begun under Carter, which Reagan has used for sermons against totalitarian devils. They never expected anyone so quick to rant against evil empires to betray them and pay homage to the SS, even in passing and by accident. Elie Wiesel, the Chairman of the Commission, publically pleaded with Reagan not to go. Reagan went.

The West German capitalist class is largely made up of ex-Nazis and their children, and it is hard for them to really sell patriotism with that background. The best they can hope for is a sort of let's bury the past attitude, and that was what Bitburg was supposed to do for them. The Republicans don't get the Jewish vote, and if they even lost a few additional Jewish votes, so what? Reagan knew that Israel is a U.S. arms junkie, therefore the Establishment would not dare to continue to agitate against him after the grotesque episode. They need him more than he needs them.

He was correct. Midge Decter wrote an overlong piece for *Commentary*, taking him to task, but since the Establishment shares his world view, she ended up saying nothing and nonsense:

> What does it mean to "remember" the Holocaust? . . . It requires a continuing alertness to certain political . . . lessons. There is the lesson of Munich . . . about the need to resist totalitarianism. . . . Any Jew who decrees, as many Jews nowadays do, that the democracies should divest themselves of the power to threaten and discipline intransigent totalitarianism, especially of the Soviet variety, has forgotten the Holocaust. Any Jew who believes . . . that Israel must extend a hand of appeasing friendship to those who have sworn to destroy it . . . has forgotten the Holocaust—and forgotten himself as well.[88]

There is something cockeyed about a modern woman writing about *any* Jew forgetting *himself*, but then again she is a leading

lady opponent of feminism. At any rate, what our he/she forgot
was that Arafat and Gorbachev did not go to Bitburg. Reagan did.
Nowadays the PLO lays wreaths at Warsaw ghetto monuments,
and within days of Bitburg the Soviets celebrated their defeat of
those same SS.

The Israeli government was no better. The May 7, 1985, *New
York Times* reported that it had been "restrained" prior to the
cemetary visit, hoping it would be cancelled, but the paper went
on to say that "there is a great reluctance to criticize Mr.
Reagan . . . in light of his reported decision . . . to approve . . .
the Israeli request for $1.5 billion."[89]

By May 10, four days after Bitburg, Secretary of State Shultz
was laying another wreath, at the Yad Vashem in Jerusalem, and
prattling on about the Holocaust again, and *The New York Times*
reported that Prime Minister Shimon Peres—and of course his
Foreign Minister, Shamir—"seemed determined not to dwell on
criticism of Mr. Reagan."[90]

"I Was Not Too Eager to Find Dr. Mengele"

It was pressure by American Jews, including the Establishment,
which led to the renewed world interest in rounding up the
remnants of Hitler's criminals, and ultimately this led to the reve-
lation of Mengele's death in Brazil. On May 7, 1985, Israel
offered a $1 million reward for his capture, but this was a sham,
as the May 11 *New York Times* revealed. At that time it was
Paraguay, not Brazil, that was thought to be harboring him, if he
was still alive, and the paper reported that "After Paraguay joined
the . . . Security Council in 1968, Israel took pains not to antagonize . . . Stroessner . . . and did not press the Mengele case."[91]

The former Israeli ambassador to that country, Benno Varon,
had written an article, in May 1979, for the B'nai B'rith's
National Jewish Monthly, describing his policy while in Asun-
cion:

> I developed a standard answer: The Israeli government was not
> searching for Dr. Mengele. . . . I must confess that I was not too
> eager to find Dr. Mengele. . . . A *bungled* abduction would not
> have been worth the penalties. Besides, bringing Eichmann to jus-
> tic was a one-time operation. . . . I did not believe a replay of the
> Eichmann trial would add anything.[92]

The B'nai B'rith's Anti-Defamation League is supposed to be the Establishment's Nazi fighters, yet they certainly have not made an issue of Israel's indifference to the tracking down of surviving war criminals. They are hardly in a position to do so, as the ADL's real passion is fighting here against growing sympathy towards the Palestinians. For this they utilize—and must utilize—the CIA, and that organization is infamous for working with Nazis. The December 11, 1984, Jewish Telegraphic Agency *Daily News Bulletin* reported that the ADL

> defended its use as a panelist on international terrorism a former deputy director of the CIA who . . . supported American utilization of Nazi war criminals. Dr. Ray Cline was a featured participant at a news conference on world terrorism organized by the A.D.L.[93]

The Future of the Past

Jacobo Timerman tells us that Israeli wits, "using the word *Shoah,* which is Hebrew for Holocaust," say of the American Jewish Establishment, that, truly, " 'There's no business like *Shoah* business.' "[94] We should not be surprised that they are hustlers. For no pompous Establishment is ever able to heed King Lear, and take political physic, learning the profound lessons to be taught by society's pitiless social storms. For who lives more in the here and now than the rich? And what more can be expected of them than that they should try to utilize the past to defend their present interests? No modern capitalist elite can have a consistent insight into its history for the simple reason that their class domination has been outmoded since it was challenged by the rise of 19th-century Marxism. To be sure, Hitler could never have come to power if the crisis of capitalism had not also simultaneously turned out to be the crisis of the working class movement, whose failure to unite in Germany was crucial to his triumph. That certainly raises questions as to whether civilization can progressively resolve its explosive social contradictions. However, the Jewish capitalists were not one whit less politically bankrupt for their leftist enemies' own egregious failure.

If the American Jewish Establishment and Zionism could not play a progressive role in the Hitler epoch, when the Jewish capitalists were a pariah elite, they certainly cannot play a progressive role today, when they are integral components of the decaying capitalist world order. Once again they are under challenge from the left, which reestablished its historic relevance by its role in defeating U.S. imperialism in Indochina, and which is once again reviving in response to the world historic explosion in South Africa. We have seen that the Establishment is in deep difficulty already over their predecessors' role, and we may be certain that the left will continue to put them to route on this issue, among others, in the future.

Notes

1. Ben Hecht, *Perfidy,* pp. 194–5, 268.
2. Ibid., pp. 270–1.
3. Ibid., p. 19.
4. Ibid., p. 8.
5. Shlomo Katz, "Ben Hecht's *KAMPF, Midstream,* Winter 1962, reprinted in *Perfidy,* supplement, pp. 3, 10.
6. Ibid., second supplement, p. 3.
7. Moshe Shonfeld, *The Holocaust Victims Accuse,* pp. 105–6.
8. Hannah Arendt, *Eichmann in Jerusalem,* p. 48.
9. Ibid., p. 296.
10. Ibid., pp. 58–60, 62.
11. Jacob Robinson, *And the Crooked Shall Be Made Straight,* p. 178.
12. Ibid., pp. 365–9.
13. Ibid., p. 278.
14. Ibid., pp. 207, 333.
15. Gideon Hausner, *Justice in Jerusalem,* p. 465.
16. Ibid., p. 295.
17. Adolf Eichmann, "I Transported Them to the Butcher," *Life,* Dec. 5, 1960, p. 146.
18. Hausner, p. 341.
19. Ibid., p. 367.
20. Ibid., p. 465.
21. Marie Syrkin, "What American Jews Did During the Holocaust," *Midstream,* Oct. 1982, p. 6.
22. Vincent Canby, "Film: American Roles During the Holocaust," *NY Times,* April 19, 1982.
23. "Attitude of Zionists Toward Peter Bergson," State Department memorandum 867N.01/2347, May 19, 1944.
24. Syrkin, pp. 11–12.
25. Lucy Dawidowicz, "Indicting American Jews," *Commentary,* June 1983, pp. 40–4.
26. Alex Cockburn, "What Was to Be Done," *Village Voice,* March 1, 1983.
27. Yaakov Rodan, "Holocaust Panel: 'Network' Looked to Destroy Group," *Jewish Press,* Jan. 21, 1983, p. 1.
28. "Comments by Rabbi Morris Sherer," *American Jewry During the Holocaust,* Appendix 3, p. 15.

29. *American Jewry During the Holocaust,* p. 19.
30. *AJDTH,* p. 21.
31. Edwin Black, *The Transfer Agreement,* p. 277.
32. *AJDTH,* p. 23.
33. Ibid., p. 30.
34. Ibid., pp. 15–6.
35. Saul Friedman, "The Power and/or Powerlessness of American Jews, 1939-1945," *AJDTH,* App. 8, p. 23.
36. *AJDTH,* p. 13.
37. Arthur Goldberg, "Foreword," *AJDTH,* p. 1.
38. Maurice Carr, "The Belated Awakening," *Jerusalem Post,* May 5, 1964, p. 3.
39. Edwin Black, "A Deal With the Devil," *Washington Post,* April 29, 1984, p. 16.
40. Black, "The Startling Story of The Transfer Agreement," *The Jewish Monthly,* May 1984, p. 20.
41. Arnost Lustig, "A Passionate Longing for Truth," Ibid., p. 23.
42. Henry Feingold, "The Agony of Witness," *Congress Monthly,* Sept. 1984, p. 16.
43. "Excerpts from Address," *NY Times,* June 29, 1984, p. 12.
44. Black, *Transfer,* p. 253.
45. Ibid., pp. 374, 376.
46. Black, *Jewish Monthly,* p. 22.
47. Abraham Margaliot, "The Problems of the Rescue of German Jewry During the Years 1933-39: The Reasons for the Delay to Their Emigration from the Third Reich," *Rescue Attempts during the Holocaust,* pp. 255–6.
48. Ibid.
49. Ibid., p. 253.
50. Yoav Gelber, "Zionist Policy and the Fate of European Jewry (1939-42)," *Yad Vashem Studies,* vol. XII, p. 199.
51. Ben Halpern, "The Transfer Agreement," *Moment,* May 1984, pp. 59–61.
52. Lustig.
53. A.J. Sherman, "Coping With a Cruel Dilemma," *NY Times,* June 10, 1984, p. 26.
54. Feingold, pp. 16–17.
55. Richard Levy, "Dealing With the Devil," *Commentary,* Sept. 1984, pp. 68–71.
56. *Judaica,* Fall-Winter 1984-85, pp. 18, 20.
57. Eric Breindel, "The Price of Rescue," *New Republic,* February 18, 1985, pp. 39–41.
58. Carr.
59. Dawidowicz, p. 44.
60. "Letters from Readers," *Commentary,* Sept. 1983, p. 8, 25.
61. Letter to Dawidowicz, Jan. 4, 1983.
62. *Choice,* July 1983, p. 1641.
63. "Letters," *Choice, April 1984, p. 1104.*
64. "Ban for Brenner," *Jewish Chronicle* November 18, 1983, p. 15.
65. "Brenner's complaint," *JC,* Dec. 2, 1983, p. 34.
66. *Guardian,* Dec. 12, 1983.
67. Edward Mortimer, "Contradiction, Collusion and Controversy," *The Times,* Feb. 11, 1984.

68. Louis Rapoport, "Fantasist," *Jerusalem Post Magazine,* February 17, 1984.

69. Letter to *Jerusalem Post,* March 5, 1984.

70. "Shamir's Underground Record," *Village Voice,* July 24, 1984.

71. Gerold Frank, *The Deed,* pp. 91–3, 124, 139.

72. Christopher Walker, "Shamir Defends Terrorist Past," *The Times,* Oct. 21, 1983, p. 24.

73. "Jews to Counter Campus Racism," *National Student,* Early November 1984, p. 3.

74. "Grotesque Notion," *National Student,* Late February, 1985, p. 8.

75. Neil Cohen and Matthew Kalman, "Waiting in the Wings," *Jerusalem Post,* June 17, 1985, p. 5, and "Opening the flood gates," Ibid., June 18, 1985, p. 5.

76. Letter to *Jerusalem Post,* July 2, 1985.

77. Breindel, pp. 41–2.

78. Letter to Breindel, April 2, 1985.

79. *Fall/Winter 1984 Books and Tapes of Revisionist History.*

80. Letter from Institute for Historical Review, 8 March 1985.

81. Letter to Institute for Historical Review, April 11, 1985.

82. "Transfer Disagreement," *NR,* April 29, 1985, p. 6.

83. Letter to Edwin Black, April 25, 1985.

84. Alex Cockburn, "One-Way Street," *Nation,* June 29, 1985, p. 789.

85. Eric Breindel, " 'Energetic, If Not Enlightening' " (Letters), *Nation,* Aug. 31, 1985, p. 130.

86. Alex Cockburn, "Cockburn Replies," *Nation,* Aug. 31, 1985, p. 130.

87. Midge Decter, "Bitburg: Who Forgot What," *Commentary,* August 1985, p. 23.

88. Ibid., p. 27.

89. Thomas Friedman, "Outraged Israelis Denounce Reagan," *NY Times,* May 6, 1985, p. 5.

90. Bernard Gwertzman, "Shultz, in Jerusalem, Lauds Israel As a Symbol of Victory Over Evil," *NY Times,* May 11, 1985.

91. Ralph Blumenthal, "3 Nations Joining to Hunt Mengele," *NY Times,* May 11, 1985.

92. Benno Varon, "The Diplomat and Dr. Mengele," *National Jewish Monthly,* May 1979, pp. 6–7.

93. "ADL Defends Its Use as Panelist a Former CIA Official Who Supported U.S. Utlization of War Criminals," *JTA Daily News Bulletin,* Dec. 11, 1984.

94. Jacobo Timerman, *The Longest War,* p. 15.

7

Anti-Semitism: From Nazis to Nutsies

American Jewry is the most successful grouping in the country, yet Jews still keep asking "Will it happen again." "It" is, of course, another Holocaust, and they mean, "Can it happen here?" I can understand why they should ask the question, but that many of them think that "it" will happen here is pathetic. They are not worried that the Nazis will return to power in West Germany. They worry less about East Germany. They mean here, where the Holocaust cannot happen "again" because it never happened here in the first place. Hitler came to power in 1933, more than half a century ago, in Germany, another country on another continent, with immensely different traditions. To think modern America capable of such an enormity is no better than thinking that the Spanish Inquisition can happen "again" here.

Stephen Isaacs reported that almost all of those he interviewed for his 1974 book, *Jews in American Politics*, gave approximately the same answer to the question of "it" happening again: "If you know history at all, you have to presume not that it could happen, but that it probably will," or "It's not a matter of if; it's a matter of when."[1]

Isaacs himself went on to say that much of the Jew's voting pattern would better be explained "not so much by Isaiah's ancient call to 'seek justice and relieve the oppressed' beating a tattoo inside his subconscious as he is by the fear of a tattoo on his forearm."[2] He went on to say that "Politicians know (because they are told so by the Jewish strategists they hire) that many Jews perceive Israel as their ultimate refuge, as being synonymous with survival."[3]

It is to be understood that the vast majority of the Jewish Establishment doesn't believe word one of this nonsense. They do careful surveys of America's opinions on Jews and Israel, and they know anti-Semitism is a declining force. The ADL has spies in the KKK and Nazi groups, and it says, quite correctly, that they are disintegrating. These are folk fears, deeply held by the pro-Zionist masses, particularly by the religious, especially among the elderly, but also by the most "Jewish" youth, those with the least contact, socially and politically, with gentiles of the younger generation.

Nothing better illustrates the puerile character of much of Zionism's base in this country. The notion that, someday, the American people will let someone impose a Nazi-like regime on them would be insulting if it wasn't so farcical. The roots of the fantasy lies in the old country shtetl mentality.

The Jews of the Pale saw themselves as surrounded by illiterate peasants, whom the Tsarist Okhrana, or secret police, would whip into a pogrom mob with a little vodka. To these Jews, every Christian is still just "Ivan," and if Ivan can now read, he still believes in fairy tales about Jesus. To this is added a sort of Classic Comics leftism, a remnant of the Lower East Side past: There is going to be another Depression and then the capitalists will turn around and find themselves a Hitler, just like in Germany. Then these Jews will race down to the nearest El-Al office and fly off to their Mediterranean mousehole. Never you mind the implications for America or the world, or even Israel, of an atomic U.S. in the clutches of another Hitler, because none of this has the slightest contact with reality, except for the undisputed fact that many tens of thousands of Jews, at least, think this scenario is entirely possible and even likely.

Forward—or Backward—to the West End Avenue Soviet!

There is another, equally unreal, version of the American Hitler that is believed by many leftists, particularly Jews. According to this script, the Depression hits and the wicked bosses call up Central Casting for an actor to play the Shickelgruber shtick. But the Jews play the prodigal and they return to their left-wing heritage. Then they, side by side with their "shvartzes," their Thursday-afternoon Black cleaning ladies, build barricades on West End Avenue, and the storm troopers are beaten off. The movie ends happily, with the establishment of the United Soviet Socialist States of North America.

Again, the only connection this chimera has with reality is that it is believed by many professed leftists, and liberals as well. Given the repeated economic problems of the capitalist world economy, it is obligatory to anticipate all manner of profound economic and social catastrophies in America's future. In every such case the capitalists will certainly pull every trick they know to maintain their power. But these vulgar notions of history repeating itself neglect the fact that the rich think.

Hitler lost. Why hand over power to a loser ideology, particularly one notorious for its irrational violence? The idea of a Nazi-like regime armed with the A-bomb is no more appealing to the wealthy than to anyone else. Besides, they know that wanting a dictator to crush their foes is one thing, getting him into office is quite another.

No important element in the Jewish population is now in opposition to capitalism. This is a significant plus for the post-Holocaust capitalists. Were they to start playing around with anti-Semitism again, it would push an enormous proportion of the Jews into the leftist camp. Additionally, other forces in the society would also be galvanized into sharp opposition by any such policy turn.

Fascism and anti-Semitism would only antagonize people without any profit to the system if the fascists did not crush the unions. The union bureaucrats know they would lose their power in such an event and would resist. Ditto the intelligentsia. Nor would Blacks have to be told twice what their fate would be. And they are not the isolated middle class Jews of Germany. They are a massive 12 percent minority, centrally located in all the major cities. Not a few white New Yorkers are racists, but how many of them would be interested in seeing a race riot in the subways?

More important, if, given our history, it is legitimate to speculate about a racist scenario developing in an economic crisis, anti-Semitism is another matter. In the early years of Italian Fascism, Mussolini pushed an anti-Semitic line, but his own ranks made him give it up. Historically, Italian nationalism had evolved as the opponent of the Church, which was the anti-Semitic force in Italian life, and the nationalists were philo-Jewish.

Germany, by contrast, had a long history of popular anti-Semitism, permeating the aristocracy, the middle class and the peasantry, and Hitler built on this. America is much more like Italy than Germany. The historic ideology is liberal, and anti-Semitism has been traditionally weak and is certainly so today. Anyone who thinks it is suddenly possible to conjure up such sentiments without historic roots is superficial and incapable of learning from the Italian case.

If nativist fascism ever had a chance to come to power it was in reaction to the civil rights struggle in the 1960s. And in fact there were White Citizens Councils all over the South. The vast majority made a conscious decision to stay away from anti-Semitism. Similarly, George Wallace stayed a country mile away from Jew-hatred. In the end, the believers in the idea that America will produce a mass anti-Semitic movement tell us only about themselves, their primitive understanding of European history, their isolation from the ordinary people of this country, their prejudices against them, and nothing more.

"Disaster"

Title II of the Federal Civil Rights Act of 1964 specifically exempts private clubs from its purview, and it is this which permits businessmen's clubs and country clubs to discriminate against Jews, Blacks and women. However, in 1969 Maine took things a step further, and prohibited any club licensed to sell liquor from discriminating, unless it is a specifically religious or ethnic organization. In other words, a Catholic club is legitimate, but not a club which excludes Catholics.

In 1974 Maryland passed a law withdrawing tax benefits from discriminatory clubs. Other localities bar governmental contracts with firms that subsidize their employees' dues to such clubs.

In April 1983 a "clubs bill" was introduced into the New York City Council, banning discrimination in any club with more than

100 members that offered regular meals and took money from non-members that used it for business appointments. However, the bill got stalled in committee. The Council is notorious as a collection of political hacks, who do nothing for their consti- tuents, except to register their prejudices. Many whites— including many Jews—in the boroughs dread Blacks moving into their neighborhoods. Additionally, the cops, the Catholic Church, and some Chassidic groups have been waging a fanatic fight against gay rights legislation. Therefore, although the entire Jew- ish Establishment was for the bill, and they can get the Council to support the invasion of Lebanon, they had to settle for an amend- ment exempting clubs with up to 400 members, before the Coun- cil would pass the measure in 1985.

It is no secret that America's capitalists are not the most fanatic supporters of human equality. They profited from segregation and have consistently paid women less than men for comparable work. Many of the larger businesses are deeply implicated in the doings of the apartheid regime in South Africa. But they know that they can't defend discrimination, and have reconciled themselves to government regulation on the matter.

The vast majority of Christian capitalists, particularly the younger ones, are not even remotely anti-Semitic. "Christian" capitalists is in fact a misnomer for many of the younger genera- tion. With each year, less and less of them even bother to list a religion in their entries in *Who's Who*. They go to the best schools with Jews, they work side by side with Jews and they live in the same rich neighborhoods with them. They are also in con- stant contact with them in the cultural world, and increasingly they intermarry with them.

They are not particularly impressed with the clubs. The younger generation of Americans is very informal and the clubs are too much into neckties at the table for them. And American youth do not feel at ease with their elders. If the Jewish Establish- ment had determined to fight for the original 100 limit, or even for a total outlawing of discrimination, the clubs would have been isolated even within the upper class, and probably would have caved in.

However, the Establishment was in no position to wage such a fight. Club discrimination primarily affects the upper crust of Jews, and many of these are completely indifferent to the prob- lem. They do not see themselves as suffering from it, certainly not to any significant extent. Clubs are simply not as important as they once were as meeting places. And these Jews are too prominent for anyone but a fool to want to exclude them from business deals. (Irving Shapiro, the ex-chairman of Du Pont, considers those who complain about club discrimination as "second- and third-raters who use it as a crutch.") And, as capitalists, they are not inclined to demonstrate for anyone's rights, even their own, because they identify protests and picket lines with the radicalism they detest. What is more, a substantial element of the Establishment are now "Jewish survivalists," and share the perspectives of America's richest dullard, Laurence Tisch of Loew's, who sees assimilation as a "disaster."[4] There is no pressure on them from ordinary Jews, who have no thought of going to such clubs. Even more important, many Jews don't want to have to rent apartments in their building to Blacks and Gays, and know that they can't get too sanctimonious any longer about such irrelevant discrimination against themselves without losing credibility in their fight against tougher fair housing laws.

"Warm and Friendly"

Every poll taken in the last several decades proves that the vast majority of Americans are not anti-Semitic. In 1937 Gallup asked the public "if your party nominated a generally well-qualified man for President and he happened to be a Jew, would you vote for him?" The public was evenly divided, 46 percent-46 percent. By 1958, 62 percent would have voted for a Jew, 68 percent would have voted for him in 1961, 77 percent in 1963, 80 percent in 1965, 82 percent in 1967, 86 percent in 1969. The vote would have dropped to 82 percent in 1978, when 12 percent said they would not vote for a Jew. That same year, 91 percent would have voted for a Catholic and 77 percent for a Black.

Jews are far better regarded than atheists, although even with them 40 percent would have voted for a qualified candidate in 1978, compared with only 18 percent in 1958.[5] Another Gallup poll showed the proportion of Americans who approved of marriages with Jews had risen from 59 percent in 1968 to 69 percent in 1978.[6]

In July 1981, the AJCommittee released a poll it had commissioned by the Yankelovich, Skelly and White research organization. The pollsters found "a significant decline" regarding many of the most hostile traditional Jewish stereotypes:

	1964	1981
Irritating faults	48%	29%
Shady business practices	48%	33%
Not as honest	34%	22%

However, the percentage who thought Jews have too much power increased from 13 percent in 1964 to 23 percent in 1981. Thirty-seven percent think that the Jews have "too much power in the business world." To put that in context, 17 percent think Italians have too much business power and 20 percent say that for Japanese-Americans. And while only a minority think Jews are dishonest, or too powerful, 57 percent think Jewish employers go out of their way to hire Jews, 53 percent think they stick together too much, and 52 percent think they always like being at the head of things. However, even these percentages were down from 1964, and the pollsters say that "They are not seen as particularly influential when it comes to government, politics, education and a variety of other areas."[7]

Not too much should be read into these figures. This is not Weimar Germany. America is Archie Bunker-land. Lots of folks will be quick to tell you a joke about a drunken Polack without meaning any harm. Jews are expected to have a talent for making money. And their alleged clannishness is often admired. When an Irishman comes here to raise money for the IRA he knows exactly who to hold up as a role model for the local narrowbacks: "Look at the Jews and Israel," he will say, and they will always nod their heads in agreement.

The general attitude towards Jews is highly favorable. Ninety-three percent believe Jews are hard working, 90 percent think they have a strong faith in God, which for yer typical A-murican is a positive trait, 86 percent think of them as "warm and friendly," and 79 percent say they have contributed much to American culture. In the aforementioned poll, 92 percent find them acceptable as neighbors, one percent more than Italians, 73 percent would vote for one of them for President, compared to 76 percent for Italians, and 66 percent have no objection to their child marrying one, compared to 72 percent for Italians, but only 48 percent for Blacks.

The marriage statistics tell us much about the great mass of Americans. Most of the 52 percent of the population who don't want their daughter to marry a Black are racists, although some are only concerned that mixed marriage is a tough row to hoe in this country. But the 24 percent who don't want an Italian son-in-law are still worrying about "the whore of Rome."

Very few of those who don't want their kid marrying a Jew have a Hitlerian concept of race. Many are older Blacks who share the old-fashioned Christian notion of the Jews as Christkillers. (Black-Jewish relations are so different from White-Jewish relations that the topic must be dealt with in a separate chapter.)

White Fundamentalism is a mixed bag re the Jews. The poll says they are more likely to be prejudiced, 25 percent vs. 18 percent for others, but many share Falwell's wacky notion that Zionism is part of God's design. The ones who are uptight about their kid marrying a Jew really think the only way you can go to heaven is by acknowledging Jesus as your personal savior, and they don't want any grandchild of theirs going to hell. This comes off as terribly naive to intellectuals, even to those still professing a religion, but these Bible-bashers are rarely malicious. They think Jews have a right to their own religion. They lack education and aren't philosophers—"po' people sure got some po' ways"—but life teaches them. Forty percent of all marriages involving Jews, and a higher percentage if we take in informal liaisons, are mixed marriages. We may be sure that in some cases the in-laws are Fundamentalists. When their first boy who goes to college comes home with a Jewish wife you may be sure that they are upset. But most accept her sooner or later. And if you know anything at all about these folks you know that they are going to love their grandchildren to death.

A November 1981 Gallup poll asked which groups the public thought had too much influence in an election year and, again, it is clear that vast majority of the people don't see Jews or Zionists as any menace.

Oil Companies	70%
Unions	46%
Arab interests	30%
Blacks	14%
Jews	11%
Born Agains	10%
Catholic church	9%
Zionists	4%[8]

The decisive factor in the popular attitude toward Jews is that the older generation with its prejudices is dying off, and not being replaced. The poll categorized non-Jews as prejudiced, neutrals and unprejudiced, with 23 percent being prejudiced, 32 percent neutral and 45 percent unprejudiced.

Of those 18-29, 16 percent were prejudiced, 36 percent neutral and 48 percent unprejudiced. Of those 55 plus, 32 percent were prejudiced, 37 percent neutrals and only 32 percent were unprejudiced. As the neutrals were, for the most part, Southerners and other country folks with little contact with Jews, who had neither any hostility nor positive feelings towards Jews, they can largely be discounted for our purposes.

At a time when there are now far more college students than farmers, it is the older, less educated who are the prejudiced while the new educated are increasingly unprejudiced. The pollsters make it quite clear that there has been an immense change in the popular culture since "the 1960s," i.e., since the civil rights movement and the Vietnam anti-war movement:

> Americans have grown increasingly tolerant of a variety of lifestyles and beliefs. They are more willing to accept men with beards, the rights of atheists, foreigners, etc.[9]

"Mordant Thought: Being Jewish Was Easier When It Was Hard to Be a Jew"

And what of the Jews? How do they think the American people see them? Yankelovich and his associates questioned 174 Jews: "The perceptions of American Jews regarding how non-Jews feel about them is consistently more negative than the beliefs actually expressed by non-Jews."[10]

	non-Jews' views	*Jews' perception of non-Jews' views*
Jews have more money than most people	56%	83%
Jews more ambitious	45%	79%
Too much power in business	32%	76%
Too much power in U.S.	20%	53%
Push where not wanted	16%	55%

Only 13 percent of those who know that Jews have more money than most people say they "are bothered" by that. But 77 percent of the Jews think most of them are concerned.[11]

Both non-Jews and Jews were asked if they thought an increase in anti-Semitism was possible. Seven percent of non-Jews thought it was possible in their own area and 21 percent thought it possible elsewhere in the country. No less than 40 percent of the Jews thought it possible in their own area, and 67 percent elsewhere.[12] Although polls show that the majority of Americans find Jews quite acceptable as marriage partners and potential Presidents, the pollsters report that "most Jewish respondents believe that Jews are seen as unacceptable."[13]

These statistics command frank discussion. Today a sober estimate would be that about as high a percentage of Jews are prejudiced against gentiles as gentiles are against Jews. The roots of this deep-rooted folk feeling was discussed by Nahum Goldmann in his last book, *The Jewish Paradox:*

> The Jews are the most separatist people in the world. Their belief in the notion of the chosen people is the basis of their entire religion. . . . The Jews have intensified their separation from the non-Jewish world; they have rejected, and still do reject, mixed marriages; they have put up one wall after another to protect their existence as a people apart, and have built their ghettoes with their own hands, from the *shtetl* of Eastern Europe to the *mellah* of Morocco. . . .

He explained that:

> One of the great phenomena of Jewish psychology . . . lies in having created a thoroughly ingenious defense mechanism against the politico-economic situation acting upon them, against persecution and exile. This mechanism can be described in a few words: the Jews saw their persecutors as an inferior race. . . . We lived in a rural setting, and most of my grandfather's patients were peasants. Every Jew felt ten or a hundred times the superior of these lowly tillers of the soil: he was cultured, learned Hebrew, knew the Bible, studied the Talmud—in other words he knew that he stood head and shoulders above these illiterates . . . the only thing that mattered was surviving until the coming of the Messiah, and not worrying too much about "other people's" reality.[14]

The orthodox, and many Conservatives, believe that anti-

Semitism is eternal, that other people must hate them as the Chosen People, and 20th-century anti-Semitism has only confirmed them in this sectarian absurdity. But many Jews far removed from the ancestral faith see themselves as a sort of secular chosen people, better educated and with higher incomes than the broad masses, and therefore envied by them. In the end, their assumption is just as fallacious as the openly chauvinist conception of the Orthodox. Ordinary Americans don't hate the rich, they just want to rise themselves, or at least to see their children get up in the world. Education is seen as the ladder to success and, if anything, many people want their kids to be serious students, like the Jewish youth, whom they know all go to college.

Since the Jews are in fact better educated and have higher incomes than the broad population, they don't "hang out" with workers, and don't really know how they think. What is more, as is frequently the case with atheists, they are contemptuous of those who are still religious, be they gentiles or Jews. Given the long history of Christian anti-Semitism, and given their social distance from the common herd, they assume its still out there in full force. And as with liberals in general, they are cultural elitists. They equate tolerance and higher education and tend to see the masses as unenlightened on all questions. They can't quite grasp that millions of ordinary folks have been educated, in greater or lesser degree, by the impact of the civil rights and anti-war movements, and that therefore tolerance of all minorities has risen and will continue to rise.

On one crucial question regarding gentiles, secular Jews dramatically differ from the religious. Many wouldn't dream of marrying an Orthodox Jew, because they think the kosher laws and other Talmudic restrictions laughable, but have no hesitation abut marrying Christians and lapsed Christians. On the other hand, organized Jewry, the religious and Zionists, are as intensely hostile to mixed marriage as the most fanatic Fundamentalist Bible bashers or racists.

Ancient Judaism sought proselytes, but later pressure from the medieval Church caused the Talmudists to declare that a convert is as hard to bear as a sore. Today's Orhodox and Conservative rabbis will reluctantly accept converts but do nothing to encourage them. The Reform also oppose mixed marriage, but then do try to involve non-Jewish spouses in their congregations. Reform rabbi Howard Berman described organized Jewry's atti-

tude in 1984 in *Issues,* published by the American Council for
Judaism:

> For many Jews the rising rate of intermarriage is a frightening and
> dangerous threat to the survival of our faith and our people . . .
> this is the perspective that many, many Jews have . . . perhaps
> even the majority of Jewish community leaders and Jewish
> parents. . . . Most rabbis—all Orthodox and Conservative and
> most Reform clergy—refuse to officiate at intermarriage
> ceremonies. For the traditionalists, intermarriage . . . is tan-
> tamount to treason. . . . Most Reform rabbis also see intermar-
> riages as a threat to Jewish survival, and will not participate in
> such weddings in any way. Although the Reform movement leaves
> the final decision . . . to the individual rabbi . . . the official posi-
> tion is one of strong discouragement.[15]

Nathan Perlmutter developed the Establishment's later-day
medievalism in his crank screed, *The Real Anti-Semitism in America.* Commenting on increasing gentile acceptance of mixed marriage he dryly remarked that "it is hardly good news for Jews
concerned with communal seepage through intermarriage."
Which leads this Maimonides for our times to a "Mordant
thought: Being Jewish was easier when it was hard to be a
Jew."[16]

As with their Christian counterparts, most Jewish bigots usually end up accepting their child's spouse. But this can not alter
the "mordant" reality that "official" Jewry, the sects and the
Zionists, oppose and denounce inter-marriage. On Saturday,
August 6, 1983, this writer was in Jerusalem's Independence Park
when about 50 young Americans started rehearsing skits. One
was about how a young mixed-marriage couple quarreled over
what to name their child. The next told of a young Italian who
took his Jewish wife home to a father who was anti-Semitic. They
said they were from the American Zionist youth federation.
Presumably, when they returned to the U.S. they would perform
in synagogues, as only Nazis dare rally in American parks against
mixed marriage.

Only five boys wore yarmulkes. Most of these Zionists did not
care if Jews heeded the kosher dietary laws, or any Judaic tenet,
as long as they upheld the sexual kosher law and married Jewish
blood. To be sure, most secularized Zionists do not think Jews
biologically superior to others, though many privately believe

Jews are smarter. Perlmutter and his co-thinkers abhor ethnic mixed marriage for two reasons: Intermarried Jews rarely migrate to Israel. And they know it usually leads Jews away from the American Jewish community, rather than bringing it new real strength.

"So? Is it good for the Jews?" That cynical rejoinder—actually meaning never mind if anything is good for humanity, is it good for business?—is the classic reaction of Jewish philistines to everything progressive. However, in this case, the only answer is yes. Intermarriage is good for the Jews. Of course, intermarriage on a massive scale spells the end of a separate community of any size. So what? Sexual assimilation is a disaster only to ideologues who desperately try to lock the Jews up in an ethnic/religious broom closet. Although every literate person knows his celebrated phrase, few now read Israel Zangwill's turn-of-the-century play, *The Melting Pot,* but he told the Jews and the world what was going to happen, and why it is progressive:

> MENDEL: . . . you can not marry her.
> DAVID: (In pained amaze) Uncle! (Slowly) Then your hankering after the synagogue was serious after all.
> MENDEL: It was not so much the synagogue—it is the call of our blood through immemorial generations.
> DAVID: *You* say that! You who have come to the heart of the Crucible, where the roaring fires of God are fusing our race with all the others.
> MENDEL: (Passionately) Not *our* race, not your race and mine.
> DAVID: What immunity has our race? (Meditatively) The pride and the prejudice, the dreams and the sacrifices, the traditions and the superstitions, the fasts and the feasts, things noble and things sordid—they must all into the Crucible.
> MENDEL: (With prophetic fury) The Jew has been tried in a thousand fires and only tempered and annealed.
> DAVID: Fires of hate, not fires of love. That is what melts.
> MENDEL: (Sneeringly) So I see.[17]

Studies based on the 1980 Census show 27 percent of non-Hispanic whites married to spouses whose ancestry was entirely their own. Another 26 percent married spouses whose origins partially overlap theirs. Forty-six percent are married entirely outside their ethnic group. Young white Americans born since 1960 are now 60.2 percent mixed ethnically, compared to 31.4

percent for those born before 1920. Seventy percent of children born of Italian ancestry since 1970 are of mixed parentage. Of those of Italian descent under 30 who have married, 72 percent of males and 64 percent of females have married someone with no Italian parentage.[18] More than three-quarters of the Irish in the U.S. are now marrying outside their nationality.[19] With Poles it is 80 percent.

Hispanics still tend to marry within their language grouping, but it must be remembered that many southwestern Hispanics live in counties with Spanish-speaking majorities. Nevertheless, 29 percent of all Hispanics now marry non-Hispanics.

The census asks no questions regarding religion, but we know that the intermarriage rate involving different Protestant sects is enormous. The best estimate of experts at the National Opinion Research Center at the University of Chicago is that one-third of marriages in larger urban Catholic archdioceses are interfaith, i.e., with Protestants in the main. Professor Egon Mayer, president of the Association for the Sociological Study of Jewry, declares that 40 percent of all Jews who have married in the last decade have intermarried. If we add young Jews living informally with non-Jews, we may legitimately speculate that a majority of young American Jews are presently "intermarried." Even if we proceed cautiously, we may say, with scientific certainty, that if the 50 percent mark has not yet been passed, it will be.

America is still in a racial gridlock, but this is beginning to break down. A majority of American Indians—53.7 percent— marry non-Indians, mostly whites, an astonishing figure given that many Indians live on remote reservations. Twenty-eight percent of Asians marry non-Asians. Almost 99 percent of non-Hispanic whites married whites, and 99 percent of Black women and 97 percent of men married within their race, but Black-white inter- marriage is rising.

Only 0.8 percent of Black men born before 1920 intermarried, but six percent born since 1950 intermarried. In 1970, all interra- cial couples amounted to only 310,000. By 1980 there were 613,000 such couples, or 1.3 percent of all couples. Interracial marriage is certain to rise with the general increase in education, as we already see that both for Blacks and whites those who marry outside their race tend to be better educated than those who marry within.[20]

Naturally, it goes without saying that hard-core anti-Semites do not hate Jews because Jews do not want to sleep with them. Or because Zionists are fanatic in their zealotry for Israel. Nevertheless, Jewish chauvinism definitely reinforces the milder antipathies that still linger on. In 1964, 39 percent of America thought its Jews were more loyal to Israel than to the U.S. Yankelovich says 48 percent now believe it. To be sure, gentiles involved with the broad spectrum of Jews know many are indifferent to Zionism and some even oppose it. They know the majority of Jews do not despise non-Jews, that the bulk of the young are exploding away from Jewishness, with many of David's philosophy. But it is easy to see why gentiles should see the imploding minority of Mendels—who proclaim themselves *the* Jews—as indeed the Jews. Ditto the broad public, reading letters to the editor from presidents of "American Jewish" organizations, defending Israel's latest war crime, or listening to Meir Kahane on some talk show.

If readers doubt that this minority exists, infinitely more loyal to Jews than to humanity at large, they are urged to go to Orthodoxy's pride, Yeshiva University in Manhattan. Some of the professors and students will be only too happy to tell them: America exists for one purpose alone—to arm Israel. Beyond that, its sons and daughters are *shagetzes* and *shiksas:* "blemishes."

"No Discernable Political Motivation"

The Anti-Defamation League issues an annual *Audit of Anti-Semitic Incidents.* The ADL started issuing the audits in 1979, when there were 129 vandalisms, including attempted bombings and arsons and cemetary desecrations. The number that year and 1980—377—may have been on the low side, as many Jewish organizations and individuals were still reluctant to give any publicity to such events, particularly the minor ones.

The number reported jumped to 974 in 1981, but declined to 829 in 1982 and further declined to 670 in 1983. The incidents rose again, by 6.7 percent, to 715 in 1984. That same year there were also 369 threats, by mail or phone, and assaults against Jewish individuals, or institutions, an increase from 350 in 1983.

Most of the incidents were minor: swastika graffiti on synagogues or tombstones, or crank mail and the like. Of the incidents involving institutions in 1984, only three were bombings, one was an attempted bombing, nine were arsons and eight were attempted arsons. Between 1979 and 1984 only five of the 3,694 incidents involving vandalism, arson or bombings showed evidence of being the work of organizations. Under pressure from Jewish organizations and others, several states have passed laws making it a special offense to desecrate religious institutions, and generally speaking the police often now go to considerable lengths to catch the perpetrators of even the most minor of graffiti incidents.

As a result, 115 people were arrested in 1983 and 84 in 1984. As in previous years, the vast majority, 73 of 84, or 87 percent, in 1984 were teenagers.[21] For all the Establishment's never-ending denunciations of "Black anti-Semitism," a 1981 report by the AJCommittee said most incidents had "no discernable political motivation" and were the work of "white teenagers," many, as on Long Island in New York State, "between 14 and 16 years old."[22] In New York City, most of these kids were Catholics.[23]

Segregation Is Utterly Dead and No One Wants It Back

The Nazis' defeat, coupled with the enormity of the Holocaust horrors, profoundly discredited all forms of anti-Semitism. The Catholic Church's subsequent repudiation of its anti-Semitic tradition further isolated the Jew-haters. But is was not until 1965 that the U.S. abandoned its own racist immigration laws, in the wake of the Black civil rights explosion.

America has dramatically changed since the 1960s. New York and San Francisco now have Jewish mayors. Los Angeles, Chicago, Washington and many other central cities have Black mayors. Millions of immigrants, legal and illegal, have poured in from the four corners of the world, radically altering the demography of the U.S. There are now hundreds of thousands of foreign students here. Hindus now own half the motels in the country. Tennessee and other southern states eagerly court Japanese investors, and a 1985 poll showed most Americans think Japan produces better quality goods than their own country.

All polls show that hostility towards Blacks is shrinking. Even George Wallace, once the arch-segregationist, says segregation is utterly dead and no one wants it back. But racism has not vanished. While O.J. Simpson racing through airports is the symbol of efficiency, and most white Americans only wish that they had enough money to move into *his* neighborhood, tens of millions of whites do not want Blacks moving onto their block. Whites know millions of Blacks are deeply religious, and think the Blacks they know on the job are OK, but they dread the Black lumpen-proletariat, with its colossal crime rate.

White Americans are thus of two minds. Blacks and other minorities have made irreversible gains, yet deep-rooted antagonisms exist. The contemporary condition of the KKK and the Nazis therefore reflects present-day reality. Millions of whites are racist, millions more just don't want Blacks around them. These facts give the fascists a toehold in politics. Nevertheless the Black position is so powerful in the central cities that it is impossible for the ruling class to even contemplate subsidizing any movement to restore segregation, much less to destroy democracy and create a concentration camp regime. Without hope of ever gaining the patronage of the rich as in Italy and Germany, native fascism has been reduced from Nazis to nutsies. The racist gangs are charging off the political stage, but they are going out shooting.

In November 1984 the ADL issued a 1984 Status Report, *The KKK and the Neo-Nazis*. It declared the KKK "weaker and more isolated and fragmented than it was two years ago." It no longer had the ability to conduct large rallies as it did in the early 1980s. "An aura of defeatism hovers over the hooded order."

Imperial Wizard Robert Shelton of the United Klans had to go to work as a used-car salesman. Apparently the UKA was severely hurt by the publicity around the lynching conviction of one of its activists in 1981, for murdering a Black youth. In 1983, another Klan, The Invisible Empire, filed for bankruptcy. Another rival Klan, the Knights of the Ku Klux Klan, has been torn by splits since the imprisonment of its leader for his role in a failed Klan-Nazi attempt to invade Dominica in the Caribbean.

The Klans are in steep decline in their traditional southern strongholds. Another Klan group, the paramilitary "Camp My Lai" in Alabama, went out of business after 10 Klansmen were indicted for a 1979 shootout with civil rights marchers in Decatur, Alabama. The only exceptions to the sharp decline in the region were in northern Georgia, where a Klan unit has grown from 100 to 300 in three years, and in North Carolina, where the Carolina Knights, a neo-Nazi grouping with members who were involved in a 1979 shootout in Greensboro, when five members of the Communist Workers Party were killed, remains stable at about 120 members.

Decline is evident elsewhere. In Connecticut a Klan was able to attract 200 sympathizers to a rally in Meridan in 1981. A faction fight has brought it down to where it only attracts 30. Klans are virtually inactive in New York, New Jersey, Pennsylvania and West Virginia. Two groups have 25 members each in Maryland. In Illinois, there is only one active Klan, with less than 100 members. Involvement in violence and subsequent arrests have hurt Klans in California and Colorado.

The ADL's analysis for the decline of the Klans is correct:

> The basic reason . . . has been its inability to find a viable means to achieve its segregationist goals, or even influence the course of events in that direction. . . . The key battle was waged, and lost, in the 1960s. . . . The KKK's limited revival of the 1970s and early 1980s was an effort to exploit discontent over such issues as busing, racial quotas and immigration in the hope that America's progress in race relations could be reversed. That hope . . . was a pipedream.[24]

The Klans are caught in a time warp. They can't restore segregation, but if you want to stop busing and quotas, Ronnie is your kind of guy, not a hooded used-car salesman, and its sympathizers have been going into "respectable" racist politics, i.e., the Republican Party.

The neo-Nazis are even more isolated. At its height, George Lincoln Rockwell's American Nazi Party had no more than 1,000 members. The party began to splinter after his assassination in 1967 and today the ADL's spies estimate that all of the groups combined do not add up to 500 nationwide. The KKK is deeply rooted in American history, but the Nazis strike even most racists as a foreign ideology, and many Nazis drifted off into the Klans.

These later-day fascists know from the beginning that they are joining movements dedicated to violence. When they read about terrorist actions, by friend or foe, they ask themselves when they are going to stop talking and pick up the gun. Now, more isolated then ever, and reduced to hard-core fanatics, they reinforce each other in their madness. Eventually they become little more than murder waiting to happen. Here is a list, by no means complete, of some of the crimes committed by these nutsies in recent years:

October 21, 1979: Joseph Franklin, ex-Nazi and Klansman, murdered an interracial couple in Oklahoma City. On January 12,

1980, he murdered a Black in Indianapolis. Two days later he killed another Black. On August 20, 1980, he murdered two Blacks who were jogging with white women in Salt Lake City.

March 21, 1981: Henry Hays of the KKK murdered a Black youth, chosen at random, "to show Klan strength in Alabama."

April 1981: John Hinckley, Jr., who had been photographed at a 1978 Nazi meeting in St. Louis, attempted to assassinate Reagan.

October 13, 1982: Perry Wharthan murdered a fellow member of a neo-Nazi group whom he suspected of being an informer.

In 1983 Gordon Kahl, a tax-protest loon and anti-Semite, killed two federal marshals and then a sheriff when finally surrounded in a concrete bunker.

The ADL's spies reported that these murders actually began to inspire the remnant groupings. Eventually The Order was organized in 1983, in Hayden Lake, Idaho, a split-off from a nation-wide network known as the Aryan Nation. Time it was for "stout-hearted Whitemen" to rise up against the "Zionist Occupation Government." By the time 23 survivors were indicted, they machine-gunned a Jewish talk show host in Denver, killed a suspected informer, committed two armored car robberies, counterfeited some cash to pay for their revolt, firebombed a Seattle porno house, set fire to a Boise synagogue, and killed some G-men and smokies as the damned ZOG closed in on them.

Readers may think this is all out of a movie about Pretty Boy Floyd and other rural folk heroes of the 1930s, and certainly that was an important part of their self-image. But a number of them looked like typical modern bearded college students. They used some of their hot cash to set up a racist computer network, and one of their problems was how to keep the troops from blowing their money on cocaine.

"Fritz the Cat . . . Contributed to the Atmosphere of Anti-Jewish Denigration"

Of all Jewish legends, that of the *Golem* is the best known to the wider world. As the tale goes, a 16th-century cabalist, rabbi Judah Low of Prague, created an unbeatable protector for the Jews by molding clay into the form of a man, and giving him life by putting a script with the secret name of God in his mouth.

The creature, Yosef Golem, soon routed the Jew-haters. As

Jews were pious then, the rabbi took care to make sure that Yosef dutifully observed the sabbath by taking out the script. Except that once he forgot, and the creature ran himself into the ground. Supposedly the legend is the basis of Mary Wollstonecraft Shelley's *Frankenstein*. The Anti-Defamation League is the Establishment's golem. Also its Frankenstein monster.

Although the ADL was organized in 1913 to deal with anti-Semitism, its literature virtually never even hints at its role during the Hitler era. This is understandable, given that it put up no defense worthy of the name. Its parent, the B'nai B'rith fraternal lodge, opposed boycotts and demonstrations against Germany in the 1930s. Nor did the ADL organize Jews against the violence of the native fascist Coughlanite Christian Front and the German-American Bund. It did not demonstrate against the Bund when it met, 20,000 strong, in New York's Madison Square Garden, on February 20, 1939. Only the Trotskyists of the tiny Socialist Workers Party called for a confrontation, but at least 50,000 Jews and others showed up. Despite 1,780 cops who tried to protect the brownshirts, the enraged demonstrators drove the Nazis off the streets. The Bund's nation-wide organization campaign was stopped dead.

The ADL has learned absolutely nothing in the ensuing decades. It wants government support for Israel, so its defense strategy is still strictly legalist and official. It calls for "broad-based community denunciation" of the KKK and Nazis, meaning statements from the political and ministerial windbags. As more than mere words are required, the ADL urges increased FBI spying on them, laws against vandalizing religious buildings, and, as the Klans always claim they are organizing against future Communist-inspired rioting, the outlawing of private paramilitary camps. But the most effective form of opposition to the racists is always strongly condemned. The ADL claims that "street brawls contribute nothing to the solution of the problem." They "have provided the Kluxers with an alibi to justify their possession of weapons." They denounce leftists who do fight the fascists as "seeking to exploit the issue of right-wing extremism in order to strengthen the forces of left-wing extremism."[25]

The ADL's avowed purpose is to defend Jews against anti-Semitism, and it freely admits that the left fights the Jew-haters, yet it openly proclaims that it sends spies into radical organizations. In the book, *The New Anti-Semitism,* two directors of the

ADL, Arnold Forster and Benjamin Epstein, brazenly described closed conventions of the Socialist Workers Party and declared that:

> The ADL has traditionally viewed close monitoring of extremists activities as part of its obligation to the Jewish and American communities. Therefore its representatives often attend open meetings, conventions and conferences of extremist groups (left wing and right wing).

They rationalize their spying:

> The SWP . . . take(s) umbrage when its anti-Israel, anti-Zionist extremism is called anti-Semitism. . . . Its domestic political course has been clearly anti-Jewish. . . . Although its spokesmen have been careful to avoid the use of crude anti-Semitic phraseology, the SWP's program and activities . . . have been totally hostile . . . whenever Jews have been under attack from anti-Semites who happen to be black, the SWP has consistently joined the fray against the Jews. . . . In this respect, the Trotskyists offer salvation to individual "revolutionary" Jews in the same way that bygone reactionary clerical regimes in Europe offered immunity to "their" Jews, by allowing them to convert to Catholicism.[26]

Of course! Now let's try to keep up with the fancy footwork. The SWP busts up Nazi rallies. It is "careful" not to utilize anti-Semitic phrases. It welcomes Jews into its ranks and indeed into its leadership. Therefore it is "clearly" anti-Jewish, and the ADL has the solemn right and duty to spy on it. Get it? No? Well, then, maybe a few more such gems from the ever-brilliant duo will make it clear, once and for all, just who are the great enemies of the Jews in these perilous times:

> Film cartoons—like the X-rated *Fritz the Cat,* which was translated to the screen from one of the new "comix" and which had a tasteless synagogue sequence . . . contributed to the atmosphere of anti-Jewish denigration, along with anti-Jewish stereotyping found in such full-length 1972 feature films as Woody Allen's *Everything You've Always Wanted to Know About Sex, Such Good Friends* and *Made for Each Other* in addition, of course, to *Portnoy.* . . . Capping and capitalizing on the vogue for sick "ethnic" humor and dehumanization was . . . *The National Lampoon* . . . October 1972. A major item was a mock comic

book entitled *"The Ventures of Zimmerman,"* a put-down on folk-singer Bob Dylan, drawn with Jewish features, blue yarmulke, and portrayed as a scheming, avaricious, money-hungry "superman" type who poses as a simple idealistic folk singer. . . . The mock cover . . . bore a "seal" reading "Approved by the Elders of Zion." . . . Are the editors of *Lampoon* anti-Semitic? Probably not. But they have made a signal contribution to the perpetuation of those destructive stereotypes—like the *Stuermer* cartoons—so intimately associated with the annihilation of European Jewry.[27]

"No . . . Congressional Committee Has Shown Any Interest"

The truth is that although the ADL still monitors the for-keeps Jew-haters, these are no longer seen as a threat. Hence Forster and Epstein's talk about the "new" anti-Semitism, and the Perl-mutters' "real" anti-Semitism. The ADL's "real" passion is Israel, thus the *1984 Audit*'s homily on how to "really" look at anti-Semitism:

> It should be borne in mind that while the Audit provides a useful yardstick . . . it is not the only such yardstick. Anti-Semitism in the United States manifests itself in various ways: In . . . political campaigns: In the anti-Semitic rhetoric of various Arab representatives in . . . the United Nations; In the anti-Semitism promoted around the world by the Soviet Union in the guise of "anti-Zionism"; In the anti-Israel and anti-Zionist propaganda carried on by pro-Arab and pro-PLO organizations in the U.S. that often tends to mask hostility to Jews; In the propaganda activities of organized right-wing anti-Jewish hate groups. . . ; In the activities of radical leftist organizations such as the Communist Party USA whose propaganda against Israel and Zionism attacks the most basic concerns of the overwhelming majority of Jews.[28]

There are several glaring errors in the statement. For openers, the "overwhelming majority of Jews" are not sacred cows, not if you believe in democracy. Don't minorities have the right to oppose majorities? And clearly, as American Jews have no right of veto over the policies of the American people vis-à-vis the Middle East, American radicals, including Jewish radicals, have every legal and moral right to oppose Zionism and Israel.

The statement is in factual error re the CP. It opposes Zionism as an ideology, but insists that Israel has a right to exist. In fact it is denounced by other leftists for its conservative stand. Various policies of the Soviet Union concerning its Jews and Israel have already been dealt with.

When discussing Arabs at the UN, it must be recalled that there are 19 Arab states. They are not united any more than are the Spanish-speaking nations of Latin America. In fact most are, if anything, overcautious in distinguishing between Zionism and Judaism and Jews.

This writer has published in *Arab Perspectives,* the publication of the Arab League's UN office, as have many other Jews. On one occasion, concerning an article, "The Growing Crisis of American Zionism," in its July 1981 issue, the editor insisted that I delete a remark that young Jews dislike the ostentatous synagogues of the Conservative sect and feel that they should be sold and the money used to help the poor. The statement is true, and I explained that no one would dare to criticize the magazine for my saying so. Many Jews would come to its defense if it did so, because they would either agree with the youths or at least agree with my right to report the facts. No matter, the editor would not permit even a factual criticism of Judaism in the publication.

There have been very few anti-Semitic statements by Arab diplomats, as anyone can see by reading Forster and Epstein and the Perlmutters. The two major offenders are Libya and Saudi Arabia. The December 9, 1983, *New York Times* reported an incredible comment by the chief Libyan delegate:

> It is high time for the United States in particular to realize that the Jewish Zionists here in the United States attempt to destroy Americans. Look around New York. Who are the owners of pornographic film operations and houses? Is it not the Jews who are exploiting the American people and trying to debase them?

The paper went on to say that "Dr. Treiki's comments were described by some officials here as extraordinary in tone, even in an organization that regularly hears angry attacks on Israel."[29] Qaddafi is looked upon by the vast majority of educated Arabs as a head case, especially so after he told the leaders of the PLO that they should have committed suicide rather than withdraw from Beirut in 1982. Domestically, his only impact is on the Black Muslims, whom he has loaned five million dollars. But they are not even mentioned in the *Audit,* and rightly so, since they are never involved in attacks on Jews.

The February 11, 1985, *New York Times* ran an ad by the ADL, quoting a remark by Maarouf Al-Dawalibi, a Saudi delegate, speaking at a UN Seminar on Religious Tolerance and Freedom no less, claiming that "If a Jew does not drink every year the blood of a non-Jewish man, then he will be damned for eternity."[30] It is to be understood that the Saudi regime is one of the most reactionary in the world and that for a Christian or Jew to enter Mecca means the death penalty. Women are forbidden to drive cars. Saudi Arabia is an absolute monarchy.

No better proof of the depraved nature of the American government exists than the fact that it sells arms to these criminals, and has made it clear, at every turn, that it would send troops to Saudi Arabia to defend the royal gangster family against revolution.

As is known, the ADL and the Establishment do not object to this stance by our own criminals, they likewise have no desire for the left to overthrow the Saudis. The lobby only opposes sales of those weapons to the Saudis that might be used against Israel. At any rate, the Saudis are loathed by the immense majority of Palestinians here, and are seen by all progressive Americans as nothing more than creatures of the State Department. Aside from some tenuous connections with right-wing anti-Semites, their real ties are to the oil industry, which, for all its other sins, is not involved in pushing anti-Semitism here. At their worst, they are naturally unwilling to send Jews to work in Saudi oilfields.

The PLO has been previously faulted for its profound errors re terrorism, but the ADL's charge that "propaganda" by pro-PLO groups here "often" masks anti-Jewish attitudes is untrue, and there can be no doubt that the ADL is deliberately misleading the public. The PLO has observer status at the UN, and often speaks there, always in the tone of Arafat's November 14, 1974, speech to the General Assembly:

> We deplore all those crimes committed against the Jews; we also deplore the real discrimination suffered by them because of their faith. In my formal capacity as chairman of the Palestine Liberation Organization and as leader of the Palestinian revolution, I proclaim before you that when we speak of our common hopes for the Palestine of tomorrow we include in our perspective all Jews now living in Palestine who choose to live with us there in peace and without discrimination. We offer them the most generous solution that we might live together in a framework of just peace in our democratic Palestine.[31]

That speech, and all subsequent PLO statements at the UN, are in keeping with its conscious policy regarding its world-wide propaganda. The leading Zionist specialist on contemporary anti-Semitism is Professor Yehuda Bauer, Director of the International Centre for the Study of Antisemitism at the Hebrew University in Jerusalem. In October 1984, the savant published an article in *Midstream:*

> A footnote is necessary here: the PLO, apart from the 1968 Palestine Covenant with its clearly anti-Jewish definitions of the right of the Jews not only to Palestine but to considerations as a separate national entity, has desisted very carefully from employing anti-Semitic imagery in the past few years. Violent as the attacks on Israel and its policies may be, official PLO propagandists seem to have avoided any statements that could be interpreted in any way as anti-Jewish.[32]

The PLO's left-wing student supporters here, and their American sympathizers, battle the Jew-haters in the streets. On November 27, 1982, 40 Kluxers tried to march through Washington. As is well-known, the right of murderous racists to march through a 70 percent Black city is a sacred right, for which Black soldiers have willingly given their lives in wars. Therefore, local Black Democrats could do no less than have their cops defend the KKK in Washington.

The pro-Israel *Jewish Week* decried the fact that:

> Some 500 pro-Palestine Liberation Organization supporters . . . joined a mob of anti-Ku Klux Klan demonstrators in last Saturday's three-hour riot . . . reporters have evidence, supported by photos, that the 500 PLO sympathizers were in the forefront of the mob . . . some of them also hurled pro-Arafat banners at officers.[33]

What monsters! The Palestinian and American Bolshies had originally planned to demonstrate in New York but decided to go to Washington for the anti-KKK protest because, as their spokeswoman told the press, "racism and oppression, be they on a national or international level, require a united and cooperative opposition."[34]

Most people would think that the Establishment would at least maintain a dignified silence if they could not hail the Palestinians for taking on the Kluxers. Instead, the *Jewish Week* complained

that " no member of Congress, let alone any congressional committee, has shown any interest in trying to pinpoint the source of
funds for such mass trips . . . ostensibly . . . to protest the KKK
but actually to undermine U.S.-Israel relations."[35] Washington's
Black Democratic congressional delegate Walter Fauntroy
denounced the "Tarzan complex" of "white outside agitators . . .
inciting our youth."[36]

Nor in fact do most Jews support breaking up hate-mongers'
rallies. A 1981 poll by San Francisco's Jewish Community Relations Council revealed that 82 percent of the local Jews
disagreed, 56 percent "strongly," with busting up Nazi meetings.
This aroused the ire of one of the local community leaders, Earl
Raab, who, in his earlier leftist phase, had been one of those at
the Garden punch-up in 1939. He pointed out that they simply
didn't think they were in any danger. He was right. A few years
before, in the 1970s, the local Nazis set up a bookstore across the
street from a synagogue in the same city. The middle-aged,
middle-class congregation, many of them originally from Germany, carefully thought it over, decided that they had a responsibility to act—and they took crowbars into the den and battered it
to pieces. But this type of action is the exception. Within the
Zionist milieu, only the terrorist Jewish Defense League and the
split-off Jewish Defense Organization fight Nazism. Such actions,
which contrast with the passivity and legalism of the major organizations, give the arch-rightists legitimacy in the eyes of many
youths, and others as well.

"The Question Is," Said Humpty Dumpty, "Which Is to Be the Master—That's All"

Most liberals, not merely Jews, believe that Nazis and Klansmen
are fully entitled to freedom of speech. They are fond of quoting
Voltaire: "I disapprove of what you say, but I will defend to the
death your right to say it," and have indeed made that tag into
their secular religion. Thus Noam Chomsky feels free to say that
"I, for one, would certainly not deny the right of free expression
to Hitler."[38]

They are quite wrong, on a number of grounds.

The left has always fought the fascists on principle, but it also
has a perfectly valid special reason to fight them now. At present
the nutsies are no danger to either Jews or Blacks as groups, or to

democracy. Were they to murder even a handful of Jews or Blacks on purely racial grounds, they would be rounded up. In fact when a synagogue is defaced by swastikas we see politicians rushing to appear to wash away the paint, ever quick to denounce the forces of evil when in fact they are reasonably certain the forces of evil is some acne-faced kid of 15. But when a left-wing group's office is shot into, these same worthies are nowhere to be seen, and the cops, who hate the left, usually just go through the motions of making an investigation. Few right-wing terrorists ever seem to get caught. In "attacking" the fascists, the left is actually defending itself.

There is another, more important, reason for bashing them. Objectively racism is a long-term losing proposition. But the nutsies don't want to accept that. Given that there are still millions of racists, they can still recruit even if we know they cannot win. At this stage, 40 crackpots were easily routed in Washington by thousands of Blacks, Palestinians and "Tarzans." But "nits will be lice." Were they to grow, even to a few hundred in some localities, their potential for violence would be enormous. Bash them now and they stay small and demoralized. Let them rally means let them recruit. To let them recruit means, inevitably, that they will kill.

Nor can the problem be solved by calling on the authorities to outlaw or infiltrate them. If they do that, they will then use it as justification for spying on left wing "terrorists" or "friends of terrorists." The duty of defeating fascism falls to us, not the politicians, who suddenly get especially solicitous of freedom of speech when it comes to Nazis.

While the Jewish Establishment, and the Voltaireans and the ignominious Fauntroy may denounce the left, Blacks have sense. They turn out by the thousand to bust Klan heads.

What is more, for all the politicians' citations of Voltaire's line, there is one thing we will never see, not even if we live to be 100: The liberals will never—repeat never—lift one little finger to actually defend the Nazis when the wrath of the people descends upon them. Here, as per usual, our liberals are full of what might be called high temperature atmosphere. And it is just as well, for what more disgraceful death could there possibly be than dying to protect some lunatic's right to incite racial hatred? But that they actually espouse such a doctrine tells us what they really represent. Here are the Jews, Blacks, the left. There the fascists.

And in the middle, the liberals, wearing their striped shirt, blowing hard on their whistle: "Foul on the fascists for offside racist
violence. Two free throws for the oppressed! Foul on the
oppressed for illegal interference with freedom of speech for
murderers. Two free throws, Nazis!"

These learned fellows mean well, but they do not understand
what politics is all about, or what they are all about. Freudians
have no difficulty in diagnosing them as orally fixated. They are
in the word business, and oral fixation is their black lung disease.
They become preoccupied with words, which take on magic qual-
ities in their unconscious. If only the world were like them,
always willing to listen. But it is not, and never will be, for
which we thank whatever Gods may be. In politics, words are
about something. Lewis Carroll summed things up for all time to
come, in his *Through the Looking Glass:*

> "I don't know what you mean by 'glory,'" Alice said.
> Humpty Dumpty smiled contemptuously. "Of course you
> don't—till I tell you. I meant 'there's a nice knockdown argument
> for you!'"
> "But 'glory' doesn't mean 'a nice knock-down argument,'"
> Alice objected.
> "When *I* use a word," Humpty Dumpty said, in a rather scorn-
> ful tone, "It means just what I choose it to mean—neither more
> nor less."
> "The question is," said Alice, "whether you *can* make words
> mean so many different things."
> "The question is," said Humpty Dumpty, "which is to be the
> master—that's all."

Yes. That is all. In the summer of 1985, a remarkable letter
appeared in *The New York Times,* from Dumi Matabane, the
Washington representative of the African National Congress:

> In reply to Mr. Viguerie's question if the A.N.C's goal was demo-
> cracy, I said, yes, democracy is our goal, *but* that did not neces-
> sarily mean the democracy that is practiced in the United States.
> That is, we are not interested in a democracy that protects the Ku
> Klux Klan, Nazi parties, white citizen councils, etc. Certainly, in
> our future free South Africa, the laws protecting freedom of
> speech and association will *not* include pro-apartheid propaganda
> or the broederbond. For this, our people need make no apolo-
> gies. . . . The only solution is to drive a stake through the heart of
> the apartheid scourge.[39]

Voltaire, even with his limitations, was brilliant. But he lived in his time as we in ours. He represented liberalism in its heroic age, when it expressed the expansive philosophy of a rising class, then at the head of the people, in the struggle against aristocracy. Today liberalism is a hair on the tail of that same capitalist class which has become the ancien régime.

Freedom of speech is defended only by defending the people against their enemies, not the other way around. To those liberals who sincerely want free speech, the left says it is not free, it costs dearly. It will cost billions to educate the poor of a world which is still 41 percent illiterate. It will cost billions even to teach the tens of millions in the United States who are functionally illiterate, or barely literate, and thereby incapable of making head or tail of the news even when they can see it, without reading, on TV. And in the end it will cost lives, as revolution always does.

Mobilize those who are now willing to smash racism, rather than prattle about free speech in the abstract while defending murderers in the concrete. Freedom of speech? Of course!! Any movement to rip out injustice in the U.S. must be a movement of millions, with all their different experiences and levels of consciousness. We never could get, and do not want, all those heads under one hat. The freest discussion must be the norm, so that people will feel free to take part, gain confidence in themselves and then pass the truth along to their co-workers, rather than merely sit and listen to intellectuals orate at them, as is the case today. But they who tell us we must adhere to Voltaire's phrase, which was so much a part of his times, traduce his spirit. We in our times go, and must go, with Matabene, who is our Voltaire: a stake through the heart of racism and anti-Semitism.

Notes

1. Stephen Isaacs, *Jews and American Politics*, p. 15.
2. Ibid., p. 141.
3. Ibid., p. 144.
4. G. William Domhoff and Richard Zweigenhaft, "Jews in the Corporate Establishment," *NY Times*, April 24, 1983.
5. George Gallup, "Prejudice in Politics Is at an All-Time Low," *San Francisco Chronicle*, Sept. 25, 1978.
6. "Feelings Towards Jews Found More Favorable in a Survey by Gallup," *NY Times*, April 16, 1981.
7. Yankelovich, Skelly and White, *Anti-Semitism in the United States*, vol. I, p. 32.
8. Geraldine Rosenfield, *The Polls: Attitudes Towards American Jews*, pp. 438–39.

9. Yankelovich, p. 9.

10. Ibid., p. 27.

11. Ibid., p. 64.

12. Ibid., p. 70.

13. Ibid., p. 28.

14. Nahum Goldmann, *The Jewish Paradox*, pp. 8, 12–13.

15. Howard Berman, "Open Hearts and an Open Door," *Issues*, Winter 1984, pp. 2–3.

16. Nathan and Ruth Ann Perlmutter, *The Real Anti-Semitism in America*, pp. 74, 286.

17. Israel Zangwill, *The Melting Pot*, pp. 95–6.

18. Glenn Collins, "A New Look at Intermarriage in the U.S.," *NY Times*, Feb. 11, 1985, p. 16.

19. Stephen Steinberg, *The Ethnic Myth*, p. 68.

20. Barbara Wilson, "Marriage's Melting Pot," *American Demographics*, p. 45.

21. *1984 Audit Of Anti-Semitic Incidents*, p. 6.

22. Alisa Kesten, Milton Ellerin, Sonya Kaufer, *Anti-Semitism in America: A Balance Sheet*, pp. 1–2.

23. Perlmutter, p. 224.

24. *The KKK and the Neo-Nazis*, p. 8.

25. Robert Thomas, Jr., "Klan Is Considered No Present Danger," *NY Times*, Nov. 11, 1979.

26. Arnold Forster and Benjamin Epstein, *The New Anti-Semitism*, pp. 137–8, 140, 336.

27. Ibid., pp. 113–4.

28. *1984 Audit*, p. 3.

29. Richard Bernstein, "Libya and Israel Clash at the U.N.," *NY Times*, Dec. 9, 1983, p. 11.

30. "An Open Letter to King Fahd of Saudi Arabia," *NY Times*, February 11, 1985.

31. "Arafat: democratic Palestine Is goal of Our Struggle," *Militant*, Nov. 1, 1985, p. 17.

32. Yehuda Bauer, "Anti-Semitism Today—A Fiction or a Fact?," *Midstream*, Oct. 1984, p. 27.

33. Walter Lewis, "Pro-PLO Mob Joins Rioters in Washington, Undercuts Israel," *Jewish Week*, Dec. 3, 1982.

34. "Twin demos: Pro-PLO, Anti-KKK," *Guardian*, Dec. 8, 1982.

35. Lewis.

36. Ike Nahem and Linda Mohrbacher, "Debate Rages Over D.C. Anti-Klan Protest," *Militant*, Dec. 17, 1982, p. 3.

37. Perlmutter, pp. 222.

38. Noam Chomsky to Lenni Brenner, Aug. 5, 1981.

39. Dumi Matabane, "A Stake Through the Apartheid Dracula's Heart," *NY Times*, Sept. 11, 1985.

8

Blacks and Jews
Maids and
Muggers, Landlords
and Lawyers

If, at the end of WWII, anyone had predicted that the themes of "Black-Jewish hostility" and "Black anti-Semitism" would become major topics in American journalism, few would have believed it possible. But then again, not even a prophet would have predicted that America would see a day when the mayors of New York and San Francisco would be Jews, and the mayors of Washington, Chicago, Los Angeles, Philadelphia, Atlanta, New Orleans, Detroit and many other cities would be Black. American ethnic relations have undergone an immense metamorphosis since the end of WWII, and so have both Blacks and Jews. The dramatic changes in their relations are but part of those transformations.

Countless thousands of Africans were brought here in colonial times as slaves by Sephardi merchant-shippers like Newport,

Rhode Island's Aaron Lopez and Jacob Rivera. Later, when "King Cotton" dominated the South, Jews began to enter the planter class in substantial numbers. Later yet, many German-Jewish peddlers went into the commercially underdeveloped South and several became prominent cotton traders.

While Baltimore rabbi David Einhorn and perhaps some other rabbis opposed slavery, Reform leader Isaac Wise feared abolitionism as "warmongering." According to the *Encyclopedia Judaica,* "Southern rabbis, in conformity with their surroundings, supported slavery fully."[1] However, the Jewish role in ante-bellum slavery must never be overemphasized. Jews were an insignificant proportion of the slave trading or slaveholding elements.

Judah P. Benjamin, who was never a member of any synagogue and who took no part in Jewish affairs, may not have been "the most prominent nineteenth-century American Jew," as the *Encyclopedia Judaica* calls him, but certainly he was the most important Jew on either side in the Civil War, first as the Confederacy's Attorney-General, then its Secretary of War and finally its Secretary of State.[2] Ten thousand Jews fought in the epic struggle, with 500 dying. Seven thousand soldiered in the Union Army, many of these in German-language units. Many of these were deeply committed to abolitionism, not because they were Jews, but because they were German '48ers, who tended to be light years ahead of most northern whites in this regard.

Given the profound sectional split in post-Civil War America, it is not surprising that the Jews were likewise divided on the race question. If Bernard Baruch's father, Simon, the former Quartermaster-General of the Confederacy, was a member of the KKK, the '48ers were overwhelmingly Republican and many favored the radical reconstructionist wing of the party led by Thaddeus Stevens.

Most historians are in agreement that even in the South the foreign-born German Jewish merchants tended, at least in degree, to be less racially antagonistic than the frequently rabid native-born whites. From the 1880s on, most of the Yiddish immigrants settled in northern cities, which then had very small Black populations, and therefore most Jews had very little direct contact with Blacks. Coming as most of them did from the Tsarist pogrom empire, they tended to be instinctually sympathetic to the Blacks, rather than to their lynchers.

The Economics of the Conflict

Significant modern contact between the two groups took several forms. Jewish philanthropists, such as Julius Rosenwald of Sears, Roebuck, a supporter of Booker T. Washington's Uncle Tom accommodationist philosophy, gave millions to Tuskegee and other Black schools. Jewish liberals and pink socialists were among the founding members of the integrationist National Association for the Advancement of Colored People. Two of these early Jewish activists, Joel and Arthur Springarn, later became presidents of the organization. Most of the Jews involved in the NAACP were extremely opposed to Zionism. What they wanted, for Blacks and Jews, was equal rights in America.

Professor David Lewis of Howard University writes that:

> There is less exaggeration than truth in an American Jewish Congress lawyer's assertion that legal briefs, local ordinances, and federal laws beneficial to Afro-Americans "were actually written in the offices of Jewish agencies, by Jewish staff people, introduced by Jewish legislators and pressured into being by Jewish voters."[3]

This patronage was important in molding the opinions of the "talented tenth," the intellectual leadership of the beleaguered Blacks. But popular inter-ethnic contact began in the post-WWI period when Blacks moved into Jewish neighborhoods, as in New York's Harlem and San Francisco's Fillmore, as the upwardly mobile Jews moved out, eventually leaving only storekeepers and landlords behind.

By no means all landlords in slum neighborhoods were or are Jewish, but many were and are. In April 1964, at the height of the civil rights struggle, a Jewish group called the Zealots demonstrated at the New York Board of Rabbis, demanding they denounce slumlords within their congregations:

> The majority of buildings with 50 or more violations listed in the *New Times,* January 24, 1963, have identifiably Jewish landlords. . . . We have submitted to the rabbis a list of 250 Jewish landlords who own 500 slum buildings in Manhattan.[4]

In 1964, only two of the over 300 stores on 125th Street, Harlem's major shopping artery, were owned by Blacks, but very many of them were owned by Jews.[5] However, after the 1960s Black rebellions, which frequently took the form of looting of such stores, Jewish commercial involvement in the ghettoes declined sharply. Jews have been replaced by some Blacks and Chinese, Koreans, Palestinians and other Arabs.

In New York City, American Blacks, Puerto Ricans and Haitians are the vast majority of workers in Jewish owned loft-factories in the garment center. Although Jews make up a minuscule percentage of employees in these sweatshops, the ILGWU's top bureaucrats are still Jews.

We have previously cited Seymour Martin Lipset's 1969 statistic, that the majority of the rich, outside the South, with full-time servants, are Jews. And that about half of middle-class Jews have a Black woman come in one day a week to clean house. No more contemporary statistic exists. It might be thought that the increased number of Jews in their twenties and thirties who live alone—and the rise of feminism—would have lowered the percentage who employ domestics. However, personal contact has taught this writer that many of these "swingers" still have their "shvartzes."

American Jewry is the most intellectualized stratum in the society and anyone familiar with Freud knows where to look for the black lung disease of the educated: oral fixation. And one of the characteristic symptoms of that neurosis is dishevelment. Anyone familiar with this milieu knows I do not exaggerate when I categorically insist that with many of these big babies there are only two choices: domestics or derricks to pick up after them.

Peasant maids were a Jewish middle-class tradition in Eastern Europe, and even in Brooklyn in the early 1940s this writer's family had a live-in Polish maid. In modern America with its informality, this penchant for maids is anomalous and, when it is combined with liberal protestations, as it all too frequently is, it is, perhaps, the most ludicrous aspect of Jewish life. However, it assumes larger significance in that every Black intellectual knows of this reality, and it colors, as it were, their picture of Black-Jewish relations. On the other hand, has even one Black ever had a Jewish maid? The image is so amusing that it is amazing that no Black has ever thought to utilize it as a comedy shtick.

In the heyday of the blue-collar Jewish working class, a Black would encounter Jews either as fellow workers or as superiors. Today blue-collar Blacks never work side by side with Jews. As the educated Black stratum expanded it moved massively into the civil service, where it found the least prejudice. In New York in particular, Black teachers do have Jewish colleagues, but the principals, and the American Federation of Teachers bureaucrats, are far more likely to be Jewish than Black.

We may generalize that today's class relationship between the two groups is one in which the Jews are almost invariably in the superior social position. Few Jewish students ever have more than one Black teacher, if that. Almost no Jews patronize Black stores, which do not exist outside Black neighborhoods. Few have ever been treated by a Black doctor, and Jews virtually never have Black lawyers.

"Black and White Together, We Shall Overcome"

Immediately after Jesse Jackson's "Hymie" remark, Democratic Socialist Jack Newfield wrote a widely discussed article in the March 20, 1984, *Village Voice:* "All we can do now is try to convert this calamity into something positive." For, after all:

> The logical morality of Black-Jewish coalitions is overwhelming to me. Blacks and Jews share a history of persecution. Slavery and the Holocaust should demonstrate to everyone what intolerance and racism can lead to. . . . There is no more haunting symbol of that collaboration than the buried bodies of Goodman, Chaney, and Schwerner—two Jewish activists . . . and a Black activist . . . who were murdered together by the Ku Klux Klansmen . . . 20 years ago, during the freedom summer of voter registration. . . . But memory, sentiment, or moralism, by themselves, are not enough to refashion this coalition of conscience. There has been too much pain inflicted: because of the 1968 school strike, because of the firing of Andrew Young, because of the rise of Koch, because of the habit of Jesse Jackson. But realism can help rebuild this coalition . . . maybe the most helpful glue can be facts. Simple facts. A most significant fact to understand is that Jews are still, by far, the most liberal group of whites . . . despite the images of Podhoretz, Koch and Kahane.[6]

The above was nothing but a liberal *maisela,* a fairy tale written to gull Blacks, to convince them their interests, today, are the same as the richest ethnic group in the country. Allegedly these common concerns required that they "retire Reagan," i.e., vote for Mondale after Jackson lost.

Both Blacks and Jews have been persecuted. But they do not "share" a common past. Every Jew knows that Hebrews were slaves in Egypt. That never stopped Aaron Lopez or Judah P. Benjamin or Simon Baruch from owning Blacks. The Holocaust occurred decades ago on another continent. It never prevented Jewish slumlords from ripping off Blacks.

But let us go further. If Jewish history will never unite Jews with Blacks, neither will slavery unite Blacks with Jews. It was not instructive enough to dissuade dozens of leading Black entertainers, from Ray Charles on down, from playing in Sun City in South Africa. The only Jews such Black opportunists—as thick as thieves in show biz and politics and elsewhere—are interested in uniting with are booking agents and others who can help their careers.

So much for remote history. But were most Jews ever allied to the Blacks during the civil rights struggle? The movement always tried to show that the call for equality was broadly supported. Therefore, the major rallies invariably had white Protestant ministers, Catholic priests and rabbis speak from the podium. Some of these clergy were deeply committed and tried to mobilize their flocks to attend. Others spoke but were too naive to grasp that they were under any obligation to go beyond oratory. It is universally agreed that a higher percentage of Jews were involved, to one degree of commitment or another, with the movement than any other white ethnic or religious grouping. But it must be categorically stated that those involved were only a minority of the Jews. Even so, in 1963, rabbi Balfour Brickner of the prestigious Stephen Wise Reform Temple in New York, confessed that "non-synagogued groups have been involved in civil rights issues prior to the awakening of Jewry's religious groups."[7]

In 1985, Henry Siegman, executive director of the AJCongress, conceded that as far as religious Jews were concerned

> the social, educational, and economic distance that separated Blacks and Jews in the 1960s was so large that the term "shared interests," as commonly understood, had no political content even in the heyday of Black-Jewish cooperation. If Jews nevertheless championed the cause of civil rights . ... they did so because they understood that a society that abuses its racial minorities is not likely to protect its religious minorities. To recognize this self-interest is not to deprecate Jewish motives.[8]

Siegman is not specific as to whether those religious Jews who were involved were Reform or Conservative. We know that southern Jews, of any stripe, were rarely involved. Notoriously they feared for their social position vis-à-vis their white neighbors if they went to the side of the Blacks.

Without any statistics to go by, we nevertheless can presume that a higher percentage of northern Reform were involved than Conservatives, though both groups formally indorsed the campaign and rabbis from both groups spoke at demonstrations. But the vast majority of Orthodox were never part of the civil rights coalition. Again, here is Siegman: "There was no Orthodox involvement to speak of in the American civil rights struggle."[9]

As serious politicals understand that the civil rights struggle was one of the central events of modern times, Siegman's accusation is damning, and David Luchins, Chair of the Communal Relations Commission of the Union of Orthodox Jewish Congregations, was compelled to try to rebut it by saying that he

> was one of the several Orthodox teenagers who were proud to wear our *kipot* (skullcaps) as we were arrested in Alabama—just as we, and many others, wore them as we marched on Washington with Martin Luther King. . . . "If an Orthodox Jew," Rabbi Soloveichik declared at the 1964 Convention of Young Israel, "is a racist, it is not because of the Tora . . . but because of the Tora that he has not yet learnt." It was this theme that sent Orthodox Rabbis and laymen to Selma in 1965.[10]

Siegman quite correctly replied that his

> article dealt with . . . the failure of Orthodox religious leaders— the *roshei yeshiva* (heads of yeshivas) and *gedolei hador* (prominent leaders)—not individual Orthodox Jewish. . . . If Luchins can point only to one or two *roshei yeshiva* . . . who encouraged participation . . . that should say something to him, should it not, as to where the overwhelming weight of Orthodox Jewish religious authority stood on this issue. (I am familiar with Rabbi Aaron Soloveichik's public statement . . . I am also aware, as Dr. Luchins should be, that it was seen as a bizarre aberration by most other *gedolim*.)[11]

In his *Jews and the Left*, Arthur Liebman categorically states that "Jews were approximately two-thirds of the Freedom Riders that went South in 1961. In 1964 they represented from one-half to two-thirds of the Mississippi Summer volunteers"[12] It must be recalled that there were several thousand college students in Mississippi. No statistics exist as to how many were religious, nor are there any statistics as to their political breakdown. While beyond doubt some, like Luchins, were Orthodox or members of the other Jewish sects, nevertheless any candid observer would have said that a far larger percentage were red diaper babies, members of varying Marxist groups or New Left independents.

Again, no statistics exist as to how many members of Zionist groups went South. It is unreasonable to think many did, but many New Lefts would have described themselves as pro-Israel, and certainly the liberal Democratic politicians who took part were pro-Zionist. However, until the Black Power currents developed, in the immediately following years, Zionism was not an issue within the civil rights movements. The crucial foreign preoccupation was Vietnam, not Palestine.

While the South was the prime arena of the struggle, much of the mobilizing and most of the fund-raising took place in the North. And many sit-ins were held in the North and West. This writer was arrested, along with many hundreds of others, at sit-ins in the San Francisco Bay Area, where Blacks were severely under-represented even as chambermaids in the major hotels. While Jews were well represented in these demonstrations, very few, if any, religious Jews were among the activist leaders, certainly not in the Bay Area. Among the adult non-students, liberals predominated and many of these were pro-Israel. But again, there did not seem to be any overt Zionist organizational presence.

Street Crime and Modern Racism

If any year can be said to be the year of the beginning of the Black-Jewish split it was 1966, when 55 percent of New York's Jews voted against a civilian police review board proposition favored by the vast majority of Blacks.[13] What with enormous poverty, then and now, in the Black ghettos, the crime rates there were and are monumental. Given the blatant racism of the police, North and South, in those days, it is completely understandable that the Black community was outraged at what they saw as a betrayal by the Jewish masses.

By and large, it was the lower class of Jews, particularly those who lived in proximity to Black neighborhoods, who voted against the Review Board. While there had been a strong criminal element in the early Jewish slums, and many graduates of those gangs were well represented in the higher echelons of organized crime in the 1960s, Jewish street crime was a thing of the past. These lower-class Jews saw the cops as their defenders against Black lumpen males who were ripping them off to get money to buy heroin. They didn't see them as racial inferiors, as many other whites then did, and no one thought these muggers and burglers were anti-Semitic. Black street crime, not any Black attitude toward Israel or affirmative action, or even any Black anti-Semitism, has moved the lower stratum of American Jewry to the right on the race question.

Given the economic deprivation of the Black ghettos, a considerable amount of such street crime is to be expected. But the massive proportions of Black crime is largely due to heroin or, more precisely, the fact that it is illegal. More precisely yet, it is due to the fact that America's politicians refuse to establish free clinics for the controlled distribution of heroin to registered addicts.

According to an article in the February 20, 1981, *New York Times:*

> Researchers at Temple University discovered recently that 243 heroin users in Baltimore committed more than 500,000 crimes over 11 years—an average of 200 crimes by each of them each year.[14]

As long as heroin clinics are not set up, crime will continue to rage in America's streets. The bulk of the Black masses, the prime victims, loathe junkies as much as the white masses. But of course they don't hate them as Blacks. Many whites do, since the majority of junkies are either Black or Hispanic, and they feel that if there aren't any Blacks in their neighborhood there won't be any criminals around to prey on them.

Yes, indeed, "poor people do have some poor ways." They lack the subtlety to grasp on their own that the solution is clinics. And, of course—individual exceptions aside—American politicians lack both the brains or the morality to propose any answer to any problem that would make them unpopular, at least at first. On this, the Black Democrats, as with Harlem's Congressional

representative, Charles Rangel, are among the worst. His reports
to his constituents are largely devoted to his Sisyphean labors in
trying to stop poppy growing in Pakistan and elsewhere, while he
virtually ignores the vast range of other problems confronting
Black Americans. And the white liberal Democrats, Jewish and
otherwise, have inexorably abandoned their principles, increasingly voting for greater penalties against criminals, instead of putting the ax to the root of so much of the crime problem, by establishing free distribution of heroin.

The traditional left parties have also failed in this regard,
though by no means to the extent of the capitalist politicians.
Some, as with the Communist Party, are prigs, bitterly opposed
to the use of marihuana or other drugs, addictive or not. Others,
as with the Trotskyist SWP, do formally support free clinics. But,
far from putting any priority on the question, they see drugs primarily as a security problem for their organization. They expel
members who use even marihuana. They do nothing to raise the
heroin question in public.

For all their prattle about Marxism as a theoretical science, it
would be difficult to put together *even a short pamphlet* of articles
on the impact of drugs on America—particularly its race
relations—from the press of all these self-styled revolutionary
groupings *combined*. Nevertheless, it must be said, over and
over again, that "street crime" is one of the most important
"material bases" for modern style white racism, and at the heart
of such crime is heroin.

Similarly, it must be said, over and over again, that heroin is a
cancer within the poor Black neighborhoods and those who do not
shout for such clinics fail those neighborhoods, quite regardless
of whatever other meritorious actions they take or advocate. Historians of the future will be unable to understand why virtually
the entire spectrum of political ideology, with the exception of a
few independent leftists and others of libertarian approach, were
so utterly silent in our day on this question.

Does the above appear as a digression from the topic of Black-
Jewish conflict? Not if you go to the Upper West Side in Manhattan or Boro Park in Brooklyn and talk to Jews. Whatever they
think of Jesse Jackson or Louis Farrakhan, they dread neither.
They are afraid of Black junkies.

According to the May 16, 1985, *New York Times:*

New York is a city charged with fears about crime, and fears tend to constrain relations between people of different races, according to a *New York Times*/WCBS-TV Poll. The poll indicated that residents of all races believed that crime was the most important problem facing the city. . . . Jack Lictenfeld, an 85-year-old white from the Upper West Side, agreed . . . "You get mugged three or four times by blacks and you get very angry and you get a bad feeling." . . . Seventy-one percent of the whites and 51 percent of the blacks said they would feel unsafe if they encountered several loud, teen-age black boys on a subway car. When asked about noisy white youths, 55 percent of the whites and 49 percent of the blacks said they would be concerned.[15]

Black Power

The review board referendum was the first overt sign of the popular Jewish shift to the right, but Black politics were also changing. That same year Stokely Carmichael of the Student Non-violent Coordinating Committee began popularizing the Black Power slogan, instead of merely talking about civil rights. Until then the Black Muslims had been virtually the only Black current which had raised questions about American Jews and strenuously opposed the Israeli state as such. Black Communists were not very influential, and while the CP was opposed to the rightward thrust of Israeli policy, they categorically favored the continued existence of the state.

The NAACP had always been bi-racial and W.E.B. Dubois, one of its founders, was pro-Zionist. However Walter White, the organization's leading figure in the late 1940s, when the question of an Israeli state became a domestic American issue, was much more ambivalent, as he candidly revealed in his autobiography, *A Man Called White:*

> Both the wisdom and the practicability of partition were doubt-ful. . . . I did not like the self-segregation of Zionism. . . . But I reluctantly supported partition only because Palestine seemed the only haven . . . for nearly one million Jews of Europe.[16]

He told of being "bombarded" by Zionists seeking his help to get Haiti and Liberia to vote for partition. He did significantly intervene and later, when he went to Israel, was warmly wel-comed by the government in gratitude. Nevertheless, he was profoundly disturbed by much of what he saw. His wife, Poppy Cannon, wrote about his concerns in her own book about her husband.

She quoted him:

> "I did what I did with some reservations. On principle I am against segregation, whether imposed from within or without. I still don't know" . . . Several young men eyed us from the doorways. "Those are friendly Arabs. They are glad we are here." . . . Walter shook his head. "I've seen that look too often on the faces of colored men down South who are supposed to be happy with their lot. Friendly? No, I don't like it."[17]

However, for all his doubts, when asked if he still favored the existence of the new state, he answered unhesitatingly: "Of course. You can't unmake a baby."[18]

Given that Egypt is African, there was remarkably little Black outcry against Israel for its part in the 1956 Sinai invasion. Instead, hostility was focused primarily on the British and French, with the Israelis seen as their pawns, pushed into their service by Arab intransigence. Middle Eastern politics were still obscure to most Black intellectuals. Only the totally isolated Black Muslims identified with the Arabs in a full way.

Additionally, the domestic civil rights struggle was beginning to unfold, and the participation of Jewish liberals and donors was genuinely appreciated by the old-line Negro leadership. When they thought at all about Israel they naturally enough projected onto Zionism the still genuine liberalism of their Jewish Establishment allies here.

Castro's triumph in Cuba was crucial in the development of the new Black politics. Hispanics were always seen as fellow sufferers from white racism and when he stood up to the "Yanquis," many Black politicals sympathized. When he came to the UN in September 1960, and dramatically moved into a Harlem hotel, thousands of Blacks rushed there to jubilantly cheer him. LeRoi Jones and other young militants worked in and around the Fair Play for Cuba Committee. Huey Newton and Bobby Seale, the founders of the Black Panther Party, met for the first time at a rally during the Cuba missile crisis, organized by this writer and other leftists, Black and white.

Few of the mainline Negro leaders were in favor of Kennedy's criminal Bay of Pigs invasion of Cuba. But for the most part, they were muted in their protests. They felt they needed the Democratic Administration in Washington against their own "down home" Democratic enemies in the South. A gap opened between them and the young activists, which became an abyss in the next few years.

That same period also saw the rise of the Nation of Islam to prominence. This group had been around since the 1930s but had always been dismissed by intellectual Blacks as just another of the innumerable bizarre storefront cults which arose among the least literate of the despairing masses. Their ideological baggage was quite crackpot: A sort of mad Black Victor Frankenstein had created the white race, and his creatures took over. Then Allah, a.k.a. Wallace Fard, revealed himself, in Detroit, to Elijah Poole, so that the "lost-found nation" could be saved. But they combined their uncompromising nationalist separatism with a puritanical morality which stood out in the ·chaos of the ghetto, with its endemic hustling and crime.

When they recruited a self-taught convict, Malcolm Little, they—and the Black masses—found their voice. Indeed Malcolm X was the oratorical equal of Martin Luther King, and after newsman Mike Wallace did a TV documentary on the Nation of Islam, he, more than any other person, created the new "Black" movement.

Nietzsche once said that a pregnant error was better than a sterile truth, and this was the case here. The traditional civil rights leaders were educated men. They were far too urbane to go for any monkeychatter about mad Black scientists. But they were suckers for mad white Democratic murderers, and they urged the masses to vote for Johnson in 1964. Malcolm, who for the most part downplayed the wacky aspects of the Muslim ideology, told the people that, if the Republicans were wolves, the Democrats were foxes.

Malcolm's opposition to Zionism was initially based on his group's Islamic nature and he denounced "the Jews who with the help of Christians in America and Europe drove our Muslim brothers out of their homeland."[19] He always insisted that he opposed anyone, Jew or Christian, who ripped off the Black masses.

Not being dependent on Jewish patronage, as the civil rights leaders so obviously were, he could "tell it like it is":

In every Black ghetto, Jews own the major businesses. Every night the owners of those businesses go home with that Black community's money, which helps the ghetto to stay poor.[20]

Malcolm broke with the Nation of Islam on March 12, 1964. He had come to realize that it was not enough to denounce the timid handkerchief-heads leading the civil rights campaign. It was necessary to build the movement while criticizing its leaders. His travels broadened his perspectives and in his last period he gave up the Muslims' rackety-rack about "White Devils." On May 29 he told a meeting that:

In my recent travels into the African countries and others, it was impressed upon me the importance of having a working unity among all peoples, Blacks as well as Whites. But the only way this is going to be brought about is that the Black ones have to be in unity first.[21]

On February 18, 1965, he summed up his new philosophy:

We are living in a era of revolution. . . . It is incorrect to classify the revolt of the Negro as simply a racial conflict of Black against White, or as a purely American problem. Rather, we are today seeing a global rebellion of the oppressed against the oppressor, the exploited against the exploiter.[22]

Three days later he was murdered by assassins sent by the Nation of Islam. History's eulogy was given by playwright Ossie Davis: "And we shall know him then for what he was and is—a prince, our own black shining prince, who didn't hesitate to die, because he loved us so."[23]

The 1967 New York Teachers Strike

In 1964 Albert Shanker took over as president of the United Federation of Teachers, the New York unit of the American Federation of Teachers. A former member of the Young Peoples Socialist League, the youth section of the Socialist Party, a founding member of the Congress on Racial Equality (CORE), and a participant in demonstrations in Selma, nevertheless the leader of the largest union local in America fomented one of the most intense racial conflicts ever to wrack a major northern city in the U.S.

No one could pretend New York was educating the majority of Black youth. At least 52 percent of the city's public school students were Black or Hispanic. Most attended de facto segregated schools. A massive minority never finished high school. Only 7 percent of the students in those segregated schools received "academic" diplomas, allowing them into the municipal colleges.[24] A majority of the teachers and most of the principals were Jews. Fewer than 13 percent of the teachers were minority, the lowest percentage in the country's five most important municipal school systems.[25]

In 1967, New York State authorized a school decentralization plan. Local boards would help administer their children's schools. The city gave the boards a list of names of those who had passed the *city* exam for superintendent. None were minority. The Black superintendent and board in Brooklyn's Ocean Hill-Brownsville, one of America's worst slums, decided to hire seven Asian, Black and Puerto Rican principals from the *State's* qualified principal list instead. Shanker took them to court and lost.

In May, 1968, the local board transferred 19 teachers, all Jews, out of the district for sabotaging decentralization. They were covered by contracts and couldn't be fired. It must be understood that principals routinely transferred teachers out of their districts, for many reasons, and the union usually didn't protest. But now Shanker was determined to "teach" the new local boards that they had to come to terms with him and he struck the district.

Most of the district's teachers, including most Jews, were conscientious and only 68 out of a staff of 700 joined the bogus "strike." Jeff Mackler, a Jewish Trotskyist, and a leading union opponent of Shanker, later wrote about the strike in his pamphlet *Teachers Under Attack:*

> Imagine a teachers' strike where the strikers received the full support of their employer, the police, white racist groups. . . . Imagine a teachers' strike in which "scabs" were arrested . . . in which school authorities chained the schools closed to keep "scabs" out.[26]

Eventually Shanker called a city-wide strike to compel reinstatement of the transferred 19 and the 68 Shankerites. No fewer than 11,000 teachers, many if not most being Jews, out of 55,000 UFT members, tried to keep the city's schools open. New York's Black and Hispanic communities rallied behind the local board, including the ultra-respectable NAACP and Urban League. Eventually, the courts and the cops forced the local board to take back the hated teachers.

If the police review board vote was the first sign of popular Jewish estrangement from the Blacks, there is no doubt that the Establishment broke ranks during the strike. On March 16, 1969, an ad appeared in *The New York Times,* paid for by The Jewish Citizens Committee for Community Control. It was a reprint of an article, "Exploding the Myth of Black Anti-Semitism," by Walter Karp and H.R. Shapiro. It told the story of

> a political lie . . . that . . . breeds hatred between two of the largest ethnic groups in the city—as it was meant to do. It allows the powerful to step on the powerless—as it was meant to do . . . What? . . . how can black anti-semitism be a lie? Didn't Leslie Campbell, a black teacher from the Ocean Hill-Brownsville school district, read a student's anti-semitic verse over radio station WBAI-FM? . . . And what of those ugly anti-Jewish leaflets the UFT thoughtfully flooded the city with. . . . We are told by the Anti-Defamation League . . . that "raw, undisguised anti-semitism is at a crisis-level in New York City schools." . . .

For all the ADL's ranting, Karp and Shapiro cited previous statements from the Establishment which embarrassingly revealed that:

> *From 1966 to the fall of 1968, it was the consistent policy of almost every major Jewish organization to MINIMIZE the significance of occasional reports of black anti-semitism.* . . . On April 28, 1966 . . . an American Jewish Congress spokesman coined the term "Jewish backlash" and denounced stories of black anti-Jewish sentiment as "overblown." . . . To black criticism of Jewish merchants and ghetto landlords the Union of Hebrew Congregations replied . . . with open criticism of . . . "those Jewish slumlords and ghetto profiteers." . . . *Now* . . . *when Ocean Hill was actually HIRING scores of Jewish teachers, the B'nai B'rith begins crying up black anti-semitism.* . . . As late as October 22, a spokesman for the American Jewish Committee could publically accuse Shanker of "using the Jewish community" for his own purposes. . . . As late as October 23, 1968 . . . the ADL . . . reported the results of its intensive study of anti-Jewish leaflets and found no evidence of any organized effort behind them. . . . Now let us look at the dossier . . . this same organization has compiled for its January report. . . . *It notes now that the*

leaflets "had early origins and distribution and were recirculated" during the strike. . . . Since the UFT undeniably recirculated them, it is obvious that the union had saved them up . . . and unleashed them in a frightening barrage. . . . As the strikes grew more bitter . . . the ever-useful leaflets . . . were now unleashed in Jewish neighborhoods. . . .

The two journalists described how the leaflets panicked older Jews: "To such people a single racist leaflet looks like the high road to Auschwitz. All sense of reality flees." Then:

The decisive moment occurred when this tide of Jewish fears and hatred began exerting its inevitable pressure on the most illustrious Jewish organizations. These groups may make flossy pronouncements about national policies, but for all their political pretensions they are no more nor less than Jewish protective societies, mere ethnic mouthpieces. . . . If their members wanted their fears confirmed . . . then that is what the membership would get. . . . What is more, having accepted Shanker's story, these Jewish spokesmen are permanently wed to it, for to tell the truth now would expose their complicity.[27]

There is no doubt the Establishment did do a sharp turn on Black anti-Semitism. In an article subtitled "New Study Confutes Widespread Sensational Beliefs," the June 1967 *ADL Bulletin* had run a study done for the ADL by the University of California's Survey Research Center. The pollsters claimed that:

Negroes are less anti-Semitic than whites. . . . To the degree that Negroes distinguish between Jewish and non-Jewish whites, they prefer Jews . . . the more militant a Negro is, the less likely he is to be anti-white.[28]

In his 1974 book, *Jews and American Politics,* Stephen Isaacs also cited several sources to the effect that the Establishment yielded to pressure from its constituency. But there were other factors at work as well. Israel had won the 1967 war. The militant wing of the Black movement had opposed the conquest of the rest of Palestine. Johnson had supported the Israelis and they wanted his continued patronage. They began to secretly pressure Jewish leaders to quiet down Jewish opposition to the Vietnam war. Norman Podhoretz was already "breaking ranks" with liberalism.

Nevertheless, the reality was that most Northern Jews had been only passively for the Blacks, and only as long as they were demanding legal equality in the South. When the issues went beyond mere formal equality, the least educated and most traditional Jews turned against the Blacks. They may have been stampeded by Shanker, at least in New York, but they were not following any instructions from the Establishment. Liberalism on the race question became primarily the preserve of the educated youth, the "limousine liberals" and the secularized suburbanites. Even with them, their solidarity with the Blacks began to consist of little more than voting for moderate Black Democrats in mayorality campaigns against white—and even Jewish—incumbents.

Hydrants Pissing on the Dog

Karp and Shapiro mentioned that Leslie Campbell, Brooklyn coordinator for the African-American Teachers Association, an important element in the community struggle for decentralization, had read an anti-Semitic poem over the radio. The episode was perhaps the single most directly damaging example of the "rapology" that afflicted the younger militants in the post-Malcolm years.

On December 26, 1968, Campbell read the piece, supposedly by a 15-year-old, on a show moderated by Julius Lester, on radio station WBAI. It was "dedicated" to Shanker, and called "Anti-Semitism." It read, in part:

Hey, Jew boy, with that yarmulke on your head
You pale-faced Jew boy—I wish you were dead;
I got a scoop on you—yeh, you gonna die.
. . .
I'm sick of hearing about your suffering in Germany.
. . .
Jew boy, you took my religion and adopted it for you,
But you know the Black people were the original Hebrews.
. . .
Then you came to America, land of the free,
And took over the school system to perpetuate white
supremacy.
. . .
I hated you Jew boy, because your hang-up was the Torah,
And my only hang-up was my color.[29]

There was a huge outcry. Al Vann, president of the AATA, defended Campbell. The poem was "critical of Jews" but had "no anti-Semitic overtones."[30] Nevertheless, the poem did not represent the policy of the local board. Seventy percent of the new teachers taken on by the board were white and 50 percent were Jews.[31] Although it would be wrong to blame the incident alone for Shanker's victory, it was a major propaganda coup for the UFT.

Malcolm had made himself, by his zeal and oratory, the embodiment of the total liberation of Black people, particularly their poorest stratum. This writer, for one, never doubted that his death was a catastrophe of world-historic proportions. Martin Luther King's later murder was likewise a tragedy. But Malcolm's death was vastly more important politically. That assessment still stands. After Malcolm's death, the main-line civil rights leaders, including King, never again were able to give leadership to the masses in the streets. Today, when we celebrate King's birthday as a national holiday, it is quite conveniently overlooked that, in the period just before his murder, he was seen by many thousands of Black activists as a spent force, as Gandhi had been at his death. Nationalism was the militants' ideology, but none of those who tried to fill Malcolm's shoes could do so.

When Malcolm was assassinated, he was a mature 40. The leaders of SNCC and the Panthers and other groups were mostly youths. As with the white leaders of the New Left youth, they lacked crucial experience, the seasoning, the strategic sense required to bring down the system. They "stormed heaven." They smashed legal racism. The poorest of the poor rose up, from Watts to Newark, and put the fear of God into the powers-that-be. But it is obligatory to insist that, for the most part, the Black militants of the post-Malcolm period repeatedly defeated themselves with their rapology.

Malcolm was the prince of the poor, not an intellectual. He once told *Playboy* that Beethoven was Black, because of his bushy hair. Many of the youthful Blacks who followed after him were better educated than he. Yet they produced no ideological Malcolm van X. They were looking for a short-cut to the masses. They mistakenly thought the special conditions of segregation and oppression had made the lumpen-proletariat the Black revolutionary class instead of the workers. They adapted psychologically to their wished-for following. Instead of converting the underclass, it converted them to its storefront nationalist cultism, with its pseudo-history and word-magic of every description.

They changed their "slave names." "Negro" was "Whitey's word." They became "Blacks." Christianity being a "Honkey" religion, they went native and converted to pseudo-African isms. Much worse, some deliberately tried to sound like the baaadest-assed pimp that ever wuz. They jived about "capitalist mother-fuckers," cursed "pig" cops, and some announced that the only position in the movement for women—Black women, not whites, whom they totally rejected—was "prone." Life was determined to imitate art. They were straight out of Ralph Ellison's master-piece, *The Invisible Man:* Ras the Destroyer and Reinhart come to life.

How different these trashmouths were from Malcolm! He had been part of that lumpen milieu, and had shared its verbalism. But in his last period he stressed that, while he was still personally Islamic, he was trying to win the people their rights, not convert them to ham-hatred. While he was emancipating him-self from rapology, they rushed headlong into it. When he got out of prison, he was so morally straight people remarked that he acted like he was still in it. He never once used vulgarity. They made a virtue out of the people's vice. Malcolm had become a serious revolutionary. They were frequently little more than the hydrant pissing back at the dog. He denounced those Jews who battened off the ghetto's misery. But he would never have read some outright anti-Semitic prattle in the middle of a deadly seri-ous battle with a clique of Jewish bureaucrats, at the exact time that the local board was hiring Jews to teach Black children.

Malcolm is still honored, and justly so. But who still reads—or should read?—such as LeRoi Jones's 1966 "Black Art":

We want poems
like fists beating niggers out of Jocks
or dagger poems in the slimy bellies
of the owner-jews . . .

. . . Setting fire and death to
whities ass. Look at the Liberal
Spokesman for the jews clutch his throat
& puke himself into eternity . . .

Put it on him poem. Strip him naked
to the world? Another bad poem cracking
steel knuckles in a jewlady's mouth.[32]

Jones, now professor Amiri Baraka, is still active. He is sadder but wiser. He and a few of the other then notables, like Carmichael (now Kwame Ture), played an important part in America's "1905," for all their errors, and they may yet have crucial roles in its "1917." But most of the other ideologues proved to be temporary immortals and have lapsed into mouse-like reformists or even machine hacks, Democrats in any case. Others, like Eldridge Cleaver, who never stopped ranting about "Zionist motherfuckers" and "the Jewish Mafia," are now hopeless religious fanatics. Others merely faded into well-deserved oblivion.

None of this is unusual in politics. If their own ravings defeat them, demoralized extremists frequently swing over to an equally useless minimalism as a reaction formation. This is exactly what happened to the three involved in the WBAI episode. Campbell, now Jitu Weusi, is a reform Democrat, as is Vann. Vann now admits he covered for Campbell, and that he let anti-Jewish insults get into the organization's paper. But that was then. Today Vann is a Democrat and the Black darling of the hopeless reformists at the *Village Voice,* and has taken to getting arrested at Zionist demonstrations at the Soviet consulate. But most ludicrous of all is Julius Lester, who has converted to Judaism. Nice work reb Julius! Now, all you have to do is get the *millions* of lapsed Jews to also convert to Judaism, and we'll be all set.

At any rate, Shanker won and "Oh, 'twas a famous victory." A generation of poor Blacks were deprived of any chance of an education and now the next generation suffers in turn; as in the biblical saying: "The fathers have eaten a sour grape, the children's teeth are set on edge."

The truth is as was said in *Current Biography's* 1969 article on the suddenly famous Shanker:

> The strike . . . left an indelible scar on race relations in the city, because of growing hostility between Negroes and Puerto Ricans . . . and Jews, who dominate the UFT.[33]

"What Would Happen to the Overrepresented? . . . Was the Worry Misplaced?"

If the Establishment was pushed from below into supporting Shanker, it was pushed exactly where it had to end up, given its own class composition. From then on it has been locked in battle with the entire Black movement from the NAACP over to the nationalists and Marxists. Blacks won legal equality but the masses were still obvious second-class citizens. The pols were forced to set up procedures increasing minority and female participation in economic sectors where they had been underrepresented or excluded.

Even under Nixon, the Department of Health, Education and Welfare would freeze funds to universities if they didn't come up with serious plans to increase their employment of minorities. Courts began to throw out "culture bound" civil service exams because they favored the better educated whites, and started substituting "job-related" tests. Even the Democratic Party got into the act, adapting quotas for such groups' delegate strength at its conventions.

The Establishment opposed all this. Murray Friedman, the *American Jewish Year Book's* annual commentator on intergroup relations, gave their side in 1973:

> To many Americans . . . a quota system was anathema. . . . Social critic Norman Podhoretz had been warning of the dangers of quotas . . . in *Commentary*. . . . The issue aroused deep anxieties among Jews in particular. Quotas had been used as a form of discrimination against them. . . . Two specific developments moved the organized Jewish community to assume leadership . . . in an attack on the quota movement. . . . HEW had been debating revision of its guidelines on the hiring practices of colleges. . . . These guidelines . . . encouraged or permitted . . . rigid quota systems for hiring minority or female employees. . . . At the Democratic National Convention . . . concern was voiced about a story . . . that Senator McGovern had pledged 10 percent of federal patronage jobs to blacks.[34]

What is this Gawd a'mighty world comin' to? Them niggers can't even keep their cotton pickin' hands off our graft! Seriously, the crucial statement is the declaration that "the organized Jewish community" assumed "*leadership*" in "an attack on the quota movement." That means exactly what it says: Podhoretz and Co. took it on themselves, in the name of Abraham and his seed, to *lead* the fight against both the Black and women's movements. And they did this all on the basis of a totally false analogy.

Anti-Semitic regimes had used quotas to *exclude* Jews, and these were wrongly equated with affirmative action quotas, which were designed by governmental agencies to *include* and insure opportunities for Blacks and other previously disadvantaged groups.

As Jews are not deprived in modern America, they do not benefit as such from today's "quotas." But neither do they suffer discrimination, as Jews, from them. Insofar as quotas benefiting Blacks may affect job opportunities for whites in general, Jews may or may not be affected. But in no way are they a target for such effects. Indeed, many of the legislators who enacted these affirmative action guidelines, and the administrators of them, were Jews.

By condemning affirmative action quotas as racist, putting them on a par with the Tsar's *numerus clausus,* or closed number, the Establishment reveals its *raison d'être.* It presumes to speak for all Jews, but like every Establishment it exists to defend and extend its class privileges. In this case it does so in the supposed defense of "equality of merit." They would say it is OK for money to be spent on raising the reading level of the most backward students, whoever they may be, provided there is no ethnic basis for spending the money. Then whoever passes the test gets the job.

Their zeal for "merit" goes only so far. None of the richest Jews, or the 400 richest Americans, or, for that matter, any capitalist, took a competitive written examination for the job of being a multi-millionaire. In the end, their passion for "equality before the law" boils down to this: If Lester Crown of General Dynamics should take to sleeping in subways, the AJCommittee will sternly insist that the police arrest him, exactly as they should arrest any shopping bag lady, Jew or gentile, Black or white.

Most Jews or Americans do not appreciate the depth of feeling Black intellectuals, even moderates, bring to the question of affirmative action. According to the May 21, 1984, *Times,* Benjamin Hooks, certainly one of the most mouse-like Black leaders, insisted that:

> It was vital that Jews recognize the importance that blacks attached to . . . placements without strict regard to qualifications and often by use of quotas. "Affirmative action is to the black community what Israel is to the Jewish community."[35]

In 1979, Andrew Young, America's Black UN Ambassador, met with the PLO's Ambassador and did not report the meeting to the State Department. Israeli agents observed the meeting, the word got out, and Young felt constrained to resign. The incident provoked an explosion in the entire Black leadership, and after an historic across-the-board leadership meeting their grievances against the Establishment began to pour out. Jesse Jackson, among many others, spoke out, in various media, denouncing the Establishment's attack on affirmative action, or quotas, call it as you will. With his characteristic moral obtuseness, Nathan Perlmutter of the ADL duly collected these statements in a "Not for Publication" exposé memorandum to his henchmen in the League. However, there is not the slightest doubt that the vast majority of Black leaders agreed with Jackson then, and agree with him now:

> When there wasn't much decency in society, many Jews were willing to share decency. The conflict began when we started our quest for power. Jews were willing to share decency, not power. . . . Jews called them quotas and opposed us. Even as we were expected to support jets for Israel, Jews had no problem with an expanding relationship with South Africa and sitting across the table from us on quotas. . . . In other words, with all the talk of the black-Jewish alliance, we don't own radio stations together, we don't own TV stations together, we don't own banks together, we do not share in the ownership of the industries. . . . Around a moral struggle to move IN (public accommodation, voting rights, open housing) blacks and Jews marched and died together. But in the economic struggle to move UP (equity and parity, shared power), Jewish resistance to affirmative action and minimum quotas of inclusion for blacks into law, medical and other professional schools—which Jews historically viewed as a means for their own exclusion—has put black and Jewish interests in conflict. Thus, Jewish intellectual and legal opposition to black upward mobility in the DeFunis, Bakke and Weber cases made popular the demagogic terms "reverse discrimination" and "preferential treatment." . . . Many Jews disagree on each of these issues—Jews comprise no monolith—but their profile is much too low. These are serious matters, and no one should underestimate the depth of the black-Jewish division. On the other hand, no one should overestimate the need for reconciliation to heal these wounds.[36]

In short, the Jews have made it, fair and foul, in American ways: Slaveholding, slumlording, bribing, etc., as well as sweating and studying. Now the Establishment demands a higher standard from Blacks: Study and toil and only study and toil, if you please. There is one little thing wrong: Under capitalism, if all lil' Blacks did their homework, and their mammies and pappies worked like slaves, they will still *never* as a group be the economic equals of whites in general or Jews in particular. As liars figure but figures don't lie, here are the statistics for the property status of Blacks:

They are 12.1 percent of America. But John Johnson, publisher of *Ebony* and *Jet,* AND manufacturer of Fashion Fair Cosmetics for Blacks, is the only Black among the 400 richest Americans. He is 0.25 percent of the 400. By comparison, Jews, 2.54 percent of the people, make up 23 percent.

There were a piss poor 339,239 Black businesses in 1982. The 100 largest *combined* did $2.5 billion sales in 1985. If they were one firm it would only be 150th on *Fortune's* list of the 500 largest corporations.[37] Forty-four are car dealers, and they did one-third of that $2.5 billion. They lack the capital to expand their share of the market to any appreciable extent.

Less than 1 percent of Black businesses had annual receipts of $1 million in 1982. Nearly half had receipts of *less than* $5,000 per year. Only 10 percent had *any* paid workers. Two-thirds were in retail or services, i.e., rib joints, grocers, laundromats and the like.[38] No less than 9 percent are barbershops and beauty parlors.

The millions of southern Black country folk have been reduced to 57,000 farmers, owning *1/10th of 1 percent* of the nation's agricultural acreage. Nor is Black participation in the real, white, economy of any consequences. The combined stocks, bonds *and* bank accounts of all Blacks come to *less than 0.7 percent* of the national total.

Bluntly: you can believe in economic racial equality. Or you can believe in capitalism. But not both at the same time. It is not hard to believe in both, it is *IMPOSSIBLE!!*

These statistics are results of racism, not any Black incapacity as workers or businessmen. Most of the craft work on the plantations was done by slaves. Between the Civil War and the end of the 19th century, Blacks predominated in many trades in the South. But they were then driven from them. Similarly, they were excluded from many skilled craft unions in the North until the 1960s and even later. The money spent on the segregated southern schools was in the way of a joke, and it has never been much better for the northern ghetto schools. Under capitalism, the

educated are overwhelmingly children of business people, professionals and skilled workers. It is now less than two decades since
King was assassinated. To expect any substantial equalization of
social status to have taken place in that insignificant span without
quotas was, and is, sheer fantasy.

There are programs to assist Black businesses. But these are
not the basis of the conflict with the Establishment. Black capitalists are so few and weak that the Black community does not normally think of working for them. Blacks want jobs with white
corporations and governmental institutions. The Black movement
struggles for quotas in the skilled trades for the masses and in
professional schools for intellectuals.

While the Establishment fights against quotas at all levels, its
main battle ground is in the intellectual field, as that is where the
Jews are now concentrated. We will recall that at least 20 percent
of the country's MDs and lawyers are Jews. Only 2.6 percent of
its doctors are Black.[39] In 1984 only 1.5 percent of the attorneys
in the nation's 100 largest law firms were Black.[40]

In 1971, Marco DeFunis, a Jew, sued the University of
Washington, which had rejected him for its law school. It had set
asides seats for minority applicants and he claimed better
qualifications than some of the students admitted. A lower court
made the university admit him. By the time the Supreme Court
got the case it was moot, as he was about to graduate, but the
lines had been drawn.

By no means did all Jews support DeFunis. The Reformed
Jews of the Union of American Hebrew Congregations backed
the school. So did the National Council of Jewish Women. There
are Jewish women opposed to the women's movement. Midge
Decter, Podhoretz's wife, is a dead-end anti-feminist, and most,
but not all, Orthodox women are hostile. But Betty Friedan and
many other Jews were among the founding mothers of modern
feminism, and a substantial minority of Jewish women are seriously active on the issue.

We have cited a poll showing that 64 percent of Jews are
opposed to quotas, and only 22 percent favor them. Even if, as
suggested, the polling sample probably did not have enough
organizationally unaffiliated Jews, a more accurate sample would
not have resulted in any appreciable difference. There was no
breakdown of those in favor of quotas, but it is legitimate to
speculate that a majority of the favorable are women—more pre-

cisely, young women. But even a majority of Jewish women as a whole would seem not to favor them. Again, many young Jewish men have been "educated" by their feminist girl friends on this. Some fellas learn—quick enough!—that if they say one word against quotas, some feminists are just liable to inform them that they have used up their lifetime quota of sex. And if they don't like it, they can go complain to Midge Decter about it.

It was the hard core of the Establishment, the ADL, AJCongress and AJCommittee, that submitted *amici curiae* briefs for DeFunis. A gaggle of Italian and Polish "white backlash" outfits signed the AJCommittee's brief.

In the most famous case, Allen Bakke sued the University of California at Davis. Sixteen seats in the medical school had been set aside for minorities. In 1978 the Supreme Court ruled that the school's plan discriminated against whites. The ADL, the two AJCs and Shanker's AFT submitted briefs, along with some "unmeltable ethnics" and right-wing groups like the Fraternal Order of Police, the Chamber of Commerce and Young Americans for Freedom.

To be sure, the Establishment supports remedial programs for disadvantaged students, and they are for scholarships for the poor but deserving. But this is just mucho hot air. The real-world lobbying efforts of the Establishment are for bucks to Israel and aid to Soviet Jews, as well as for a bombs away U.S. military budget. The AJCongress is not as reactionary as the other two stalwarts, but it is hardly in the front line trenches in the fight for scholarship money to students, or increased billions for our schools.

Many Jews, and other whites, have difficulty with quotas because they seem to violate equal protection before the law. They too call for increased spending for all the poor, rather than supporting racial quotas. No doubt, *if* the government had enacted such a program in the 1960s, the country would be far down the road to racial equality. But, as everyone knows, the U.S. soon after entered into an epoch of budget cuts.

Most of those who have bleated about aid to the poor in general rather than quotas can scarcely be said to have shown themselves to be terrorists, as it were, in defense of the innumerable programs stifled by Carter and then slashed by Reagan. And it must be remembered that we are talking here about existing programs, not new ones. The "dump Reagan" criers of 1984 had selective memories. They somehow forgot that Blacks were second-class citizens economically under Carter.

De facto opponents of quotas have no program for racial equality. They are simply opposing the Blacks' agenda. They are electorally opportunistic. Except that everyone knows that veterans have traditionally been awarded points on civil service tests when many of them did nothing more meritorious during some war than hand out laundry on some military base in New Jersey.

How many of those who now decry "reverse discrimination" ever did anything about the veterans' pass, or failed to take advantage of it, if eligible? Average white Americans are unpolitical. Other than voting in their unions to go on strike, they never lift a finger on behalf of human equality, including their own.

The Black movement is absolutely correct in seeing the Establishment as its enemy. But we must also ask if their opposition to quotas was really in the interest of Jews. One of the leading opponents of quotas is Harvard sociology professor Nathan Glazer. In an August 1985 *Commentary* article, the savant ruminated on that very question:

> Students of American Jewry confront . . . a sociological literature filled with forebodings about a group whose history . . . has gone very well indeed. . . . Most Jewish organizations opposed a strict statistical basis for allocating positions in higher education and in employment—quotas —as a matter of principle, but there were pragmatic considerations as well. Jews were already "overrepresented" in the institutions that were becoming battlegrounds. . . . If it were to be generally conceded that each ethnic/racial group should be represented proportionately . . . what would happen to the overrepresented? . . . Was the worry misplaced? . . . Affirmative action certainly pointed in the direction of hurting Jewish interests, or rather the interest of individual Jews. But . . . females were one of the groups designated as beneficiaries of affirmative action. Thus . . . one could argue that Jewish women were as much helped by affirmative action as Jewish men were hurt, or helped even more than Jewish men were hurt.[41]

Translated into plain English, the reactionary pedant was confessing that, in spite of the fanatic opposition of him and his co-thinkers, and their tortured equation of affirmative action quotas to anti-Semitic restrictions, Jews have been net gainers from quotas. *And* they gained in spite of the hostility to quotas by the overwhelming majority of Jews, including the majority of women. Yet Jack Newfield and other liberal Democratic hustlers have the temerity to tell us that the majority of Jews are—get this!—"The most likely coalition allies with minorities."[42]

"The Most Commonly Expressed Reason"

Why have the Jewish Establishment and the Black leadership become so estranged on the Middle East? Martin Peretz has told us, in an editorial in *The New Republic,* in 1979, in the wake of the Andrew Young affair:

> The decision by several black civil rights leaders to embrace the cause of Palestinian nationalism . . . appears to stem more from petulance than from any careful examination of the issues. . . . The facile equation of the American civil rights movement with the PLO's cause is the sort of oversimplification that comes easily to those unfamiliar with the murky complexities.

But, not to worry. Because "the interest that black political leaders recently have taken in the Middle East will, we suspect, be temporary." Having in a few deft strokes proven that them darkies don' know sheeeet, and will forget the whole damn thing in ten seconds flat, since it's all too much for their feeble minds, the powerful Semitic brain of Marty Peretz worked on to give us the real poop: "Supporting the PLO has only symbolic significance. What lies beneath the symbolism is an attack on American Jews."[43]

Foreign readers may not know who Marty is, but in America it is widely agreed that he is an embarrassment not only to Zionism but to capitalism. Freedom of the press and "free enterprise" mean a system where any idiot with money can buy an established magazine, and turn it into a vehicle for his inanities, and that is what happened to *The New Republic.*

We are fortunate to have the results of a serious study of a significant portion of the Black leadership that gives us a real picture of their concerns. In 1984 the World Jewish Congress and the World Zionist Organization commissioned Kitty Cohen to poll the Congressional Black Caucus. The results of her interviews with 16 of the then 21 Black Representatives appeared in the April 1985 issue of the WJC's London magazine, *Patterns of Prejudice:* "The most commonly expressed reason for a deterioration in the cooperation between Blacks and Jews was Israel's ties with South Africa."[44]

Naturally enough, Blacks are not of one mind re the Middle East. But by now innumerable leaders have visited the region. Of course they have studied its complexities! And, regardless of other differences, they *all* oppose Israel's South African policies to one degree or another. Even Bayard Rustin, absolutely Israel's most zealous Black American partisan, voiced his "deep sense of concern and disturbance" when the Israeli government brought Prime Minister Johannes Vorster of South Africa to the Wailing Wall in April 1976.[45]

Israel's apologists try to blame Israel's links to Pretoria on the Black African states. Israel was not especially close to South Africa in its early years. In the 1950s, Tel Aviv realized that it needed the votes of the emerging Black African states at the UN, and eventually there were thousands of Israeli technicians in the sub-Sahara region, and many thousands of Africans studied in Israel at various institutions. In return for Black African support, Israel voted for sanctions against South Africa.

Black African estrangement from Israel began with the 1967 war, when Israel conquered the Sinai, part of Africa. Egypt demanded that its fellow members of the Organization of African Unity take action. Most did not break ties immediately, but after the next war (1973), almost all Black states that had not already done so severed diplomatic relations. A few of the more conservative regimes kept up overt or covert economic links.

Israel had preemptively invaded Egypt only after Nasser made blustering threats. Israel did not start the war to conquer Sinai, and reasonable people understood this. Given this, and the considerable Israeli economic aid to Africa, many Black Americans thought the subsequent break was unjustified. But that aid was never in Africa's interest. On February 22, 1977, *The Wall Street Journal* ran an article on the CIA:

> *The Wall Street Journal* has learned that the agency provided large sums to the Israeli government. The purpose of the Israeli payments . . . was to finance "foreign aid" projects in African nations. The operation apparently was intended to bolster Israel's political standing on the African continent. In past years— including at least the period from 1964 to 1968, and perhaps beyond—the CIA has paid Israel a total estimated in the millions of dollars. The money was then to be channeled to the African recipients.[46]

The connection actually goes back at least to 1961, when the CIA used the AFL-CIO to send $300,000 to the Histadrut for its Afro-Asian Institute for the training of ex-colonials in union organizing.

Most African politicals didn't want to get too close to the US, the ally of Britain, France and Portugal, then still in Africa. But they didn't want to link up to the Soviets either. They knew little of Zionism's history. When they thought of Israel it was in terms of its having won independence from Britain. They admired the kibbutzim. They thought of Israel as a "third force."

The Americans' prime concern was to keep them away from the Soviets, so the CIA picked up the tab for Israel's penetration of the continent. All went well until Sinai. No amount of chatter about Zionist-socialism could alter the reality that Israel had conquered a piece of Africa. Or that imperial Washington was openly pleased with Israel's triumph.

It was Palestine and stepped-up diplomacy by the Arab states, not South Africa, which finally motivated the break in relations. Once the rupture took place, Israel moved rapidly towards Pretoria. The immediate result of Vorster's visit was an Israeli-South African joint cabinet committee to push trade. By now the links are extensive. Israeli investments are admitted in desalination plants and electronic equipment. The International Monetary Fund reported only $69 million for Israel's 1983 exports to South Africa, but this omits weapons. However, a report for Tel Aviv University's Jaffe Institute for Strategic Studies puts arms sales to Pretoria at $350 million per year.

South Africans have invested in Israeli hotels, housing and port development, and joint Israeli-South African companies for iron and steel processing and chemical and fertilizer production. Air and sea shipping links are extensive. Israel is the world's leading diamond cutting center, but South Africa's $750 million per year uncut diamond sales appear as a transaction between Britain and Israel because the gems first go through the DeBeers Ltd. Central Selling Organization in London. Only $142 million of Israel's imports go on the books as coming from South Africa.

Coal and iron are the major non-diamond commodities. Counting "official" exports and the diamonds, South Africa's exports to Israel came to $892 million in 1983, more than its exports to West Germany.[47] Additionally, South Africa beats the world anti-apartheid boycott by shipping products like formica to Israel where it is finished and goes out as Israeli tables.

The South African *Financial Mail* for September 14, 1979, reported that "Both countries benefit by increasing exports, there's . . . access to European and U.S. markets where South Africa can't otherwise easily compete."[48]

There can be no doubt that Israel ignores the UN's arms embargo of South Africa. In 1977, Foreign Minister Moshe Dayan told some American professors that Israel "will not abandon South Africa because of President Carter's position" favoring the ban. "It is not the business of the President of the United States whom we have for friends so long as we are within the limits of the law." That was a little raw, and a statement was rushed out announcing that "if there is a Security Council resolution Israel will not violate it."[49]

No sane person believed Israel obeyed the ban. Sure enough, on December 14, 1981, *The New York Times* reported a "recent 10-day visit by Israel's defense Minister, Ariel Sharon, to South African forces in Namibia along the border with Angola." In an interview, "Sharon . . . reported that South Africa needed more weapons if it was to fight successfully against Soviet-supplied troops."[50]

Sharon did not mean for some other country to get rich in this worthy cause. Weapons sales are secret, but it is admitted that they included Reshef patrol boats, armed with Gabriel-2 missiles, Ramata patrol boats, remote-pilot drone scout planes, radar stations, alarm systems, electronic "anti-terrorist" fences and other surveillance systems. Uzi machine guns are locally produced on license.[50]

A report in the Israeli government-owned Jewish Telegraphic Agency's June 27, 1984, *Daily News Bulletin,* pulled up the curtain of secrecy, at least in part. Writing of trade between the two countries, it said that:

> Israel's largest export items, being classified as electronic equipment and metal products and machinery, fuel speculation that Israel contravenes the United Nations embargo. . . . Two months ago, the *Sunday Times* of London . . . claimed that around 300 Israeli advisors are in South Africa helping to train soldiers, sailors and pilots, and that Pretoria and Jerusalem cooperate in the nuclear field on the basis of South African uranium being exchanged for Israeli technology. . . . A South African strategist . . . said South Africa and Israel share information on missile development and counter-insurgency.[51]

On September 22, 1979, an American spy satellite detected an atomic flash off Africa. South Africa used a GC-45 155mm howitzer in its test and Israel had smuggled it out of the U.S. to Antigua, where a South African ship picked it up. The episode was revealed in 1980 by British Independent Television (ITV). Israel denies the story but in 1985 Wolf Blitzer, the *Jerusalem Post's* well-informed Washington correspondent, wrote that while Israel denies involvement,

> few people in Washington—either in or out of the government—have taken those denials very seriously. . . . Jack Anderson, writing in *The Washington Post* on April 26, said the United States "had prior knowledge that South Africa and Israel would explode a small nuclear device in the fall of 1979." . . . Rep. John Conyers (D. Mich.) issued a report on May 22. . . . He charged the Carter administration with covering up the alleged Israeli-South African nuclear cooperation.[52]

The report was by Ronald Walters, professor of political science at Howard University, and formerly Jesse Jackson's main issues advisor during his campaign. It explained why the Democratic administration covered up the explosion:

> If it became public that Israel had the bomb the administration might have been pressured to cut off U.S. military aid there (present law would require it). . . . The administration did not need any new complications in garnering Jewish votes during the upcoming Democratic Party primary campaign against Senator Edward Kennedy."[53]

Until the beginning of the present revolution in South Africa, Israel didn't hide its alliance with the racists. In May 1984, the Israeli Defense Forces hosted the 2nd Annual Congress of Free World Paratroopers. A high point was the presentation of a wreath to their "fallen brothers." Robert Brown of *Soldier of Fortune* joined Major General duPlessis, Chief of Operations for the South African Defense Forces, in presenting the wreath.[54]

By November 5, 1984, the situation in South Africa had changed. When South Africa's Foreign Minister Roelof Botha met Israeli Foreign Minister Yitzhak Shamir, in Jerusalem, it was officially called a "private meeting." Except that *The New York Times* reported that he was met at the airport . . . by Mr. Shamir and provided with an official limousine and all the usual courtesies of an official visit, including a dinner.[55]

On August 13, 1985, the Israeli Foreign Ministry brought Chief Gatsha Buthelezi to Jerusalem. He is chief minister of KwaZulu, the biggest puppet Bantustan. The *Times* described his visit

> He is considered among the least militant of South Africa's black leaders. . . . His nonviolent approach has earned him the enmity of the more militant black organizations. . . . The Zulu leader saved some of his most bitter remarks for Americans. . . . painting the more nonviolent leaders like himself as "stooges." . . . Israeli officials clearly want to maintain contact with moderate blacks . . . which is what is behind the invitation to Chief Buthelezi.[56]

The December 1985 issue of *Israeli Foreign Affairs* reported that Israel announced that it would provide development aid to the KwaZulu Bantustan. The Histadrut has established links to unions led by Buthelezi's Inkatha gangs. These bogus unions are bitterly opposed by the real Black unions. No country in the world is as deeply involved with the Bantustans as Israel, and it is no wonder.

In 1984 the Jews-only West Bank settlement of Ariel was twin-citied with Bisho, the capital of the "Ciskei" puppet state. Yosef Schneider, the Bantustan's Israeli representative, declared that it was "symbolic that no country in the world recognized Ciskei, just as there is no country in the world that recognizes the Jewish settlements in Judea and Samaria."[57]

South Africa's revolution is a turning point in world history, as important as the American, French and Russian revolutions. The profound world ramifications have already emerged in our domestic politics. The Black movement has been powerfully energized; no one still talks about campus apathy. Reagan, who won so handily in 1984, is now on the defensive as his "constructive engagement" swindle has collapsed. The liberal Democrats, completely demoralized after their Mondale fiasco, have all duly rushed down to the South African embassy to get themselves photoed while being arrested. They fondly hope to channel hatred of apartheid into votes for them.

The Establishment feels the immense pressure. If the anti-apartheid movement focuses on the Israel-South Africa connection, Zionism will be faced by a domestic opposition of huge proportions. They fear that a considerable number of their Jewish supporters may abandon them rather than come into conflict with an aroused Black population. Blitzer wrote in August 1985 that "Quietly, there have been some American Jewish representations made to Israel urging a more forceful Israeli expression of opposition."[58]

They got their answer from Shamir at a September 26, 1985, meeting of the Conference of Presidents of Major American Jewish Organizations:

"We are not going to change the character of our relations with South Africa" . . . Shamir said there was a large number of Jews living in South Africa "and we are a small country." . . . Asked about pressure on South Africa to change apartheid, Mr. Shamir said Israel would leave it "to the world powers to tackle this problem."[59]

Talk about South African Jewry is just an excuse. Jerusalem trotted out Iranian Jewry to justify sale of spare American weapon parts to Khomeini. Shamir gave his real thinking earlier in the year, as reported in *Working Class Opposition,* a revolutionary publication:

"If South Africa goes, all of Africa goes with it." Those were the words of Israeli Foreign Minister Yitzhak Shamir when asked to comment on . . . the NBC television on November 7. . . . "It's necessary for our allies to understand that Israel and South Africa are essential countries in their respective areas of influence. If South Africa disappears, if its government doesn't find a way to overcome its current problems, all Africa will go with it. In the same way, if Israel succumbs to the attacks of its enemies, the West will no longer have access to the Middle East."[60]

The Establishment has divided somewhat over the anti-apartheid struggle. According to a story in the December 6, 1984, *New York Times,* "some religious groups—particularly Jews—say they have seized upon the South Africa issue to repair their ties to the Black community."[61] The Synagogue Council of America, which claims to represent the reform, Conservative and most

Orthodox Jews, issued a statement in December 1984 denouncing apartheid. There is no reason to doubt that they are opposed. But the resolution went no further than to "urge the American Government to continue its current initiatives and utilize all appropriate actions at its disposal to impress upon the Government of South Africa, our repugnance at these racial policies."[62] Everyone who could think knew Reagan had no such initiatives going and that he was quite supportive of the Pretoria regime. And, of course, there have been no statements denouncing the Israeli-South African connection.

It is difficult to estimate the total Jewish participation in the anti-apartheid movement, which is very strong on our campuses. It is reasonable to assume the percentage of Jews involved reflects their percentage, or a little higher, in the schools concerned. But, compared to the 1960s, Jews are not as prominent in the leadership. Blacks and radicals have initiated many of the local coalitions. Jewish students involved are overwhelmingly not affiliated to the organized Jewish community.

Nowhere is the participation of any sector of the Establishment as important as their participation in the civil rights movement was. Again, we see rabbis and delegations from the AJCongress marching, particularly at the South African Embassy. But they were not part of the April 20, 1985, demonstration in San Francisco and Washington, which involved tens of thousands. When they do picket it is frequently with Black Democrats, and the talk gets to revivin' the good ol' Black-Jewish coalition. But the rabbis know not to appear at mass Black events, where they fear to be challenged on the Israel-South Africa link.

The weakness of the Establishment liberals is best seen when they try to organize Jewish anti-apartheid events. Thus, the Northern California Board of Rabbis and the Jewish Community Relations Council of San Francisco called such a rally on August 25, 1985, with additional nominal sponsorship from the local AFL-CIO Council, some Black politicians and Christian clergy. The local community paper editorialized: "It would be helpful if more Jewish groups were represented . . . sporting banners and posters. . . . In the '60s Jews were in the forefront of the civil rights movement." The *Jewish Bulletin's* report of the event gave the attendance as "about 200 in San Francisco's Union Square."

The *American Jewish Year Book* gives 75,000 as San Francisco's Jewish population. While many are unaffiliated, it is easy to see why so few of the organized showed up. The editorial calling the demonstration talked of healing "the schism opened up by Jesse Jackson and Louis Farrakhan." It went on how "Israel also has voiced its opposition to apartheid countless times." But then it had to say that:

> True, Israel continues to trade with South Africa. But so does the United States and much of Black Africa—in far greater quantity than Israel. In Israel's present economic straits, it can't afford to pass up any lucrative trading partners. But . . . Israel, as noted, hasn't refrained from criticizing apartheid.[63]

Liberal rabbis and the like are not, it must be confessed, politically sharp. They do not understand that you cannot run with the fox and hunt with the hounds. Jews who believe you can will not come to anti-apartheid demonstrations. And you cannot hope to heal any schism with the Black masses if all you will tell them is "Sorry, no hard feelings, but Israel simply must trade with white racists."

In fact, how liberal is the liberal wing of the Establishment? Stephen Solarz, a member of the Board of Governors of the AJCongress, is the Representative of Brooklyn's 13th Congressional District. This is the only district in the country with a Jewish majority. As a member of the House subcommittee on Africa, he has always spoken against apartheid. But he is not talking in favor of majority—i.e. Black—rule, which is what the African National Congress insists upon. He let it all hang out in an October 8, 1985, *New York Times* Op-ed:

> Most South African Whites would reject a unitary state based on the principle of one-man, one-vote. . . . But they might well accept a system of checks and balances based on a combination of majority rule and minority rights, with Federal arrangements providing for a devolution of power to regional and local authorities. While such a formula clearly falls short of maximum black aspirations, it would probably be an acceptable starting point for a long overdue dialogue between the races.[64]

Acceptable to the ANC? This is another moderate *maisela*. But it is the real position of the Democratic Party wing of the Establishment. *The New Republic* made this clear in a September 9, 1985 editorial:

The one-man, one-vote electoral formula that the insurgent leadership has fixed on is designed for simple appeal to democrats
everywhere. . . . But the formula is not an authentic solution. . . .
What we are suggesting, in short, is that "separate development"
need not be a code phrase for continuation of apartheid . . .
although each group needs the other economically . . . they fear
each other politically. Reasonable people . . . will be willing to
explore the fears, even if it leads to contemplation of territorial
divisions and federal schemes with wide local autonomy and
reciprocal citizenships as alternatives to the mesmerizing dream of
a singular wealthy South Africa under a central pluralist government. The very idea mocks reality. . . . To meet the black
grievance, partition would have to be . . . a genuine reallocation
of the wealth and power. . . . None of the entities born under a
partition plan would be likely to meet all the standards . . . that
we demand for ourselves. But . . . still, blacks and whites should
only be lucky enough to achieve something so distant from their
present dreams of dominance and avenged justice.[65]

It is to be emphasized that this comes from the liberal wing of
the Establishment. The "Neo-Conservative" view was put in the
September 1985 *Commentary* by Paul Johnson, a British Tory:

Disinvestment . . . is an absurdity in itself, and a cruel absurdity. . . . South Africa differs from the rest of the continent . . . it
is in many respects a free country. . . . Both the rule of law and
democracy are subject in South Africa to important qualifications.
But it is the only African country where they exist at all. . . . The
judiciary is independent—very much so—non-whites can get justice against the state, something they are most unlikely to secure
anywhere else on the continent. . . . For instance, the circumstances in which . . . Steve Biko died in detention have been
subjected to a degree of minute security in the courts which would
be rare even in America. . . . There is overwhelming evidence
that South Africa has been moving away from apartheid . . .
apartheid could be dead and officially buried in five years. . . . A
successful campaign of disinvestment would simply drive the Afrikaners back into the *laager*. . . . The forces of reform within the
regime would lose their electoral base and the reform movement
itself would come to a halt. . . . The primary opponent of
apartheid in South Africa—its only effective opponent, in
practice—is capitalism. . . . There is, in fact, a common interest
for blacks and business to dismantle apartheid. . . . The present

situation . . . can thus be seen as a race. . . . There are those within the regime . . . who want to dismantle apartheid . . . but they must move slowly, because they have to carry the bulk of the Afrikaners with them. On the other hand, there is the ANC. . . . Its terror campaign . . . is strongly reminiscent of the . . . efforts by the Grand Mufti and his killers to destroy the forces of Arab moderation in prewar Palestine.[66]

At last we laity may understand a fact long known to ornithologists: It is impossible to distinguish two bird songs. That of the cuckoo and that of the British Tory in full throat, whistling his little head off, in praise of his beloved capitalism.

The amusing thing is that Podhoretz ran this *meshugas,* this madness, because he agrees with it. He lists his religion as Jewish, whatever that means. He actually believes in two secular idols: world capitalism and Israel. Both are implicated up to their jockey shorts with the criminals in Pretoria. Therefore Botha and Co. are not sworn enemies of human equality. They are its best friends. Fanaticism can go no further.

Those committed to the defeat of apartheid clearly see the right wing of the Establishment as enemies. They do not and cannot see its liberals as allies. Their loyalty is to Israel, not the oppressed in South Africa.

Israel's South African policy is evil to the nth degree. *No one* in the Establishment will break with Zionism over Israel's ties to Pretoria. Some kid themselves that they can remain publicly silent about that alliance and simultaneously pose as opponents of apartheid. The right wing is not that naive.

Democratic liberals and their henchmen in the unions tell us not to speak of Israel and South Africa, as that, they claim, would divide the anti-apartheid forces. As per usual, they are wrong. For us to be silent would be to declare to the world that we have a higher loyalty to Israel's deluded sympathizers than to the Blacks in South Africa. This we can never do. Politics is as much a matter of morale as strategy. If we tolerate a double standard—that it is shameful for Americans to sell candy in Pretoria, but that it is understandable for Israel to sell candy and weapons to Pretoria—we will go nowhere. We cannot go before Blacks, the natural bedrock for our cause, and tell them they must be silent to please any Jews or Democrats or union piecards. "You cannot serve two masters." Full stop, period.

Black Politicians and the Jews

Black nationalism still exists as a folk phenomenon, and sometimes it takes on a dramatic mass character. But the nationalists
have not been able to get their act together. Practically, nationalism has been degraded into nothing more than the crudest skin
politics, the electing of Black Democrats. However Blacks are the
caboose of the economic train and cannot be otherwise under this
system. Therefore, these officials have nothing to offer their supporters, neither program nor results. In 1984, the National
Conference of Black Mayors backed Reagan's call for a subminimum teenage wage as a cure for Black unemployment. "If
$2.50 an hour is all we can go with at this time, we'll take what-
ever we can," said Mayor Johnny Ford of Tuskegee, Alabama.[67]

Nor do these Democrats have a thing in the way of strategy re
South Africa. In October 1985, the "graying leaders of the American civil rights movement," as *The New York Times* described
them, organized an anti-apartheid march in Atlanta. Benjamin
Hooks, head of the NAACP, John Lewis, ex-head of SNCC,
Mayor Young, Julian Bond, et al., were all there. Lewis summed
up their collective vacuity: "I do think we have an obligation, but
what can you do from so many thousands of miles away?" Not
having done anything for the people in over a decade, they have
no following:

> "You've got to have a large coalition, particularly of students in
> the colleges," Mr. Hooks said. But like the civil rights leaders
> themselves, most of the 700 to 800 marchers were middle-aged.[68]

Naturally these Democrats have nothing more to offer re the
Middle East than they do on domestic politics or South Africa.
Mayor Tom Bradley of Los Angeles greeted Begin at the airport
on his last trip to the U.S., in November 1982, after the grisly
Beirut massacre. Might the fact that, as *The New York Times* so
delicately put it, "Jewish financial contributions have been a
mainstay to his political campaigns," have had a tiny bit to do
with his identity with Begin?[69] Certainly his pro-Begin stance was
perfectly in character. On January 7, 1983, the *South African
Digest,* the organ of the Ministry of Foreign Affairs, published a
photo of him, captioned:

The Mayor of Los Angeles, the Honorable Tom Bradley (right), recently presented the key of the City of Los Angeles to the South African Consul General in Beverly Hills, Mr. Sean M. Cleary.[70]

Few, if any, other Black Democrats are such dark traitors as to be giving out keys to South African consuls. But many are quite shameless, if more open, when it comes to South Africa's intimate ally. This was clearly seen during the June 1984 Berkeley, California, vote on "Proposition E," which would have put the city on record as calling for a cut in U.S. aid to Israel in proportion to the amount Israel spent on settlements in the occupied territories. Of course, Bradley denounced the measure. So did Oakland's mayor, Lionel Wilson, and Willie Brown, the Speaker of the State Assembly. Every Black elected official in the state was either loudly opposed or neutral, except Berkeley's own Mayor, Gus Newport.

By far the most crucial of the "neutrals" was Congressional representative Ronald Dellums, a Berkeley resident. The referendum put the most famous member of the Democratic Socialists of America on a cross. His district is mostly white. Many of his campaign contributors are Jews, and when it comes to Israel they run the gamut from purblind apologists to cynical opportunists.

Dellums must vote on Middle Eastern matters in Congress, and he votes no to "all arms transfers and sales to any nation in the Middle East, because such actions will escalate the violence."[71] He must take this position because his district takes in the University of California at Berkeley, with one of the largest antiwar movements of any school in the country. If he didn't oppose arms to Israel in Congress, he could expect left-wing electoral opposition. But his Jewish fund-raisers and contributors would never support him if he *unnecessarily* antagonized pro-Zionist Jewish voters by supporting the proposition.

With the proposition on the ballot, a local Zionist leader put him on the spot with a letter declaring "90 percent of your Jewish constituents oppose this initiative as a disguised attempt to push the Israeli people into the sea." The Zionist insisted he believed in a Black-Jewish coalition. But "the Jewish people will consider mere neutrality on this issue as insensitivity."

Dellums could not denounce the measure, as that would have infuriated his left supporters. However, his "neutrality" was clearly an attack on the proposal. His

gut reaction is that the problems of the Middle East are so complex that it is of questionable value to approach solutions in such a
piecemeal fashion. Such efforts seem better calculated to cause
anguish and divisiveness than to move us to a realistic position of
solving these problems. On a personal level I resent being pushed
into kneejerk positions on ballot initiatives that are irrelevant to
any political solution to the problem. When I think of it in that
vein, a neutral position makes perfectly good sense.[72]

Defying the entire Black Democratic spectrum, including Jesse
Jackson, who campaigned in the state just before the vote, but
kept silent on the Berkeley poll, 42 percent of the Black voters
supported Proposition E, compared to 36 percent of the city's
voters as a whole

One month later, Irving Kristol, the neo-con guru, discussed
Jackson in *Commentary,* and warned his readers that they had to
understand that the enemy was not Jackson but the Black masses.
He was preaching a "Third World view of politics." Kristol per-
ceived that "if he cannot do this within the Democratic party he
will either desert that party or his enthusiastic followers will
desert him."[73]

Kristol is right. The complete hacks, like Bradley and Rangel,
who votes Israel's way 90 percent of the time on weapons bills,
opposed Jackson from the beginning and the masses went right by
them to Jackson. Then there is Jackson himself, who does speak
out for the Palestinians, but who is a reformist with no strategy
for getting the Black masses what they need, let alone the Palestinians.

Finally there are the people. By no means are most of them
activists, certainly not yet. But they have plebeian egalitarian
instincts, which leads many of them to side with the oppressed
everywhere, even if passively. If they don't get the leadership
they need from Jackson, they will go past him as well. The
Berkeley vote was one of the first signs of that.

The historic dependence of both the Democratic Party and the
old line civil rights organizations on Jewish funding is well
known to Black intellectuals. Many of them hope to free themselves of their addiction and, naturally enough, some of them
look in the Arabs' direction. After the Young affair, Jackson met
with representatives of Arab-American groups and Arab governments and practically shook them down. If they didn't put bucks

into the Black community, "We will all learn to recite the alphabet without three letters: P-L-O."

A Chicago *Sun-Times* reporter interviewed both the Arabs and Jackson:

> He was telling us: "If you don't support me, I won't support you." . . . Jackson confirmed the solicitation. . . . "My challenge to them was that if they wanted to be part of the human rights struggle . . . they must join it with dollars and bodies."[74]

Similarly, Los Angeles Representative Mervyn Dymally, one of only six Representatives, all Black, who protested the 1985 bombing of the PLO headquarters in Tunisia, told *Al Fajr,* a Palestinian paper, that:

> The wealthy Arab governments need to invest in programmes that are responsive to the needs and aspirations of minorities in the U.S., such as providing loans through a corporation for building houses or helping private black universities.[75]

There is an unreal quality to all this. There is a small Palestinian community here. Most of it is middle class—grocery store owners and academics and the like. They naturally are a financial support for their hard-pressed people in the Middle East. They can hardly be a serious financial base for a Black movement here.

There are other Arabs here. Many are Lebanese Maronites, and many of these are supporters of the right-wing Phalange—that is to say, those who perpetrated the Sabra and Shatilla massacre. At any rate, most Arab-American voters are Reaganites and are not going to be the moneybags for any Black Democrats.

Right-wing Arab governments have spent some money on anti-Zionist propaganda, but not nearly as much as the public might think. And they, of course, are pro-capitalist and want to be the friends of Reagan and his ilk. They are not about to jeopardize their links with Washington by any kind of massive interference in the internal affairs of this country, certainly not on behalf of the Palestinians, whom they don't like and whom they see as political disrupters. Still less would they risk their relations with official America for its Blacks.

Most of the "progressive" Arab states are not very progressive and at any rate are not very rich after the collapse of oil prices.

Libya does have money and has given sums to the Muslims, most recently lending Farrakhan $5 million which he intends to use setting up Black businesses. However, anyone who knows the Arab world can testify that serious Arab intellectuals look on Qaddafi as a joke. He was born in a tent and their attitude is that he is their desert prophet. They feel every nationality should have one of these around, just to keep reminding everyone what simplicity is like. For the Black movement to rely on him or any other Arab regime would just be asking for disaster.

Both the Arab national movement and the Black movement are in catastrophic *ideological* shape. Until they get their acts together programmatically and strategically, no amount of money is going to help either. The Black movement couldn't make it with the heroin of Jewish money, and it will never make it with the methadone of Arab money.

"Welcome to Hymietown: Population 2,000,000 Jews—and a Few Goyim"

Someone had to be awfully interested in the fortunes of Jesse Jackson to have read "it," an article by Rick Atkinson in the February 13, 1984, *Washington Post*. The piece was all about his quarrels with the Establishment during the campaign over affirmative action and Palestine. He told how he could identify with Arabs and Israelis, about how he had "not taken an anti-Israel's right to exist policy. Never did." And then, in the 37th paragraph in an otherwise not very exciting article, came a geography lesson that is now a permanent part of the language of this country:

> In private conversations with reporters, Jackson has referred to Jews as "Hymie" and to New York as "Hymietown." "I'm not familiar with that," Jackson said Thursday. "That's not accurate."

At the foot of the piece was a note that "Staff writer Milton Coleman contributed to this report."[76] Coleman is Black and was the source for the Hymie quotes. Jackson had used the terms, short for Hyman, a name common among Jews of another generation, in an informal "Let's talk Black" discussion.

On February 26 Jackson admitted using the terms, in an apology made in a synagogue. But the damage was done. Not so much by the statements, which, after all, were said in a bull session. "Talkin' Black" *means* using slang. The public's problem came in the fact that *Reverend* Jackson lied about it on February 19 on the "Face the Nation" TV show: "It simply is not true, and I think that the accuser ought to come forth." The lie raised natural questions as to the sincerity of his apology. What made matters worse was that Farrakhan had rushed to Jackson's defense before his apology.

After demonstrations by the Jewish Defense League, Farrakhan had, according to *The New York Times,* "warned Jewish organizations that there would be retaliation 'if you harm this brother.' " Soon Perlmutter was demanding that Jackson repudiate Farrakhan, which he refused to do, saying he was only reflecting Black anger at the previous assassinations of Medgar Evers, Malcolm and King.[77]

Until the Democratic convention in August, there was a steady journalistic flow about Jackson's statements, his relations to Farrakhan, and the Muslim's remarks as well. "Hymietown" was an unknown phrase until then. Suddenly a new place existed, Hymietown-on-the-Hudson. A Jewish friend joked once that he read it so many times that he began to see signs on the freeway: "Welcome to Hymietown: Population 2,000,000 Jews—and some goyim."

Jackson kept insisting that he was not an anti-Semite, telling the press that "I'm Judeo-Christian. My ethos is Jewish. My identification with the Jewish people and their struggles is in my bloodstream and in my religion." But no one can fool Nathan Perlmutter: "Let us say it plainly. We are dealing with a person whose recorded expressions are those of an anti-Semite."[78]

There is no reason to bore American readers with petty details of all this. They know it. Whole Canadian forests were chopped down so that we could get every nuance of the saga. Fortunately, it is finally over. On November 19, 1985, one Mikhail Gorbachev, sinister head of the evil empire, was in Geneva for a summit with our own Ronnie. Jackson had gone there on behalf of anti-war groups that had gathered over a million signatures calling for a nuclear test ban, and he met the monster. They made small talk, about nuclear tests, South Africa and other petty matters, until Jackson brought up what *The New York Times* called

the plight of Jews in the Soviet Union. This last subject had to be mentioned, Mr. Jackson said, because "There is a great anxiety among the American people about the plight of Soviet Jews."

If that anxiety could be eliminated, "it will go a long ways to establish the bonds of mutual trust." Later Jackson again expressed his—or rather "our"—"real, earnest anxiety" about the human rights of Soviet Jews.[79]

Jackson later claimed he brought up the Soviet Jews because "Gorbachev had to know that he did not have some 'dissident,' a pro-Gorbachev guy he could ease through the back door."[80] Yeah. Except that few have any doubt Jackson was getting the Establishment off his back. Certainly the organizations that sent him over didn't ask him to bring up Soviet Jews.

How much anxiety is there in the U.S. over Soviet Jewry? Aside from the Zionists, Falwell, the AFL-CIA tops, and the politicians, there is little popular interest. Of course, this being the land of the freak, home of the knave, we may be sure every single politician who has done time in prison in the last 20 years for bribery can prove that he made at least one statement on Soviet Jews.

In the real world, the first Jew in space was Col. Boris Volynov, who went up on January 15, 1969, and again in 1976. America's first Jewish astronaut, the late Judy Resnick, didn't go up until August 30, 1984. Talking about Soviet Jews in the U.S. has little to do with their real problems, which are primarily those of the entire Soviet people; the domination of their society by a caste of bureaucratic parasites. But talking about Soviet Jews here has everything to do with showing American Jews that you are a friendly native. That is the only real significance of Jackson's Geneva episode.

Jackson succeeded in getting out from under the anti-Semitism charge. Daniel Thurz, vice president of the B'nai B'rith, the parent organization of Perlmutter's ADL, praised Jackson for presenting the case "so persuasively and effectively."[81] We must now therefore ask if Jackson ever was an anti-Semite? The answer is no. Perlmutter's memo lists his alleged sins. Jackson denies ever saying that he was "sick and tired of hearing about the Holocaust and having America being put in the position of a guilt trip. We have to get on with the issues of today and not talk about the Holocaust." The statement was allegedly heard by two people whom Perlmutter described as "Jewish activists" and who seem to have been plants in Jackson's entourage on his 1979 trip to Israel.

Even if he said it, so what? Professor Israel Shahak of Hebrew University, a Warsaw ghetto and Bergen-Belsen survivor, a former Zionist, now an outspoken opponent of Zionism, has repeatedly said what needs to be said on this matter: The Holocaust is constantly trotted out by Israeli politicians as their excuse for all manner of crimes, public and private, up to and including the 1982 Lebanon invasion. Here in the U.S., every miserable bribetaking alderman has made his speech denouncing Adolph Hitler. Jackson is accused of saying, after his tour, that he had "seen very few Jewish reporters that have the capacity to be objective about Arab affairs," and that they challenged him "without conversation."

Whether this is true or not is incidental. Certainly it doesn't exactly place Jackson in the same league as Bogdan Zinovy Chmielnicki and his Cossack pogrom hordes. He is accused of thinking Nixon henchmen Ehrlichman and Haldeman were Jews.[82] So? Jews could have made that error, given the enormous number of Jews with German names. Perlmutter and Co. knew Jackson listed the Jews as part of his hoped-for rainbow coalition. They knew he involved the New Jewish Agenda and other critics of Israeli policy in his campaign. None of that mattered. Jackson's real sin was speaking out for the Palestinians and, it must be stressed, for affirmative action.

The Establishment were hypocrites in their denunciations of Jackson. This was revealed by a more or less liberal member of its inner circle, Brandeis professor Leonard Fein, in an editorial in his *Moment* magazine:

> It is inappropriate for those who regularly refer to "shvartzes" sanctimoniously to condemn those who use "Hymie." The exemplary public declarations of Jewish organizations on the matter of civil rights ring hollow when contrasted to the sanction we have come to give bigotry in our private attitude and behavior. . . . It is time, and then some, for us to stop pretending that our history of persecution has immunized us against prejudice.[83]

Shvartzes is Yiddish for Blacks. But *every* Yiddish speaker knows it has taken on a deprecatory quality when used *in English*. When American Jews use it in English it means the nigger, the inferior. One says, "My shvartze can't come tomorrow. But I need the place clean for the party. Give me your shvartze's number." Fein is correct. Shvartzes is constantly used in organized Jewish circles.

Jackson's Hymie remarks and the subsequent denials put him on the defensive for the rest of the campaign and, therefore, like the WBAI poetry reading, they were setbacks for the entire Black movement. But Jackson's failings in this regard were by no means as important as his overall ideological and strategic weakness. He had no solution to the problems of America, its Blacks or the Palestinians.

Jackson is a reformist to the nth power. He knows America's foreign policy is imperialist, but such moderates are always concerned with being "realists." In December 1983 he announced his opposition to any increase in the military budget for the next five years, other than for inflation. Translated into English, an America under Reagan or, as he hoped, a Democrat, would have still had "more nuclear weapons than it needs" and it would still have had "the world's largest network of bases across the world."[84]

He ended up supporting Mondale, who backed the invasion of Grenada, which militant Blacks, including Jackson, opposed. He knew—and said—Blacks won *nothing* at the convention. But when Ronald Walters then proposed that Blacks write in his name for president, he opposed the idea. We say that smart rats abandon sinking ships. A reformist mouse like Jackson insisted on jumping on Mondale's boat when it was already 20 fathoms beneath the waves.

For him, as with everyone, foreign policy is an extension of domestic politics. Naturally he extended his purblind reformism to the Palestine question. He came into the convention calling for "recognition of the right of the Palestinian people to a homeland with the provision that it be a weaponless state."[85] This sounds OK *if* you are a liberal, trying to sell something human to a party you know is incurably imperialist.

In the real world, Palestinians will never permanently reconcile themselves to the notion that an inch of their homeland, where they were the born majority, belongs by right to someone else. Still less will they accept a Bantustan, even temporarily. Sovereign states are equals. If Israel has a right to an army, so does a Palestinian state, as does every state.

In his reformism, Jackson neglects two tiny considerations: The Zionists know the Palestinians will never reconcile themselves to the loss of Jaffa. And they know that any Palestinian state would get guns at the first opportunity. Therefore they will never grant a West Bank state. It will be Zionist Israel *or* a democratic secular Palestine, never Israel *and* Palestine. But, of course, not even this wretched Bantustan was ever his operative program. He always knew he would end up supporting whomever beat him for the nomination, be it Mondale or Hart, both fanatic opponents of any kind of Palestinian state.

Farrakhan

On May 19, 1984, Benjamin Hooks told the Union of American Hebrew Congregations that "Black folks don't give Farrakhan all that much importance. He is the leader of 10,000 people."[86] Today Louis Farrakhan is world famous, entirely due to the campaign against him by the Establishment.

Louis Eugene Wolcott was born in the Bronx, in New York City, in 1933, to an Episcopalian from Bermuda. He was a calypso singer when he was recruited to the Nation in 1955 by Malcolm. He stayed loyal to the movement after Malcolm abandoned it. Although there is no one who claims he was personally involved in the subsequent assassination of Malcolm X, he wrote in the December 1964 issue of *Muhammad Speaks,* "The die is set and Malcolm shall not escape . . . such a man is worthy of death."[87]

After Elijah Muhammad died in 1975 his son, Wallace Muhammad, gave up his father's ideology for Islamic orthodoxy. As Muhammad is supposed to be the last of the prophets, Elijah Muhammad was no longer called a "Divine Messenger." The group, renamed the American Muslim Mission, abandoned Black nationalism. In 1978 Farrakhan broke with the AMM to reconstitute the Nation.

For all his Black separatism, Farrakhan immediately supported Jackson's Democratic candidacy and registered to vote for the first time. His security squads, the Fruit of Islam, provided protection for Jackson, who received death threats, and suffered severe harrassment by Meir Kahane and his JDL terrorists. According to the *Chicago Tribune,* which taped his March 11, 1984, radio broadcast, he called Coleman a "traitor" and a "Judas." "What do you intend to do to Milton Coleman?" he mused.

At this point, no physical harm . . . one day soon we will punish you with death. . . . When is that? In sufficient time. We will

come to power right inside this country one day soon. And the
white man is not going to stop us from executing the law of God
on all of who fall under our jurisdiction."[88]

There was naturally a huge outcry and Farrakhan had to personally call Coleman to tell him, "There have never been threats
to your life, brother, or your family. That will go on the
record."[89]

On April 11, the *Tribune* published another excerpt from the
March 11 talk:

> Here the Jews don't like Farrakhan, so they call him Hitler. Well,
> that's a good name. Hitler was a very great man. He wasn't great
> for me as a Black person, but he was a great German. . . . He
> rose Germany up from nothing. Well, in a sense you could say
> there's similarity in that we are rising our people up from noth-
> ing.[90]

Again there was an outcry and Farrakhan had to clarify himself. Hitler "was indeed a great man," but he was "wickedly
great."[91] Jackson declared his disagreement with all of this, but
refused to disassociate himself from Farrakhan the man.

On June 24 Farrakhan was taped again.

> This I want the Jews to know and we want the world to know:
> that they are not the chosen people of God. . . . The Holy Koran
> charges the Jews with taking the message of God and altering that
> message and giving the people a book written by their own
> hands. . . . I'm not anti-Jew. I am pro-truth, but in this serious
> hour, the truth must be told so that the true people of God may
> come up into the view of the entire world. These that have stolen
> our identity, these that have dressed themselves up in our gar-
> ments must be defrocked today. . . . The Zionists are those Jewish
> persons who wanted a homeland for the Jews . . . but they wanted
> to fulfill the vision without fulfilling the preconditions. . . . It was
> your cold naked scheming . . . against the lives of a people there
> in Palestine . . . you pushed out the original inhabitants. . . . Now
> that nation called Israel never has had any peace . . . because
> there can be no peace structured on injustice, thievery, lying and
> deceit and using the name of God to shield your gutter religion
> under His holy and righteous name. . . . You hate us because we
> dare to say that. . . . It is the black people in America that is the
> chosen people of Almighty God.[92]

The gutter religion attack was too much for Jackson and he sharply disassociated himself from the remark:

> Such statements . . . have no place in my own thinking or in this campaign, and I call upon all my supporters to join me in speaking out in support of my stand.[93]

Jackson was trying to put together a rainbow-hued alliance and he was trying to do it in a party crucially dependent on Jewish donors. Therefore he had to suffer politically from his tardiness in breaking with Farrakhan. But the Muslim in no way suffered from the repudiation. All he was ever interested in was

> the despised, the rejected, the unloved, the unwanted, the lost sheep of the Bible, the Prodigal Son of the book; the Black people of America, you are the people of Almighty God!!

Farrakhan couldn't care less what Jackson, or anyone else thinks of him, for he has Allah's unlisted phone number:

> I said to America and to those Jewish persons who don't like Farrakhan, and Black persons too . . . that I am not before you of myself, but I am indeed backed by the power of that which upholds the universe . . . the very God that you call upon . . . is my support, my protector, my defender. . . . I answer to no one but to Almighty God Allah and His Christ. . . . I took the money from Libya and I dare you to say I am wrong in doing what I did. I don't bow down to you! I don't bow down to Saudi Arabia![94]

The Muslim is not just answerable to Christ. He is like unto him. He told 25,000 people in New York's Madison Square Garden on October 7, 1985, that, just as

> Jesus had a controversy with the Jews. Farrakhan has a controversy with the Jews. Jesus was hated by the Jews. Farrakhan is hated by the Jews. I am your last chance, Jews. You can't say "never again" to God, because when He puts you in an oven, you are in one indeed![95]

Farrakhan's notions of both Arabs and Jews are crackpot. He pontificated in an interview in *The National Alliance:*

> The word itself, Semitic, deals with Afro-Asian people. If I am anti-Semitic I am against myself. You have Arabs and they are

called Semitic people. Semi means half. They are in-between. There is a mixture of the blood of Africa and Asia and Europe in there and you have what you call a Semitic people. . . . Now, most of these that call me anti-Semitic are not Semites themselves. These are Jews that adopted the faith of Judaism up in Europe; they're called Ashkenazi Jews. They have nothing to do with the Middle East—they're Europeans. . . . They are *not* Semitic people. Their origin is not in Palestine.[96]

Crackpots are just like everyone else—only more so. Calvin Coolidge said America's business is business and, for all its separatism, the Nation of Islam is as A-murican as they come. Farrakhan's solution is POWER: People Organized and Working for Economic Rebirth. The $5 million loan from Qaddafi is going into setting up a sort of Islamic Arm & Hammer to sell soap, toothpaste, and Black beauty aids. Blacks would then subscribe more money.

Marxists have made "petty bourgeois" the most overused term in the political lexicon, but this hoary "buy Black" notion is the ultimate petty bourgeois utopia. In today's business world, $5 million gets you a cup of coffee and a Danish. Leave the waitress a decent tip and there is no change. But John Johnson, a firm believer in the old maxim "part a prophet from his money and make yourself a profit," was going to manufacture the goods for POWER. Until October 23, 1985, when it suddenly occurred to the Johnson Products Company that a lot of their other customers are Jewish-owned department stores. The deal fell through. "We knew we could not offend our distribution channels."[97]

This creates enormous problems for Farrakhan, as there is no other Black firm that is already set up to do the job, and he scarcely wants to do business with whites. But money talks, and perhaps he will be able to get the goods produced abroad? But so what, under any circumstances? There are almost 29 million Blacks in the U.S. Twenty cents a head isn't even the start of a start of a solution to the problems of Black America.

Obviously, Farrakhan is a loose cannon. But that doesn't mean he can't hit a few targets. In 1985 he toured America, speaking to over 120,000 people, overwhelmingly Black, filling the Garden in New York and other auditoriums in Los Angeles, Washington and elsewhere. They cheered him and his attacks on Jews for two reasons. Obviously, they see him as a Black who is being attacked by Jews in particular and whites in general. But Stanley Crouch, a Black writing in the *Village Voice,* was also quite right in writing that his emergence

> seems a comment on the failures of black, liberal and conservative politics since the Nixon era. . . . The result is a black lower class perhaps more despairing and cynical than we have ever seen. . . . In this atmosphere, Farrakhan's broad attacks are political rock and roll—loved more for the irritation they create than for their substance. . . . When Farrakhan . . . baited Jews . . . he . . . plumbs the battles that have gone on between black people and Jews for almost 20 years. He speaks to (though not for) those who have fought with Jews over affirmative action, or have felt locked out of discussions about Middle East policy by Jews as willing to bully and deflect criticism with the term "anti-Semite" as black people were with "racist" 20 years ago. . . . Obviously, black leaders have failed. . . . As one black woman, infuriated by Farrakhan, said, "We should be putting our feet in the pants of these politicians. Get this dope out of here. Get these schools working. Clean up these neighborhoods. Do what we need done."[98]

Farrakhan is no danger to the Jews. For all his badmouthing, the Nation of Islam is not accused of attacking a single Jew. Nor will they, for Farrakhan knows the authorities would crack down on him in a hot second if he attacked any white people. It might be assumed that someone in his audience might hear him raging against Jews and take it upon himself to attack Jews. This could well happen. But so far there have been no such reports in the press.

This writer is not privy to the innermost thoughts of the Establishment. But past contact with some of them leads to the belief that some of the smarter of them are sorry they ever made such an outcry against Farrakhan. They were going after Jackson and he started out as a handy stick to beat a dog. Now, as he says, "I am sorry, you are going to have me to contend with for the rest of your natural life."[99] Nevertheless he is not going to become the next Malcolm or King, and he is not going to bring them down. In the end, he is just another rapologist. He does not mobilize the masses to demonstrate in the streets against white racism in general, or against the Jewish Establishment, or against Israeli consulates.

The ones who are going to be most damaged by him, directly and indirectly, are going to be the Black politicians. The Trotskyist *Militant* condemns him as an anti-Semite, but it pointed out why he will inexorably hurt them: "He goes after one thing for which they have no defense—their political corruption and collaboration with the enemies of Blacks."[100]

Those, like Jack Newfield, who preached about a fabled Black-Jewish coalition, have a problem. In the real world, a "coalition" between 20 percent of our doctors and lawyers and their cleaning ladies could never be an equal alliance. Such a thing is a sociological absurdity. The only coalition between such disparate groups that could ever happen in this world was the one that did happen: the Democratic Party. Except that Mondale tried to out-Reagan Reagan by emphasizing the federal deficit. Except that the Democrats in Congress are not exactly lions and tigers in defense of social programs benefiting the poor. The masses are getting nothing out of these Black Democrats.

Whenever Farrakhan comes into a town, the local Jewish Establishment rushes to them to get them to denounce him. In the overwhelming majority of cases they succeed. But in the end the auditoriums are filled for him as they never have been for the Black Democrats who denounce him. And they never will be filled for them, not even if their wives danced naked in the aisles. Because they are indeed do-nothings. The masses don't expect Farrakhan to do anything. After all, he isn't in City Hall, he isn't in Congress. They are. All he has to do to look better than them is denounce them.

Warm and Friendly International Bankers

What do the ordinary Black people of America think about Farrakhan and Jews and Israel? The Simon Wiesenthal Center in Los Angeles commissioned Market Fact Incorporated of Washington, D.C., to do a nationwide telephone poll of 500 Blacks in October 1985.

When asked to name a Black leader, 59 percent said Jesse Jackson. Next came Atlanta Mayor Andrew Young. Then came Farrakhan with only 7 percent.[101] But he ranked ahead of Tom Bradley, Benjamin Hooks, Julian Bond and Coretta Scott King. Forty-one percent said they wanted his influence to increase. But 25 percent wanted it to decrease and 34 percent disapproved of him as a spokesman for Blacks, seven times higher than any other prominent Black. His greatest support comes from the poorest and least educated.

According to the Center, the poll showed that Blacks are no more suspicious of Jews than non-Jews. It was claimed that in fact Blacks "are viewed as receiving better treatment from Jews than from non-Jews." But, while 30 percent of those aware of what was going on in the Middle East were pro-Israel, 23 percent were sympathetic to the Palestinians, a far higher percentage than among whites. Thirty-eight percent believed Jews have too much power in the U.S.[102]

In 1981, 31 percent of Blacks told Yankelovich that Jews had too much power, compared to 23 percent of the population as a whole.[103] Thus most Blacks don't think Jews are too powerful, but the percentage is higher than for whites and it has grown. It is reasonable to think that this is due to Farrakhan.

In July 1984, a Lou Harris poll showed that Blacks were more negative toward Jews on a number of issues than whites were, but not on all. Thus, according to Harris:

> By 2-1 the public as a whole does not think that most slum owners are Jewish, by a narrow 36-30 percent most Blacks think they are. Whereas most Americans deny by 46-33 percent that when it comes to choosing between people and money, Jews will choose money, by 59-19 percent Blacks agree with that view. . . . A 41-30 percent plurality of all Americans . . . deny . . . that Jews are more loyal to Israel than to America, by 43-20 percent, most Blacks believe it. Whereas by 60-22 percent, a majority of the public . . . deny . . . that Jewish businessmen will usually try to pull a shady deal on you, by a narrow 38-34 percent, Blacks tend to believe it.

However, while the general public denies, by 52-34 percent the claim that Jews must work harder because they are discriminated against, by 44-38 percent Blacks believe it. More important, while 39-33 percent of the public believe that Jews have been more supportive of civil rights, 43-23 percent of Blacks think so.[104]

The 1981 Yankelovich poll also showed that 63 percent of Blacks think that "Jews are more loyal to Israel than to America," compared to 45 percent of whites. Sixty-seven percent believe that "international banking is pretty much controlled by Jews," while 40 percent of whites think so. Forty-three percent say "Jews don't care what happens to anyone but their own kind." Eighteen percent of whites think that. However, 82 percent of Blacks believe Jews are "warm and friendly people," compared to 89 percent of whites. Only 34 percent think Jews "should stop complaining about what happened to them in Nazi Germany," while 40 percent of whites feel so.[105]

The Wiesenthal Center doesn't begin to understand the mentality of the Black ghetto. It claimed Blacks to be no more suspicious of Jews than non-Jews. In reality it is just the other way around. They are at least as irrationally suspicious of Jews as non-Jews. Black observers could have told them about a real phenomenon called "Black paranoia." Like the classic shtetl mentality of Eastern European Jewry, it is the end product of discrimination and isolation and ignorance.

A 1982 poll showed 67 percent of Blacks to believe that Saudi Arabian investments threaten U.S. economic independence, compared to 47 percent for the public as a whole.[106] Yankelovich reported that no less than 26 percent of Blacks thought Italian-Americans have too much power and 12 percent think Japanese-Americans have too much power. To anyone who knows this country, the last is slapstick in itself, but even more Blacks—55 percent—say Japanese-Americans have "too much influence in certain professions."[107]

Many of the polls previously cited in this book clearly show that tens of millions of Americans, Jew and gentile, are not exactly brilliant when it comes to politics and still less when it comes to understanding the rest of the citizenry. The same must be said of Blacks who seem to think of Jews as a bunch of warm and friendly international bankers. Maybe they've seen a movie the rest of us haven't: Woody Allen playing Shylock. The older generation, like whites, has a lot of Bible bashing notions of the Jews as Christ killers. But Yankelovich is quite correct in saying that Christian anti-Semitism is sharply down in the younger generation. He says hostility to Jews among Blacks is

> at least in part, a specific expression of a more general conflict between the "have's" and the "have not's" . . . the perceived business power of Jews is responsible for feelings about Jews held by blacks. . . . Social contact with Jews is generally associated with lower levels of anti-semitism, [while] among blacks, the nature of social contact with Jews produces somewhat higher levels of anti-semitism. . . . Relative to whites, blacks are more likely to interact with Jews in impersonal settings (shopkeepers, doctors, dentists) rather than in more truly social settings such as clubs, friendships.[108]

Black anti-Semitism, such as it is, is very different from classical European anti-Semitism or its white American shadow. Neither Farrakhan nor anyone else is attacking Jews, no one is calling for depriving Jews of their political rights, and no one is trying to take away their property.

In the 1960s ghetto rebellions, the few Black shopkeepers would try to protect their stores from looters by putting "soul brother" signs in their windows. Black rioters may or may not have thought to ask themselves whether or not any particular store they broke into was Jewish, but any white store in a Black neighborhood was fair game in an outbreak. More important, looting was the spontaneous action of the lowest stratum of the masses. It was not the policy of Malcolm, or the Black Muslims after he left them, nor any organization of any weight.

European anti-Semitism was always strongest among capitalists and professionals who saw Jews as rivals rather than as exploiters. They wanted quotas on Jews, or wanted them out of the country so that they could control "their" national market. Farrakhan is the last leader of any importance who still calls for a Black economy but even his program in no way calls for quotas against Jews. And no one thinks the POWER proposal is the basis of his appeal. The rest of the Black movement calls for affirmative action which is total integration into the white economy.

Glazer and the Establishment may have had a "foreboding" that quotas for Blacks would lead to quotas against Jews. But that was a crackpot anxiety, to say the least. That never was a demand of any Black movement nor was it ever in the minds of the whites who dominated Congress in the salad days of affirmative action. In the real world, it was they, the Jewish Establishment, who have been waging a ferocious economic war against the Blacks, with their never-ending attacks on affirmative action quotas.

The Fate of the Establishment

There is an old Jewish proverb, "After the destruction of the second temple, prophesy was left to fools." Nevertheless only a fool can be blind to the problems facing the Establishment. The poll of the Black Congressional Caucus foretells their fate. They more or less won their fight against quotas. They put Jackson on the ropes after the Hymie incident. Farrakhan can't do them serious harm unless he changes his isolationist line. But the African

National Congress is not a pack of reformist wimps à la Jackson, nor are they just a-talkin' as with Farrakhan. As they fight in South Africa, they will mobilize thousands of Blacks here. And others as well, including Jews. As attention is focused on South Africa, Israel's connection to the Pretoria criminals, and the Establishment's defense of their holy land, will undergo the severest scrutiny. Nothing on this planet can prevent this. Those who believe in human equality will see to this. Indeed we shall shout it from the rooftops.

Jews, Blacks, Americans, Israelis, whatever, have one choice and only one choice: with the Blacks in South Africa or against them. There is no middle ground. And because there is none, it will be impossible to run in two directions, towards the Blacks and, simultaneously, towards the intimate ally of their tormentors. This time 'round there will only be winners and losers. Woe to the vanquished!

Notes

1.   "Negro-Jewish Relations in the U.S.," *Encyclopedia Judaica*, vol. 12, col. 932.

2.   "Benjamin, Judah Philip," *EJ*, vol. 4, col. 528.

3.   David Lewis, "Parallels and Divergencies: Assimilationist Strategies of Afro-American and Jewish Elites from 1910 to the Early 1930s," *Journal of American History*, Dec. 1984, p. 559.

4.   "Remarks by Discussant Morris U. Schappes," *Negro-Jewish Relations in the United States*, p. 62.

5.   Ibid., p. 61.

6.   Jack Newfield, "Blacks and Jews," *Village Voice*, March 20, 1984, p. 16.

7.   Schappes, p. 57.

8.   Henry Siegman, "Jews and Blacks: Reconciling the Differences," *Congress Monthly*, Jan. 1985, p. 3.

9.   Siegmann, "Jewish Ethics and Terrorism," *Jerusalem Post*, Aug. 5, 1985, p. 17.

10.   David Luchins, "Orthodox Jewry and the Fight for Social Justice," *Post*, Sept. 23, 1984, p. 2.

11.   Siegmann, "The Orthodox Leaders," *Jerusalem Post*, Oct. 6, 1984.

12.   Arthur Liebman, *Jews and the Left*, p. 541.

13.   Roberta Feuerlicht, *The Fate of the Jews*, p. 163.

14.   Robert Curvin, "What If Heroin Were Free?" *NY Times*, Feb. 20, 1981.

15.   Maureen Dowd, "Fear of Crime Seems to Strain Race Relations," *NY Times*, May 16, 1985, p. 22.

16.   Walter White, *A Man Called White*, p. 353.

17.   Poppy Cannon, *A Gentle Knight*, pp. 90, 96.

18.   Ibid., p. 103.

19.   Robert Weisbord and Richard Kazarian, Jr., *Israel in the Black American Perspective*, p. 45.

20.   Ibid.

21. Malik Miah, "Malcolm's Legacy: Black Freedom Struggle Is Part of World Revolutionary Process," *Militant*, Feb. 25, 1983, p. 8.
22. Ibid.
23. Ossie Davis, "Malcolm Was Our Manhood, Our Living Blackhood," in Philip Foner (ed.), *The Voice of Black America*, p. 1012.
24. Jeff Mackler, *Teachers Under Attack*, p. 21.
25. Ibid., p. 17.
26. Ibid., p. 23.
27. "Exploding the Myth of Black Anti-Semitism," *NY Times*, March 16, 1969, p. 7E.
28. "How Negroes Feel About Jews," *Jewish Digest*, December 1968, p. 49.
29. Arnold Forster and Benjamin Epstein, *The New Anti-Semitism*, p. 61.
30. Ibid.
31. Martin Mayer, *The Teachers Strike*, p. 76.
32. Forster and Epstein, p. 200.
33. "Shanker, Albert," *Current Biography 1969*, p. 394.
34. Murray Friedman, "Politics and Intergroup Relations in the United States," *American Jewish Year Book 1973*, p. 175.
35. Robert McFadden, "Reform Jews Ask Healing of Split in Ties to Blacks," *NY Times*, May 21, 1984, p. B10.
36. Nathan Perlmutter, *Memorandum*, Oct. 6, 1983, p.. 3–5.
37. Milton Moskowitz, "Black Businesses Far Behind," *San Francisco Chronicle*, May 31, 1985.
38. "Blacks Owned 47% More Businesses in '82 Than '77," *Wall Street Journal*, Oct. 8, 1985, p. 49.
39. "Lawyer Asks Wider College Desegregation," *NY Times*, Apr. 8, 1984, p. 29.
40. David Margolick, "Bar Group Is Told of Racial Barriers," *Times*, Feb. 16, 1985.
41. Nathan Glazer, "On Jewish Forebodings," *Commentary*, Aug. 1985, pp. 32–4.
42. Newfield, p. 16.
43. "Blacks and the PLO," *New Republic*, Sept. 1, 1979, pp. 5–6.
44. Kitty Cohen, "Black-Jewish Relations in 1984: A Survey of Black U.S. Congressmen," *Patterns of Prejudice*, Apr. 1985, p. 12.
45. Weisbord and Kazarian, Jr., p. 94.
46. Edward Behr, "CIA Reportedly Gave Israelis Millions While It Was Paying Jordan's Hussein," *Wall Street Journal*, Feb. 22, 1977. p. 2.
47. Alex Cockburn, "Beat The Devil," *Nation*, Aug. 17, 1985, p. 103.
48. "Special Report Israel Supplement," *Financial Mail*, Sept. 14, 1979, p. 20.
49. Weisbord and Kazarian, Jr., pp. 108–9.
50. Drew Middleton, "South Africa Needs More Arms, Israeli Says," *NY Times*, Dec. 14, 1981, p. 9.
51. Sheldon Kirshner, "Envoy Says Israeli Relations With S. Africa Overblown by Detractors," *JTA Daily New Bulletin*, June 27, 1984, pp. 3–4.
52. Wolf Blitzer, "Does Israel Have a Nuclear Weapons Arsenal? Probably," *Northern California Jewish Bulletin*, May 31, 1985, p. 39.
53. Ronald Walters, *The September 22, 1979 Mystery Flash: Did South Africa Detonate a Nuclear Bomb?*, May 21, 1985, p. 15.
54. Kevin Steele, "Winning Israeli Wings," *Soldier of Fortune*, Oct. 1984, pp. 57, 59.

55. "South African Holds Talks With Shamir," *NY Times,* Nov. 6, 1985, p. 3.

56. Thomas Friedman, "Zulu Leader Sets Primary Demands," *NY Times,* Aug. 14, 1985, p. 3.

57. "Israel and the Bantustans," *Israel Foreign Affairs,* Dec. 1985, pp. 2, 5.

58. Blitzer, "Black Leaders See Israel as a Supporter of Apartheid," *Jewish Bulletin,* Aug. 23, 1985, p. 11.

59. David Bird, "Israel Won't Act Against Pretoria," *NY Times,* Sept. 27, 1985, p. 4.

60. "Reform of Apartheid or a Socialist Azania?," *Working Class Opposition,* March 1985, p. 18.

61. David Sanger, "Anti-Apartheid Rallies Reviving Rights Coalition, Organizers Say," *NY Times,* Dec. 6, 1984, p. 20.

62. Rabbis Condemn Apartheid Policy," *Amsterdam News,* January 5, 1985, p. 4.

63. "Join the Apartheid Fight," *Jewish Bulletin,* Aug. 23, 1985, p. 10, and "Jews Can't Let S. African Blacks Suffer, Rabbis Proclaim," *Ibid., Aug. 30, 1985. p. 3.*

64. Stephen Solarz, "Tackling Apartheid from the Inside," *NY Times,* Oct. 8, 1985. p. 27.

65. "The Partition Solution," *NR,* Sept. 9, 1985, p. 6.

66. Paul Johnson, "The Race for South Africa," *Commentary,* Sept. 1985, pp. 27–32.

67. "Black Mayors Back Subminimum Wage for Youth," *NY Times,* May 6, 1985, p. 25.

68. Dudley Clendinen, "South Africa Violence and Memories of Selma," *NY Times,* Oct. 25, 1984.

69. Judith Cummings, "Meeting Planned in Los Angeles by Black Muslim Stirs a Debate," *NY Times,* Sept. 14, 1985, p. 7.

70. *South African Digest,* January 7, 1983, p. 5.

71. Ronald Dellums, *Letter to the 8th Congressional District,* Aug. 1985, p. 3.

72. Jock Taft, "Sifting the Berkeley Left," *Merip Reports,* Jan. 1985, p. 27.

73. Irving Kristol, "The Political Dilemma of American Jews," *Commentary,* July 1985, p. 28.

74. Perlmutter memo, p. 11.

75. Ghassan Bishara, "U.S. Congressman Swims Against Pro-Israel Stream," *Al Fajr,* Nov. 1, 1985, p. 7.

76. Rick Atkinson, "Peace With American Jews Eludes Jackson," *Washington Post,* Feb. 13, 1984, pp. 4–5.

77. Howell Raines, "Jackson's Candor Is Praised but Remark Is Criticized," *Times,* February 28, 1984, p. 20.

78. "Jackson's 'Hymie" Remark Deplored by 58 Percent of Blacks, Poll Says: ADL Leader Denounces Candidate," *JTADNB,* June 4, 1984, p. 4.

79. Joseph Lelyveld, "Jackson, in Impromptu Session, Presses Gorbachev on Soviet Jews," *NY Times,* Nov. 20, 1985, p. 1.

80. Lelyveld, "Jackson and Diplomacy: Embracing the Nuances," *NY Times,* Nov. 21, 1985.

81. "B'nai B'rith Praises Jackson for Asking Gorbachev to Release Jews," *Northern California Jewish Bulletin, Nov. 22, 1985, p. 22.*

82. Perlmutter, *Memo,* pp. 8–10.

83. Leonard Fein, "Jesse Jackson and the Jews," *Moment,* April 1984, p. 14.

84.   Ronald Smothers, "Jackson Proposes Military Freeze," *NY Times*, Dec. 25, 1983, p. 22.

85.   Raines, "Parties Study Jackson Role in Convention," *NY Times*, April 8, 1984, p. 38.

86.   McFadden.

87.   Milton Ellerin, *Minister Louis Farrakhan, Leader of the Nation of Islam*, p. 8.

88.   Alan Schwartz, "Who Is Louis Farrakhan?," *ADL Bulletin*, Sept. 1984, p. 10.

89.   Ellerin, p. 6.

90.   Schwartz, pp. 10–11.

91.   Ellerin, p. 7.

92.   "Excerpts from Address," *NY Times*, June 29, 1984, p. 12.

93.   Akinshiju Ola, "Farrakhan Controversy Won't Just Fade Away," *Guardian*, July 11, 1984, p. 9.

94.   Louis Farrakhan, "Message from the Washington Convention Center," *Final Call*, Sept. 1985, p. 18.

95.   Salim Muwakkil, "Louis Farrakhan and the Rhetoric of Racial Division," *In These Times*, Oct. 23, 1985.

96.   Farrakhan, "We are not against Jews. We are against Exploitation," *The National Alliance*, Dec. 27, 1985, p. 13.

97.   "Farrakhan Plan Setback," *NY Times*, Oct. 24, 1984, p. 34.

98.   Stanley Crouch, "Nationalism of Fools," *Village Voice*, Oct. 29, 1985, pp. 23–4.

99.   Farrakhan.

100.   Doug Jenness, "Unions Must Look to Entire Working Class," *Militant*, Dec. 27, 1985, p. 9.

101.   "People's Politics," *People's World*, Jan. 4, 1986, p. 8.

102.   "Blacks Rate Farrakhan as a Top Leader, Poll Finds," *Jewish Bulletin*, Dec. 27, 1985, pp. 1, 28.

103.   Yankelovich, Skelly and White, *Anti-Semitism in the United States*, vol. I, p. 68.

104.   Louis Harris, "Poll Shows Presidential Election Can Go Either Way," *Amsterdam News*, July 7, 1984, p. 40.

105.   Yankelovich, pp. 65–8.

106.   Yosef Abramowitz, "Black Support for Israel," *Near East Report*, March 23, 1984, p. 46.

107.   Yankelovich, p. 68.

108.   Ibid., pp. 25–6, 40.

9

Religion

"What Have You Done? The Voice of Your Brother's Blood Is Crying unto Me"

For centuries Judaism acted as a portable homeland, uniting the scattered Jews of the world. Today, not only doesn't Judaism unite American Jewry, but there are now three major Jewish sects, as different as chalk from cheese. And all of them, combined, are an ever diminishing factor in Jewish society.

The same phenomenon so glaringly apparent in every other aspect of Jewish life especially applies here: There is an imploding minority which is becoming increasingly inward looking. But the exploding majority doesn't care about Judaism in any form. To be sure, the sects will continue on in weakened condition into the foreseeable future. Nevertheless, history's judgement on Judaism is irrevocable: Not even a miracle from God can save the world's oldest monotheistic faith from its inexorable disintegration. No form of Judaism can successfully compete in the free market of ideas.

Orthodoxy

Judaism is ancient. "Orthodoxy" is not. The word was borrowed from Christian usage in 1795 to describe the rabbinical opponents of the Enlightenment.[1] When France conquered Holland that year and converted it into the Batavian Republic, Amsterdam's rabbis were so frightened of the dangers presented by complete freedom that they circulated a petition denouncing equal citizenship for Jews as contrary to the Bible. More than 1,000 Jews signed the curious document.[2] In that same epoch, Shneur Zalman, founder of the HaBaD chassidic cult, now commonly known as the "Lubavitchers," supported the anti-Semitic Tsar against Napoleon:

> If France should win, riches will increase among Jews and they will prosper. But they will become estranged from God. If Alexander wins the war, the Jews will become impoverished, but their hearts will be joined with God.[3]

Two centuries have elapsed, but Orthodoxy has not changed, nor will it, nor can it. It will always be incompatible with a libertarian mentality.

The 1971 National Jewish Population Survey estimated that 9 percent of America's Jews were Orthodox.[4] As all Jews are only 2.54 percent of the people, Orthodoxy is about 0.025 percent of all Americans. However, over half the Orthodox live in the New York metropolitan area. While even there they are a flyspeck in terms of the general population, they are an important component of organized Jewish life.

According to the Federation of Jewish Philanthropies, there are 230,000 Orthodox in New York City, Westchester, Nassau and Suffolk Counties, and they are 13 percent of the region's Jews. More than half of them, 128,000, live in Brooklyn, where they are 27 percent of the Jews.[5] Twenty percent of Bronx Jews are Orthodox, 12 percent of Queens' Jews, 11 percent of Staten Island Jewry, but only 8 percent of Manhattan's Jews are Orthodox.[6]

Charles Silberman, an Establishment scholar, did a further breakdown of the NJPS statistics in his 1985 book, *A Certain People*. Orthodoxy declined from 11 percent of second generation American Jews to 3 percent of the third. In most of the country the generational decline is continuing, the exceptions being New

York, Baltimore and Cleveland, where there have been "small increases," and Los Angeles, Miami and Washington, where new communities have arisen. "There is, at most, a stabilization of numbers after three-quarters of a century of steady decline."[7]

They take the biblical injunction "be fruitful and multiply" literally and do not practice birth control. Nevertheless an analysis of the NJPS in the *American Jewish Year Book 1973* shows there has been no significant growth, even with their prodigious fertility. By household heads, Orthodoxy made up the following percentages of American Jewry:

Under 30	=	4.8%
30-39	=	4.8%
40-49	=	6.2%
50-59	=	9.0%
60-69	=	12.4%
70+	=	16.1%
Age unknown	=	10.1%
All Jews	=	8.9%[8]

Few young Orthodox are descendants of the 1880-1924 immigration. Most are second generation children of those who came as refugees from Hitler or as DPs after the war. Previously the Orthodox rabbinate here resigned itself to the disintegration of the faith. However, the "Lubavitcher rebbe," the intellectual star of Chassidism, was rescued from Poland in 1940. In 1947 the "Satmar rebbe," an intense anti-Zionist, set up in the Williamsburg section of Brooklyn. While the two loathed each other's position on Israel, their movements provided the initial drive to stabilize the entire Orthodox element.

For all their unbounded zeal, the newcomers could never have established themselves if America had not undergone a fundamental transformation on the Jewish question. Prior to the Holocaust, anti-Semitism was quite strong in New York. Chassids feared walking about in their outlandish garb. After the slaughter, and especially after the creation of the Israeli State, anti-Semitism became extremely isolated and the Chassids gained confidence. Today their communities usually adjoin Puerto Rican or Black neighborhoods.

Most Puerto Ricans are little more than nominal Catholics, with no anti-Semitic tradition. The Williamsburg Chassids have a problem with Puerto Rican burglars, given the huge crime rate in the *barrio*, but there is no anti-Semitic content to this. The Chassids strike their neighbors as weird, to say the least, but most Jews see them the same way.

There is considerable antagonism between the Lubavitchers along Eastern Parkway and the surrounding Blacks. The rebbe realized, years ago, that if his followers moved away because of crime, it would only be a matter of time before they assimilated into the indifferent Jewish population of the city. He organized his people into street patrols, and the problem has become much more manageable. However, this has generated organized anti-Lubavitcher demonstrations, as when vigilantes beat up Victor Rhodes, an innocent Black.[9] But the Lubavitchers are extremely well organized, and are connected with both Democratic and Republican politicians, including some Black Democrats, and they can never be dislodged. Beyond this, anti-Semitism in New York is not worth spitting at. No New Yorker looks twice at a Chassid on a subway.

As they have become a visible presence again in New York life, it is frequently assumed that at least some of their increase comes from recruitment. Articles on them usually quote some *baal teshuvah* or penitent about how he foreswore marihuana for Moses and an impression has arisen that the synagogues are packed with similar types. However, only the Lubavitchers try to win Jews back to their ancestral faith.

Pollster Steven Cohen calculates that no more than "several hundred" young assimilated were recruited in the 1970s.[10] Silberman, who constantly tries to see a revival of all things Jewish, nevertheless has to be candid about most of these:

> Those who have had contact with Orthodox *baalei teshuvah*, (rabbi Ralph) Pelcovitz wrote, "can attest to the mercurial moods of some of these penitents and the ever-present danger of their leaving us as suddenly and abruptly as they arrive." . . . Some have been with cults, others with drugs; they seek a safe harbor as well as some meaning and purpose for their lives. . . . The attrition rate is not documented," he writes, "but one gets the feeling that it is substantial."[11]

The Chassids

Numerically insignificant as Orthodoxy is, it is nevertheless fractured into rival camps—the Chassids, an intermediate cluster who are frequently referred to as the strict Orthodox, and those known as the modern Orthodox. Each current is yet further divided.

No one is certain as to the exact number of Chassids in the country. But an educated estimate would be about 100,000, with 90,000 in New York, most of these in Brooklyn. All Chassidim claim to be spiritual followers of Israel ben Eliazer, a woodcutter, a mystic in mid-18th century Poland, known as the *Baal Shem Tov,* He Who Has a Good Name.

Polish Jewish piety had become overwhelming. A common saying declared that "He who studies Talmud 100 times is not to be compared to he who has studied Talmud 101 times." Their language, Yiddish, alienated them from common life, lacking many elementary terms for tools and objects of nature. The Baal Shem Tov sought to put joy into the mummified religion with dancing and ecstatic prayers. His followers minds were filled with *caballa,* esoteric numerical meanings for each letter in the Bible, revealing hidden interpretations of the scriptures.

With his death the movement soon splintered into innumerable subsects, each grouped around its saintly *zaddik.* The *Judaica* describes how these "wonder rabbis" provided illumination for their communities, each blessed one from

> his own all-pervasive radiance, attained through his mystic union with God . . . the zaddik is . . . the ladder between heaven and earth . . . hence his absolute authority, as well as the belief of most hasidic dynasties that the zaddik must dwell in visible affluence.[12]

Today the "Satmarim" are the largest American chassidic sect, with about 25,000 supporters, mostly congregated in Williamsburg in Brooklyn. As with all such groups it is named after its "court," in the old country, in this case the little Magyar town of Satu Mare, just over the border in Rumania. The only way to describe them is as the Jewish Amish. Six days a week most men wear long black coats and round black felt hats with yarmulkes underneath, as they go off to work in Manhattan. Within their own neighborhood many replace the felt hats with fur hats, winter or summer.

On Saturdays many older men, and some younger ones, wear knee breeches and white silk stockings as they stroll to and from the synagogues. Married women shave their heads and cover them with wigs and kerchiefs. The old country quality of the community is emphasized on weekdays by the bedding that these ultimate housewives air out their windows. Signs are in Yiddish. Although all the children and most of the adults know English, Yiddish is the language of the neighborhood streets.

Their singularity extends far beyond quaint costume. The high point of their annual Purim carnival is the burning of an Israeli flag. They and a periphery of other Orthodox are organized politically into the *Neturei Karta,* the "Guardians of the City." Judaism, they say, is not defended by soldiers but by its Torah scholars. Along with all other Orthodox, they believe God drove the Jews from their homeland for their sins.

Opposition to Zionism is based on the further authority of Tractate *Ketubot,* folio 3, of the Babylonian Talmud. According to this, when God expelled the Jews he made them take an oath to obey him on three things: not to rebel against the gentiles among whom they would live, not to try to hasten the Messiah's arrival by excessive prayer, and not to try to go up to the Holy Land in a column, i.e., try to take it by force.

In their eyes, Zionism is the profoundest sin. It has delayed the arrival of the Messiah and is responsible for the Holocaust. Their most important statement in English, rabbi Moshe Shonfeld's *The Holocaust Victims Accuse,* solemnly informs us:

> that our people were brutally murdered by beastly agents of the Angel of Death . . . would be totally inexplicable to us, if it were not for the understanding we derive from our holy Torah that all of this was, indeed, from the Almighty. . . . The rabbis of Hungary, squeezed together in the cattle cars to Auschwitz . . . saw the awesome fulfillment of these dire warnings . . . maintaining that it all happened to us because we didn't come out strong enough against the Zionists.[13]

The Zionists' crimes during the Hitler era are dealt with, in small measure, in this book, and elsewhere. Nevertheless, it is obligatory to say that this theory is crackpot. It is only a variation on the common Orthodox rabbinical conception of politics in which the deity's intentions, past, present or future, are, ultimately, decisive.

Can the community survive, given its archaic and fanatic character? As of now it grows through natural increase. However, some of its leaders are pessimistic for the future. They hate Zionism for its crimes, real and imagined, but they know that they have no way to bring it down. Meanwhile, closer to home, they are bedeviled by street crime. And, of course, America flaunts its manifold iniquities before their pious eyes. Their observance of the stricture forbidding rebellion against gentile authority means that they must be passive in the face of these monstrous moral provocations. They fear their youths are not going to be forever satisfied with hollow-sounding preachments about accepting the will of God.

This writer was born in Williamsburg, Brooklyn, and has observed these Chassids for many years. I will permit myself one remark on their destiny. Most assuredly some youths will inevitably become dissatisfied with a voluntary ghetto where everything has meaning but nothing is allowed. However, what will attract them to a surrounding America in which nothing has meaning but everything is allowed? Demoralization will set in, but it will be many years before they fully collapse.

The Lubavitchers

Although they are only the second largest Chassidic sect, the Lubavitchers are by far the best known, at least to their fellow Jews, especially in New York. Lyubavichi, a little town in Smolensk oblast, in what is now the Russian S.F.S.R., became the seat of HaBaD Chassidism after Shneur Zalman's son settled there in 1813. The predecessor to the present rebbe was sentenced to death by Stalin in 1927. President Coolidge and others intervened and the rebbe and his son-in-law, Menachem Mendel Schneerson, now the seventh rebbe, were allowed to leave the country for Warsaw.

The young Schneerson went on to study mathematics and physics and finally engineering at the University of Berlin, the Sorbonne and Cambridge. During his student days the future rebbe abandoned their distinctive costume. Menachem Mendel was in France when it fell in 1940, fled into unoccupied Vichy, and left for the U.S. in 1941. He took over the group in 1951 and has made it the most energetic Orthodox faction. He is, of course, descended from the movement's founder, Shneur Zalman.

Estimates of the cult's strength are vague, but 30,000 worldwide would be a reasonable guess. There are about an estimated 20,000 in Brooklyn. Most of them live in Crown Heights, near Lubavitch headquarters, at 770 Eastern Parkway. The movement is zealous in its efforts to convert Jews to Judaism. They have published some 10 million books and pamphlets and have set up HaBaD Houses near hundreds of universities in the U.S. and abroad. Their "Mitzvah mobiles," young enthusiasts with vans, are frequently parked in downtown Manhattan. Schneerson's disciples rush up to Jewish-looking passersby and try to get them into the vans where they are given a crash course in elementary Judaic rituals.

HaBaD is an acrostic for *Hakmah, Binah, Da'at,* cabalistic phrases meaning germinal, developmental and conclusive. As per standard script, the rebbe is the link between God and ordinary Jews. But HaBaD has always been the most theoretical of these mystical sects. Its basic document is Zalman's *Ha Tanya,* written in 1796. Its doctrine is the ultimate in theological racism:

> In every Jew, whether righteous or wicked, are two souls. . . . There is one soul which originates in the *kelipah* [husks— LB]. . . . From it stem all the evil characteristics. . . . This soul . . . is derived from *kelipat nogah,* which also contains good. . . . The souls of the nations of world, however, emanate from the other, unclean *kelipot* which contains no good whatever, as is written in *Etz Chayim,* Portal 49, ch. 3, that all the good that the nations do, is done from selfish motives. So the *Gemara* comments on the verse, "The kindness of the nations is sin."[14]

Now we can understand why their relations to their Black neighbors are infinitely more antagonistic than the Satmarim's with the Puerto Ricans. Similarly, in Israel, the Neturei Karta community in Jerusalem has the friendliest relationship with the Palestinians, while the local Lubavitchers are notorious for their hatred of Arabs. However, Blacks have far more rights than Arabs do in Israel, and far more votes than Jews do even in Brooklyn.

Will it come as a surprise that, given their own perverted notions about the evil nature of the goyisher soul, the Brooklyn Lubavichers are in cahoots with the most corrupt Black Democrats? They tied in with State Senator Vander Beatty, who ended up doing what New Yorkers call restful time in an enclosed rural environment.

According to Irving Howe's *Dissent* magazine, which hardly can be accused of anti-Jewish sentiments:

> Leaders of the Lubavitcher Hasidim . . . allied themselves with

Beatty through such notoriously corrupt antipoverty organizations as the Crown Heights Jewish Community Council. . . . Beatty protected such operations in exchange for unwavering Hasidic support at the polls, and had several Hasidic leaders serve on his local school boards, though no Hasidic child attends public school. . . . When some Hasidim were cited by the city and the federal government for harassing minority tenants, Beatty helped block a suspension of funds.[15]

Readers may have put reb Schneerson in the same category as Jim Jones and the Moon. But how can that be? For did not that powerful theological mind—Jimmy Carter—declare Schneerson's 78th birthday "Education Day, U.S.A."? And did not God's political vicar on earth—Ronnie—proclaim his 80th birthday a "National Day of Reflection"?[16] If we reflect we might think them two of a kind: ignorant demagogues, doing a little chasing after Jewish votes.

The Misnagidim

Next over from the chassids are a grouping known as the "strict" Orthodox. These are descendants of the *misnagidim,* or opponents of the early chassids. They dress like ordinary folks, except for the men wearing a yarmulke or a hat. Most people, including Jews, think that shaving is a breech of Orthodoxy, but this is incorrect. It is forbidden to use a razor because you might nick yourself and marring the face is a vanity. But shaving machines are allowed.

These Orthodox do not think their rabbis are holy men, and they have no esoteric doctrines beyond the Talmud. They differ from the next group over, the self-styled "modern Orthodox," in that the "strict" are more concerned that their boys learn Talmud then that they go to college. Their strongholds are Borough Park and Midwood in Brooklyn. Because they are less distinctive than the Chassids, and their neighborhoods include many non-Orthodox, it is difficult to assess their numbers. But their children will certainly tend to orient towards college, hence towards modern Orthodoxy.

The modern Orthodox are also *misnagidim.* Their strongholds are in Midwood and Canarsie in Brooklyn. But they have also set up colonies in the suburbs. One of their most important clusters is in West Orange, in Essex County, New Jersey, 15 miles from

New York. The settlement there is a merger of remnants of Newark congregations, mostly descendants of 1880-1924 immigrants, and children of DPs coming out from New York.

Again, most people, including most Jews, think of Orthodoxy as incompatible with science. But this was never really literally true. In country after country the court physicians of the middle ages were Jews. Modern Orthodoxy follows in this tradition. Yeshiva University's Albert Einstein Medical School is a world-class institution, with Nobel Prize winners, including an Orthodox woman. The Jersey moderns include a substantial element working in that state's chemical and pharmaceutical industries, as well as engineers and computer programmers.

Professor Edward Shapiro is quite correct in describing the ideological quirks of these people:

> It is not surprising that many . . . are scientists since their fields pose less of a threat to traditional Judaism than do the humanities. . . . The scientific orientation . . . is responsible, in part, for the community's intellectual flaccidity, a characteristic which, according to the sociologist Charles Liebman, afflicts Yeshiva University also. . . . There is very little desire for education per se . . . for intellectual challenges, for ideological dialogue. In fact, education, in contrast to training, is suspect since it supposedly threatens religious pieties and leads to intermarriage. This anti-intellectualism is strengthened by the social background of many . . . Orthodox which leads them to place an inordinate importance on financial success.[17]

These suburbanites are afraid of assimilation, but they definitely do not want to be identified with their less cultured co-religionists. There is a tiny "black hat" element in the Jersey settlement and these professionals dread an influx of them because, in the end, they are what has been described as "cosmopolitan parochialists." In other words, they may fear the word "assimilation," but they are too far along in the process not to be concerned over what gentiles—and assimilated Jewish intellectuals—think of them.

While they shun the embarrassing external forms of fanaticism, sectarianism is the raison d'être of their community, and it has a logic all its own which drives them ever onward into a mental world inhabited by no one except themselves. Shapiro writes that they are divided on sectarian niceties. Their quarrels are

A microcosm of the divisiveness within the larger American Orthodox community and stem from the same source—religious one-upmanship. Status among the Orthodox is achieved in part by being more *frum* [pious—LB] than one's neighbor. This results in continual religious bickering which is viewed with incomprehension, if not ridicule, by the non-Orthodox. This . . . is particularly prevalent among newer and younger members. . . . One achieves religious status by the size and nature of his *kippot* [yarmulke—LB], by wearing a *tallis* [prayer shawl—LB] over the head during the silent devotion, and by *shokling* [swaying while praying—LB]. . . . No specific religious issue has bedeviled Ahawas Achim [Congregation Brotherly Love—LB] more (and this is true of other modern Orthodox congregations) than the size and configuration of its *mehizah* [partition segregating women— LB]. . . . When a dinner was held to honor the person responsible for building the new *mikveh* [ritual bath for women—LB], a group insisted on separate seating for themselves and their wives even though the dinner's major speaker sat at a table with women. . . . At one time the synagogue even had square dances. As the community moved to the right . . . there has been no mixed dancing.[18]

Now and Then, Here and There

These references to Orthodoxy and women compel some blunt words: *ALL* Orthodox men are male chauvinists. Every day each male prays: "Blessed are thou, O Lord our God, king of the universe, who hast not made me a woman." Each day every woman recites: "Blessed are thou, O Lord our God, king of the universe, who hast made me according to thy pleasure."

All Orthodox synagogues have segregated seating. In the Lubavitcher synagogue women must sit in a screened balcony. As a frumer yid *constantly* looks at his rebbe, naturally it is behind the men so they should not be corrupted by a glimpse of a woman through the screen. The debates in the synagogues referred to are over where to put the women, how high the partition must be, etc.

The Wailing Wall in Jerusalem, Judaism's holiest shrine, is segregated. However, as Zionism is a political hustle, when extremely prominent women, like Elizabeth Taylor, visit the wall, they are allowed to walk on the men's side of the partition. If a celebrity were barred, she might make a stink, and the world press would play it up.

As it is, when such exceptions are made, there is usually mention made in the Israeli papers and Jewish community weeklies here, and sometimes there is a little muttering on the part of lady Zionists, "Why her and not us?" However, Zionist feminism is intimately connected to Betty Friedan and Bella Abzug of the National Organization for Women—NOW. Or now and then, as some call it. They share NOW's political vice: all talk and no do. If they marched onto the men's side of the mehizah it would, one might say, put Zionism on a cross. Would the government jail them before the world press? However, just as you can lead a horse to water, but you cannot make him drink, so you can propose action to a liberal Zionist, but you cannot make her think.

Some might think Friedan and Abzug would have suggested this to them. Friedan did march—once—with some Israeli Jewish feminists, not Jewish and Arab feminists. But not for nothing is NOW called now and then. It does call marches—now and then—but it doesn't yet understand that for America's women to get their Equal Rights Amendment they must become full time "streetwalkers." No. Friedan and Abzug are hardly the ones to tell their Zionist cronies to get "off their backs." Instead they are Israel's unpaid defense attorneys at international women's conferences, denying it is racist.

Orthodox Feminism, Such As It Is

The mikveh referred to is a bathhouse to which women must repair one week *after their period is completely over.* Until then they are *ritually* unclean and sex would defile the man. Because of this, many Brooklyn Chassids have their own buses to take them to work in Manhattan. They might unknowingly touch a menstruating Jewess on a subway and be defiled. (God doesn't give a damn if they touch a menstruating shiksa). As the cost of living is now higher than a cat's back, Chassidic women work, and many also take these buses. Of course, they are segregated and, as this writer has seen, some buses have curtains partitioning the women away from the menfolk.

Not all Orthodox go to the extremes of these Chassids, but it is to be repeated that all Orthodox males are chauvinists. This reality has become the troublesome point for the better-educated younger women. There are now women's *minyans* among these rebels. You must have a minyan, 10 *men,* to have group prayers in an Orthodox synagogue. These would-be feminists allow themselves to be segregated in regular synagogue services, but hold their own outlaw services, in which they do all the things men do in for-keeps synagogues.

Blu Greenberg has written an article for *Lilith,* a magazine named after the legendary first wife of Adam, who got rid of her because she insisted they were equal as they "both come from the earth."[19] Her piece fully expresses the hopelessly double-gaited mentality of these "weak sisters" of feminism:

> I could no longer accept that apologetic line so popular among those in the traditional Jewish community who were attempting to deal with feminism. Different role assignments? Yes, that part was true. But genuine equality? There was simply too much evidence to the contrary. On the other hand . . . I discovered that there were some feminists who relished criticism of the Jewish tradition but would brook no naysaying of feminism. . . . I thought of them as "orthodox" feminists, for feminism was to them a religion. . . . They were the vociferous minority. . . . Two things I know for sure. My questioning never will lead me to abandon tradition. But . . . I never can yield the new value of women's equality.[20]

I also know two things—for sure: 1. Orthodoxy is incompatible with feminism. Rabbis here will never grant equality to women in their synagogues. And Israel's soil will soak up blood before they ever grant equality to Jewish women. 2. It is disgraceful to equate those fighting for equality with fanatics denying it. She believes in liberation everywhere except in her synagogue. Orthodoxy is more important than her rights. More crucially, attaining full equality for all women, in America, in the Middle East and everywhere else will take an immense effort. That demands "monotheistic" devotion of a sort she depreciates in her feminist betters. There can be no two idols in freedom's temple.

We must assist young women from Orthodox homes who seek to emancipate themselves psychologically. But there cannot be the slightest sympathy for the likes of Greenberg. A full-grown adult must act like one. When she wakes to the fact that Orthodoxy is nothing better than a "family disease," as the great apostate Heinrich Heine so poetically called Judaism, she "votes with her feet," exactly as *millions* of Jews have done before her.

Raisin' Hell in the Holy Land

A phrase by Nathan Glazer, "Israel has become *the* Jewish religion for American Jews," is now universally cited in the literature, and is indisputably true.[21] Certainly this is not so for the Neturei Karta and for some other Chassids, and for a few other individual *misnagidim,* who retain the traditional anti-Zionist position identified with classic Orthodoxy. But it is true, in varying degree, with the bulk of Orthodox.

The Lubavitchers were anti-Zionists in the old country. Today, however, it is routine for Israeli politicians on the lecture circuit here to stop off at Eastern Parkway to chat with the rebbe. How sincere are they in courting this fanatic? Let's put it this way. Israel's most successful slogan is that it is "The only democracy in the Middle East." In other words, put the same credence in a visit to a rabbi by an Israeli politician as you would in a visit with a clergyman by an American politician. Just as here, a minority of politicians are intensely religious. But, just as here, most simply are hustlers. If they had to, they would pray to the rain god to get votes.

Although the rebbe is identified with the Israeli religious right, Zionism is not central to his movement. He personally has never been to Israel, and the overwhelming aspect of his work is religious. No one would think of going to his movement if they wanted to get information about Zionism. And most Zionists are a little embarrassed by such black hats. The real strength for Zionism is among some of the younger modern Orthodox.

Zionism has achieved several things once thought impossible even by its founders. Jews now politically dominate much of their ancestral homeland. The Israeli military is certainly one of the most efficient in the world. Religiously the impact of Zionism has been even more dramatic. Orthodoxy, which was losing ground everywhere in the pre-WWII Jewish world, is now the official religion of one-fifth of world Jewry, even if most Israelis are not Orthodox, or fully so, by the rabbis' exacting standards. Hebrew, a purely liturgical language for the overwhelming majority of Orthodox in the pre-Holocaust era, is now the street language of millions of Jews—and 710,000 Israeli Arabs. Zionism has given the outdated past a future.

Israel is a reactionary utopia, albeit a success, combining bronze age theocracy with nuclear weapons. Such a profound change in Orthodoxy's fortunes is little short of a secular miracle.

Inevitably it had a staggering impact on the political and theological thinking of what was once one of the world's most politically passive religions. Given their intense sectarianism, it was only to be expected that many Orthodox should see the hand of God in all this. Several thousand American Orthodox, at least, are so fanaticized that not only do the Palestinians have every right to be fearful, but many thoughtful Israeli Zionists are thoroughly convinced that their influence has irreversibly converted Israel into a lunatic asylum.

The more traditional Orthodox Zionists merely express the shtetl mentality "dizzy with success." The gimme-take vulgarity of ghetto Jewry at its worst is instantly recognizable in this 1974 editorial from the shrewdies over at *Jewish Life,* the organ of the Union of Orthodox Jewish Congregations of America:

> But the more we think about this, the more an important question comes to mind. Why is all this oil found there? Why did Divine Providence—for this cannot be mere coincidence—place the world's energy treasure right at Israel's doorstep? Pondering this question is enough to convince even the skeptic that we are somehow witnessing a drama whose script was written a very long time ago.[22]

A very long time ago. And in Hebrew, no doubt. The language Eve and the snake chatted in. The West Bank settlers are another matter. They too try to root their politics in biblical terms, but there is a modern, fascist, quality to their thinking that was still missing in the pious greed of the *zaides,* the grandfathers, of the Union. Here is Yedidiah Segal of the *Gush Emunim* (Bloc of the Faithful), in September 1982:

> The atheism of humanism has nothing in common with the Torah. The Torah is not humanist. If the Torah demands vengeance upon its enemies—as is written, "Happy shall he be, that taketh and dasheth thy little ones against the stones" (Psalms 137:9)—how can one view it as humanistic. The Torah's approach is based on fundamentally different ethical standards than those accepted by the western world.[23]

Part of Psalm 137 is constantly cited as the central biblical injunction for Zionism. Segal has quoted the line that embarrasses more civilized Zionists. Let us give it in full, from the King James Bible, as this is how it has entered into the language:

By the rivers of Babylon, there we sat down,
yea, we wept, when we remembered Zion.
We hanged our harps upon the willows in the midst thereof.
For there they that carried us away captive required of us a song:
and they that wasted us required of us mirth, saying,
Sing us one of the songs of Zion.
How shall we sing the Lord's song in a strange land?
If I forget thee, O Jerusalem, let my right hand forget her cunning.
If I do not remember thee, let my tongue cleave to the roof of my mouth;
if I prefer not Jerusalem above my chief joy.
Remember, O Lord, the children of Edom in the day of Jerusalem;
who said, rase it, rase it, even to the foundation thereof.
O daughter of Babylon, who art to be destroyed; happy shall he be,
that rewardeth thee as thou hast served us.
Happy shall he be, that taketh
and dasheth thy little ones against the stones.

"Terror"

The maddest of the mad is of course Brooklyn's own Martin Kahane. Until recently, many Orthodox would give their children an English name for the goyisher state's birth certificate, and a Jewish name as well. Marty was Meir. As Kahane is a variant of Cohen, or hereditary priest of the temple, our kid is of the chosen of the chosen.

Meir would agree: Zionism and busting in the heads of gentile brats, that is what Judaism is all about. Here he is, in New York's *Jewish Press*, the organ of the entire Zionist right:

> Let us look at events through *Jewish* eyes . . . 1) Lebanon: . . . A war was begun against a "Palestinian" enemy—*an entire people*—which seeks to wipe out the Jewish state and the vast majority of its Jews. It was . . . a war unto the death, the utter destruction of the enemy, the instilling of total fear, *terror,* until he capitulates and acknowledges the L-rd.[24]

Kahane's line is simplicity itself. Israel is a Jewish state, it discriminates against Arabs:

> What kind of liberal mind is so contemptuous of Arabs that it cannot understand that no Arabs can ever happily accept living in a country . . . whose national land can be rented to Jews alone. . . . What kind of obtuse intellectual cannot understand that the Arab . . . believes that the Jews of Israel are thieves?[25]

Not only that, he proclaims, they breed like—let's say it—
Arabs, and someday they will be able to vote Zionism out of
business. Democracy and Zionism being totally incompatible, we
must drive them out. Until then, let's make life miserable for
them. On March 21, 1985, the Mapam Party paper *Al Hamishmar*
compared Kahane's proposals to the 1935 Nuremberg Laws in
Nazi Germany:

> KAHANE'S PROPOSAL: Jewish men and women . . . are forbid-
> den to marry non-Jews, either in Israel or abroad. Such mixed
> marriages shall not be recognized as a marriage.
> NAZI LAW: Marriages between Jews and citizens . . . of German
> blood . . . are forbidden . . . also if they have taken place abroad.
> KAHANE'S PROPOSAL: Jewish men and women . . . are forbid-
> den sexual relations of any kind with non-Jews, even out of
> wedlock . . . punishable by two years imprisonment.
> NAZI LAW: A non-Jew who has sexual relations with a Jewish
> whore or with a Jewish male, is liable to fifty years imprison-
> ment.[26]

Palestinians naturally see Kahane as the end product of Zionism. And he is. But he is also a product of Orthodoxy. On
October 16, 1974, I met him, in the JDL office in San Francisco.
I was there when he came in after a lecture, and he initially
assumed I was a friend of the group. We continued to chat, in a
friendly manner, after he realized I was skeptical.

Terrorists, people who attack innocent civilians, are much
maligned. The public thinks they are filed-toothed cannibals. But
they are really like everyone else—only more so. From right to
left they are eager to explain themselves, to show that they are
not really crazy. If you want a soothing half hour, talk to any
representative of any terrorist group. Don't tell them you are one
of the hated enemy. (That might not be healthy.)

At any rate, we chatted amiably. The rabbi is convinced there
will be another Holocaust, this time in the U.S. That will drive
American Jews to Israel.

"But if that is true," I remarked, "Israel's ass will have had it.
Because the U.S. is its only patron and ally."

"Oh no," he immediately replied. "Israel will survive no
matter what because God is on its side."

"Well," I responded, "he sure wasn't on the side of the Jews in
1939."

Suddenly, for the first time, his finger shot into the air: "That's because they weren't in their homeland. The prophecies say he will only protect them in their own land."

He said much more after that, but I remember nary one word. A line like that drives everything else out of your head. The idea of a God is an opinion. The notion that he/she/it intervenes in modern affairs is an even more disputed opinion. But the conception that there is a God who could have rescued the 6,000,000, but did not, because they lived in Europe, is not an opinion. It is a blasphemy. It is what happens to many of those who try to inject a supernatural force into mundane affairs.

Funny, isn't it? If the bible basher is anti-Zionist, God is punishing the Jews for Zionism. If he is a Zionist, its the other way around.

Kahane embarrasses the Establishment. They know Americans. As long as they can keep the discussion on Palestinian terrorism, they've got it made. This guy not only says he is a terrorist, he justifies himself as one of a long line of Zionist terrorists. And he points to Foreign Minister Yitzhak Shamir and his Stern Gang as his best example. Worse yet, he openly discusses today's discrimination against Arabs in "the only democracy in the Middle East." But what is even more shocking is that Kahane is by no means the only American Orthodox terrorist in Israel. And these terrorists have thousands of supporters here.

The October 4, 1984, issue of *Hamavaser,* published by the Jewish Studies Divisions of Yeshiva University, was devoted to a debate on the legitimacy of terrorism in Israel, after 27 Orthodox were jailed there. The topic is of burning interest at the school, the citadel of modern Orthodoxy and a prime recruiting ground for the JDL and Gush Emunim. The atmosphere there is discussed by rabbi Walter Wurzberger:

> If any evidence were necessary to show that the resurgence of extremist fundamentalism has penetrated even into such bastions of moderation as Yeshiva University, we need only point to the fact that *Hamevaser* considers terrorism in the State of Israel a fitting subject for debate. . . . It may be painful for us to see the Omar Mosque standing on the site of the Bet Hamikdash on the Temple Mount. Yet we must muster the courage to denounce terrorist plots, even if they are inspired by Messianic pretentions.[27]

The reader must know that the Romans, not Arabs, destroyed

the Temple. The Muslims who conquered Jerusalem were aided by thousands of Jews who saw them as liberators from Christian tyranny. The crazies want to restore the Temple so that we can get back to the good ol' days of animal sacrifices. Most people, including hundreds of thousands of secularized Israelis, do not at all find it painful to see the Mosque of Omar standing there. It is one of the most exquisite buildings on the planet. Some of the crazies tried to blow it up.

Some of the wackoes tried to murder three Palestinian mayors, blowing the legs off two of them. Three students were murdered by random firing at a West Bank university. Bombs were planted on buses. But now that we have heard from a wimpering softie, let's get some of that real Judaism. Hear ye the Lord's anointed, rabbi Moshe Tendler: "The attack on the mayors deserves a standing ovation as does the attack on the college or the placing of bombs on the Arab buses."[28]

In the November 11, 1985, *New Republic,* Leon Wieseltier points to the nationalist mysticism of rabbi Abraham Kook, the Ashkenazi chief rabbi under the British, as the ultimate source of the present "militant millenarianism." The *Judaica* describes Kook's philosophy:

> Jewish nationalism differs from that of other nations in that its mainspring is . . . divine. The "sacred connection" between the Jewish nation and the land of Israel cannot be compared with the natural connection that every nation has with its country. Thus the relationship of Jews to Israel is essential to the divine scheme. According to Kook, just as the people of Israel possesses an immanent holiness so does the Land of Israel.[29]

Most early Zionists were not Orthodox. But Kook understood what few others grasped. Zionism would come to terms with religion. If a movement keeps talking about Zion, which is a biblical concept, and keeps trying to win over Orthodoxy, in time it has to attune itself to its would-be clients. Wieseltier tells us that, when Zionism conquered the Wailing Wall in the 1967 war, Zvi Yehuda Kook further developed his father's conception. According to Wieseltier:

> The messianic doctrine of Maimonides is frequently cited as the basis for . . . the politics of the settlers. "The messianic age is this world," Maimonides wrote, "and the world keeps to its customs,

except that sovereignty will be restored to Israel . . . there is no difference between this world and the messianic era except the subjugation of the (other) kingdoms." . . . Rabbi Shlomo Aviner . . . characterize(s) the politics of the settlers as "messianic realism" . . . civil rights is a Western incrustation upon the Jewish revival; the tolerant among them are those who search the classical sources for categories of second-class citizenship for Palestinians. But the prevailing view consists in a tacit consensus about the desirability of their expulsion.[30]

These madmen, for that is what they all are, could not exist without the support of a significant minority of American Orthodoxy. In the November 12, 1985, *Village Voice,* Robert Friedman told us that:

One of the best kept secrets in America's ostensibly liberal Jewish community is the tremendous support it has given to Gush Emunim and Rabbi Kahane. . . . the Gush Emunim . . . has reaped . . . hundreds of thousands of dollars. . . . Kahane has collected millions of dollars from American Jewish businessmen. Among the wealthy Jews who have supported the JDL is Reuben Mattus, the founder and president of Häagen-Dazs ice cream. "If they needed money, I gave it," Mattus said. . . . "The emotional and financial level of support for Kahane in my district is tremendous," says Assemblyman (Dov) Hikind, whose district [the 48th, in Brooklyn—LB] has the largest Jewish constituency in New York State.[31]

As Matzohs Are to Bread

What is the real relationship between the ideology of these crackpots and that of the Old Testament? Kahane and Co. are absolutely correct in insisting that Judaism was a tribal religion, replete with hereditary priests performing animal sacrifices. It was genocidal to the Amalekites, and tried to be so toward the Canaanites. There was much else in it that was fanatic and racist. Simply put, it was the product of a barbaric world.

Nevertheless it evolved. The humane values of some of the later prophets are far removed from much of the earlier brutality. This leavening is *utterly lacking* in the thinking of today's Orthodox right, and it is this which makes their "religion" no more Judaism than a matzoh is bread. They cherish the savage bronze age lines because they provide rationale for their own murderous hatred of Palestinians.

When do they righteously rage against the ruling class of their Israel in anything like the terms Isaiah used to denounce Judah's ruling class?: "What mean ye that ye beat my people to pieces, and grind the faces of the poor?" At the very most, they only attack the Israeli Labor Party as representing the "Ashkenazi Establishment." To be sure, it must be denounced. Amongst its many crimes, it saw the Oriental Jews, particularly Yemenites and Moroccans, as so many asses to carry their load. But this is no more than demogogic populism. None of them call for the expropriation of the rich and the reorganization of society. Were they to come to power, that Establishment would retain *every penny* of the wealth they stole from the Palestinians and sweated out of the Orientals.

Their right-wing chauvinism is no more ancient Judaism at its highest than Falwell's pro-apartheid sentiments are Christianity. To be sure, it is impossible to transform modern society by using the prophets' thinking as our program. But that is another matter. The point is that present-day Orthodox nationalism is reactionary even in terms of Isaiah. The saying is that "the devil can quote scripture." Indeed Kahane constantly cites the Bible in his regular column in New York's *Jewish Press*. But *not once* has he ever quoted the "left" cries of the prophets. Find me, in any of his articles, *one word* of the most famous passages from Isaiah:

> Hear the word of the Lord, ye rulers of Sodom;
> give ear unto the law of our God, ye people of Gomorrah.
> To what purpose is the multitude of your sacrifices unto me?
> saith the Lord:
> I am full of the burnt offerings of rams, and the fat of fed beasts;
> and I delight not in the blood of bullocks, or of lambs, or of he goats.
> . . .
> Learn to do well; seek judgement, relieve the oppressed,
> judge the fatherless, plead for the widow.
> . . .
> for out of Zion shall go forth the law,
> and the word of the Lord from Jerusalem.
> And he shall judge among the nations,
> and shall rebuke many people:
> and they shall beat their swords into plowshares,
> and their spears into pruning hooks:
> Nation shall not life up sword against nation,
> neither shall they learn war any more.

If the rightists insist their faith is in Zionism and braining babies, who can gainsay them? But their religion is not Isaiah's Judaism.

Conservative Is the Perfect Word

The Conservatives are the largest American Jewish sect. The National Jewish Population Survey gave them 23 percent of all Jews in 1971.[32] As with the Orthodox, their percentage of Jewish household heads drops off sharply in the youngest age cohort:

Under 30	=	13.4%
30-39	=	21.4%
40-49	=	26.6%
50-59	=	27.1%
60-69	=	25.7%
70+	=	18.2%
Age unknown	=	22.1%
All Jews	=	23.1%[33]

The sect is irreversibly declining. A 1979 survey revealed that only 39 percent of their married children join their synagogues.[34] Most worshippers are women, a blinking red sign that they are going to go out of business.[35] When the men of a religion don't think praying is important, it isn't, as anyone familiar with Italian Catholicism and similar cases will testify. The cult-temple and its male ritualists get a reputation for bookish foolishness. As feminists, the next generation of their young women will join their brothers in hiking out the door.

Elliot Dorff, writing in *American Jewish History,* has best described the grouping: "As a Conservative rabbi . . . I must admit that the vast majority of these lay people are . . . acting from sociological and not ideological motives."[36] They are Goldilocks and the three bowls of porridge. This one is too Orthodox and old-fashioned. This one is too Reform and goyisher. This one is just right!

Their rabbis accept the authority of Talmudic *halakha* but believe they must keep it abreast of the times. As they evolved from Orthodoxy and dispersed geographically, the rabbis allowed Saturday driving, to the synagogue only. But since the grouping is indeed little better than a sociological reaction to Orthodoxy and Reform, it inevitably has two wings, each one flying towards one of those poles. It is therefore impossible for them to get their theological act together.

In the 19th century, those who moved away from Orthodoxy were fond of the maxim "Be a man in the street but a Jew at home." Now Conservative rabbis have reworked the old mot: It is forbidden to be a fool in front of goyim, but it is compulsory in the synagogue.

Genesis insists "God created man in his own image, in the image of God created he him." Then a wag had man creating God in his own image. Now women recreate ancient religions in their lovely image. In 1985 these eternal come-latelies ordained their first woman rabbis. But they were only able to do this because halakha had never bothered to denounce such a self-evident violation of Judaism's total male chauvinism.

Despite female rabbis, they cannot square their circle. The Talmud expressly forbids female witnesses in judicial matters except in the rarest circumstances. Women are also specifically exempt from some commandments. Because a mother's work is never done, they do not have to stop to pray three times daily. However, normally if you are excused from obligations you are not allowed to perform for someone not released. They appointed a commission to debate whether a woman could lead men in prayers she wasn't obligated to perform. After much hair-splitting, it decided being a witness or conducting services was not the critical task of a rabbi, who is supposed to be a spiritual leader. Besides, an eligible male is usually available to testify, or run a portion of a service. A rabbi figured out an ingenious way around their problem. If a woman made a statement that she considered herself obligated in all ways men are, she could be admitted to their rabbinical school. Daily services, wearing a prayer shawl and wrapping *tefillin*—amulets, strips of parchment inscribed with texts from the Bible—around the forehead and arm near the heart, were the most significant mandates assumed.

Now some of the female seminarians ask why they must sign a pledge not required of males. They have come full circle. They fought to exercise such male privileges. Now refusing to put on tefillin and shawls is their way of demanding equality. However, as with the Orthodox, these are not truly feminists but fools of the female persuasion. Most Jewish women don't have this non-problem. Nor need they. If they are in a sectarian pit, it is of their own digging. No one is keeping them there.

"No Longer Welcome"

The Conservatives' problems are not exclusively theological. Their members are the biggest UJA contributors and Israel Bonds purchasers, but their co-thinkers are not recognized in Israel. Israeli Conservative rabbis cannot perform a legal marriage or divorce or bury their dead. As Yanks they believe in religious equality. With one lobe they know they should be out there picketing. But they are aptly named and are the ultimate in bourgeois respectability.

They would never dream of demonstrating, certainly not against the Jewish state. At most they are only trying to prevent further humiliations. On May 10, 1985, their Rabbinical Assembly announced that 51 members of the Israeli knesset, including Ariel Sharon and Yitzhak Shamir, "are no longer welcome as speakers or honorees" at their 850 Congregations. These had voted that only those converted to Judaism by Orthodox rabbis would be recognized there as Jews under the Law of Return, which grants instantaneous Israeli citizenship to Jewish immigrants.

The Conservatives made it clear they were not boycotting Zionist fund drives.[37] However, these politicians are practical and work under the old proverb: "If I don't give the begger what he wants, what will he do to hurt me?" As long as these theological Tories keep sending bucks to Jerusalem, they can whine all night long. As Reform suffers from similar discrimination, more will be said on this.

"To the Vulgarity of Bar Mitzvahs There Is No End"

As Conservativism is little better than a sociological grouping in search of an identity, we must go past the theological world of their rabbis and look at the folkways of their laity to get a real feel for the sect. The following appeared in the May 15, 1978, *New York Times*. As it is so gross, and it was about a youth who need not now believe in all this nonsense, we have omitted his first name:

> Nearly 60 years ago, Robert Cohen's bar mitzvah party was held in a noisy and crowded tenement flat on Manhattan's Lower East Side. Last night, Mr. Cohen stood on the 50-yard line of the Orange Bowl at the lavish bar mitzvah of his grandson

_____ . "It doesn't matter, I guess, where a bar mitzvah party is held so long as there is love and family and joy," Mr. Cohen said after a 64-piece band, cheerleaders, and pompom girls from a local high school stormed onto the field blasting football marches and "Happy Birthday, _____." . . . Earlier . . . at a Conservative temple where no press cameras were permitted, _____ had completed the traditional recitation of Old Testament passages. . . . But the spending of nearly $20,000 . . . was certain to raise questions about propriety. . . . Sixty of _____ 's friends, all veterans of the bar mitzvah circuit, were brought to the stadium by school bus. "A Jewish kid around the age of 13 goes to more parties than Jackie Kennedy," said one adult.[38]

No Orthodox family would think of having a bevy of shiksas shaking pompoms, and much else, at their son's bar mitzvah. There was no sectarian label on the next drollery, from *Moment,* so it could be either a Conservative or Reform blast. While by no means all congregations would tolerate this, there is no doubt the psychology is widespread in both sects:

Michael . . . became a bar mitzvah . . . the party theme was derived from the University of Georgia football team, nicknamed the "bulldogs." . . . Mom informed the paper that "we're having a Bulldog Bar Mitzvah" . . . a 14 × 8 foot runthrough poster "depicting a bulldog dressed in a tux with red tie and cummerbund was painted with the inscription, 'How 'Bout That Michael.'" . . . Michael will come charging through the poster dressed in tux complete with red tie and cummerbund to the strains of—what else?—'Glory, Glory to Old Georgia."

Moment's piece, resignedly titled "To the Vulgarity of Bar Mitzvah's There Is No End," regales with a further tale about "barn mitzvahs" in Los Angeles. These feature live chickens, steaks with the kid's name branded on them and musicians dressed as "Wild West rabbis." At one of these affairs, an 83-year-old, celebrated his second bar mitzvah. This Yankee Doodle Yidl came on complete with cowboy boots, holster and gun. *Moment* says "the consultant fees for theme parties range from $10-40,000."[39]
Orthodox Jews would have difficulties with a bulldog bar mitzvah because the team plays on Saturday, which is the only day of the week they would never turn on a TV set. Thereby they

reveal the falsity of Judaism because, as every A-murican will tell ya, that is the day *God wants ya'll to watch* Southern Methodist play Texas Christian.

Reform: The Faith That Doesn't Even Move Molehills

I once asked a rabbi what denomination he represented and he replied that he was Orthodox, the synagogue was Conservative and the congregation was Reform. The joke points to the biggest distinction between Conservative and Reform clergy and laity. The rabbis are aware of the theological dilemmas confronting them. The ranks are united on only one thing. They think of themselves as Jews, and want to pass this on to their kids. With both groups, there tends to be a fall-off of membership after their kids get bar/bat mitzvahed. *The New York Times* reported that there was concern at the 1985 convention of the Union of American Hebrew Congregations for Reform's wide reputation for vacuity. The movement is "sensitive to criticism that it does not demand much of its adherents."[40]

In the decades after it laid out its theological positions in its 1885 Pittsburgh Platform (see Chapter 1), Reform sought to attract the Eastern European immigrants and their children. However, those who wanted a secular philosophy passed it by. Those who joined came from more intensely Jewish environments than the classic German-Jewish reformers. They grew up in Jewish sections of New York and other cities that did American service for ghettos. Their families had spoken a language that only Jews spoke and practiced rituals that many Reform had abandoned in Germany.

The early reformers wanted to remain Jews but were negative about everything specifically Jewish. The new recruits liked Reform's freedom to pick and choose what to hold onto, but they wanted to be more distinctively Jewish than the founders of the American grouping. Reform actually lost members after 1930 and the newcomers argued that the movement was unable to satisfy the religious feelings of the typical Jew. Pressure from below induced their Central Conference of American Rabbis to revise their basics in 1937.

"The Guiding Principles of Reform Judaism" were very different from the Pittsburgh Platform. Although they were still convinced that the Bible and Talmud could not be taken literally, the Talmud, the oral law, was seen as a "depository of permanent spiritual ideals." In 1885 they had declared that Jews were a religion and no longer a nation. In 1937 they still thought of the Jews as primarily a religion but recognized "the group loyalty of Jews who have become estranged from our religious tradition." Whereas in 1885 they had explicitly declared that they did not expect any Jewish return to Palestine, in 1937 they affirmed an "obligation of all Jewry to aid in its upbuilding as a Jewish homeland" and "a center of Jewish culture and spiritual life." There was new emphasis on

> prayer in both home and synagogue . . . preservation of the Sabbath, festivals and Holy Days, the retention and development of such customs, symbols and ceremonies as possess inspirational value . . . the use of Hebrew, together with the vernacular.

The Guiding Principles shared the Pittsburgh Platform's highfalutin rhetoric about society, advocating "harmonious relations between warring classes on the basis of equity and justice."[41]

There was a little here for everyone. Jewish public opinion was becoming increasingly ethnic rather than religious, hence secular "group loyalty" was now approved, and Zionism endorsed. The phraseology about ritual was broad enough to satisfy those wanting "emotion" in the services. The social rhetoric was in perfect keeping with the New Deal. But regressive talk about rituals could not solve their problem. What prayers, Holy Days, ceremonies were essential to Judaism?

They allow their temples virtual autonomy, so many have added some Hebrew and symbolism to their ceremonies. But that has meant little. Even though they tried to snuggle up to tradition, they actually went further from it. They now have women rabbis and have fully purged themselves of male chauvinism. They don't approve mixed marriage but accept it as a reality and try to involve non-Jewish spouses in their congregations.

Because so many followers are out-marrying, they now consider children of Jewish fathers as Jews. As long as they recognized exclusive matrilineal lineage there was bottom-line ethnic unity with Orthodoxy. Now they are as different as a store front Pentacostal church and the Vatican. Their relations can only get worse. Their problem vis-à-vis Conservativism is unimportant because they know them to be little more than slow-moving reformers. Ten years from now the Conservatives will have their position, exactly as they followed after them re women rabbis.

The Anti-Zionist Remnant

As with the Orthodox, they are not of one mind regarding Zionism. The original Reformers, in Germany and the U.S., wanted only to integrate into their capitalist classes. Emotionally, Palestine meant nothing to them. When Zionism came along they saw it as a threat because it raised questions as to Jewish loyalty to their countries of birth or abode. But some Reform rabbis, as with Stephen Wise, were Zionists even before the movement changed its position. With American recognition of Israel in 1948, and the subsequent pandering after Jewish votes, the dual loyalty fear lost all meaning.

There are only two organizational remnants left of the once-dominant anti-Zionist current in Reform. As the U.S. became increasingly identified with Israel, and Zionism became the dominant tendency within organized Jewish life here, the American Council for Judaism pulled in its horns. They have no quarrel with the existence of the Israeli state or the U.S. alliance with it. They object only to the belief that Israel's interests should be central to Jews here. However, hyper-moderation did not save it from decline from an organization of a few thousand members in the early 1940s to a mere handful still loyal to the shadow organization.

The AJC sank into oblivion after its Director, rabbi Elmer Berger, resigned in 1968. He felt it wasn't enough to oppose Zionism because it made specious claims to the loyalty of U.S. Jewry. It was crucial to directly solidarize with the victims of Zionism, the Palestinians. When the ACJ refused to do this, Berger set up American Jewish Alternatives to Zionism, which now exists primarily to support his personal efforts. Although in his mid-seventies, he still speaks for student and other groups around the country. However, his impact on his fellow Reform is close to zero.

"Competing with Recreational Options"

Reform is unique in the monotheistic religious world in not having a fixed sabbath. They learned long ago that their kind of Jew was too busy working or getting ready for the big game to show up on Saturday mornings. So they have Friday night and/or Saturday and/or Sunday services.

In theory, there is no reason why a Reform synagogue couldn't have a woman rabbi conduct a Tuesday morning ham and eggs sabbath breakfast. No one would come no matter which day they observed. Although the NJPS gave them 13.5 percent of household heads, rabbi W. Gunther Plaut, immediate past president of the CCAR, reported in 1985 that "only 6 to 10 percent of Reform Jews go to temple regularly." *The New York Times* had him saying that:

> "Even the Almighty" must find the Friday evening temple service "utterly boring." . . . services "are neither filled with drama nor intellectual acuity, and instead feature set rituals which the rabbi dreads and the small congregation endures."

He wanted to get back to Saturday mornings, but his successor, rabbi Jack Stern of Scarsdale, New York, said his temple pulled 80 to 150 Fridays but only 12 to 15 Saturdays.[42] "Other rabbis said they were now competing with recreational options."[43] Folks got to get ready for the big game. And so does God.

Get Ready for Some "Holy Accusers"

> It is the Messianic task of Israel to make the pure knowledge of God and the pure law of the morality of Judaism the common possession and blessing of all the peoples of the earth. We do not expect . . . they would give up their historic characteristics . . . similarly we shall not permit the Jewish people to give up its innate holy powers . . . so that it might be assimilated.[44]

Thus Samuel Holdheim, one of the leading figures in 19th-century German Reform. The 19th-century reformers no longer believed in the Messiah. They had to justify the continued existence of a Jewish sect. Their very dispersion created their new mission. They were still the chosen people, the light unto the nations. To this minute Reform believes this. Here is W. Gunther Plaut giving *The Case for the Chosen People:*

> Jewish history is world history condensed to its quintessence. . . .

If all is well with Israel, the world is well; if Israel is ailing, mankind is ill. . . . It is a grand if "unreasonable" conception. But then, is grandeur ever reasonable? . . . But make no mistake about it: grandeur is always and forever a position of responsibility. . . . If the God of Sinai is the desperate invention of a desperate people, then not only is this people's existence the cruelest joke perpetrated on . . . men . . . then the impossibilities of Jewish history are made possible by the maintainance of a fiction, a final grandiose Zero. . . . It cannot be so. I believe in a God of history, I believe in a Covenant, albeit the venture of my faith may differ in many ways from that of my fathers.[45]

This is not to be mistaken for the simple-minded chauvinism of a Kahane. We are reassured: "the reality of divine encounter between God and Jesus, Paul, or Mohammed is as plausible as the vision of Isaiah."[46] They may not have gotten everything straight, but that is another matter.

Does he really believe this childish 'I'm a prophet, you're a prophet, he's a prophet too'? Might God pick up the phone and call Plaut? He granted gentiles chosenness only to protect his own turf. He really was defending the notion that God *has* most definitely had an "encounter" with the Jewish *PEOPLE* at Sinai. He acknowledges that most Jews now ridicule the fantasy.

That's OK. Individuals can choose not to be chosen. But Jews Inc. cannot, and he chooses to carry on the collective calling. And because the Jews were so chosen, they believe they should "walk in the way of the prophets." So, get ready for the righteous rage of some of Plaut's "holy accusers."

Israel denies Reform equality with Orthodoxy. But, according to rabbi Ady Assabi, the coordinator of Israeli Reform, speaking in 1976, "Secularism in Israel, and not Orthodoxy, is the greatest foe."[47] Get it? Those who believe in religious freedom are the enemy, not the people who deny it. The December 14, 1976, *Jerusalem Post* told of the Jerusalem convention of their World Union for Progressive Judaism:

For years now the leadership . . . has been waging a fierce internal battle. The policy has been to damp down public criticism of Israel's denial of religious recognition . . . from a reluctance to add to Israel's troubles in these grim years of grave danger. . . . There were sharp intramural discussions before this year's convention. . . . In the end the "quiet" policy prevailed.[48]

In the 1970s, a group, *Breira,* or choice, arose within the ranks of organized American Jewry, in reaction to the oppression of the Palestinians. On May 21, 1976, the Israeli paper *Ha aretz* reported some comments by rabbi Alexander Schindler, later president of the UAHC. Harken ye unto a prophet in his wrath:

> He proposed to Breira to renounce its public criticism of Israel, which causes great damage. He wants to open channels of communication for it with the Israeli leadership and with the Jewish Establishment in the U.S.[49]

There came a day of reckoning, the Lebanese invasion, which these liberals opposed. Then came the tearful mea culpas: Schindler, by then president of the UAHC, was forced to confess that:

> We haven't been *completely* silent in the past, but we've certainly been reticent. I fear that our past *public* support of the government of Israel, no matter its policy, and no matter our private reservations, was used by the Israelis to project a world Jewish community completely in accord with its goals and methods. We were used like cows. We were milked, both for financial and moral support—and for the influence we could bring to bear on Washington—and when we were used up we were put out to pasture. Yes, it is fair to say that we have been treated with contempt—and we've gone along willingly. But we've crossed a watershed now, and our open criticism will continue and increase.[50]

Better late than never. Except that Schindler is Schindler and with him late is never. On August 27, 1983, 300,000 people demonstrated in Washington to commemorate Martin Luther King's famous 1963 "I had a dream" speech. Virtually the entire Jewish Establishment initially opposed the demo because the convening call, signed by Jackson and former Senator James Abourezk, a leader of the American-Arab Anti-Discrimination Committee, included an innocent enough statement:

> We oppose the militarization of internal conflicts, often abetted and even encouraged by massive U.S. arms exports, in areas of the world such as the Middle East and Central America, while their basic human problems are neglected.

UAHC still had ties to the old guard civil rights leadership because it is for affirmative action, and it supported the demo. But they lobbied their moderate Black friends until they got a statement from Coretta King that, "where a divisive act or statement is made, e.g. one that is anti-Israel, anti-Semitic . . . the co-chairs will publicly disavow such a statement."[51]

Schindler was even allowed to give the closing benediction at the march. However, according to Morris Rodenstein, writing in New Jewish Agenda's magazine, UAHC "made no attempt to bring people to Washington."[52]

Not surprisingly, Plaut and Schindler supported Mondale in 1984, in spite of what they knew was his blatant demagoguery re moving America's embassy to Jerusalem. Schindler reminded the *Times's* readers that:

> Traditionally, most Jews have backed the Democratic Party because it represented a liberal political philosophy that translated the ethical imperatives of the Hebrew prophets into programs to feed the hungry, heal the sick and house the homeless.[53]

Yay, verily. If Isaiah were alive, he'd be a Democrat. Although Democrats do go overboard housing the homeless. Sometimes they house people who already have homes. Like the Japanese-Americans they threw into concentration camps in WWII. Schindler is literate and knows of numerous such Democratic crimes. But prophets in our age are wiser than of old. What did they know of honest-to-God lesser evils?

But the greatest zealot for justice of them all is doubtlessly rabbi Arthur Lelyveld, former president of the American Jewish Congress. He had been very active in the NAACP in the civil rights campaign and had been beaten in Mississippi in 1964. He spent months in South Africa in 1985 and then toured the U.S. Even the San Francisco *Jewish Bulletin,* not noted for criticizing Israel, gagged at his effrontry:

> In response to a question about Israel's economic relationship with South Africa, Lelyveld offered statistics that have been criticized by some sources: "Since 1976 Israel has scrupulously observed the sanction against military assistance of South Africa. Its trade with South Africa is minimal, and almost 80% less than the trade

carried on by the black nations of Africa with South Africa. The whole world trades with South Africa.[54]

Days after Lelyveld's Bay Area appearance, Bishop Desmond Tutu spoke in San Francisco, before the AJCongress and, according to the San Francisco *Chronicle,* "Condemned Israel for continuing to sell millions of dollars in arms to South Africa."[55] The Israeli consul downplayed the alliance, but admitted that:

> Three years ago . . . Israel sold South Africa missile boats for that country's external security, which he said was a limited transaction, and did not affect South Africa's internal policies.[56]

Of course not! Lelyveld could have asked Israel for the facts before he made a fool of himself. He could have learned yet more from anti-Zionist specialists on Israel's arms traffic, including Haifa University professor Benyamin Beit-Hallahmi and Hebrew University's Israel Shahak. Lelyveld *does not want to know the truth.* Reform had never said more than boo about Israel's denial of its own rights. After a while ostrichism becomes a way of life.

America's Reform Jews are Yankees down to their tippy toes. They know exactly what an A-murican is supposed to do if anyone messes with his right to pray to the rain god of his choice: You are supposed to take the rifle down off the wall, boy, an' ya'll better know it! Seriously, no one expects these elderly rabbis to go racing through airports, shooting up El-Al ticket counters, but the unwillingness to "prophetically" denounce Israel demonstrates that, as with the Orthodox terrorists, their religion is no more Judaism than a matzoh is bread. Against who but the rulers of ancient Israel and Judah did the prophets rage?

It is easy to see that ethnicity, not God, has become their religion. Glazer's mot must be modified somewhat: The Jews have become the religion of organized Jewry. They are tribalists— racists, to be honest. Israel can do *anything* to the Blacks in South Africa, to the Palestinians, even to them. It is Jewish, and when it is denounced by goyim it is time to circle the wagons. To be blunt: Reform Judaism is no more moral than a New York Reform Democratic club. And very often they are the same people. New Yorkers will find the analogy perfectly apt. Both spout idealism. Neither has a principle worthy of the name.

"Deeply Honored"

Perhaps the most bizarre effect that Zionism has had on American
Jewry has been to make allies of the right-wing of the Jewish
Establishment and the Fundamentalists around Jerry Falwell. The
vast majority of Jews do not go along with this and even many
within the inner circles of the Establishment have opposed this
orientation.

Readers will have noticed that occasionally I've slipped into
country dialect, when trying to ridicule someone. Marx once
called the illiterate peasantry of his day "rural idiots," and that is
how most city slickers see Fundamentalists. Of course there are
not a few city idiots, some Jews among them. But, be that as it
may, anyone selling Country & Western to Jews would end up
with his belly flappin' against his backbone. This must be appreciated to understand how even unpolitical Jews see coddling
Falwell.

On February 6, 1985, Benyamin Netanyahu, Israel's UN
representative, addressed the National Prayer Breakfast in Honor
of Israel during the National Religious Broadcasters Annual Convention. It must be understood that Jews think these guys would
be hilarious if they weren't so dangerous. Imagine some mountain
William gettin' up before a mike and telling "all you folks out
there in Biblelan' to send money to me down here at WKKK in
Texarkabama, Mississippi," and all them folks doing it! From
Brenner to Kahane, all Jews stand together on this: anyone sending them money is indeed an idiot. Now diplomats are supposed
to lie for their country. But many wonder how he could say with
a straight face that "I am very grateful to you, and deeply
honored, to accept this Proclamation of Blessing on behalf of the
people and government of Israel." Even Netanyahu admitted,
"Many have been puzzled and surprised by what they consider a
new found friendship."[57]

If diplomatic usage permits this in a foreigner hustling support
for his government, accommodating these dangerous yokel reactionaries by an American Jew is an infamous act. And that is how
most Jews see it. Yet that is what neo-con Irving Kristol did in
the July 1984 *Commentary:*

> The rise of the Moral Majority . . . baffles Jews. . . . But . . . why
> should Jews care about the theology of a fundamentalist

preacher . . . what do such theological abstractions matter as against the mundane fact that this same preacher is vigorously pro-Israel? . . . One reason for the peculiar Jewish reaction here is that . . . the Moral Majority is simultaneously committed to . . . school prayer, anti-abortion. . . . How does one go about balancing the pros and cons. . . . Support of the Moral Majority could . . . turn out decisive for the very existence of the Jewish state. . . . But the expediential point of view is not enough if the Moral Majority's support . . . is not to wither and die. . . . That will happen if it continues to evoke so . . . embarrassed a response. . . . Jews really do need to revise their thinking about some, at least, of these . . . issues. . . . It is time they did so . . . Moral Majority or no Moral Majority.

Since the Holocaust and the emergence of . . . Israel, American Jews have been . . . moving away from . . . universalist secular humanism. . . . But while American Jews want to become more Jewish, they do not want American Christians to become more Christian. This is . . . untenable.[58]

Kristol and the Reaganites over at *Commentary* are not alone in this. Nathan Glazer said the same thing in the October 21, 1985, *New Republic,* the organ of the Democratic faction within the Establishment's right wing:

When the Court decides that a Christmas crèche can be displayed on public property, I see no threat of the establishment of religion . . . About 95 percent of the country is Christian, by birth or practice. That this should find some expression in public life seems not unreasonable. . . . Having listened to the readings and heard the prayers . . . when the Supreme Court did not stand so sternly against establishment, I didn't see the harm in being silent, or learning that one is different—because one is a Jew, or a Catholic, or an atheist. A country such as ours can be held together only by tolerance and by deals.[59]

This turn toward the evangelicals does not sit well with many among the Establishment. Israel might think it gained new strength in American politics by the ties, but they live here and their children will as well. What is "good for the Jews," i.e., Israel, is not "good for the Jews," i.e., them. Schindler was the leading representative of the dissidents:

Most Jewish leaders are willing to forgive anyone anything so long as they hear a good word about Israel. . . . The reason I am reluctant to work with such groups . . . is that in their domestic program the main objects of their attacks were some of our staunchest supporters among liberals in Congress. So even their support of Israel is flawed in this respect.[60]

Despite the lamentations of the liberals, Israel went on playing up to the crackpots. And of course, for all their qualms, the liberals stayed loyal to Israel. But then, on August 19, 1985, Falwell met President Botha of South Africa. According to *The New York Times:*

> Falwell came away saying he was firmly supportive of the South African leader's limited racial reforms and was opposed to proposed American sanctions . . . when he returned to the United States his organization would urge "millions of Christians to buy Krugerrands."[61]

There was a huge outcry. Many hundreds of anti-apartheid demonstrators rushed to picket Falwell's church in Virginia. He became an unperson in most Establishment circles. It remains to be seen if the Israeli government will break all ties with him. But his name rarely appears now in American Jewish publications. They are having trouble enough with the Blacks over Israel and South Africa. If they hang in with him, even the moderate Black Democrats would turn on them.

The liberals like Schindler feel vindicated. In reality they are exposed as bankrupts, although in a different way than the right-wing hacks who sat in his pew and did not notice the odor. Their Israel treated him like a statesman up to the minute he unzipped his political fly and exposed his racism. Yet not even this leads them to break with Zionism.

Love—"This Cancerous Growth"

It must always be remembered that the immense majority of American Jews are not affiliated with *any* sect, Jewish or otherwise. The 1971, NJPS reported that 5.7 percent of all Jews were atheists, another 2.3 percent answered "a little" when questioned if they believed, 5.5 percent were listed as doubtful, and 12.6 percent said they "somewhat" believed in a deity.[62]

They did not break down the respondents by age, but all evidence points to an increase in atheism in the younger generation and in the better educated. At any rate, intermarriage is gaining and Egon Mayer, an Establishment sociologist, estimates that there are already between 400,000 and 600,000 children of mixed marriages.[63]

In providing a secular purpose for Conservative and Reform congregations, Zionism slowed the disintegration of American Judaism. But it is a losing battle and now its leaders are beginning to rant. In 1980, Charlotte Jacobson, head of the American section of the WZO, declared that:

> Ever since Jewish emancipation . . . in every country assimilation has grown generation by generation. We American Jews . . . thought we would escape this cancerous growth. But we haven't.[64]

Cancer kills. Young Jews are assimilating, falling in love with their neighbors, doing anything but dying. Judaism is dying, Zionism is dying.

Will they go over to Christianity? Of course not. For two reasons. Christianity's historic crimes against Jews are too well known. And more important, American Christianity is also dying. In the March 1984 issue of *Gallup Report,* George Gallup, Jr., related that, although about 90 percent of Americans believe in God, and about 80 percent call themselves Christians, only half could name more than half of the ten commandments. About the same percentage can tell you who gave the Sermon on the Mount. The future belongs to the youth, but two-thirds of American teenagers cannot name the four gospels. Twenty-nine percent of all teenagers don't know why Christians celebrate Easter, "and about 20 percent of those who attend religious services regularly."[65]

The Gallup poll has always had an intense interest in the state of religiosity, and George Gallup's conclusions, in the May 1985 *Report,* is irrefutable:

> Certain basic themes emerge from the . . . data collected over . . . five decades:
> • The gap between belief and commitment, between high religiosity and low ethics
> • The glaring lack of knowledge
> • What would appear to be a failure, in part, of organized religion to make a difference in society in terms of morality and ethics
> • The superficiality of faith[66]

Jacobson and others are correct: tribal religion cannot survive in a cosmopolitan and tolerant society. But Judaism's assimilation into "the Judeo-Christian heritage," that p.r. hustle coined to sanctify American capitalism, and Israel's membership in "the free world," which includes Wall Street's gallant Muslim, Buddhist and other allies, could not save it. It only became an official part of a psychologically disintegrating social order. The ignorance revealed by the polls cited testifies to that. Even among the better informed a profound malaise is glaringly evident as the intellectuals' voodoo incantation—"vote for the lesser evil"—fails in the "real world" they prattle about. This is crucial for Conservativism and Reform, both bastions of this vacuous secular faith.

There is a saying: "No one's religion ever survived their immorality." We can update this: No one's religion ever survived their wretched politics. American Judaism tied itself in with two false secular Gods: liberalism and Zionism. Now both are in profound crisis. Neither will even begin to solve America or Israel's problems. There will still be some believers decades from now. But such shards mean nothing sociologically. American Judaism is irrevocably doomed.

Notes

1. "Orthodoxy," *Encyclopedia Judaica,* vol. 12, col. 1486.
2. Heinrich Graetz, *History of the Jews,* vol. V, p. 454.
3. Lucy Dawidowicz, "Politics, the Jews & the '84 Election," *Commentary,* Feb. 1985, p. 30.
4. Will Maslow, *The Structure and Functioning of the American Jewish Community,* p. 25.
5. Kenneth Briggs, "Orthodox Judaism Is Buoyed by a Resurgence in New York," *NY Times,* March 29, 1983.
6. Paul Ritterband and Steven Cohen, "The Social Characteristics of the New York Area Jewish Community, 1981," *AJYB 1984,* p. 153.
7. Charles Silberman, *A Certain People,* p. 239.
8. Fred Massarik and Alvin Chenkin, "United States National Jewish Population Study," *AJYB 1973,* p. 282.
9. Joe Klein, "The Power Next Time?," *New York,* Oct. 10, 1983, p. 44.
10. Steven Cohen, *American Modernity and Jewish Identity,* p. 2.
11. Silberman, p. 268.
12. "Hasidism," *EJ,* vol. 7, col. 1400–1.
13. Moshe Shonfeld, *The Holocaust Victims Accuse,* pp. 5–6.
14. Schneur Zalmen, *Tanya,* pp. 3–5.
15. Jim Sleeper, "Black Politics in Brooklyn," *Dissent,* Spring 1983, p. 148.
16. "Schneerson, Menachem Mendel," *1983 Current Biography,* p. 358.
17. Edward Shapiro, "Orthodoxy in Pleasantdale," *Judaism,* Spring 1985, p. 166.
18. Ibid., pp. 168–9.

19. *Lilith*, Spring 1982, p. 1.

20. Blu Greenberg, "How an Orthodox Woman Evolved Beyond 'Woman of Valor' to Become a Fervent Feminist," *Lilith*, Spring 1982, pp. 7–8.

21. Nathan Glazer, "American Jews: Three Conflicts of Loyalties," Seymour Martin Lipset (ed.), *The Third Century: America as a Post-Industrial Society*, p. 233.

22. "Oil, Providence and Israel," *Jewish Life*, Spring 1974, p. 3.

23. S. Zalman Abramov, "Gush Emunim and the 'Underground' Terrorists," *Jewish Currents*, Oct. 1985, p. 16.

24. Meir Kahane, "Brief Thoughts of Vision and Donkeys," *Jewish Press*, Oct. 1, 1982, p. 37.

25. Meir Kahane, "Is Israel's Soul Imperiled? Yes, by Liberal Jews," *NY Times*, Dec. 20, 1985.

26. "Kahane's Proposals Compared with the Nazi Laws," *Al Hamishmar*, March 21, 1985.

27. Walter Wurzberger, "The Case Against Terrorism," *Hamevaser*, Oct. 4, 1984, p. 4.

28. Moshe Tendler, "Judge By Torah Standards," Ibid., p. 7.

29. "Kook, Abraham Isaac," *EJ*, vol. 10, col. 1187.

30. Leon Wieseltier, "The Demons of the Jews," *New Republic*, November 11, 1985, p. 20.

31. Robert Friedman, "In the Realm of Perfect Faith," *Village Voice*, November 12, 1985, p. 16.

32. Maslow, p. 25.

33. Massarik and Chenkin, p. 282.

34. Jack Wertheimer, "The Conservative Synagogue Revisisted," *American Jewish History*, Dec. 1984, p. 129.

35. Ibid., p. 125.

36. Elliot Dorff, "The ideology of Conservative Judaism: Sklare After 30 Years," *American Jewish History*, Dec. 1984, p. 103.

37. Ari Goldman, "Israeli Officials Face Restrictions," *NY Times*, May 11, 1985, p. 9.

38. Jon Nordheimer, "Miami Bar Mitzvah Has 'Love and Family and Joy'—and Cheerleaders," *NY Times*, May 15, 1978, p. D10.

39. "To the Vulgarity of Bar Mitzvahs There Is No End," *Moment*, April 1984, p. 10.

40. Joseph Berger, "Reform Jews Urge Day School Option," *NY Times*, Nov. 5, 1985. p. 7.

41. Sylvan Schwartzman, *Reform Judaism in the Making*, pp. 137–41.

42. Goldman, "New Focus Urged for Reform Judaism," *NY Times*, June 25, 1985, p. 13.

43. Goldman, "Reform Rabbis Reject Call to Alter Services," *NY Times*, June 26, 1985, p. 17.

44. W. Gunther Plaut, *The Case for the Chosen People*, pp. 108–9.

45. Ibid., 81–5.

46. Ibid., p. 89.

47. Judy Siegal, "Reform Movement Suppresses Bid to 'Abolish Chief Rabbinate'," *Jerusalem Post*, Nov. 22, 1985, p. 2.

48. Arthur Super, "Reform and the Aliya argument," *Jerusalem Post*, Dec. 14, 1976, p. 8.

49. *Ha aretz*, May 21, 1976.

50. Michael Kramer, "American Jews and Israel: The Schism," *New York*, pp. 28–9.

51. Lawrence Bush, "Conscience and Coalition," *Jewish Currents,* Oct. 1983, p. 6.

52. Morris Rodenstein, (Letter), *Agenda,* Summer 1984, p. 4.

53. Alexander Schindler, "Beyond the Dilemma of Jewish Voters," *NY Times,* July 3, 1984, p. 15.

54. Tamar Kaufman, "Oakland Leaders Hear Rabbi's Personal View of South Africa," *Jewish Bulletin,* Jan. 24, 1986, p. 24.

55. Mark Barabak, "Tutu Says Time Is Running Out," *Chronicle,* Jan. 23, 1986, p. 22.

56. Ira Kamin, "Tutu's Anti-Israel Comments Condemned by Israeli Envoy," *Jewish Bulletin,* Jan. 31, 1986, p. 6.

57. "Christian Zionism," *Catalyst,* vol. I, no. 1, p. 7.

58. Irving Kristol, "The Political Dilemma of American Jews," *Commentary,* pp. 25.

59. Nathan Glazer, "Church-State Bargain," *New Republic,* Oct. 21, 1985, pp. 17–8.

60. Richard Bernstein, "Evangelicals Strengthening Bonds with Jews," *NY Times,* Feb. 6, 1983, p. 40.

61. Alan Cowell, "Botha In Meeting With Churchmen," *NY Times,* Aug. 20, 1985, p. 6.

62. Massarik and Chenkin, p. 300.

63. Berger, "Interfaith Marriages: Children's View," *NY Times,* Dec. 2, 1985, p. 19.

64. Charlotte Jacobson, "The Dynamics of Zionism," *American Mizrachi Woman,* Jan. 1980, p. 5.

65. George Gallup, Jr., "Commentary on the State of Religion in the United States Today," *Gallup Report,* March 1984, pp. 8, 14, 75–6.

66. Gallup Jr., "Fifty Years of Gallup Surveys on Religion," Ibid., May 1985, p. 12.

10

"Hath Not a Jew Credit Cards? Ph.D.? Uzi Machine Gun?"

The Intelligentsia, Israel, and the Jews

Modern America's culture is simply unthinkable without the massive and disproportionate contribution of its Jews. It is almost as if the Jews assimilated America rather than the other way around.

The physicists who produced the A and H bombs were overwhelmingly Jewish (as were the scientists who designed the first Soviet bomb).[1] For the last 15 years Jews have won approximately 40 percent of America's Nobel prizes.[2] In a 1965 *Commentary* article, Milton Himmelfarb, an editor of the *American Jewish Year Book,* cited an estimate that "something like a quarter of the buyers of books in the United States are Jews."[3] There is no reason to think the figure is lower now.

In the 1930s, Arthur Rubinstein declared that a majority of the world's concertgoers were Jewish. Since then Jewry lost one-third of its number in the Holocaust, and the audience for classical music has greatly expanded. But there can be no doubt that even today Jews are disproportionately represented in the classical music world in Europe and America. Go to any performance in New York's Lincoln Center. The audience majority is Jewish.

In his 1964 *Culture Consumers,* Alvin Toffler reported that his conversations with administrators of artistic institutions showed that the growth of the Jewish population of a city meant a rise in the level of cultural activity. "A museum director in San Antonio says: 'The vast majority of collectors here are Jewish.' "[4]

These statistics fuel the secularist version of the Jews as the chosen people. For many Jews the notion of their intellectual superiority is really all they have left of their separatist heritage. Philip Roth, one of the severest commentators on American Jewish life, put it very simply. Most youths get nothing specifically Jewish from their families. "No body of law, no body of learning and no language, and finally, no lord." They "received . . . a psychology, not a culture . . . and the psychology can be translated into three words: 'Jews are better.' "[5]

You would be rich if you had a penny for every Jew who is proud that Jesus was a Jew. Along with the baptized Christian Marx, the atheist Freud and of course Einstein. Are they not the intellectual pillars of civilization? To be sure, few read the New Testament. Or *Capital* or *The Interpretation of Dreams.* Fewer yet understand Einstein. No matter. Chauvinism is always absurd.

For the Jewish professionals, this modernized chosenness fulfills a class need. The Jewish intellectual ethic is their equivalent of the Protestant work ethic. Their modern God—more precisely their new golden calf—culture—is pressed into psychological service as the ideological rubric to justify the income of parasitic corporation lawyers.

Jews in the Media

Given the immense thrust towards the intellectual life in general, it is scarcely surprising that Jews play an enormous role in all media. Bernard Kalb is Reagan's press secretary. Although only about 3.1 percent of America papers are owned by Jews,

The New York Times, easily the most important daily, is owned by the Sulzbergers. Katherine Graham, of Jewish descent, owns the *Washington Post* and *Newsweek.* Walter Annenberg owns *TV Guide,* the world's largest selling magazine. *US New and World Report* and *The Atlantic Monthly* are owned by Mort Zuckerman. Leonard Stern owns the *Village Voice.* Sam Newhouse owns *Vanity Fair, Vogue, Gentleman's Quarterly, Mademoiselle* and *The New Yorker.*

Editors and writers for mainstream publications are legion. Side by side with them are the ideological journals. Of these, *Commentary* is the only specifically "Jewish" publication (it is owned by the AJCommittee), to have a broader appeal. Reagan appointed Jeane Kirkpatrick U.S. Ambassador to the UN on the basis of an article of hers that he read in the magazine.[6] *Dissent* is a democratic socialist (read Democratic Party) publication, seen by the public as an extension of Irving Howe's persona. Marty Peretz is the owner-editor of *The New Republic.* Victor Nevasky edits *The Nation.* The list is endless. Bernard Avishai is correct; the people of the book have become the people of the magazine.[7]

Jews founded the three TV networks. CBS is still strongly Jewish, with Loew's Larry Tisch now the largest stockholder, followed by founder William Paley and Ivan Boesky. However ABC has merged with Capital Cities Communications. NBC was founded by David Sarnoff, but now that it has merged with the even more gigantic General Electric Company the specifically Jewish element in its ownership is quite small.

We are seeing the working out of two fundamental principles of modern capitalism. A wave of mergers and buy-ins has taken place in all media and communications industries as capitalism has entered a final stage that can only be described as industrial feudalism. A feature of this inexorable concentration of wealth has been the increasing merger of Jewish and Christian capital, and this is nowhere more evident than with ABC and NBC.

Is there any political significance in the enormous role Jews play in the media? Certainly the owners are for capitalism, but that scarcely distinguishes them. Beyond that, they and Jewish editors, TV producers, etc., are not united on any issue, including Israeli politics. That the bulk of Americans are politically illiterate is clearly demonstrated by the polls cited herein. Certainly the media, including that part owned by Jews, has dismally failed to educate the public.

All major popular media owners see Americans as in the circus ad: children of all ages. Most papers don't even try to educate their readers. Only about 15 dailies have even one correspondent abroad. They cost money. But *The New York Times,* the wire services and the networks are serious. If a reporter digs up a scandal, they usually run it. But they are profoundly committed to the system and do not hire journalists with razors out for its neck. And if owners and editors do not see their own government as evil, they do not see its allies as sinister, especially those with a democratic mask. Support for the status quo is axiomatic in such cases.

The New York Times has editorially moved right, even making a holy ass of itself ballyhooing Mehmet Ali Agca's loony charge of a plot to kill the Pope: "Evidence of Bulgaria's involvement is circumstantial but credible . . . What is unthinkable is that its Caligulas would have raised a hand . . . without Soviet agents wanting it."[8]

For all this anti-Communist *meshugas,* when it comes to the Middle East, if the *Times* (and most other media tycoons) had its druthers, it prefers a liberal Israel. Right-wing Israeli regimes have their own agenda, whereas the *Times* wants an Israel that will come to a modus vivendi with the reactionary Arab regimes in the interests of anti-Sovietism. And, of course, whatever the regime there, the *Times* is never for revolution, not there or anywhere. The *Times* never supported a single demonstration here against Hitler and it will always remain true to its vile traditions.

The Israeli government is never pleased when the *Times* exposes some outrage. It is concerned about what readers might do, not because it is afraid the paper will call for protests, or even cuts in military aid.

Joseph Kraft has described the post WWII status of those fortunate enough to work in news for the major media:

> We have been among the principal beneficiaries of American life. We have enjoyed a huge rise in income. . . . We have become a kind of lumpen aristocracy.[9]

Grossly overpaid, their economic interests are far removed from those of the common people of this earth, and many feel exactly like their employers. In November 1976, Israel Bonds put on a fashion show in Washington. Among the models were Mrs.

David Brinkley, Mrs. Martin Agronsky, and Mrs. Dan Rather. It is also revealing that some of the other models were Mrs. Henry Jackson, wife of the pro-Israeli "Senator from Boeing," Mrs. Joseph Sisco, wife of the ex-Under Secretary of State. Present were the wives of the Chief Justice of the Supreme Court, the Secretary of Defense, the Attorney-General, and the head of the Federal Reserve Board.[10] Obviously some leading TV news people are too close to the Zionists. But aren't they also far too intimate with the entire power structure in this country?

However, news broadcasters and editors do not make up news. Nor do they try to censor what the people in the field look for in the way of stories. They are on the spot and see Palestinians as ordinary folks. At least on the West Bank, they do not see the typical Zionist settler as Mr. Nice Guy. And he is not. When *any* settler, religious or secular, opens up his mouth, out comes chauvinist madness.

Nevertheless, even if newsmen are for Palestinians getting some rights, they are usually psychologically incapable of going beyond hoping Israel will change its policies because the government and/or the people will decide that a new approach would really be in Israel's interest. That is to say, they look upwards to the powers-that-be or alternatively to "progressive Zionists" to be the motor for their wished-for changes.

They are for democracy and secularism here, but the notion of a democratic secular Palestine gives them the whim-whams. They are not sinister in this, merely consistent, although it would appear otherwise. That is because they are also for lesser-evilism at home, meaning they do not fight for those democratic secular principles even here. What they are doing is consistently extending their domestic methodology abroad. Therefore, although they are more sympathetic to the Palestinians than their employers, they join their quest for the ultimate Palestinian "moderate" who will convince his fellows to "recognize Israel."

One and all, they are "realists." Do they try to overthrow Washington, merely because it repeatedly commits felony murder? Surely then a sensible Palestinian would do as they do—or not do as they not do.

Their penchant for moderates is well-intended but it prevents them from understanding the internal dynamics for the Palestinian movement. In the modern world, oppressed nations don't wait for Lady Bountiful to come along. This writer lectures for Palestinian student groups, the future leaders of their nation. Most believe Arafat has capitulated to U.S. imperialism and Arab reaction. *All* believe in armed struggle. I constantly criticize their overemphasis on militarism. It gets in the way of mobilizing their masses for street demonstrations and the development of working unity with progressive Jews there. But I do not counterpose "moderation" because no one will listen, and rightly so. Liberal journalists can't grasp this because of their equally profound misunderstanding of their own country.

However, it must be stressed that their limitations do not blind these professionals to the monstrous oppression that is routine in Palestine. Incidents of Zionist brutality are frequent in *The New York Times,* today, if less so in regional papers. The *Times's* mid-East coverage is huge. There is more on that region, day after day, year after year, than on any other part of the planet.

The shame—for such it is—lies not with that paper's publisher or editors, for all their severe faults. It rests with the intellectuals who read it. They read David Shipler's story on how Israeli censors suppressed Rabin's account of his expulsion of *50,000* civilians in 1948. They saw a photo, on April 30, 1979, captioned "Ismail Ajweh, Arab journalist, taking polygraph test in Jerusalem. Administering the test is Mordechai Gazit, former Chief Examiner and acting director of the Police Headquarters polygraph laboratory." The accompanying piece told how Ajweh was held *without charge* for 120 days, how he was beaten for 18 days, how *Ha aretz,* the country's leading paper, had Gazit test Ajweh, and how Gazit categorically declared that "it seems to us that Mr. Ajweh told the truth and in fact was tortured during his investigation."[11]

"Or Even As a Reporter Who Is Sympathetic to Jewish People"

Even in the worst years, before 1967, there were a very few people in the media who weren't buying the okey-doke. And one was a Jew. Mike Wallace had a Palestinian, Fayez Sayegh, on his *Night Beat* talk show in 1957. Wallace had bailed out of Reform Judaism as a teenager, but at that time he was typically pro-Israel. However, he listened to the scholarly Palestinian, and he realized that at least there was another side, even if he still remained pro-Israel. Soon he started doing interviews in the Middle East, with both Arabs and Israelis. His most controversial was in 1975, in Syria.

Damascus and Aleppo have a friendly rivalry. Both claim to be the oldest continually inhabited city in the world. And both have Jewish communities going back at least 2,500 years. Wallace had heard stories, from Jews here, that the 4,500 remaining Syrian Jews were virtual prisoners, and he went to have a look for himself. Of course the stories were false. They had been oppressed but Hafez Assad had lifted almost all restrictions. They could not serve in the army, or freely emigrate. Beyond that, they were free. Wallace ran the story on *60 Minutes* in February 1975. Later, in his book, *Close Encounters,* he wrote that "never before had I been swamped by such a deluge of intense and negative reaction. . . . I in particular and CBS News . . . had become 'dupes of the Arabs.' "[12] The AJCongress filed a complaint with the National News Council. The controversy would not stop and Wallace went back to Damascus in 1976. The second show drove home the point made the first time, and the AJC was forced to withdraw their charge.

Wallace was justifiably outraged at the attack on his integrity, and gave an interview to the *Christian Science Monitor* when the second show was televised:

> I had heard stories of atrocities—lies; that the doors of Jewish homes were painted a certain color—lies; that Jews can't get driver's licenses—lies; that no Jew could get a telephone—lies; that Jews can't go out after curfew—lies; that Jews can't study Hebrew—lies; that the Jewish cemetery was bulldozed—lies. Of course, some of those things were true at one time, but not now. That's all I say.[13]

Even though the AJC backed down, *Near East Report,* the organ of the American-Israel Political Action Committee, persisted in drawing an analogy which, Wallace relates, he "found obscene, they compared our broadcasts to 'films in which Goebbels portrayed the clean and tidy barracks in the idyllic concentration camps.' "[14]

They still hate him. In their February 10, 1984, issue, the *Report* claimed that:

> In 1975 Mike Wallace did a . . . segment on the condition of Jews in Syria. Wallace concluded . . . that "today, life for Syria's Jews

is better than it was in years past." This ridiculous statement about the terrorized Jewish community in Syria caused a sensation. In fact, Wallace felt compelled to do a second segment . . . one in which he tried to back away from his earlier pro-Syrian report. . . . But Wallace didn't learn much from that episode. In his Jan. 8 (1984) report, he mouths Syrian propaganda. . . . So what is Wallace's problem? . . . Does he feel that he has to bend over backwards to prove that he is no secret Zionist? . . . No one thinks of him as a Zionist or even as a reporter who is sympathetic to Jewish people.[15]

Foreign readers must understand that Wallace is thought of by most Americans, including most Jews, as their country's leading TV investigator. Anyone raving against him sounds crazy to them. If they carry on so against him, Zionists will surely not listen to me. Nevertheless I'm going to tell them something. Not argue. Tell them.

I went to Syria in October 1981, after reading the article, "Syrian Jewry Cries Out Now," in the September 25, 1981, New York *Jewish Press*. The piece had "foreigners who reach Israel" talking of "the destruction of most of the ancient synagogues, murder, rape, attacks, robbery, etc.—these are the latest conditions under which the 5,000 remaining Jews in Syria live today."[16] As Wallace said in his reports, the government gives each journalist a translator. One was with me when I interviewed the chief rabbi. However, I returned to the Jewish quarter— alone—at least a dozen times. I interviewed him again. Additionally, Jews recognized me from my visit to a synagogue and would insist on my having coffee with them in their stores. We talked in strict confidence. "Assad freed us" was what I was constantly told. Their only worry was that he might be overthrown. "You can tell Americans," the rabbi said, in private, "that we are on average better off than the Muslims." I asked him how things compared to when Wallace had been there. "Better."

I have eyes. I can see. And I can think. They were at perfect ease. Assad is in error for not drafting them into the military. If he did, it would be a huge step forward in the democratic secular Arab revolution, so needed in the region. And, if it is reasonable to think that one or two Jews might spy for Israel, it certainly already has less obvious agents in Syria. At any rate, such spies would be a small price to pay for the further secularization of Syria. And to put Zionism irrevocably on the ideological defensive.

Paradoxically, as long as Israelis are confronted by ethnic Arab armies, the government can convince most Israelis that it's tribal war to the end. If Jews are active against them, in Syria, the ideological nature of the struggle would become clear. Nevertheless, Assad doesn't retain this lingering inequality because he hates his Jewish citizens. It is simply that he is not a revolutionary, for all the rhetoric of his Baath Party.

One Jewish coppersmith told me Assad bought a celebrated tray his father made, and had the son present it to a visiting head of state, and how they had become friendly as a result. I drank coffee with him and his customers, mostly Muslims. Damascenes in particular are very secularized and many are politically left of the government. There are anti-Jewish elements. Not Palestinians, but Syrians. Members of the Muslim Brotherhood. Assad is an Alawi Muslim and these fanatics try to stir up the Sunni majority against him, He therefore treats all attacks on minorities, including Christians and Jews, as mortal dangers to his regime.

Assad is not some softie like Reagan or Gorbachev. He hangs enemies in public squares. When the Brotherhood rose up against him in Hama, he wiped out entire neighborhoods. Anyone thinking of murdering a Jew for being a Jew—in Arab Syria!—knows exactly what the punishment will be: Not some iffy thing like death. Or some maybe thing like certain death. But absolute, certain death.

"If We Went Ahead, It Very Well Might Affect Fund Raising"

Is there any literate adult who does not know that Vanessa Redgrave is one of the world's greatest actresses? Among her many awards was an Oscar for her role in *Julia,* in which she played an American involved in the 1930s German anti-Nazi underground. She won an Emmy for her part as a Jew in an inmate orchestra at Auschwitz in *Playing for Time.*

Any rational person would think her pro-Jewish. But when she appeared at the Academy Awards ceremony, the JDL hung her in effigy, and Zionists in the hall booed. When CBS hired her for *Playing for Time,* it came under immediate fire from the AJCongress, the ADL and other Establishment mouthpieces. Later CBS Vice-President Harvey Shepard said that the show resulted in "enormous financial loses to the network." It is believed that they had to cut their 30-second prime time ad rate from $90,000 to $30-35,000.[17]

None of these critics complained about her performances. That would be absurd. They hate her for her solidarity with the Palestinians, not for anything said or done to or about Jews anywhere else besides Israel.

In 1982 she was hired by the Boston Symphony to narrate an oratorio. Then in April, just before she was to perform, she was fired. She sued, claiming her civil rights were violated, and her contract breached. The case went to court in 1984. The Symphony claimed they cancelled her appearance only after threats of disruption from the JDL and discovering that members of the orchestra would refuse to play. Her lawyer, who was Jewish, said a key role in the dismissal was played by Irving Rabb, a leading figure in Boston's Jewish Establishment, and a member of the Symphony's board of trustees, who pressured the general manager.

That gentleman, one Thomas Morris, testified that one player out of 106 refused to play, and of course they received a threat from the JDL. And, "If we went ahead, it very well might affect fund raising."

The Symphony's lawyer argued that any disruption would have ruined the event. But Peter Sellers, who hired her and who was to have directed her (and who is now artistic director of the American National Theatre at Washington's Kennedy Center), categorically opposed this conception of the solemnity of art. "If the Boston Symphony Orchestra acts this way, no one is safe. Across the course of musical history, there is a rich history of disruption."[18]

The jury rejected the Symphony's claim that it acted under circumstances beyond its control and awarded Redgrave the $27,500 fee she would have received and $100,000 in damages. They did not find for her on the civil rights issue but only because of the court's final instructions. In a later letter to the court, the jurors explained that:

We were convinced that there was indeed an abrogation of Ms. Redgrave's civil rights by the BSO. We were convinced that one of the primary reasons . . . was that the agent(s) who acted for the BSO . . . were willing to cooperate with members of the broader community to fire Ms. Redgrave because, and only because, of the disagreement by that group with political views that Ms. Redgrave had publically expressed.[19]

The verdict was a major victory for civil liberties, as this was the first time anyone had won money after trial in a blacklisting case. However, the federal judge then threw out the damages award, holding she was only entitled to the contract payment. She was then ordered to pay the orchestra's court costs.[20] The judge ruled that an artistic institution is "entirely free" not to hire anyone for exclusively political reasons.[21]

Actors Equity, the Screen Actors Guild, the ACLU and the Committee for Civil Rights Under Law of the Boston Bar are supporting her appeal. Whether she will win remains to be seen. These are prestige organizations, the kind that impress judges. But foreign readers must know that federal judges are appointed by our Presidents. That means they are of no better quality than the politicians who pick them. This Supreme Court is loaded with ideological henchmen of Nixon and Reagan. She *could* win. But until that happens readers would do well to learn the old proverb: " 'Virtue in the middle,' said the devil, sitting down between two Supreme Court judges."

For us, the question is why did the Orchestra fold like an accordion before Zionist pressure, while the movie industry gave Redgrave an award and CBS was willing to suffer a large loss? As we have seen, the classical music world is disproportionately Jewish. Nor is it a secret that many rich Jewish patrons are philistines, showing off their wealth. Classical music is crucially dependent on their philanthropy. If they decided not to donate, even the Boston Symphony would be in real trouble.

Show biz is another scene. Pro-Zionists abound. New Yorkers argue that the greatest political joke of all time is the line in *The Sleeper,* about how the world blew up when a nut named Albert Shanker got his hands on an atomic bomb. However, when his named appeared on a pro-Israel Nat PAC ad in 1983, it was asked if the world will really blow up after a nut named Woody Allen gets a hold of the bomb.

For every political jerk there is an Ed Asner, who was outraged at how "little *geschrei*" (outcry) there was against Israel's Lebanon crimes.[22] He was then head of the Guild, whose members remember the Hollywood 10, purged during the McCarthyite witch hunt. He rallied the union in Redgrave's defense. Even the studio bosses understand they can face boycotts from Fundamentalist and Catholic wackoes over porn. The networks also have no use for the boycott mentality. They can lose on one show. It won't break them. They have a seller's market. If Mr. SuperJew businessman feels an urge to cut off his nose to spite his face and not advertise, they will be pleased to hand him a razor.

It is not necessary to explain that one of the world's great actresses has an absolute right to work in her profession. Or that it is the duty of all intellectuals to rally in defense of her rights. Indeed it is a symptom of the backwardness of America's political intelligentsia that the orchestra affair never became a cause célèbre.

If Ms. Redgrave was fired for left-wing politics in general, there would have been an outcry. It was her anti-Zionism that, somehow, semi-demi-hemilegitimatized the witch hunting by the "respectable" Establishment. And yet, all she is doing is denouncing oppression and solidarizing with the PLO as the organization of the oppressed. She takes the traditional Marxist position against individual terrorism: "I am absolutely opposed to terrorism," she told the court. There is no reason to disbelieve her.[23]

And of course she is not anti-Jewish. She hopes to utilize *Zionism in the Age of the Dictators* for a documentary on Zionist collaboration with the Nazis. I was naturally concerned that such a film be accurate and was more than reassured. She wants to do a massive treatment of the Nazi period, examining not only the role of the Zionists, but the ruling class in Germany, Britain and the U.S., and even of the CP-USSR, in the Jewish tragedy.

It became apparent that what she has in mind might be too huge a project, a Wagnerian Ring cycle, which might take so long to produce that its impact on the Zionist-Palestinian struggle would be remote. But, be this as it may, it attests to her concern for balance and accuracy. She wants to document the crimes against the Jews, not commit a crime against them. Which makes the Zionist assault on her character as obscene as their rabid denunciations of Mike Wallace.

The Village Voice

The editorials in American dailies are too moderate to seriously effect intellectual public opinion. Nor are the vast majority of daily political columnists more commanding. They are rarely cited in the scholarly literature on the Middle East. It is to some of our periodicals that politicals look for in-depth analysis of events there, but most of these are explicitly political publications. One, however, the *Village Voice,* is more general, although it devotes a disproportionate amount of attention to the Middle East and to topics of interest to Jews.

On June 17, 1981, the *Voice* ran a front-page article by Jack Newfield, "Anti-Semitism and the Crime of Silence." The article attacked several liberals and leftists, including another *Voice* columnist, Alex Cockburn. Although Newfield confessed that he "did not write enough" about anti-Semitism, and although he conceded that he did "*not* believe Alex is prejudiced," he accused him of being "anti-West, which leads him to despise America's ally, Israel." That being so, Cockburn has become "a political accountant who keeps two sets of books." He had become "deaf to the problems of Jews."

> Alex has written virtually no words of protest about Anatoly Shcharansky . . . or other casualties of Russia's savage anti-Semitism. No . . . censure for the PLO's murder of schoolchildren at Ma'alot, or pregnant women at Kiryat Shmona. No essays about the unequal status of women in Arab nations.

Newfield insisted he did not object to criticism of Israel. He conceded that Cockburn had "accurately" pointed out "abuses of the rights of Palestinians." But he had "a healthy amount of ethnic pride." Israel seemed to him "a necessary sanctuary from a future Holocaust." To him, "Zionism is a defensive response to anti-Semitism."

On one thing there could be no argument: "The Zionism-equals-racism slogan is one of the great lies of this century of great lies." He allowed that people of good will could disagree about a solution fair to Arabs and Jews. Nevertheless,

> my own identity as a Jew, and my sense of justice in the world, does not depend on, or derive from, Israel always being virtuous. All it requires is that Israel exist to work out its own problems. Certainly no one argues that the misdeeds of Pol Pot and Idi Amin are justification to liquidate Cambodia and Uganda as sovereign entities. And in the ethical measure of nations, Israel is still better than most.[24]

By any reckoning, Cockburn is one of the world's most controversial journalists and he dotes on attacks. His rejoinder appears in the following issue:

> The article was evidence not of what Newfield described as his suddenly alerted journalistic conscience in the face of anti-Semitism, but of an intellectual blindness which tells us so much about American liberalism. . . . He is kind enough to say that I am "not prejudiced." . . . A red, a supporter of terror, the first person up for examination in an article on anti-Semitism . . . but "not prejudiced." But Newfield knows exactly what he is implying . . . this side of straight-forward slander . . . that the terms "Cockburn" and "anti-Semitism" seem to have ended up in his same file. . . . Newfield shares his courage in denunciation of Shcharansky's treatment, or PLO horrors, with about 99 percent of the American press. . . . If my readers expect anything from me, it is . . . emphasis upon subject matter that is not simultaneously dealt with . . . by every other newspaper . . .

Having defeated Newfield's assaults on his political character, Cockburn moved to the offensive on point after point:

> Newfield talks about women's rights in Saudi Arabia and gay rights in Cuba. . . . I will join Newfield in demonstrating . . . in front of the consulates of those two countries, if he will then accompany me to the Israeli consulate. . . . There are distinctions of which Newfield does not seem to be aware when he evokes "modern Zionism" as a "defensive response to anti-Semitism." . . . In a report by Anatol Shub which appeared in *Harper's* in May of 1972 [Shub wrote] . . . "Israeli authorities . . . firmly discourage any attempts by Soviet Jews to take up the cause of their Russian friends. . . . Israelis distinguish between 'Zionist' and 'anti-Soviet' activities. . . . The Soviet authorities . . . are . . . permitting 'Zionists' to emigrate, while sending 'anti-Soviet democrats' to prisons. . . . The Israelis go along . . . even when the persecuted anti-Soviets are Jewish"[25]

There were final retorts the next week. These debates go in all directions and they discussed Israel's and the Soviet Union's links with the then Argentine junta. Cockburn made it clear what he thought of the Soviets as he additionally challenged his detractor to demonstrate with him at the Soviet and Argentine consulates as well:

The Soviet regime is one of the most bureaucratic and repressive on earth. . . . Newfield appears concerned only by the lot of Soviet Jews. . . . Surely the central task here is to support democratic opposition.[26]

It was Newfield's article that induced this writer to contact Cockburn to offer the use of my files on Jewish matters for his rebuttals. Additionally, I made the proposal that he challenge Newfield to go to the consulates. It had two purposes. The proposition would show Alex was no apologist for the Arab regimes or the Soviets. And, if Newfield accepted, we would make an event of it, drawing in other writers.

There is wide agreement in literary circles that American writers must use their freedom on behalf of oppressed writers abroad. But these good intentions rarely get off the printed page. However, while despots don't like articles against them, what they really fear is demonstrations.

Newfield accepted. As it had been my idea, and as I never make proposals I'm not prepared to assume responsibility for organizing, he was put in contact with me. He was enthusiastic. He had discussed the walk with Nat Hentoff, another *Voice* scribe, who was also interested in going to the consulates. We worked on setting a mutually convenient date.

Yet the march never happened. Apparently Jack had agreed before consulting his colleagues in the Democratic Socialists of America. They have a Jewish committee, whose head, Jo-Ann Mort, is a member of Americans for a Progressive Israel, affiliated to the Israeli Mapam Party. It frequently disagrees with Israeli policy but is an absolutely loyal opposition. It members have been prominent in the military there and, it is reasonable to assume, in the security agencies there and abroad.

At any rate, they have two principles here. They never demonstrate at Israeli consulates. And they never work with anyone who opposes the continued existence of the Israeli state. Jack had no idea what my politics were, but they did, and when they told him he was violating their policies, he cancelled the entire idea.

I tried to find out if he was also a member of API, and got conflicting answers from bureaucrats in their office. Let's split the difference and say that he is at least extremely close to them. Clearly he had no objection to demonstrating at the Israelis until Mort of API laid down the law. By the time he backed out, most

ment from which the above is excerpted, about Judaism, Israel or Jews, except that incongruous insistence on his being positive. His negativism was so obvious that he was asked where any positive attitude could have come from, and he could only confess that he was "really not sure. I always had it."[38]

At the same time there was much vague muttering about his subjective instincts, motives and reactions. This line of unreasoning was elevated into a political philosophy by Ellen Willis:

> Ellen: Jewishness is obviously not just a religion. Secular Jews can feel every bit as passionately, viscerally involved in the question of being Jews. . . . It's not a nation . . . so what is it? In a certain way it's like a big extended family.
> Jack: Right.[39]

Now let's return to Newfield's *Voice* description of his relationship to Israel: "My own identity as a Jew, and my sense of justice in the world, does not depend on, or derive from, Israel always being virtuous. All it requires is that Israel exist to work out *its own problems.*" Now we understand. In the real world, Israel is the problem. And the Palestinians are oppressed by that problem. But these tribalists have cathected their emotions onto it. They see a political entity as a "family" matter. That is why Israel doesn't have to "always" be virtuous. What he really means is that it doesn't have to *ever* be virtuous.

The best of these tribalists is Nat Hentoff. But even when he cries out against Israeli policy, as he did in 1982, in the immediate wake of the invasion of Lebanon, he reveals the emotional, irrational attachment they have for Israel. He was raised a Zionist and he writes "as a Zionist." But, when he grew older,

> my identification with Israel was somewhat abstract. . . . It felt good to know there was one place in the world that had to take me in. But I knew more about the British Labor Party than about the Israeli Labor Party. . . .
>
> In 1967, I was trying to learn how to be a pacifist. . . . Then came the Six Day War. "How are we doing?" I'd ask. . . . I wasn't asking about the state of the nonviolence in the world. . . .
>
> I want . . . Israel to survive . . . Yet, I am increasingly afraid of what it will become. . . . How does it sit, the Jewish conscience, in the United States? . . . Where are you, American Jews who would save Israel?[40]

Note well the common characteristics. When he said he knew more about the BLP than the ILP he was saying that he really knew *nothing* about Israel. But, as with many others, it would be his mousehole on the Med. And again, as with so many, he was a pacifist here, where he knew something about the society, and for a war in the Middle East.

By 1982 some of the *emotion* had worn off. But the tone of his article and his politics is how terrible it is that Israel is so hard on the Palestinians because that is bad for Israel. The liberal tribalist is like unto the Puritan who hated bear-baiting. Not so much because of the bear's pain as because of the onlooker's pleasure. In their minds, Palestinians have about as much to do with stopping their oppression at Zionist hands as bears have to do with stopping bear-baiting.

Having equated anti-Zionism with anti-Semitism, these tribalists now see themselves as surrounded by Jew-haters, even as the entire range of observers, from the ADL on, discuss the decline of anti-Semitism. The Holocaust is reduced to their pretext for non-stop sermonizing in today's world.

Here is Paul Berman, a once-upon-a-time anarchist. A foolish philosopher had said anti-Semitism differed from racism in that anti-Semitism is hatred of the almost same while racism is loathing for the different. Berman pontificated on the inane distinction:

> The hatred that arises from saying to someone "you believe you are like us, but you are not" is extreme, more extreme even than hatreds that arise from saying "you are different." . . . in the feelings of black anti-Semites . . . the deepest points of commonality seem the sorest points of all.[41]

An outraged Jew wrote in. Let me assure gentile readers that Jews of Eastern European descent instantly recognized his *buba:*

> Berman's recent article . . . only served to establish his own moral narcolepsy. . . . Why couldn't Berman simply say that hatred of Jews is extreme? Why does it have to be *more extreme* than that of Blacks? . . . Berman reminds me of my grandmother. She never suffered. *She suffered more than everyone,* and she never could accept anyone else's pain as being as serious as hers.[42]

Narcissism was the essence of the shtetl mentality and narcissists is what they all are, despite their worldly veneers. Forget about any other explanation of their frothing loyalty to Israel regardless of its crimes, which they acknowledge. The world is picking *on them* when it denounces Israel, even if the world is right. A hard-core tribalist doesn't really believe non-Jews have any right to criticize Israel. That is the meaning of Newfield's canard that left anti-Zionism is "interchangeable" with anti-Semitism.

Berman finally upped periscope to denounce Joan Peters's fraud, *From Time Immemorial,* but only after innumerable others had already done so. And even then to deny Alex the right to attack it, even though he was *the first* major media journalist to draw attention to Norman Finkelstein's analysis of its cooked statistics:

> No one protested against the people who did acclaim it. Alexander Cockburn spoke out, let it be acknowledged, though Cockburn's own reputation on Israeli matters is not such as to lend weight to what he says.[43]

Schneiderman, a liberal tribalist, had a more benign attitude. He thinks Israel's politics are not in its own interest. When the paper's editors interviewed Mondale in 1984, they got into an argument with the rabid demagogue. They were not satisfied with his down-the-line support for Israel:

> M: What have you got as an alternative?
> V: Well, to begin with, some degree of American pressure . . . that would say something about settlements. . . . It's not a matter of imposing a settlement. In Israel . . . at least 50 percent . . . wants to trade off those lands and settlements. What you are doing is ensuring stalement.[44]

And Alex's outspokenness sold. But he was warned off me. Not because there were any errors in my research—we knew the columns would be scrutinized and we covered our assets, as they say, double-checking facts—but because questioning Zionism's Holocaust bone fides is tampering with tribalism's sacred excuse for everything. And when he committed the eighth—aye, and deadliest—sin, working *for* Israel's victims, his head rolled. After all, to do a book for an Arab scholarly institute always "compromises the integrity of any journalist." Always. But for the *Voice* to endorse a political panderer like Mondale, who *it* said "vie(d) without dignity or restraint to please the most intractable supporters of a belligerent Israel," never compromised its integrity.[45] Never.

Of Anti-Zionist Writers and Pro-Zionist Reviewers

Willis shares Newfield's my-country-right-or-wrong attitude towards Israel and his hostility towards the left. Hear her in *Response:*

> I . . . came to the conclusion that the anti-Zionist position that Israel should not exist was essentially an anti-Semitic position. . . . Left-wing anti-Semitism . . . assumed that since most Jews were middle class, Jews could not really be oppressed. . . . Left anti-Semitism and Right anti-Semitism really work together symbiotically.[46]

Hear her again in *The New York Times Book Review* for October 3, 1982. She utilized a critique of the Perlmutters' *The Real Anti-Semitism in America* to slander her betters:

> *The Real Anti-Semitism* makes some valid points. It is true that at present Jews have less to fear from overt anti-Semitic malice than from impersonal, institutional anti-Jewish bias. It is also true that liberals and leftists have been guilty of perpetuating such bias under cover of a righteous concern for peace and justice. Uncritical support of the PLO, indifference to Israel's vulnerability and insensitivity to Jews' realistic fears about quotas all reflect the left's refusal to take anti-Semitism as seriously as other kinds of oppression.[47]

Not feeling particularly guilty that day, I sent in a letter to the paper, which they ran on November 7, 1982:

> Not one word of this is true . . . the Communist Party disagrees with the PLO's end goal of a democratic, secular Palestine. . . . The Socialist Workers Party . . . disagrees with the PLO's attacks on civilian targets. . . . Willis additionally maligns the left when she accuses it of indifference to domestic anti-Semitism. She surely knows that leftists are always in the van of the demonstrations against the Ku Klux Klan and the Nazis.[48]

Clearly Willis has a strong attitude re "left anti-Semitism" And readers can well imagine her feelings about me after the letter.

All the more reason for an editor of the *Voice Literary Supplement* to be sure that *Zionism in the Age of the Dictators* was exposed as the hate tract it surely is. But the *VLS* kept a discreet silence.

No one has ever accused me of being shy, so I called her, after it had already received 40 reviews, asking why it hadn't been discussed there. "We don't review everything. If you don't like it, go start your own review." She did not dare attack it because she knew well enough that I'd have sent in another letter exposing her, this time in her own publication.

In the end the book was discussed in so many prestige journals that the *VLS's* cowardice scarcely mattered. But passing over anti-Zionist books is the norm with liberal publications. Noam Chomsky is indisputably one of the world's most famous political scholars. When he speaks on a campus, hundreds of students automatically attend. Yet here is how his *Fateful Triangle,* which deals with the U.S., Israel and the Palestinians, was dealt with, or not dealt with, by the critics:

> *Fateful Triangle* was reviewed in just about every major or minor journal in Canada, it was widely reviewed in England and Australia. . . . In the U.S., apart from the *N.Y. Review* . . . it was reviewed in the *Boston Globe* . . . and a minor southern California newspaper, after a huge fuss. That's it. Even the left press— *Village Voice, Nation,* etc.—won't touch it. . . . To take an earlier case, Ed Said was a regular reviewer for the *N.Y. Times* book review on literary topics, and after a long series of Zionist reviews asked to be allowed to review some contemporary things. . . . My book *Peace in the Middle East* was coming out. . . . They said fine. He called me some months later and asked whether the book had been delayed since he hadn't heard from the *Times.* . . . It was already out. He checked . . . he would not be allowed to review any books of the sort. . . . That is typical; the *N.Y. Times* is a highly disciplined operation, since they know that reviews there determine what a librarian in Des Moines will order. . . .
>
> It is not simply a matter of Jewish pressure, though that is great; rather it reflects the deeper fact that since 1967, the liberal intellectuals who dominate most of the mainstream ideological institutions have been deeply enamoured with Israel, which demonstrates how one should deal with third world upstarts. And, of course, serves willingly as an instrument of U.S. power and violence. . . . It is an unbeatable system, particularly because

much of the left goes along . . . *The Nation,* for example, Cockburn and Hitchens aside.[49]

It is usually not the editors of these publications, still less their owners, who determine which books get discussed. Book sections of broader journals are almost invariably autonomous Baronies. *The New York Times Book Review* didn't even mention Roberta Feuerlicht's *The Fate of the Jews,* which was published by Times Books, a division of the New York Times Book Company. But plainly preserving the integrity of these departments is not served by autonomy if such publications hire partisans to edit the reviews.

The bias only appears more jarring with self-styled liberal outfits like the *Voice* and *The Nation,* where autonomy is an excuse. When *The Nation* did not review my book I contacted Victor Nevasky and asked for one, or a chance to write an article on the implications of Israel having a Foreign Minister who wanted to go to war on Hitler's side. He promised a review, which never happened. When I again asked to do an article, it was explained that

> we assigned your book in good faith and it didn't work out. Alas, we have already assigned a series of Middle East pieces and are so overloaded that we can't commission any more for the foreseeable future.[50]

Alas. Fortunately Alex used the occasion of *The New Republic's* refusal to run my rebuttal to their attack on me to also hit Nevasky, whom he frequently exposes as an opportunist:

> I should add, in the interest of fairness, that *The Nation* has not reviewed Brenner's books, preferring in the case of at least one of the editors the safer expedient of private slander. But then *The Nation* has not been notable for its courage in this area, having found itself unable to review Noam Chomsky's *The Fateful Triangle* or Joan Peters's *From Time Immemorial.*[51]

Perhaps this led to Edward Said's attack on Peters. And at least Chomsky's name has appeared on a rare article. That is better than the *Voice,* which allowed Berman to denounce him in a June 10, 1981, horror story, "Gas Chamber Games," in which he declared Chomsky's civil liberties defense of a French crackpot, Robert Faurisson, of the no Holocaust school, was "hopelessly fouled by a defense of him on other grounds as well." And, as everyone knows, of late Chomsky's books have begun to decline, "beginning with *Peace in the Middle East?,* which seems to me blind to certain issues, such as anti-Semitism's bearing on Israel."[52]

Note the date. In two successive issues, Schneiderman allowed two pro-Zionists, Berman and Newfield, to claw Chomsky, Cockburn, and, in Newfield's diatribe, William Kunstler, Amiri Baraka, and Richard Falk, as well as sundry rightists. Naturally only the leftists replied, as our "P.T. Barnum" calculated they would, with long letters for which our Barnum does not pay. Now we have the secret of how to get your rag a reputation for being in the center of things. Only nothing happened. Except two screwballs savaged serious people over bullshit, to use the scientific term for bovine feces. Chomsky explained:

> The scale of the attacks on Faurisson contrasts strikingly with the reach of his own writings. How many readers have come across a line he has written, or heard his name, apart from these attacks? . . . Berman's comments about Israel and anti-Semitism . . . suggest the . . . interpretation that this is just another chapter in the disgraceful effort to conjure up anti-Semitism to deflect criticism of policies of Israel, in a style reminiscent of earlier episodes of state worship.[53]

"When a Whore Repents, She Becomes a Madam"

Truly, it must have been excruciating for Newfield to be sold, with the ol' *Voice* plantation, to honest Lenny Stern in 1985. As the Ever Omniscient One has informed us, "Jews do not own any of the corporations that have become symbols of greed and misconduct."[54] Except that the *Times* had Stern's Hartz Mountain Industries settling two anti-trust suits, in 1979, for $100 million. And he (Stern) "was forced to pay $640,000 in back pay to workers as part of a settlement of a 1974 union-organizing fight." And, "Last year Hartz Mountain agreed to plea bargain with Federal prosecutors . . . in connection with one of the anti-trust suits." Seems the outfit "pleaded guilty to perjury, subornation of perjury and obstruction of justice."[55] *Forbes* reported the perjury involved "hiring of hookers."[56] Hartz Mountain's canaries are happy canaries!

According to the *Times*, "among the largest contributors" to campaigns of members of New York's Board of Estimate, which includes Ed Koch, the city's court jester, was one Lenny Stern. The Board "approves all . . . land-use changes" and—would you believe!—for $132,000 Hartz "received permission to convert a commercial loft into housing for artists." But, not to worry. "I don't think there is anything immoral about that at all," Koch announced. "From me, they got nothing." Of course not! Anyway, even though there wasn't "anything immoral" going on, "since he purchased the weekly newspaper, Mr. Stern was no longer making campaign contributions."[57] Truly, "when a whore repents, she becomes a madam."

On the surface, the *Voice* does well. Stern bought it for $55 million. Not just coffee and cake money. *The New York Times* used the sale as occasion to interview some staff. People buy the *Voice* primarily for film and music coverage, and only then for politics. "Readers are getting older," and sales are "stagnant" for the crucial 24-year-olds and younger.

Why should they buy it? "Some staff . . . say . . . articles are often too long and often predictable.[58] Meaning Schneiderman pushed Alex out and kept Hentoff, the dullest writer since Sumarians started scratching mud. And while all *Voice* politicals suffer from severe self-regard, none are holier-than-Hentoff, the supreme referee of the universe:

> At Harvard on May 2, 200 students prevented South Africa's con-
> sul general in New York from leaving a meeting room for an hour
> by barricading the door. The Harvard student action was way
> beyond the scope of either the free speech or peaceable assembly
> clauses of the First Amendment. And it's bad strategy as well—
> protesting repression by engaging in repression, however
> limited.[59]

Gosh. When the sheet started it had a singular motto, "A newspaper designed to be read," a sneer at its simple-minded local predecessor, which it put out of business. Big as it is, a new paper, with less initial resources, but combining service journalism with dynamic politics, would end up doing unto it what it did to its extinct competitor.

The Nation: "Power . . . Only When Palestinians Decide to Work Within the System"

Victor Nevasky proudly tells audiences *The Nation* lost money for 120 years and is willing to lose more over the next 120. Nevertheless, circulation is now growing. Cockburn is the better part of the explanation. There are significant articles on other topics but, Cockburn and Edward Said aside, rarely on the Middle East.

Not because Victor is a Jewish chauvinist. Far from it. But he is the world's foremost proponent of *maus-politik*. In February 1986 he told a Berkeley audience the magazine was conducting a debate between liberals and radicals. "Which are you?," asked innocent I. "I'm a progressive." Translated from his native tongue—evasion—into English: He will run with the Democrats until enough "respectable" intellectuals abandon the sinking ship. Then he will tail after.

He merely extends his pallid pink domestic reformism into the Middle East. Thus he ran a front-page article by Meron Benvenisti, a "progressive Zionist," on "How Israel Can Reverse 'Annexation,'" in the January 16, 1986, issue. Benvenisti put the choices as majority tyranny, i.e., what exists now; power sharing, i.e., a bi-national state of equals; or partition, something on the order of the 1967 situation:

> The aversion to a binational state also needs to be analyzed. I agree that such an arrangement could be a recipe for eternal strife, as the experience of many multiethnic societies shows. . . . Partition would necessitate a fundamental change in political perceptions, however, it seems the only permanent resolution. . . .

But, alas, partition, i.e., a West Bank statelet, does not appear imminent. So, in the meantime, to head off worse, Palestinians should utilize their not inconsiderable staying power, their "communal power, the true potential of which will be realized only when Palestinians decide to work within the system."[60]

Wonderful. Except that is *never* what any progressive tells the oppressed. We leave that to their open enemies. Not even a mouse like Victor would run such advice to Blacks in South Africa. True, it is worse there than on the West Bank. But how many more rights do the natives have on the West Bank, that this

can be called dignified advice? And besides, why chop down pre-
cious Canadian timber just to run conservative advice that *absolutely* will not be accepted by the majority of Palestinians?
Bluntly: such preachments are like unto a guided tour of a dead
man's skull.

On February 6, 1982, *The Nation* sponsored a speakout for
Solidarnosc at New York's Town Hall. To be sure, Jaruzelski is a
dictator, and there was nothing improper in organizing a meeting
on Poland. But as Alex remarked re Shcharansky, there is nothing
really difficult about denouncing Stalinism in New York. However, as Professor Edward Said, America's most prominent Palestinian intellectual, remarked in a controversy over the gathering:

> So far as I know, no right-thinking group of prominent American
> intellectuals has met at Town Hall to protest the denial of Pales-
> tinian rights.[61]

This writer proposed such an event to *The Nation,* suggesting
that Ralph Schoenman, who organized the Polish affair, and I
handle the details. Schoenman is an outspoken anti-Zionist. Yet,
for all his prattle about liberal-radical debates, Victor has shown
no interest in the proposition, despite the fact that it is well
known that Israel-Palestine is the most divisive question facing
liberals and radicals.

The Middle East is a long way off and the consequences of
their follies re Palestine are therefore not apparent to these
liberals. But the Democrats are not fighting Reagan. Even these
"realists" can see that. However, as certified "crackpot realists"
they can never abandon a large party for a small one, which any
new party would necessarily be in its earliest stages. To be sure,
the Democratic Party may or may not die as I think it will, even
if slowly. But that scarcely matters. As it exists now it is a walking mummy, the bandaged past, incapable of looking the present
in the eye, to say nothing of the future.

A case in point. On February 20, 1986, John Zaccaro, Jr., was
arrested for cocaine dealing. Does anyone expect his mom to now
call for legalization of the drug? Or her party? The younger
Democrats are permeated with cocaine. So are the younger elements on Wall Street. And the entertainment scene. And the
sports world. Younger Jews. And, and, and.

The party has preached a sort of folk patriotism to the masses,
as opposed to the Republicans' business chauvinism aimed at the

middle class. Democratic populism is no more in touch with the world than the Republican gospel. For them to come now to their dupes and admit the cocaine world of the youth *is the world,* like it or not, would only stun these "kind hearts and gentle people."

What has this to do with liberalism? Merely that it was an Enlightenment doctrine, proclaiming that ordinary people could think rationally. Yet its party deals demagogically with drugs, with Palestine, indeed with so many other issues. The liberals' unwillingness to break with that party means that liberalism is already corpse dead, regardless of the fate of the Democratic Party. So much for the self-flattering image of the majority of Jews as liberals!

The God of Moses = The Politics of Reagan

For several decades the American right had difficulty producing a credible publication. Bill Buckley was cultured and had a gift for sarcasm. But what was *National Review* selling? The first thing that came to mind was *God and Man at Yale.* Given the enormous Jewish intellectual contingent, Buckley's semi-secularized Catholic conservativism automatically isolated itself from them. Another significant portion of the educated elite was of Buckley's Irish background, except it isn't a secret that many such think the worst thing that ever hit Ireland was St. Patrick. And Buckley is too obviously an upper class Tory, even educated in British private schools. He seemed a sort of priest with a Hoover collar.

NR has finally achieved a substantial circulation, but that doesn't mean much to intellectuals who have an aversion to middle brows. But *Commentary,* and even many of its enemies say it, is much more sophisticated. That is important. Preaching to the converted is just a waste of time.

That *Commentary* is a Jewish magazine legitimatizes it with many intellectuals of Christian background, particularly of the older generation. One ex-Catholic explained to me, "My first Jewish girl friend put my cap on right. Until then I thought Voltaire was the head devil." For these the Jews are not only the secular educated chosen people, they are the secularist political chosen people. Even now, the magazine is identified with neo-conservativism rather than the straight stuff.

Podhoretz's father was a milkman and Norman was a liberal in the late 1950s and early 1960s. They are not fighting Roosevelt as Buckley seems to be doing. If Podhoretz is a reactionary, many intellectuals feel that at least he came to it through life rather than inheriting it from daddy like Buckley.

For all this, the magazine is often pathetic. Here is Richard Grenier, reviewing *Reds* in 1982. Grenier spent six pages trashing a movie everyone from Reagan to Brenner liked. He denounced Warren Beatty for going beyond artistic license to create several myths about revolution and feminism. "In the apotheosis of Louise Bryant . . . this calculated strategy to flatter the female public . . . involves distortion of the historical facts." Then he turns around to tell us that:

> In actual fact . . . scenes . . . between Louise Bryant and Eugene O'Neill after her return from Russia obviously never took place. Nonetheless, one of them is among the best things in the film . . . because it provides a note of cynicism in . . . a very syrupy movie. . . ."Something in me tightens," he says drily, "when an American intellectual's eyes shine at the mention of Russia. I say to myself, 'Watch out. I am being offered a new version of Irish Catholicism.' "

That's having it both ways. But here is having it all your way. Like what men in white suits come after you for:

> This Congress, called to foment anti-imperialism, was thronged with Persians, Turks, Caucasians and Arabs. . . . The actual trip to and from Baku was one of the first glimpses . . . of just how rapidly the Bolshevik bureaucracy had adapted itself to its position as the new privileged class: expensive foods, rare wines, beautiful Caucasian prostitutes. According to a report attributed to Reed, old Muslim women boarded the train and stripped their charges, lovely girls, some barely fourteen years old, before the delegates. . . . It all ended, said Reed, in a drunken sex orgy. . . . What seemed to disgust Reed was mainly that the girls had been paid for. Now if they had been fine Russian girls who had chosen to engage in sexual intercourse with the delegates, he said, that would have been something else.[62]

You say what you will, but I think this sounds like a great idea. I've often told my leftist friends that we will get nowhere with dull classes and boring meetings. "Let's have naked dancing girls. Then we will have fun. And so will they. The world needs wild parties, not political parties."

Do they listen? Seriously—if it will ever be possible to be serious again after this cockamamy tale—this is how *Commentary's* inner circle thinks—or doesn't think. They believe what they want to believe, and only what they want to believe. Another perfect case in point is Irving Kristol.

After some years as *Commentary's* managing editor, he cofounded London's *Encounter* in 1953, with Stephen Spender, and edited it until 1958. In 1966 *The New York Times* ran a story that the organ of the Congress for Cultural Freedom was secretly subsidized by the CIA. Kristol, Spender and Melvin Lasky denied it: "We know of no 'indirect' benefactions."[63] But by February 11, 1968, Kristol had a piece in the *Times Magazine,* explaining away his involvement with the CIA:

Were there no signs of the C.I.A. presence? Were there not . . . rumors of secret government subventions? Why did I not believe them? . . . but they were not particularly credible. Most . . . issued from sources—left-wing, anti-American or both—that would have been happy to circulate them, true or not, and one discounted them in advance.

Of course. If anyone tells him his fly is open, he asks their politics. If they are Communists he never zips up because they would say it anyway. We understand. He says that had he known they were putting up the bucks he wouldn't have taken the job, but

Not, I hasten to add, because I disapproved of the C.I.A. or even of secret subsidies (at certain times, in certain places, under certain conditions, for specific and limited purposes). . . . Perhaps it will be said that my . . . political opinions were so clearly "safe" . . . that censorship was superfluous. Maybe so. . . . Looking back on the cold war of the nineteen-fifties against Stalinism, I can at moments feel positively nostalgic for the relatively forthright way it posed unambiguous moral issues. . . . I am pleased to have had a small part in it.[64]

He was quite right. There was—and is—no need for the CIA to give him orders. A member of *The Wall Street Journal's* Board of Contributors, capitalism, not Israel, is his real religion. Of late he has been hustling Reagan's foreign policy, using Israel's alleged defense needs as bait whenever he sees a potential Jewish customer. This emerged quite clearly in his July 1984 *Commentary* piece:

> Can anyone believe that an American government which, in
> righteous moralistic *hauteur,* refuses to intervene to prevent a
> Communist takeover in Central America, will intervene to
> counterbalance Soviet participation in an assault on Israel. . . . We
> are constrained to take our allies where and how we find them—
> even if they are authoritarian (e.g., Turkey), even if they are total-
> itarian (e.g., China). . . . If American Jews truly wish to be nonin-
> terventionist, they have to cease being concerned with Israel, with
> Jews in the Soviet Union. . . . To demand that an American
> government be interventionist exclusively on behalf of Jewish
> interests . . . well, to state that demand is to reveal its absurdity.
> Yet most . . . Jewish organizations . . . cannot even bring them-
> selves openly to support . . . a large and powerful military estab-
> lishment that can, if necessary, fight and win dirty, little (or not so
> little) wars.[65]

Kristol's article is the ultimate in *realpolitik.* But like most
practitioners of the science, he is just another crackpot realist. In
theory B follows A. Logically all Zionists should recognize that
the requirements of the anti-Soviet struggle compel the U.S. and
Israel to take allies where they must. But in the "real world" in
which we live, but which he—alone—understands, this won't fly.

Close observers have already told us that most rank and file
American Zionists, Hadassah ladies and the like, are unsophisti-
cated. They believe in vulgar Jewish nationalism. They will not
sign on to march shoulder to shoulder with the Chinese Communist Party. Still less will Kristol convince most Jewish college
youth, who do think. They are not about to back open-ended alliances with any passing devil that Ronnie might take a fancy to.
Certainly not in the name of either Israel or Jewishness, about
which they do not give even a little damn.

In the end, what is the Jewishness the magazine is trying to
protect? When capitalism was on the rise and represented progress, its image of the Jews was Shakespeare's classic humanism:

> Hath not a Jew eyes? Hath not a Jew hands, organs, dimensions,
> senses, affections, passions; fed with the same food, hurt with the
> same weapons, subject to the same diseases, healed by the same
> means, warmed and cooled by the same winter and summer, as a
> Christian is? If you prick us, do we not bleed? If you tickle us, do
> we not laugh? If you poison us, do we not die?

For the bard, the Jew is an integral part of humanity. Not so with Kristol and Podhoretz. Jews have two special "interests": their wealth and Israel. Or, if you like, Israel and their wealth. Their Jew is a hideous inversion of the Shakespearean character, truly a Shylock for our time. "Hath not a Jew plastic credit cards? Ph.D. thesis? Uzi machine gun? If he shoots you, do you not bleed?"

Fortunately, Podhoretz and Co. are having difficulty in peddling tallith-draped Reaganism even to *Commentary's* cynical intellectual readers. Circulation has dropped from 70,000 in 1970 to 47,000 in 1985. When you print a letter from Nixon, even give it pride of place, as the magazine did in January 1986, when he wrote in to say how much he admired Paul Johnson's article on South Africa, all you do is isolate yourself.

Ronnie will renew his subscription. But many professors will not. You can get them to believe all Jews are brothers. But it's hard to get even the dumbest academics to believe our bank accounts are sisters.

Of Eccentric Publishers and Respectable Editors

It's not really necessary to take much time discussing Marty Peretz and his *New Republic*. Even its senior editor, Michael Kinsley, acknowledges that he is off. "I happen to have had the experience of being owned by a foundation at *Harper's* and by a rich eccentric," he told a 1985 conference of journals of critical opinion,

> and despite the fact that many of the disadvantages of the rich eccentric happen to involve my particular employer, I would still vote for the rich eccentric over the foundation any day.[66]

Good for you Mike. At any rate, that is Peretz's reputation. And we must always remember the old saying. "When you're poor you're crazy. When you're rich you're eccentric." About the best thing that can be said for the magazine is that its existence is not really an argument against Zionism. After all, doesn't every movement have its lunatic fringe?

The New York Review of Books was once a fairly liberal outfit. Chomsky was welcomed into its pages. But that was over a decade ago. Since then it has become increasingly conservative, stodgy and even cowardly. It attacked Peters only after everyone else. It finally got around to doing an article on Kahane, again

after he was old news. They were one of the few publications in
the country to review Chomsky's *Fateful Triangle,* but again only
after their sister publication, *The London Review of Books* had
run a piece on it. And when they did run something it was by an
Israeli hack, who was brazen enough to complain that

> for Chomsky . . . there is no real difference . . . between the
> Alignment and the Likud, only the difference between hypocrisy
> and brutality. Yet between the sane hypocrisy of the Alignment
> and the self-righteous brutality of the Likud, I would not hesitate
> to prefer the Alignment.[67]

If anything will set my bells off it is lesser evilism, and I had to
write in:

> A question for the editor. . . . Granted, every American editor
> thinks he or she has the right to vote, here, for some murderer as
> the lesser evil, but how did you dare to submit Chomsky's serious
> work to a Philistine, who could do no better than denounce him as
> unwilling to support a gang of hypocrites?[68]

They did not run the letter. But let's think about why they
didn't. No one is surprised if a writer is accused of being a hypocrite. But reader, have you *ever* before heard of a review which
condemned a writer for *not* being a hypocrite? The reviewer was
Israeli but editors Robert Silvers and Barbara Epstein are American Jews and their running it demonstrates the back-asswards
morality of American liberalism. They think themselves positively saintly in voting for lesser evils, and they get to breathing
rather hard when anyone challenges their curious ethics.

One of their frequent writers is rabbi Arthur Hertzberg, a leading figure in the AJCongress. Normally his articles are, at best,
only moderately interesting. However his November 21, 1985,
review of Charles Silberman's *A Certain People* deserves comment.

Given the intermarriage statistics, many Establishment scholars are pessimistic as to whether organized Jewry can survive
here. But Silberman is their Alfred E. Neuman, and like *Mad*
magazine's resident sage, he does not worry overmuch: "The
great majority of American Jews, young as well as old, are
retaining their Jewish identity."[69]

Silberman insists intermarriage is now stabilizing and even
decreasing. And he plunges deeper in announcing that such liai-

sons are even adding strength to the community. But Hertzberg isn't buying any of this. Ever since 1963 he has answered the question, whether Jewry will survive, "in the negative. History, sociology, and the emptiness of contemporary Jewish religion all point in the same direction."[70]

Now again, with his vast experience in organized Jewish life, he summarily dismissed Silberman's claims as "simply unbelievable." Silberman carried on about young Jews returning to Judaism or, at least, studying their heritage in Jewish studies courses in universities. But again Hertzberg, who has taught such classes for 25 years, dismisses Silberman: "most Jewish students are less involved . . . than college students were a generation ago." He concludes his devastating critique by remarking that, when everything is reckoned up, neither numbers nor wealth counts:

> In all of its authentic versions, even at its most secular, Judaism is the faith of those who are dissatisfied with the society around them and have a critical sense of the hollowness of worldly success— and only through such people can Judaism survive, or have reason for survival.

There is more than a little cant about the Jews' mission as a light unto the nations in this. But his article is candid. Modern Judaism is a light unto no one. The rich "giver" and the "activist," the link to the warlords in Washington, "are seen as heirs of the scholars and pietists of old."[71] American Judaism is *the* paradigm of hollow worldly success. Yet he persists in hanging on as the last of the idealistic Mohicans for a faith utterly forsworn by its young, the most educated youth in the world. They did not ask his permission to leave—and they do not give a damn if he stays on, going through the rituals of a dying religion.

And so with the *Review's* editors, who hang onto Israel like a dog worrying a bone. They are not *Commentary* or *New Republic,* dead-end defenders of the undefendable. Rather it is as if they do not read what they print. They are simply too much of the established order here to ever go beyond the most loyal of criticisms of its counterpart in Israel. They would always rather denounce its opponents for not being hypocrites than join in the struggle against the Alignment-Likud government, that is to say against the Alignment, whom *they* insist are hypocrites, and the Likud, whom *they* proclaim to be brutes.

Other examples of reactionary thinking, or the lack of it, concerning Israel could easily be gleaned from the more conservative press, and vapid handwringing could be plucked out of the liberal journals. But what has already been cited is sufficient. It is to be stressed that the "realism" of the right re Israel is only of a piece with their immorality towards the workings of the capitalist system in general. Similarly, the cynicism and/or reformism of the liberals re the Middle East is how they operate within domestic politics.

For every Cockburn and Chomsky among them, chauvinists like Newfield and insipid reformists like Nevasky are ten deep. American liberals are always noble minded when they denounce Republicans. When they deal with anything connected with the Democrats, which Israel surely is, they would rather run through the streets stark naked than even give the appearance of being idealists.

America is economically one of the most elitist societies imaginable. It is an obscene mockery of the doctrine of human equality. Given the hump on America's back, it is natural that American Jewry is likewise twisted out of shape. In the end, that Jewry is an integral part of the country, sharing most of its vices. Come election day, Jews vote for a candidate who hustles Fundamentalist Christian votes, or Jewish chauvinist votes, just like folks. Their "prophetic heritage," their "passion for secular justice," their "contribution to world culture" is just so much wood on the tribal totem pole. Nothing exempts them from being made fools of by the politicians—or making fools of themselves, if you like—in the good ol' pathetic A-murican political way.

The doctrine of human equality is universal, but it is never universally received. Under it, all ethnic groups are called, but none is chosen. The belief that American Jewry, in its majority, will play a progressive role in the future is racist and utopian. As Jews are now overwhelmingly intellectuals, they fall under sociological laws governing the behavior of the educated. At best, only a minority of any capitalist intelligentsia is ever revolutionary. Most are time servers. In fact, a significant minority of Jews will continue to play reactionary roles, as Zionism's defenders, or as Republicans or as last ditch patrons of the Democratic Party.

And so what? Who expects the bulk of Amish or Irish to play progressive roles? Or members of a million and one other ethnic or religious groups? Only with them no one cares, certainly not enlightened members of such groups, who do what they have to do as individuals. And that is the way it will be with the minority of Jews, primarily youth, who will come over to the oppressed, exploited, insulted and injured of this earth.

In the end, the future belongs to them and their intellectual comrades. There can be no looking back, no holding onto any parochial tradition, no divided loyalty. Going over to them means all the way over: "May we live for the oppressed. May we die with the oppressed. May we rise from the dead with the oppressed!!"

Notes

1. Arthur Hertzberg, "The Jewish Intelligentsia and Their Jewishness," *Midstream,* Nov. 1984, p. 37.
2. Charles Silberman, *A Certain People,* p. 145.
3. Milton Himmelfarb,"How We Are," *Commentary Reader,* p. 402.
4. Alvin Toffler, *The Culture Consumers,* p. 34.
5. Philip Roth (Discussant), "Jewish Intellectuals and Jewish Identity," *Congress Bi-Weekly,* Sept. 16, 1963, p. 21.
6. Walter Goodman, "25 Years at Commentary Inspire a Podhoretz Party," *NY Times,* Feb. 1, 1985, p. 1.
7. Bernard Avishai, "Breaking Faith," *Dissent,* Spring 1981, p. 239.
8. "The Papal Plot in Court," *NY Times,* June 1, 1985, p. 18.
9. Silberman, p. 151.
10. Wolf Blitzer, "Washington Wives Model for Israel," *Jerusalem Post,* Nov. 29, 1976. p. 5.
11. Jonathan Kandell, "Hospitalized Arab Says Israeli Police Beat Him in Jail," *NY Times,* April 30, 1979.
12. Mike Wallace and Gary Gates, *Close Encounters,* p. 286.
13. Arthur Unger, "New Mike Wallace Special Refuels a Debate," *Christian Science Monitor,* March 19, 1976, p. 1.
14. Wallace and Gates, p. 294.
15. "Mike Wallace's Problem," *Near East Report,* February 10, 1984, p. 23.
16. Lenni Brenner, "By the Street Called Straight," *Arab Perspectives,* Feb. 1982, p. 12.
17. "CBS Loses $3 million on 'Playing for Time,'" *Response,* Feb. 1981.
18. "Mix of Art and Politics at Core of Actress's Suit," *NY Times,* Oct. 28, 1984, p. 6.
19. "What Is at Stake in Redgrave v. Boston Symphony Orchestra," *AJAZ Report #50,* Dec. 1985, p. 9.
20. "Redgrave Loses Jury Award," *NY Times,* Feb. 14, 1985, p. 12.
21. *AJAZ Report.*
22. Steve Smith, "Asner Is Active Despite Anti-Semitic Slur," *Jewish Bulletin,* June 28, 1985, p. 6.
23. "Vanessa Redgrave Ends Testimony in Boston Suit," *NY Times,* Oct. 31, 1984, p. 10.
24. Jack Newfield, "Anti-Semitism and the Crime of Silence," *Village Voice,* June 17, 1981, pp. 1–97, passim.
25. Alex Cockburn, "Silence and Other Crimes," *Village Voice,* June 24, 1981, p. 1.

26. Cockburn, "Cockburn: Newfield's Continued Silence," *Village Voice,* July 1, 1981, p. 11.
27. Cockburn, June 24, 1981, pp. 21–3.
28. Martha Ackelsberg, "Pride, Prejudice, and Politics: Jewish Jews on the American Left," *Response,* Autumn 1982, p. 5.
29. David Margolick, "Critic of Israel on *The Voice* Got an Arab Institute Grant," *NY Times,* Jan. 12, 1984, p. B7.
30. Margolick, "*The Voice* Suspends Critic Over Arab Studies Aid," *NY Times,* Jan. 17, 1984, p. B3.
31. "Editorial," *Village Voice,* Jan. 24, 1983, p. 3.
32. Cockburn, "A Question of Appearances," Ibid., p. 4.
33. "Alexflap," *Wall Street Journal,* Jan. 13, 1984, p. 22.
34. "Defend the Scoundrel! *Village Voice's* Cockburn Up a Creek," *Workers Vanguard,* Jan. 20, 1984, p. 3, 14.
35. Cockburn, "Beat The Devil," *Nation,* Sept. 7, 1985, p. 166.
36. *Response,* p. 19.
37. Ibid., p. 4–6.
38. Ibid., p. 17.
40. Nat Hentoff, "The Silence of American Jews," *Village Voice,* June 29, 1982, p. 8.
41. Paul Berman, "Moral Insomnia," *Village Voice,* Dec. 17, 1985, p. 45.
42. M.L. Redman, "Black-Jewish Blues," *Village Voice,* Jan. 21, 1986, p. 6.
43. Berman, "A Discouraging Word," *Village Voice,* Nov. 6, 1985, p. 37.
44. "Here's the Beef," *Village Voice,* April 3, 1984.
45. "Endorsement: Mondale for President," *Village Voice,* April 3, 1984, p. 10.
46. *Response,* pp. 7–9, 13.
47. Ellen Willis, "Advise for Survival," *NY Times Book Review,* Oct. 3, 1982, p. 15.
48. Lenni Brenner, (Letter), *NY Times Book Review,* Nov. 7, 1982, p. 46.
49. Noam Chomsky to Lenni Brenner, April 15, 1985.
50. Victor Nevasky to Lenni Brenner, Jan. 28, 1985.
51. Cockburn, "Beat the Devil," *Nation,* June 29, 1985, p. 789.
52. Berman, "Gas Chamber Games," *Village Voice,* June 10, 1981, pp. 37, 43.
53. Chomsky, "Chomsky: Freedom of Expression? Absolutely," *Village Voice,* July 1, 1981, p. 12.
54. Newfield, "Blacks and Jews," *Village Voice,* March 20, 1984, p. 15.
55. Richard Stevenson, "*Village Voice* Is Sold to Chairman of Hartz," *NY Times,* June 21, 1985, p. 33.
56. "The *Forbes* Four Hundred," *Forbes,* Oct. 28, 1985, p. 128.
57. Josh Barbanel, "Abundant Political Gifts by Developers Faulted," *NY Times,* Nov. 27, 1985.
58. Alex Jones, "At *Village Voice,* a Clashing of Visions," *NY Times,* June 30, 1985, p. 12.
59. "Underground at Columbia," *Village Voice,* May 14, 1985, p. 2.
60. Meron Benvenisti, "How Israel Can Reverse 'Annexation,'" *Nation,* Jan. 18, 1986, pp. 48–50.
61. Harry Ring, "Susan Sontag's Conversion to Anticommunism," *Militant,* April 2, 1982, p. 11.
62. Richard Grenier, "Bolshevism for the 80's," *Commentary,* March 1982, p. 62.

63. Stephen Spender, Melvin Lasky, Irving Kristol, "Freedom of *Encounter* Magazine," (Letter) *NY Times,* May 10, 1966, p. 44.

64. Irving Kristol, "Memoirs of a 'Cold Warrior,'" *NY Times Magazine,* Feb. 11, 1968, pp. 25-6, 98.

65. Kristol, "The Political Dilemma of American Jews," *Commentary,* July 1984, pp. 27-8.

66. Elsa Dixler, "Rich Eccentrics, Red-Baiting and Jameson's Dog," *Nation,* June 8, 1985, p. 702.

67. Avishai Margalit, (review of *The Fateful Triangle*), *NY Review of Books,* June 28, 1984, p. 14.

68. Brenner to *NY Review of Books,* June 15, 1984.

69. Silberman, p. 225.

70. Ibid., p. 166.

71. Arthur Hertzberg, "The Triumph of the Jews," *NY Review of Books,* Nov. 21, 1985, pp. 18, 20, 22.

Index